Dangerous Doctrine

DANGEROUS DOCTRINE

HOW OBAMA'S GRAND STRATEGY WEAKENED AMERICA

ROBERT G. KAUFMAN

UNIVERSITY PRESS OF KENTUCKY

Copyright © 2016 by The University Press of Kentucky

Scholarly publisher for the Commonwealth,
serving Bellarmine University, Berea College, Centre College of Kentucky, Eastern
Kentucky University, The Filson Historical Society, Georgetown College,
Kentucky Historical Society, Kentucky State University, Morehead State
University, Murray State University, Northern Kentucky University, Transylvania
University, University of Kentucky, University of Louisville, and Western
Kentucky University.

Editorial and Sales Offices: The University Press of Kentucky
663 South Limestone Street, Lexington, Kentucky 40508-4008
www.kentuckypress.com

Cataloging-in-Publication data is available from the Library of Congress.

ISBN 978-0-8131-6720-6 (hardcover : alk. paper)
ISBN 978-0-8131-6721-3 (pdf)
ISBN 978-0-8131-6722-0 (epub)

This book is printed on acid-free paper meeting
the requirements of the American National Standard
for Permanence in Paper for Printed Library Materials.

Manufactured in the United States of America.

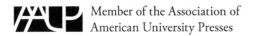 Member of the Association of
American University Presses

To the memory of Susannah Merry Hanson—
a wonderful young woman who led a wonderful life
that sudden illness ended much too soon. Suzy was not only
one of my favorite students but also one of my favorite people.
I will always remember and admire Suzy for the sterling content
of her character, her indefatigable good humor, and
her unpretentious but formidable intelligence.

December 31, 1986–November 13, 2014

Contents

Introduction

Is there an Obama Doctrine, a distinct grand strategy informing the president's foreign and national security policies?[1] Or does the search for coherence confuse rather than clarify understanding? Opinions vary. Some prominent defenders of the administration not only deny the existence of the Obama Doctrine, but also praise the president for choosing pragmatism and flexibility as an alternative.[2] In a January 2014 interview with David Remnick, President Obama responded in the same vein, saying there was no need for any new grand strategy: "I don't really even need George Kennan right now," said the president, only "the right strategic partners."[3] Conversely, some of Obama's fiercest detractors assail him for lacking sufficient interest in foreign policy to define or adhere to any core strategy.[4] Neither of these perspectives is correct. Nor does it suffice to summarize the Obama Doctrine as "Don't Do Stupid Stuff" (Thomas Friedman's formulation in the *New York Times*), or simply as a policy of American retrenchment.[5]

Like Margaret Thatcher and Ronald Reagan, President Obama came to office as a conviction rather than consensus politician. Obama aspires to transform not only the relationship between government and the individual at home, but also the role of the United States abroad. As Walter Russell Mead observes, the president has "extremely ambitious" foreign policy goals: a global climate treaty; a new relationship with Iran; nuclear arms control and disarmament; the withdrawal of American military forces from Iraq and Afghanistan without leaving chaos behind; a final settlement of the Arab-Israeli conflict; the containment of global terrorism; engagement with Russia; a benign end to the Syrian civil war; a decent outcome for the Arab Spring; a durable equilibrium in East Asia with a rising China embracing rather than menacing the regional status quo; American military restraint, except in extraordinary circumstances that require a high burden of proof to justify the resort to unilateralism of narrow coalitions of the willing; and the establishment of multilateralism, collective security, and international law as the norm for resolving international disputes.[6]

President Obama has articulated a clear, consistent national security strategy, which has crystallized into a doctrine during his second term. The president has pursued his transformative agenda with remarkable fidelity, despite the vagaries of practical politics compelling even the most consistent conviction politicians to compromise frequently.

This book will explicate and analyze the Obama Doctrine, drawing primarily, though not exclusively, from President Obama's own rationale for his policies. It will spotlight the period from his inauguration through the midterm elections of 2014. The author consciously avoids any reliance on incendiary accounts of President Obama's foreign policy that routinely place the worst possible construction on the president's motives without adequate empirical foundation.[7] For all the divergence of perspectives on the merits of President Obama's foreign policy, consensus exists that the president has dominated its formulation and implementation. This includes Obama's first term, when occasional differences occurred within his administration; Secretary of State Hillary Clinton was consistently the most hawkish member during internal debates.[8] As William Galston observes in the *Wall Street Journal,* Clinton vigorously advocated the surge in Afghanistan, the use of American airpower in Libya in 2011, and the Navy Seal raid killing Osama bin Laden. She unsuccessfully supported maintaining a residual American force in Iraq, a proposal that the president's manifest lack of enthusiasm for and the public opposition of the Iraqi government conspired to doom. Although she endorsed negotiating with Iran, Clinton also distrusted Iranian intentions—far more than the president did. President Obama prevailed handily, however, in all the major foreign policy battles within the administration while Hillary Clinton served as secretary of state.[9] Robert Gates and Leon Panetta (who served as Obama's first director of the CIA and then replaced Gates as secretary of defense) both complained in their memoirs about the Obama administration's zealous determination to "bring everything under their control."[10]

Obama has asserted his prerogative even more decisively during his second term, appointing Chuck Hagel as secretary of defense, John Kerry as secretary of state, and Samantha Power as his ambassador to the United

Nations. This trio has embraced President Obama's view of the world and the diminished role for American military power in it with even fewer reservations than their predecessors, who challenged the president on rare occasions within quite narrow bounds.[11] Consider, for example, the symbiotic political relationship between Obama and John Kerry. Like Obama, Kerry stridently opposed every one of Ronald Reagan's pivotal foreign policy initiatives—the defense buildup, SDI, the U.S. military intervention in Grenada, and his uncompromising and relentless anticommunist rhetoric. Like Obama, Kerry passionately advocated the nuclear freeze as a preferable alternative. After initially voting for the invasion of Iraq in 2003, Kerry repented, coming out categorically against the war, the Bush Doctrine, and Bush's 2007 surge. Kerry's days as an antiwar leader in Vietnam also instilled in him strong presumption—matching Obama's—for deferring and limiting the use of force in favor of multilateralism, engagement, and diplomacy.[12]

Although Chuck Hagel formerly served as a Republican senator from Nebraska, his foreign policy and national security views have long aligned more closely with the dovish New Politics wing of the Democratic Party. Hagel called for direct negotiations with Hamas in Gaza and Hezbollah in Lebanon. He supported unconditional negotiations with the Iranian regime and categorically opposed the imposition of unilateral sanctions and the use of force against it. Unlike President Obama's two Republican presidential opponents—Senator John McCain of Arizona and Massachusetts's former governor Mitt Romney—Hagel favored substantially cutting defense spending and devolving U.S. global responsibilities.[13] Hagel's resignation after the midterm elections of 2014 under pressure from the president does not signify any new direction in the administration's foreign or national security policy. Hagel left primarily because of Obama's growing frustration with Hagel's ineffectiveness rather than any major policy disagreement. Ashton Carter—Hagel's replacement—has exemplary academic credentials and extensive policy experience, having previously served Presidents Carter and Clinton before becoming President Obama's fourth secretary of defense. Carter lacks, however, either the inclination or the clout within the Obama administration's increasingly homogeneous national security team to influence or alter the course the president has firmly set.[14]

Ambassador Power's criticisms about the misuse of American power make President Obama's most apologetic statements seem tame by comparison: "U.S. foreign policy has to be rethought. It needs not tweaking but overhauling. We need: a historical reckoning with crimes committed, sponsored, or permitted by the United States. This would entail restoring FOIA to its pre-Bush stature, opening the files, and acknowledging the force of a mantra we have spent the last decade promoting in Guatemala, South Africa, and Yugoslavia: A country has to look back before it can move forward. Instituting a doctrine of mea culpa would enhance our credibility by showing that American decision-makers do not endorse the sins of their predecessors."[15]

The year 2014 witnessed a further concentration of foreign policy decision making in the White House, as multiple foreign policy crises buffeted the Obama administration: a looming cold war in Europe with Putin's Russia; a savage and emboldened Islamic caliphate in the Middle East; the collapse of Iraq; and China's mounting assertiveness and arrogance dealing with its maritime neighbors in Asia. As Mark Landler reported in the *New York Times,* President Obama responded by "leaning more than ever on a his small circle of White House aides, who forged their relationship with him during the 2008 campaign and loom even larger in the administration without weighty voices like those of Robert M. Gates, the former secretary of defense, or Hillary Rodham Clinton, the former secretary of state."[16]

This book offers a robust critique of the Obama Doctrine that is grounded in international relations theory and the annals of American diplomacy. It focuses on the record and trajectory of the Obama foreign policy in the geopolitically pivotal regions of Europe, the Middle East, and Asia. The book argues that President Obama has imprudently abandoned the venerable tradition of muscular internationalism emblematic of Presidents Truman, Eisenhower, Kennedy, Reagan, and both Bushes. Instead, the Obama Doctrine paves the way for ending the indispensable role the United States has played since World War II as what Josef Joffe calls "the world's default power," thereby defeating and deterring hegemonic threats in vital geopolitical regions; catalyzing the spread and sustenance of stable liberal democracy through trade and alliances rather than territorial acquisition; and striving conscientiously, though imperfectly, to choose the lesser moral and geopolitical evil when no plausible good alternative exists.[17]

As a caveat, this book makes no claims to certainty in interpreting the past or speculating about the future. No assessment of American foreign policy should strive for a level of precision beyond what the subject matter admits: namely, arguments based on probabilities and possibilities. Perhaps events will ultimately vindicate President Obama's gamble of establishing multilateralism as the norm if not the rule for when and how the United States engages with the world. Perhaps defining American interests worth fighting for narrowly and endowing the means to promote them modestly will reduce the costs and risks that the United States incurs. Perhaps President Obama's grand strategy will make it possible for the United States safely to accord greater priority to solving problems at home and revitalizing the economy on which all forms of power depend.

Yet the lessons of history suggest otherwise. Typically, the greatest challenges to the United States arise when dangerous adversaries perceive the United States as internationally disengaged and unprepared militarily. After World War I, American withdrawal and retrenchment did not make the world safe for democracy, but for Nazi and Soviet totalitarianism. After World War II, the United States did not make the same mistake. American power proved indispensable for winning the Cold War and extending the democratic zone of peace during the 1990s. Stephen C. Brooks, G. John Ikenberry, and William C. Wohlforth encapsulate nicely the benefits arising from the United States' remaining militarily preeminent and deeply engaged in the world: it helps "prevent the outbreak of conflict in the world's most important regions, keeps the global economy humming, and makes international cooperation easier."[18] The Obama Doctrine risks casting all this away, imperiling America's national interest, rightly understood.

Chapter 1 explicates the main tenets of the Obama Doctrine—an ambitious synthesis of rival approaches to international relations without being beholden to an unalloyed version of any single one. Chapter 2 identifies the Obama Doctrine's points of convergence with and departure from traditions such as neorealism, classical realism, declinism, liberal internationalism, and moral democratic realism—all of which have numerous variations. Chapter 3 compares and contrasts the Obama Doctrine with the rival traditions of American diplomacy. Chapters 4 through 6 analyze the record of the Obama Doctrine in the three paramount regions geopolitically for American foreign policy: Europe, the Middle East, and Asia.

These chapters also address President Obama's record of and rationale for using force, including his strategy for winding down wars while avoiding what he perceives to be excessively high costs and risks. The conclusion offers a brisk summation of why the Obama Doctrine invites peril and why a grand strategy anchored in moral democratic realism, adapted to the conditions of the twenty-first century, offers the best practicable alternative. The epilogue evaluates whether and to what extent the president has reset or doubled down on the main tenets of the Obama Doctrine since the midterm elections of 2014. It will expound briefly on the president's 2015 National Security Strategy, released in early February—particularly the theme of "strategic patience."[19] This document largely affirms the main tenets of the Obama Doctrine as this writer has rendered them.

1

The Main Tenets of the Obama Doctrine

Barack Obama's meteoric rise owes more to the appeal of his personal narrative and his protean theme of change than to a long, well-defined, controversial record such as the one that constituted Ronald Reagan's path to the presidency. Yet the Harvard historian James T. Kloppenberg, author of an admiring intellectual biography of Obama, correctly locates the president on the American political spectrum as a man of the left. He sees this reflected in Obama's formative experiences, two major books, prepresidential speeches, and progressive voting record in the Senate.[1] By his own account in *The Audacity of Hope,* Obama "personally came of age" during the Reagan presidency, defining himself politically as Reagan's antithesis.[2] His decision to become a community organizer arose from his conviction that "change was imperative," foremost "in the White House where Reagan and his minions were carrying on their dirty deeds."[3] Later President Obama came to respect Reagan's tactical acumen and steadfastness—but never his politics. On the contrary, Nancy Reagan and Obama engaged in this exchange at the White House in early 2011, which highlights the profound political differences dividing her husband and the president: "You are a lefty," Nancy Reagan remarked as President Obama signed the Reagan Commission into law. Yes, "I am a lefty," Obama replied.[4]

The designation anti-Reaganite "man of the left" also applies to Barack Obama in his early and evolving views on America's role in the world, which the progressive outlook of his mother, his mentors, and his elite education reinforced. The young Obama "bemoaned" the "effects of Reagan's policies toward the Third World," particularly with what he perceived to be the administration's support for the apartheid regime in South Africa. He also opposed the rhetoric and reality of Reagan's policy of unremitting vigilance toward the Soviet Union, particularly in the realm of national defense. The more Obama studied arms control policy, the more he "found Star Wars to be ill conceived."[5] In 1983 Obama published his first article in Columbia University's college newspaper, *Sundial,* supporting the nuclear freeze but criticizing the movement's narrow focus. He called for the United States to initiate a nuclear test ban as the first step to achieving a nuclear-free world. He blamed "the Reagan Administration's stalling at the Geneva talks on nuclear weapons" for causing "severe tension" that "could ultimately bring about a severe rift between the United States and Western Europe. By being intransigent, Reagan is playing right into Russian hands." Obama praised student activism as a valuable way to "lay the foundation for future mobilization against the relentless, often silent spread of militarism in the country."[6]

Senator Obama's 2002 speech in Chicago categorically opposing the impending war in Iraq also helped vault him to national prominence, distinguishing him from other liberal Democrats such as Senator Hillary Clinton of New York, who voted in 2002 to authorize the Bush administration's use of force to depose Saddam Hussein. In his speech Obama declared his opposition not to "all wars," but to a "dumb" and rash war in Iraq, the country's embarking on which he attributed to Karl Rove and the "cynical attempt by Richard Perle and Paul Wolfowitz and other armchair, weekend warriors . . . to shove their own ideological agendas down our throats." Obama affirmed that Saddam Hussein was a "brutal" and "ruthless" man "who butchers his own people," who serially defied UN resolutions and used chemical and biological weapons, and who coveted a nuclear capability. Even so, Obama admonished that Saddam posed "no imminent and direct threat to the United States, or to his neighbors," and he thus warranted no war to depose him. Obama predicted that an invasion of Iraq without a clear rationale and without strong international support would only fan the flames of Middle East tension and encourage the worst, rather than the best, impulses of the Arab world.[7] Senator Obama voted twice against President Bush's strategy in Iraq, predicting it would fail. He pushed for a phased but unconditional withdrawal of American troops from Iraq, to be completed by 2010—also a major theme of

Obama's 2008 presidential campaign against Republican Senator John McCain.[8]

Obama's impassioned critique of the Iraq war galvanized the Democratic Party's preponderantly liberal base, which was unreconciled to President Bill Clinton's triangulation to the center of American politics during the 1990s. His unbridled antiwar stand may have tipped the balance in his razor-thin victory over Hillary Clinton in the primary contest for the Democratic Party's presidential nomination.[9] Running for president in 2008, Obama offered a "sweeping liberal foreign policy critique," repudiating President Bush's doctrine of preemption and his reliance on narrow coalitions of the willing in favor of multilateralism, engagement, and negotiation.[10]

Obama heavily touted his "unique" credentials to improve America's image in and relationship with the Islamic world. "The day I'm inaugurated, not only the country looks at itself differently, but the world looks at America differently," Obama told New Hampshire Public Radio in November 2007.

> If I'm reaching out to the Muslim world they understand that I've lived in a Muslim country and I may be Christian, but I also understand their point of view. My sister is half Indonesian. I traveled there all the way through my college years. And so I'm intimately concerned with what happens in these countries and the cultures and perspectives these folks have. And those are powerful tools for us to be able to reach out to the world . . . then I think the world will have confidence that I am listening to them and that our future and our security is tied up with our ability to work with other countries in the world—that will ultimately make us safer.[11]

As a candidate, Obama also assigned high priority to halting the spread of nuclear weapons and achieving disarmament, which he deemed required "the active cooperation of Russia." Although not shying "away from pushing for more democracy and accountability in Russia," Obama urged the United States to "work with [Russia] in areas of common interest."[12] He promised to listen to rather than dictate to our international partners. In a constant refrain, Obama blasted President George W. Bush above all for tragically causing "people around the world" to associate freedom with "war, torture, and forcibly imposed regime change." Alternatively, he envisioned building "a better, freer world" by acting "in ways that reflect the decency and aspirations of the American people."[13]

The Obama Doctrine therefore has deep roots in the progressive wing of the Democratic Party, which has dominated the party's foreign policy since supplanting Cold War liberalism in the 1960s.[14] Despite mounting criticism from many quarters, President Obama's foreign policy has remained largely faithful to major themes he articulated during his inaugural presidential campaign.

The Tenets of the Obama Doctrine

Tenet I: Protect the world and the United States from the arrogance of American power too often justified by extravagant claims of American exceptionalism.

President Obama has radiated a significantly more ambivalent view about the merits of American global leadership since World War II than any of his predecessors. Like the antiwar left during the Cold War, President Obama frequently conveys the notion that he often considers American enemies abroad less menacing than what Senator J. William Fulbright, Democrat of Arkansas, famously called "the arrogance of [American] power." This theme, the frequent acknowledgment of "past mistakes," and the pledge to listen rather than dictate all pervade many of President Obama's landmark foreign policy speeches.[15]

Consider, for instance, Obama's address to Turkey's Grand National Assembly in Ankara on April 6, 2009—his first trip to a majority Muslim country. Obama praised Turkish democracy effusively, while highlighting the less-than-perfect record of our own. "The United States is still working through some of our own darker periods in our history," Obama said. "Facing the Washington Monument that I spoke of is a memorial of Abraham Lincoln, the man who freed those who were enslaved even after Washington led our Revolution. Our country still struggles with the legacies of . . . the past treatment of Native Americans."[16] In his landmark speech to the Muslim world delivered in Cairo, Egypt, on June 4, 2009, President Obama assigned the Western world major responsibility for this "time of tension" with the Middle East and North Africa, saying that "colonialism . . . denied rights and opportunities to many Muslims," and that during the Cold War, the superpowers treated Muslim countries "too often . . . as proxies without regard to their own aspirations." Moreover, he concluded that "sweeping change brought by modernity and globalization led many Muslims to view the West as hostile to the traditions of Islam." Obama went on to rebuke not only George W. Bush's war deposing Saddam in Iraq, but, by implication, the legacies of past leaders endeavoring to change the regimes of enemies: Woodrow Wilson in Latin America and toward Germany in World War I; Harry Truman's imposing democracy on a vanquished Germany and Japan after World War II; and Reagan's strategy to transform the Soviet regime through unrelenting comprehensive pressure. "So let me be clear," Obama told his audience. "No system of government can or should be imposed by one nation on any other."[17]

Speaking at the United Nations on September 23, 2009, Obama reiterated his categorical opposition to forcible democratic regime change, unaware of the irony of extolling in the next breath the legacy of Franklin Delano Roosevelt, who violated Obama's dictum with impunity, demanding at Casablanca in January 1943 unconditional surrender of and regime change in Germany and Japan. Obama also attributed the "skepticism and distrust" with which "many around the world had come to view America" partly to the belief that America had "acted unilaterally, without regard for the interests of others." He condemned his predecessor for using torture and prohibited its use "without exception or equivocation," declaring that under his administration, America would live its values and lead by example.[18]

At an April 4, 2009, meeting of the G-20 in Strasbourg, the president dismissed the notion of an exceptional America endowed with exceptional responsibilities. "I believe in American exceptionalism, just as I suspect that the Brits believe in British exceptionalism and the Greeks believe in Greek exceptionalism."[19] Obama also chided his fellow Americans for "failing to appreciate Europe's leading role in the world. There have been times where America has shown arrogance and been dismissive, even derisive."[20] These statements elicited ferocious criticism. Ever since, President Obama and his leading officials have not only backed off from any outright repudiation of American exceptionalism, but rhetorically reaffirmed it. Obama clearly believes, however, that we in the United

States should have more respect for "the opinions of mankind," more modesty about our own virtues, and more awareness of our own vices, which would inoculate us from the perennial human temptation for absolute power to corrupt absolutely. "The United States has a hard-earned humility when it comes to our ability to determine events inside other countries," Obama averred.[21] In a glowing account of Obama's foreign policy, Ryan Lizza concurs: "The one consistent thread running through most of Obama's decisions has been that America must act humbly in the world. Unlike his immediate predecessors, Obama came of age politically during the post–Cold War era, a time when America's unmatched power created widespread resentment. Obama believes that highly visible American leadership can taint a foreign-policy goal just as easily as it can bolster it."[22]

Or as David Remnick put it approvingly in the January 14, 2014, issue of the *New Yorker,* on the basis of a series of lengthy personal interviews with President Obama:

He has not hesitated in his public rhetoric to acknowledge, however subtly, the abuses, as well as the triumphs, of American power. He remembers going with his mother to live in Indonesia, in 1967—shortly after a military coup, engineered with American help, led to the slaughter of hundreds of thousands of people. This event . . . made a lasting impression on Obama. He is convinced that an essential component of diplomacy is the public recognition of historical facts—not only the taking of American hostages in Iran, in 1979, but also the American role in the overthrow of Mohammad Mossadegh, the democratically elected Prime Minister of Iran, in 1953.[23]

Predictably, conservatives have rebuked Obama for his predilection to concede past American sins, for distorting the historical record, and for undermining the legitimacy of American power. Not all the criticism, however, comes from the conservative side alone. Ray Takeyh—a senior fellow at the Council on Foreign Relations who served in the Obama administration and has written extensively about the Middle East— warned of the consequences of President Obama's "not well founded" declaration in this Cairo speech that "the United States played a role in the overthrow of a democratically elected Iranian government." Iranian clerics have exploited "this myth," which Takeyh argues the United States must jettison to "develop a less self-defeating approach to the Islamic Republic today."[24]

Tenet II: Embrace multilateralism rather than unilateralism or narrow coalitions of the willing as the default presumption for American grand strategy.

President Obama embraces multilateralism not as a categorical imperative but as a preferred option for addressing most foreign policy issues most of the time. From the start, Obama has expressed high regard for the capacity of collective action in general and the United Nations in particular to facilitate progress in achieving "the four pillars" he believes "are fundamental" to the future: "non-proliferation and disarmament; the promotion of peace and security; the preservation of our planet; and a global economy that advances opportunity for all people." Obama admits that the UN historically has not lived up to Franklin Roosevelt's vision "that nations of the world could solve their problems together." The UN is "made up of sovereign states . . . and has often become a forum for sowing discord instead of forging common ground." In this era, "when our destiny is shared," however, Obama supposes that the UN can overcome its default position of gridlock. "Power is no longer a zero-sum game. No one nation can or should try to dominate another nation. No world order that elevates one nation or a group of people over another will succeed. No balance of power among nations will hold. The traditional divisions between nations of the South and the North make no sense in an interconnected world; nor do alignments of nations rooted in the cleavages of a long-gone Cold War."[25]

One adviser described the president's reliance on multilateralism over unilateralism or narrow coalitions of the willing as "leading from behind." According to Ryan Lizza, leading from behind entails a nontraditional approach to leadership arising from "two unspoken beliefs: that the relative power of the U.S. is declining . . . and that the U.S. is reviled in many parts of the world," which requires "stealth and modesty" in the pursuit of U.S. interests and ideals.[26]

President Obama's commencement address at West Point on May 28, 2014—a revelatory statement of his views on the use and nonuse of force, which Tenet IV will address presently—also illuminates his broader views on the role of multilateralism generally in American grand strategy. Obama foresees few situations in which the United States must act unilaterally. "Instead, we must mobilize our allies and partners to take collective action." The United States also must broaden its "tools to include diplomacy and development, sanctions and isolation," and "appeals to international law." Obama envisions international institutions as a significant "force multiplier" that can reduce "the need for unilateral American action and increase restraint among other nations."[27] Accordingly, Obama dismisses as wrong the "skeptics who often downplay the effectiveness" of the UN and international law for fostering cooperation, resolving disputes, and punishing aggression. As successful examples of multilateralism in action, Obama cites (controversially) the American intervention in Libya in 2011, negotiations with Iran to curb its nuclear program, the international community's response to Russia's subversion of Ukraine's independence, and the efforts to disarm the Syrian dictator Bashar al-Assad of his chemical weapons capability under the auspices of the UN.[28]

In his national address of September 10, 2014, explaining his rationale for the conflict with the Islamic State of Iraq and Syria (ISIS), President Obama stressed likewise that "America will be joined by a broad coalition of partners." He defined it as "American leadership at its best . . . to enlist more partners in the fight, especially Arab nations who can help mobilize Sunni communities in Iraq and Syria. . . . We rally other nations on behalf of our common security and common humanity."[29]

Tenet III: Minimize the salience of regime type or ideology in determining friends, foes, threats, and opportunities.

The Obama Doctrine tends to discount the significance of regime type and ideology in international politics—positively or negatively. Obama does not consider, for example, the character of the Iranian regime or the ideology it espouses as insurmountable obstacles to negotiation or cooperation. "I'm not big on extremism generally," Obama told Jeffrey Goldberg in March 2014. "What I'll say is that if you look at Iranian behavior, they are strategic, and they're not impulsive. They have a worldview, and they see their interests, and they respond to costs and benefits. . . . They are a large, powerful country that sees itself as an important player on the world stage, and I do not think has a suicide wish, and can respond to incentives."[30]

This disinclination to stress ideology and regime type accounts partially for the Obama administration's lofty hopes for resetting relations with authoritarian regimes such as those of Russia and China rather than bolstering liberal democratic allies such as Canada, Great Britain, India, Israel, Japan, Poland, Germany, Hungary, the Czech Republic, Latvia, Estonia, and Lithuania. In his rhetoric and actions, the president has increasingly relegated the promotion of democracy to a comparatively minor and peripheral concern. The *Washington Post* Editorial Board described, for example, President Obama's September 24, 2013, address to the United Nations as "the most morally crimped speech by a president in modern times."[31] President Obama explicitly excluded the promotion of democracy as a core interest of the United States. For Obama, downplaying American values in foreign relations reflects sober moderation and realism and acts as a salutary corrective to the crusading idealism that plunged the United States into a war in Iraq he opposed.[32]

This disinclination to stress ideology and regime type explains, too, President Obama's extreme reluctance to acknowledge the significance of what Daniel Pipes calls Islamism, or Islamic fascism.[33] Initially the Obama administration classified as "workplace violence" army Major Nidal Malik Hasan's murderous spree at Fort Hood, Texas, in 2009, killing fifteen and wounding more than twice that number, even though Hasan himself admits shouting out "Allahu akbar" ("God is great" in Arabic) while opening fire.[34] Initially the administration wrongly blamed the September 11, 2012, attack on the American embassy in Benghazi on an anti-Islamic YouTube video. The preponderance of evidence refutes the claims of some of Obama's partisan critics in Congress that the president lied or deliberately misled the American people. Instead, Obama resisted drawing the appropriate conclusions because acknowledging that Benghazi was a premeditated attack timed for the anniversary of 9/11 controverted the president's firmly held core convictions that deny or minimize the danger of Islamic radicalism.[35]

According to Michael Hirsh, the national editor for *Politico Magazine* and former chief correspondent for the *National Journal*, the tendency of the Obama administration to "ignore, sidestep or minimize the violent actions of . . . the Islamist militias in Benghazi" also dictated its initially passive approach toward Boko Haram—the terrorist group that kidnapped more than two hundred Christian girls in Nigeria's Borno Province in April 2014. Abubakar Shekau, the homicidal Islamist leader of Boko Haram, has declared his allegiance to al-Qaeda. His group also has killed thousands of innocent civilians.[36] Yet, as Josh Rogin reports, former Secretary of State Hillary Clinton successfully opposed designating Boko Haram as a terrorist entity; her successor, John Kerry, did so in 2013. Neither she nor the president wished to contradict the administration's first-term narrative that terrorism was a narrow problem on the wane and devoid of an Islamist dimension.[37] Nor would the Obama administration acknowledge the patently Islamist January 2015 terrorist attacks in Paris against *Charlie Hebdo*'s journalistic offices and a kosher deli. Instead, Obama dismissed the deli attack in particular as having been perpetrated by "vicious zealots . . . randomly shoot[ing] a bunch of folks."[38]

Tenet IV: Use force sparingly, proportionally, multilaterally, for limited goals, with limited means, and only as a last resort. Establish a high burden of proof to justify exceptions to this rule.

President Obama is no pacifist. "We must begin by acknowledging this hard truth," the president remarked in December 2009, accepting his Nobel Peace Prize. "We will not eradicate violence in our lifetimes. There will be times when nations—acting individually or in concert—will find the use of force not only morally necessary, but justified." For all his ambivalence about American power, Obama acknowledges that the stability of the post–World War II world owes significantly to it: "The United States of America has helped underwrite global security for more than six decades with the blood of our citizens and the strength of our arms. . . . So yes, the instruments of war do have a role to play in preserving the peace."[39]

During his presidency, Obama has resorted to primarily limited strikes to achieve narrowly defined goals. He decisively ordered the bold mission that killed Osama bin Laden on May 2, 2011. The administration has significantly expanded the use of drones against al-Qaeda in Pakistan, killing many of its leaders. "If you look at this president's use of Special Forces and small interventions and partnering, you'd see he's been more comfortable in those areas," according to Anthony Cordesman, a longtime, well-regarded defense analyst.[40]

As Martin S. Indyk, Kenneth G. Lieberthal, and Michael E. O'Hanlon observe in their favorable account of President Obama's foreign policy, however, the president clearly remains wary of major "American military interventionism," particularly any intervention lacking the imprimatur of the UN or at least NATO approval.[41] Obama began his presidency with a deep skepticism about the efficacy of military power to solve problems, which his experience dealing with Iraq, Afghanistan, and Syria has crystallized. "He genuinely believes that he was elected to get America off its war footing, that his legacy is to get the U.S. away from its over-reliance on the military instrument," remarked Julianne Smith, former deputy national security adviser to Vice President Joseph Biden. "There's just a fundamental strategic framework that tilts toward not intervening and looking to see what other instruments are available to deal with a crisis."[42] As Obama has told the American people frequently: "I know well that we are weary of war. We've ended one war in Iraq. We're ending another in Afghanistan . . . we cannot resolve the underlying conflict in Syria with our military."[43] Obama has renounced the muscular internationalism of his two Republican presidential rivals—John McCain and Mitt Romney—as a dangerous diversion to his call for the country "to concentrate on the task of building our nation here at home."[44] Like a defensive neorealist also cautious about using force and dubious about the effect of ideology or regime type on the behavior of states, President Obama tends to view international conflicts through the prism of the spiral model, which posits the danger of overreacting to threats, rather than the deterrence model, which posits the danger of appeasing enemies—especially closed regimes espousing noxious ideologies.[45]

In his 2014 commencement address at West Point, President Obama expounded on his aversion to force, grounded in the spiral model. The president stressed that not every problem has a military solution. He congratulated himself repeatedly for "ending" the wars in Iraq and Afghanistan. He blamed "some of our most costly mistakes" since World War II not on our "restraint," but on our "willingness to rush into military adventures without thinking through the consequences, without building international support and legitimacy for our actions, without leveling with the American people about the sacrifices required." He added, "U.S. military action cannot be the only, or even the primary, component of our leadership in every instance. Just because we have the best hammer does not mean that every problem is a nail." Although Obama indicates a willingness to use force "unilaterally if necessary, when our core interests demand it; when our people are threatened; when our livelihoods are at stake; when the security of our allies is in danger," he opposes the United States going alone otherwise.[46]

"Leading from behind" in Libya exemplifies Obama's preferred template for using force. In 2011 the United Nations Security Council, NATO, and the Arab League authorized limited, calibrated multilateral operations to prevent the Libyan dictator Muammar al-Gaddafi from slaughtering civilians caught up in a civil war, though, controversially, the operation facilitated the more ambitious but unauthorized goal of regime change—a goal that President Obama has renounced either for Iran or for the raging, metastasizing Syrian civil war.[47]

As the Brookings fellow Thomas Wright notes, the president has yet to explain how his vision of multilateralism can work in an age when Russia and China usually will not approve decisive action in the UN Security Council, where they wield a veto.[48] Yet Obama does not consider this a fatal contradiction. His aversion to using force and his embrace of multilateralism form part of an integrated strategy. Generally, Obama considers America's position largely secure and serious threats to it historically low. "America has rarely been stronger relative to the rest of the world," said the president in his address to the West Point cadets. "Our military has no peer." Likewise, he deemphasizes the danger of traditional threats to the United States emanating from great-power rivalry. "The odds of a direct threat against us by any nation are low, and do not come close to the dangers we faced during the Cold War."[49] Accordingly, Obama's West Point address makes little mention of Russia, Iran, or China as potential rivals, or of democratic India and Japan as geopolitical counterweights.

The administration's multiple iterations of Obama's national security strategy reflect Obama's sanguine views about the largely benign security environment facing the United States. The 2010 statement of Obama's National Security Strategy emphasizes international engagement and cooperation as the first option against national security threats—a theme Obama has reprised throughout his presidency. The section titled "Security" stresses that force should be used only as a last resort. When we overuse our military might, or fail to invest in or deploy complementary tools, or act without partners, the document's argument runs, then our military is overstretched and our leadership around the world is too narrowly identified with military force.[50]

The Obama Doctrine's embrace of multilateralism serves the president's two larger purposes: significantly raising the barriers to what the president regards as protracted, costly, unnecessary, and counterproductive American military interventions, while lending critical legitimacy in the rare instance when multilateral institutions can rouse themselves to take decisive collective action. Essentially, Obama gives precedence to defining the mission to fit the coalition. He believes this stands the best chance of instilling and cultivating habits and reflexes in the international community conducive to genuine collective security, replacing the rule of force with the rule of law.

Tenet V: Rely more on soft power—*diplomacy, persuasion, and the allure of American culture*—*rather than on* hard power—*coercive economic and military power. Focus more on the danger of terrorism, nuclear proliferation generally, humanitarian concerns, and unconventional threats rather than on the imperatives of traditional geopolitics, especially the diminishing dangers emanating from traditional great-power rivalry.*

This tenet elaborates on the previous one. The Obama Doctrine subordinates traditional great-power rivalry to what it defines as the more salient imperatives: combatting terrorism, curbing nuclear proliferation, eventually eliminating nuclear weapons, and taking decisive action to address gathering unconventional threats such as global warming. The statement of President Obama's 2010 National Security Strategy does not envisage authoritarian Russia and China as potential rivals or democratic India and Japan as indispensable allies to counterbalance them. The statement and its multiple emendations call instead for engaging rather than containing China, Russia, and Iran—all rivals or, at the least, strategic competitors in traditionally vital geopolitical regions of East Asia, Europe, and the Middle East.[51]

"For the foreseeable future," Obama views terrorism—narrowly defined to exclude Islamism or rogue regimes facilitating it—as "the most direct threat to America at home and abroad." Obama claims that his administration has made tremendous progress reducing the magnitude of that threat, though he acknowledges challenges remain:

Al Qaeda's leadership on the border region between Pakistan and Afghanistan has been decimated, and Osama bin Laden is no more. . . . But a strategy that involves invading every country that harbors terrorist networks is naïve and unsustainable. I believe we must shift our counterterrorism strategy—drawing on the successes and shortcomings of our experiences in Iraq and Afghanistan—to more effectively partner with countries where terrorist networks seek a foothold. And the need for a new strategy reflects the fact that today's principal threat no longer comes from centralized al Qaeda leadership. Instead, it comes from decentralized al Qaeda affiliates and extremists, many with agendas focused in countries where they operate. And this lessens the possibility of large-scale 9/11-style attacks against the homeland, but it heightens the danger of U.S. personnel overseas being attacked, as we saw in Benghazi. It heightens the danger to less defensible targets, as we saw in a shopping mall in Nairobi.[52]

Contrast, too, the relaxed view Obama takes of traditional great-power threats with the high priority he accords to strengthening a "global non-proliferation regime." Speaking in Prague on April 5, 2009, Obama pledged to seek the "peace and security of a world without nuclear weapons." Obama abhorred the "existence of thousands of nuclear weapons [as] the most dangerous legacy of the Cold War," implying that the United States bears the major share of the blame for it. "As the only nuclear power to have used a nuclear weapon," Obama verged on repentance, "the United States has a moral responsibility to . . . take concrete steps towards a world without nuclear weapons." Thus, Obama committed the United States to pursuing the following aggressively: reducing the number and role of nuclear weapons in our national strategy; urging others to do the same; an arms control treaty with Russia that cuts nuclear arsenals deeply, setting the stage for further cuts, and eventually including "all nuclear weapons states in the endeavor"; ratification of the Comprehensive Test Ban Treaty; "a new treaty that verifiably ends the production of fissile materials intended for use in state nuclear weapons"; and ironclad safeguards to prevent terrorists from ever acquiring nuclear weapons. Although Obama also vowed to prevent Iran specifically from acquiring nuclear weapons, he stresses the broader danger of nuclear proliferation in general, rather than distinguish between responsible versus irresponsible nuclear powers.[53]

Obama excludes from his catalogue of important measures generously funding, aggressively researching, or actively deploying comprehensive ballistic missile defense—even as insurance against cheating in his nuclear-free world. Obama not only doubts the technical feasibility of a full-fledged Strategic Defense Initiative, but also worries about its potentially destabilizing effect. He gives only qualified and conditional support even for a limited strategic defense program deployed in Europe and geared to a potential threat from Iran's short- and intermediate-range ballistic missiles. "As long as the threat from Iran persists," Obama says, "we will go forward with a missile defense system" so long as it is "cost-effective and proven. If the Iranian threat is eliminated, we will have a stronger basis for security, and the driving force for missile defense construction in Europe will be removed."[54]

The president's emphasis in his 2010 National Security Statement on combating climate change markedly distinguishes his conception of national security from that of his predecessors. Unlike its relatively benign depiction of the situation prevailing between the United States and other great powers, the statement foresees "the danger from climate change" as "real, urgent, and severe." The president considers combating climate change one of the most urgent imperatives for American foreign policy: "The change wrought by a warming planet will lead to new conflicts over refugees and resources; new suffering from drought and famine; catastrophic natural disasters; and the degradation of land across the globe."[55] As Obama has reiterated with urgency throughout his presidency, "The question is not whether we need to act. The overwhelming judgment of science, accumulated and measured and reviewed and sliced and diced over decades, has put that to rest. The question is whether we have the will to act before it's too late. Because if we fail to protect the world we leave our children, then we fail in the most fundamental purpose of us being here in the first place."[56]

Obama has promised "a new chapter in American leadership on climate change."[57] The Obama administration has provided generous subsidies for green energy. During his first term, Obama submitted a bold plan—though Congress will not pass it—for a cap-and-trade scheme phasing in an 83 percent reduction in U.S. carbon dioxide emissions by

2050. The president also has employed the regulatory process to discourage exploration for fossil fuels, including canceling the Keystone Pipeline.[58] Obama has touted his extensive and expensive 2014 climate plan as a bold step to reduce carbon emissions, encourage conservation, and produce more green energy.[59] Simultaneously, Obama has worked—as yet without success—to negotiate a series of global treaties that would drastically shrink the world's dangerous emissions of greenhouse gases—even at the risk of imposing a heavy burden on a sluggish American economy in the short term. The 2009 Copenhagen Climate Change Conference ended with a nonbinding accord among only five nations rather than the template for an international agreement with teeth Obama had hoped to achieve. Even after the midterm elections of 2014, the president has continued to subordinate his differences with China over human rights to his paramount objective of securing Chinese acquiescence to a comprehensive climate change regime.[60] Finally, the Obama administration's 2010 National Security Strategy also stresses the need and justification for humanitarian interventions under certain circumstances to prevent genocides or mass killing in failed states.[61]

Tenet VI: The emergence of alternative power centers makes a substantial devolution of American responsibilities possible and preferable. America's serious economic problems make retrenchment a strategic necessity as well as a virtue.

Although President Obama has ritually and formulaically declared that American power has no peer, the Obama Doctrine implicitly presumes the unipolar era has ended. The United States remains powerful, perhaps even the first among equals. Nevertheless, so the Obama Doctrine's logic runs, the rise of China, the EU, India, Russia, Brazil, and other states will make a substantial reduction in American *hard power*—primarily military power—desirable and inevitable. The president's preferred remedy for addressing the nation's domestic problems adds urgency to the Obama Doctrine's embrace of strategic devolution. Facing soaring budget deficits and an anemic recovery from the financial crisis of 2008, President Obama has subordinated defense spending to his paramount objective of enlarging the size, cost, and scope of government at home.

The Obama administration has cut the defense budget substantially, from $700 billion when the president took office to $496 billion for 2015. The defense budget as a percentage of federal spending has fallen to below 17 percent under President Obama, compared to 52 percent under John F. Kennedy and 29 percent under Ronald Reagan. During this president's second term, Obama and his ideologically kindred secretary of defense, Chuck Hagel, have accelerated the administration's bold plan to downsize the American military in accordance with their notion of fiscal prudence and the tenets of the Obama Doctrine. Obama's defense budget for 2015 shrinks the army to its smallest levels since before World War II. It removes eleven of the navy's twenty-two cruisers from active service while they are modernized and decreases to thirty-two from fifty-two the number of small combat ships the navy can purchase. Although the navy will retain a fleet of eleven carriers for the time being, the 2015 budget removes the *George Washington* from active service for overhauling and nuclear refueling, leaving open the option of decommissioning that carrier in future years. It eliminates an entire fleet of A-10 Warthogs. It assigns low priority for research, development, and procurement of technologies, including ballistic missile defense. With considerable bipartisan support in this instance—including that of Senator John McCain, normally one of the president's most indefatigable hawkish critics—the administration also has canceled the F-35 Stealth Fighter.[62]

Secretary of Defense Hagel also has intimated that the 2015 budget marks just the beginning of steep cuts in the military budget and programs that will continue for years to come if the president has his way.[63] Defense spending will fall even more significantly if the Budget Sequester Act remains in effect. In 2011 Congress passed the sequester measure and 50/50 formula that the Obama administration proposed to address the recurring debt ceiling crisis. In theory, sequester imposes automatic cuts equally on defense and nondefense discretionary spending, but it exempts entitlement programs such as Social Security and welfare. In practice, however, a defense budget constituting less than 17 percent of federal spending—and falling—bears a proportionally heavier burden of reductions under sequester than domestic spending.[64] By 2023 defense spending will decline to 2.8 percent of the GDP with sequester or roughly 3 percent of the GDP without it—figures lower as a percentage of GDP than what the United States spent in 1940 before Franklin Delano Roo-

sevelt initiated a belated military buildup that still left the country woefully unprepared for the war to come.[65]

The U.S. Navy has borne much of the brunt of the president's down-
sizing. The navy's surface fleet has declined already to 280—the lowest
level since World War I and less than half of Ronald Reagan's 600-ship
navy. That number may plummet to as low as 230—almost 100 fewer
than what the navy deems the bare minimum needed to project power
credibly in vital geopolitical regions—unless the president and Congress
agree to modify the sequester. The administration also has announced it
will end the purchase of the Tomahawk, the navy's premier cruise missile,
as stockpiles dwindle and no replacement looms on the horizon.[66]

Even if President Obama consummates his plan, the United States
will remain the most powerful nation in the world militarily for years to
come. The United States still will spend far more on defense and security
than any other nation—indeed, more than the nine next-largest spend-
ers combined and more than one-third of the world's aggregate defense
spending. By the administration's own admission, however, the margin
of American military preeminence has already begun to diminish. That
adverse trend will become more pronounced, given the downward trajectory of the Obama administration's defense budgets coupled with the
steep rise in Chinese and Russian defense spending, among others. China's
has increased by double digits annually for more than a decade. Russia's
has increased by approximately 14 percent in 2012, approximately 16 percent in 2013, and greater than 30 percent since 2008 (a subject to which
later chapters will return in the context of how the Obama Doctrine has
worked in practice). In the Middle East, defense spending has increased
more than 14 percent annually since 2013, while the defense budgets of
America's NATO allies have continued to decline—only three countries
met the alliance's target of spending 2 percent of GDP on defense.[67]

The 2012 version of the president's National Security Strategy thus
has abandoned the Defense Department's long-standing requirement that
the United States have the ability to fight and win two wars simultaneously. Instead, the Obama Doctrine calls for a military capable of fighting and winning one war "while denying the objectives of—or imposing
unacceptable costs on—an opportunistic aggressor in a second region."[68]
Even defeating a single adversary will probably require more time and
treasure than before. "We are entering an era where American domi-

nance on the seas, in the skies, and in space can no longer be taken for granted," Secretary of Defense Hagel acknowledged. "Budget constraints have forced us to accept more risks—risks we believe we can manage at this level."[69] In "Chairman's Assessment of the Quadrennial Defense Review 2014," Martin Dempsey, former chairman of the Joint Chiefs of Staff, asserts, "The U.S. military can meet the updated national defense strategy, albeit at higher levels of risk in some areas."[70] Evidently, President Obama has made this sort of calculation: accepting such a higher level of risk is a prudent gamble, on the basis of the magnitude of the fiscal crisis, his optimism about the ebbing of great-power rivalry, and his confidence in the efficacy of diplomacy to vindicate the national interest in most places most of the time.

Tenet VII: Build bridges to engage and conciliate actual and potential rivals.

The Obama Doctrine goes beyond the principles of even his most liberal Democratic predecessors in stressing the potentialities of conciliating and accommodating actual and potential rivals. President Obama possesses a robust self-confidence in his unique and compelling abilities to transform American foreign policy—a self-confidence arising from his mediations on his formative experiences and his assessment of himself as ranking high among the best and the brightest. As his admiring biographer David Remnick has observed, Obama conceives of himself as a bridge, reconciling the races in the United States, and reconciling the United States with the world.[71] Obama started his presidency actively engaging with repressive regimes long hostile to the United States: a revolutionary Islamist Iran; a brutal tyranny in North Korea; Russia under an increasingly authoritarian Vladimir Putin; Cuba under Castro's communist despotism; Venezuela under the tyranny of Hugo Chavez; a stringently authoritarian China; the chilling and now bloody dictatorship of Bashar al-Assad, whom Secretary of State Hilary Clinton, Senator John Kerry, and other progressives initially designated as "a reformer";[72] and the Palestinian Authority under Mahmoud Abbas.

What critics assail as the administration's appeasement and inexcusable inaction the president and his defenders herald as his prudential strategic patience inoculating us from the temptation of precipitous and counterproductive intervention in disputes such as Ukraine and Iran that time and diplomacy can solve without making enmity a self-fulfilling prophecy.[73] The president's 2015 State of the Union Address reprises that theme: "When we make rash decisions, reacting to headlines rather than using our heads; when the first response to challenge is to send in our military—then we risk getting drawn into unnecessary conflicts, and neglect the broader strategy we need for a safer, more prosperous world. That is what our enemies want us to do. I believe in smarter American leadership. We lead best when we combine military power with strong diplomacy; when we leverage our power with coalition building; when we don't let our fears blind us to the opportunities the new century presents."[74]

Whether this strategy of bridging, conciliation, and "strategic patience" reflects wisdom or folly turns on the veracity of the Obama Doctrine's underlying assumptions and interlocking tenets. Suppose, for example, that the bellicosity, arrogance, and bumptiousness of Obama's predecessor truly provoked needless enmity toward the United States. Then the Obama Doctrine's more conciliatory approach toward adversaries may have much to commend it—either mitigating dangers and risks or providing the basis for genuine, effective multilateral cooperation once the United States demonstrates to the world community that we have gone the extra mile to resolve disputes cooperatively and peacefully. Or suppose that neither ideology nor regime type really affects the behavior of states. Then the Obama Doctrine's de-emphasis on these variables for identifying friends, foes, threats, and opportunities makes good sense geopolitically as well as ethically.

This book argues, however, that the Obama Doctrine violates the dictates of prudence precisely because of the flawed assumptions underlying it. The Obama Doctrine takes a huge gamble, one that the United States should shun not only because of its high cost and risk, but also because of the prudential alternatives well within our means to undertake. The ensuing chapters will explain why.

2

The Obama Doctrine and International Relations Theory

Barack Obama is no doctrinaire adherent of any single international relations theory. By designating President Obama a foreign policy realist, Fareed Zakaria markedly oversimplifies, though he does capture one essential dimension of Obama's outlook.[1] Instead, the Obama Doctrine draws from and synthesizes several alternative paradigms of international relations, including but not limited to realism.

The main varieties of realism all emphasize the centrality of power, the imperatives of geopolitics, and the virtues of pursuing fixed, finite, and limited foreign policy goals devoid of moral arrogance or the pretense of virtue.[2] President Obama's less than fervent expressions of American exceptionalism would resonate positively in many precincts of foreign policy realism spanning generations. Writing in 1951, George F. Kennan famously deplored the "moralistic-legalistic tradition" of American foreign policy.[3] He rejected the assumption integral to the Declaration of Independence and all robust assertions of American exceptionalism that "the specifics of our national tradition and various religious outlooks represented in the country necessarily have validity for people everywhere." Further, he rejected the idea that purposes of any state are "fit subjects for moral concern."[4]

In a series of books, the conservative realist Andrew Bacevich has delivered an updated and searing rendition of Kennan's critique of American exceptionalism. Bacevich condemns what he terms "the American credo" dominating American foreign policy from Truman through George W.

Bush.[5] Bacevich defines the credo as the trinity of beliefs that U.S. values are superior, should govern world order, and require unremitting vigilance and unassailable U.S. military preponderance to enforce. He holds this credo responsible for an economy in shambles, for the "Leviathan of the Imperial Presidency," and for an endless, needless, costly cycle of military interventions.[6] In the March 24, 2008, issue of the *American Conservative,* Bacevich endorsed Obama as substantially the lesser evil to Republican Senator John McCain: "The election of John McCain would provide a new lease on life to American militarism, while perpetuating the U.S. penchant for global intervention marketed under the guise of liberation."[7] In 2014 Peter Beinart, another Obama admirer who also dubiously classifies himself as a realist in Reinhold Niebuhr's tradition, hoped that "the backlash against America's special role in the world may prove heartening. . . . Over the last decade, that special mission has justified policies—such as the invasion, occupation, and failed reconstruction of Afghanistan and Iraq—that have cost the United States massively in money and blood . . . and has justified ignoring international norms."[8]

Similarly, the neorealist Stephen M. Walt goes much further than the more cautious President Obama, dismissing American exceptionalism as mostly a "myth." Walt scorned Ronald Reagan's and George W. Bush's belief in the benign consequences of American primacy, listing a catalogue of real and imagined U.S. sins to prove the point:

> Any honest accounting of the past half-century must acknowledge . . . the United States has been the major producer of greenhouse gases for most of the last hundred years and thus a principal cause in the adverse changes that are altering the global environment. The United States stood on the wrong side in the struggle against apartheid in South Africa and backed plenty of unsavory dictatorships—including Saddam Hussein's—when short-term strategic interests dictated. Americans may be justly proud of their role in creating and defending Israel and in combating global anti-Semitism, but its one-sided policies have also prolonged Palestinian statelessness and sustained Israel's brutal occupation.[9]

Likewise, John Mearsheimer equates China's attempt to dominate Asia with "the way the United States dominates the Western Hemisphere."[10]

Any endeavor to situate aspects of the Obama Doctrine within or beyond the bounds of realism must bear heavily in mind the variations among realists themselves. The realist tradition of international relations spans a wide spectrum ranging from strict neorealists—who categorically ignore ideology, transcendent morality, and regime type—to some classical realists who consent to take these variables somewhat into account. Explaining the largely successful operation of the nineteenth-century European balance-of-power model, for example, Edward Gulick and Henry A. Kissinger highlighted the importance of common aims, assumptions, self-conscious moderation, and ideological homogeneity among the major powers.[11] The classical realist Arnold Wolfers differentiates among status quo, revisionists, and self-abnegating states.[12] Writing in the realist tradition, Randall L. Schweller refines and systematically explores the implications of Wolfers's distinctions, arguing (at odds with neorealism) that states often fail to balance against threats effectively because of domestic constraints.[13]

The Obama Doctrine largely downplays these variables. Instead, it generally reflects the neorealist assumption that all states behave similarly and rationally in international politics regardless of the internal characteristics of their regimes or the proclivities of their leaders. Neorealists focus, accordingly, on distribution of power in the international system: unipolar, bipolar, tripolar, or multipolar.[14] Unlike President Obama, conversely, classical realists derive their theories from the ineradicable flaws in human nature. Hans Morgenthau roots his political realism, for example, in both the "inevitability" and "evilness of man's lust for power."[15] Morgenthau sees human nature itself, rather than faulty institutions, as responsible for misuse and temptations of power.[16]

Neorealists and classical realists disagree not only with each other, but also among themselves. Although neorealism rejects democratic peace theory—the idea that stable liberal democracies do not fight one another—the Obama Doctrine substantially embraces the outlooks of leading defensive realists, who take a more relaxed view of international relations than offensive neorealists, who, like mainstream classical realists, view international security as precarious rather than plentiful. Like President Obama, defensive neorealists tend generally, for example, to envisage China as a status quo power seeking security, whereas Mearsheimer and other offensive realists anticipate a rising China attempting to dominate

East Asia as a declining United States strives actively to prevent it.[17] Like President Obama, leading defensive neorealists impose a more stringent burden of proof for using force than traditional classical realists or offensive neorealists, who consider great powers as potentially more inherently aggressive. Viewing conflict through the prism of the spiral model of conflict, defensive neorealists, as well as President Obama, worry more about the danger of overreacting than of underreacting to perceived threats. The spiral model posits that preparedness, alliances, and other robust measures intended to enhance security can paradoxically trigger an escalating cycle, making a war nobody really wanted a self-fulfilling prophecy.[18]

The eclectic realist Randall Schweller foresees a novel security environment emerging, defined by three elements: (1) an abundance of security among great powers; (2) the devaluation of territory; and (3) a fairly robust liberal consensus. According to Schweller, "great powers will be driven" far more than in the past "by the prospect of maximizing their own absolute gain than by the" traditional "fear of relative losses or the temptation to make gains at others' expense."[19]

Notwithstanding these differences of degree, most realists enjoin the United States to maintain a lighter footprint abroad—also a major tenet of the Obama Doctrine.[20] Many major classical realists endorse neorealists' advocacy of the United States adopting a strategy of offshore balancing as a less burdensome and ambitious alternative to the muscular internationalism of the Truman, Reagan, and George W. Bush presidencies.[21] Offshore balancing entails keeping American military forces over the horizon (at sea or on bases back home), relying on local allies to counter regional threats, and intervening with military force only as a last resort if the local balance of power seriously breaks down.[22]

Barry Posen, a self-designated realist, makes a systematic case for this type of strategy in *Restraint: A New Foundation for U.S. Grand Strategy.* Posen assails the strategy he terms "liberal hegemony"—the governing American foreign policy since the end of the Cold War—as unnecessary, unsustainable, wasteful, and costly.[23] Like most realists urging restraint and even many proponents of a more robust foreign policy who reject his policy prescriptions, Posen heavily stresses geopolitics as Halford Mackinder defined it seminally early in the twentieth century: "He who controlled Eurasia would control the 'World Island.' He who controlled the 'World Island' would control the world."[24]

"Historically," Posen notes, "the main concern has been that a power with superior resources to the United States could somehow arise on the Eurasian landmass and then challenge the United States at home." Unlike more dogmatic proponents of offshore balancing, Posen concedes the necessity of American intervention to defeat or contain a potential hegemony during World War I, World War II, and the Cold War because of "the superior national power of particular expansionists." Posen counts such interventions, however, as few and far between exceptions to the general rule of staying out of military conflicts outside the Western Hemisphere. Posen's sanguine conclusions about the efficacy of offshore balancing stem from the neorealist conviction that states typically balance against threats effectively rather than form a bandwagon or pass the buck. "The many capable nation-states . . . in Eurasia" will normally combine effectively to prevent any single one of their number from achieving regional hegemony. Posen foresees no candidates for hegemony today or in the foreseeable future, not even a rising China. "There are," he assures us, "plausible balancing coalitions in the event that China proves ambitious." So Posen proposes a "phased reduction in U.S. political commitments and military deployments," the ultimate goal being to place the responsibility for the security of current U.S. allies "squarely on their shoulders." Posen recommends reducing the U.S. defense budget to no more than 2.5 percent of the GDP—less than what the United States spent on defense in 1940, before FDR initiated a major but dangerously belated buildup on the eve of World War II.[25] Owen Harries and Tom Switzer, writing in the realist tradition—though less categorically and sweepingly than Posen—also applaud Obama precisely for being more restrained in what the United States does abroad and for concentrating on putting our house in order at home. "In his reluctance to brandish America's world leadership credentials at every turn, President Obama is tapping into an interesting if frustrating strain of American history—and it just might help America learn the wisdom of great power, prudence, and humility."[26]

Kenneth Waltz, Stephen Walt, and Barry Posen go further than even the most dovish classical realists, neorealists, or President Obama in viewing with equanimity the prospects of a nuclear Iran.[27] Waltz considers nuclear proliferation benign rather than menacing, even speculating that a nuclear Iran would conduce to restoring stability in the Middle East: "Once Iran crosses the nuclear threshold, deterrence will apply, even if the Iranian arsenal is relatively small. No other country in the region will have the incentive to acquire its own nuclear capability, and the current crisis will finally dissipate, leading to a Middle East that is more stable than today. . . . Policymakers and citizens in the Arab world, Europe, Israel, and the United States should take comfort. . . . When it comes to nuclear weapons, now as ever, more may be better."[28] Walt opines, too, that Iran's getting "a few [nuclear] bombs wouldn't have that big an impact on world politics."[29] Both Waltz and Walt assume controversially that the logic of nuclear deterrence applies to the Islamic Republic of Iran in the same way it operated during the Cold War between the United States and the Soviet Union. In their estimation, a nuclear Iran would calculate risk rationally and cautiously despite the revolutionary rhetoric emanating from its Islamist, virulently anti-Western, and anti-Semitic regime.

Realists so disposed usually entrench their arguments in some version of declinism—another underlining assumption of the Obama Doctrine. Soft declinists such as Fareed Zakaria forecast that the United States will remain first among equals but will inevitably lose its unassailable preeminence with the rise of China, India, and other emerging nations.[30] Pessimistic declinists such as Christopher Layne forecast the emergence of full-fledged multipolarity, in which a diminished United States ranks as just one of several great powers. As Layne sees it, "Unipolarity's demise spells the end of 'Pax Americana,' which rested on the pillars of U.S. military dominance, economic leadership . . . ideological appeal (soft power) and the framework of international institutions that the United States built after 1945."[31] The logic of both the hard and soft versions of declinism dictates that the United States must scale back its ambitions and the military means underwriting them accordingly. Otherwise, declinists warn of a hard rather than soft landing in store for a United States unwilling to recognize the limits of American power in an impending multipolar era of international relations.[32]

Yet the Obama Doctrine defies easy categorization as realist or neorealist in any conventional sense of these terms. On the one hand, President Obama finds highly congenial defensive neorealism's advocacy of restraint, its embrace of the spiral model of conflict, its aversion to using force or incurring risk, its skepticism about American exceptionalism, its narrow definition of military threats, its declinism, and its de-emphasis of ideology or regime type for identifying friends or foes. On the other hand, Obama has greater confidence than any category of unalloyed realist in the efficacy of international institutions to foster rational, peaceful, and ordered relations among nations. President Obama also relegates the significance of traditional geopolitics and great-power rivalry to a lower level than classical realists or neorealists would ever countenance. Obama's relatively benign views on the prevailing security environment among great powers and the disutility of military force to resolve conflicts among them most closely approximates Randall Schweller's vision of emerging global multipolarity, in which the nature, as well as the distribution, of power will become more diffuse. He rejects Schweller's bleak assessment, however, that formidable obstacles to effective multilateralism and collective actions will mount rather than diminish.

Nor does Obama's advocacy of humanitarian interventions in certain circumstances under the auspices of international institutions qualify as realism in any legitimate sense of the term. Almost no realists supported the ends and means of the 2011 collective intervention in the Libyan civil war that the Obama administration acclaimed as a successful example of multilateralism in action.

Nor do most realists take the significance of "soft" or "smart" power as seriously as President Obama and leading members of his administration resolutely do. Joseph Nye Jr. of Harvard coined, refined, and developed the concept in multiple books and essays. Nye contrasts soft power—persuasion and influence—with coercion—traditionally the essence of hard power. He contrasts the three main sources of a state's soft power—its culture, its political values, and the perceived legitimacy of its foreign policy—with the primary sources of hard power—economic and military capabilities.[33] During her senate confirmation hearings in January 2009, secretary of state–designate Senator Hillary Rodham Clinton, Democrat of New York, accentuated correspondingly the importance of "what has been called smart power, the full range of tools at our disposal—diplomatic, economic, military, political, legal, and cultural—picking the right tool or combination of tools for each situation. With smart power, diplomacy will be the vanguard of our [Obama's] foreign policy."[34]

The classical realist Robert Kaplan thus warns against equating Obama's embrace of restraint with foreign policy "realism" in the tradition of "Henry Kissinger, Brent Scowcroft, and James Baker."[35] In the same vein, his fellow realist Paul L. Saunders explains that Obama deviates from the realist tradition fundamentally on the basis of his "excessive faith in international norms [and] little real appreciation of power's uses and limits. . . . Obama's repeated efforts to contrast the twenty-first century with the nineteenth century highlight his inordinate attachment to rules and norms in an environment of international anarchy where there is no supreme enforcement authority (and he is willing to seize the role of judge, jury and executioner for the United States, as many neoconservatives seek)."[36]

This prominent dimension of Obama's theory and practice shows his affinity for major features of liberal multilateralism, again with substantial qualifications. Like realism, liberal multilateralism does not constitute a homogeneous school of thought. Tony Blair's powerful multilateralism, for example, resembles President George W. Bush's outlook more than Obama's.[37] President Obama nevertheless embraces five core premises of the dominant version of liberal multilateralism popular in the Democratic Party, among Western European elites, and with large parts of the academy. First, Obama emphasizes the binding effects of treaties and international norms. Second, he believes that multilateral institutions can and should serve as arbiters of international legitimacy about when and how states use force. Third, he prefers to rely on soft power rather than wield hard power. Fourth, he is least averse to using force when in pursuit of humanitarian goals the "international community" deems legitimate. Fifth, he believes that deference to and strengthening of international institutions can instill norms that will perpetuate international order even if American power wanes.[38] Obama's comparative lack of interest in promoting stable liberal democracy distinguishes him from most liberal multilateralists, who consider upholding and spreading the democratic peace a central concern of American foreign policy. The Obama Doctrine thus strives to reconcile the lofty ends of liberal multilateralism with a deep reluctance characteristic of defensive neorealism to devote the means or run substantial risks to achieve them. The aversion to risk usually trumps all for Obama in the event of a clash between these two disparate inclinations.

Writing in the *New York Times,* David Brooks suggests that Obama's foreign policy disposition strikingly resembles that of Reinhold Niebuhr, whose Christian realism staked a middle ground between naive idealism and cynical realism. Obama agrees, calling Niebuhr "one of my favorite philosophers. . . . I love him." What Obama has said he takes away from Niebuhr is the "compelling idea that there's serious evil in the world, and hardship and pain. And we should be humble and modest in our belief we can eliminate those things. But we shouldn't use that as an excuse for cynicism and inaction."[39] Obama can claim fidelity to certain aspects of Niebuhr's thought—certainly with greater plausibility than the professed Niebuhrian, anti-neoconservative realist Andrew Bacevich, who actually derives his views from two historians on the opposite side of Niebuhr: the isolationist Charles Beard and the Cold War revisionist William Appelman Williams.[40] Obama's views on American exceptionalism and the danger of triumphalism echo Niebuhr's warning that all nations are guilty of the sin of pride, including liberal ones. Obama's speech accepting the Nobel Prize in 2009 rejects pacifism on the Niebuhrian grounds that the ineradicable flaws in human nature compounded by international anarchy will make some wars necessary to fight.[41]

Even so, the differences between Obama's and Niebuhr's dispositions dwarf the similarities. It is, granted, unjust to associate Niebuhr's legacy with specific policy prescriptions or any definite position on the American political spectrum. Although Niebuhr's thought remained remarkably consistent from 1941 until his death, his vocation as a theologian always made him uncomfortable with the conventional wisdom of the moment. Nor did Niebuhr develop a systematic geopolitical outlook or an elaborate moral casuistry applied to foreign policy. Nevertheless, the dominant trajectory of Niebuhr's thought runs counter to Obama's.[42]

Whereas the Obama Doctrine calls for strategic retrenchment, Niebuhr spent the most influential phase of his career worried primarily about the United States doing too little internationally than too much. His belated opposition to the Vietnam War late in his life is a noteworthy exception. Niebuhr's moral dichotomy between democracy and totalitarianism, his antiperfectionist ethic, and his conviction about the inseparability of power and politics impelled him to advocate policies for dealing with Nazi Germany that were largely similar to Winston Churchill's— the champion of fighting Hitler sooner rather than later and defender of the preemptive use of force against certain virulent gathering dangers. Like conservative hawks of all varieties, including Ronald Reagan and George W. Bush, Niebuhr cited Churchill—no hero to Obama—as his model of prudence.[43] In 1940, for example, Niebuhr published *Christianity and Power Politics,* a polemic advocating early American intervention in World War II and excoriating the liberal Protestant establishment for pacifism, isolationism, and the inability to make critical moral distinctions between totalitarian dictatorships and liberal democracies.[44]

Niebuhr's position on the Soviet Union evolved from a fleeting hope in the possibility of collaboration with the U.S.S.R. just after the Second World War to a general satisfaction with the Truman administration's policy of and rationale for dealing with what he considered the mortal and unappeasable threat. Notably, Niebuhr did not justify the policy of vigilant containment merely in terms of power politics alone. He also depicted the Cold War as a moral struggle, the successful outcome of which was essential to preserve Western democracy's superior capacity to achieve at least the approximation of justice.[45]

Niebuhr's stress on regime type and ideology contrasts fundamentally with the Obama Doctrine's de-emphasis of these variables. Niebuhr distinguished revisionist from status quo regimes and limited from unlimited revisionism largely on the basis of the internal characteristics and animating ideologies of powerful states. For all his warnings about the perils of hubris, Niebuhr accorded great weight to the critical moral distinctions between stable liberal democracies and their totalitarian enemies. He thus defended democracy soberly as the best practicable form of government—if not with the exuberance of Ronald Reagan or George W. Bush, then certainly with more import than the main thrust of the Obama Doctrine: "Man's capacity for justice makes democracy possible, but man's appetite for injustice makes democracy necessary. . . . The democratic techniques of a free society place checks upon the power of ruler and administrator and thus prevent it from becoming vexatious. . . . The perils of uncontrolled power are personal reminders of the virtues of a democratic society."[46]

Nor is the Obama Doctrine's confidence in the efficacy of multilateralism, engagement, and conciliation as substitutes for American hard power or the willingness to use them unilaterally or with narrow coalitions of the willing consistent with Niebuhr's sensibilities. Contrast President Obama's faith in the notion and effectiveness of the "international community" with Niebuhr's profound skepticism, which he expressed emblematically in *Moral Man and Immoral Society:*

Obviously one method for making force morally redemptive is to place it in the hands of a community, which transcends the conflicts of interest between individual nations and has impartial perspectives upon them. That method resolves many conflicts within national communities, and the organization of the League of Nations is ostensibly the extension of that principle to international life. But if powerful classes in international society corrupt the impartiality of national courts, it may be taken for granted that a community of nations, in which very powerful and very weak nations are bound together, has even less hope of achieving impartiality. Furthermore the prestige of the international community is not great enough, and it does not sufficiently qualify the will-to-power of individual nations, to achieve a communal spirit sufficiently unified to discipline recalcitrant nations.[47]

Niebuhr's staunch support for Israel stands closer to the mainstream of the post-1980 Republican Party than Obama's more mixed views about where the equities of the Arab-Israel conflict lie or the best practicable remedy for it. Niebuhr's views on this subject amount to the virtual antithesis of those of his professed realist admirer and Obama supporter Andrew Bacevich, whose antipathy toward Israel also conflicts with Obama's professed support for a two-state solution reflecting the legitimate aspirations of all parties.[48] Niebuhr deemed "the birth and growth of [Israel] . . . a glorious spiritual and political achievement. Its continued existence may require . . . policies for the resettlement of the Arab refugees. But the primary condition of its existence is our word that we will not allow 'any nation so conceived and so dedicated to perish from the earth.'"[49] Niebuhr would have abhorred Bacevich's scathing assessment of Israel under Prime Minister Benjamin Netanyahu as a nation illegitimately seeking "peace as domination" and bad for the United States to support.[50]

Essentially, the Obama Doctrine accords less well with Niebuhr's Christian realism than with an alloy of neorealism, liberal multilateralism shorn of its ideological dimensions, and antimoralistic variants of classical realism in the vein of George F. Kennan.

What defenders consider a compelling synthesis, detractors may interpret as Obama's ill-fated attempt to reconcile the worst features of contradictory doctrines. The U.S. foreign policy scholar Josef Joffe calls Obama an unrealistic realist.[51] Although largely in agreement with the substance of Joffe's criticism, this author prefers to characterize the president as an unrealistic defensive realist with a strong predisposition to multilateralism minus the mitigating grace of liberalism (see the chart on page 41).

3

The Obama Doctrine
and Rival Traditions
of American Diplomacy

The Obama Doctrine also defies easy categorization among rival traditions of American diplomacy. President Obama does not belong, for example, to any of the Jeffersonian, Hamiltonian, Jacksonian, or Wilsonian schools of thought that Walter Russell Mead posits in *Special Providence: American Foreign Policy and How It Changed the World*.[1] The Obama Doctrine also repudiates the "moral democratic realism" that Charles Krauthammer, George Weigel, and this author champion as a distinct and superior American foreign policy tradition.[2]

Likewise, the Obama Doctrine does not fit comfortably within Henry Nau's illuminating but problematic classification scheme specifying six types of American foreign policies, linking each to a particular president: (1) the *minimalist nationalism* of George Washington, a contingent strategy of isolationism opposed to entangling alliances or military adventures outside the Western Hemisphere while a fledging United States remained weak in the world of the strong; (2) the *militant nationalism* of Andrew Jackson, vigorous in the use of force and the assertion of American prerogatives within, but not beyond, the Western Hemisphere; (3) the *defensive realism* of Richard Nixon, a strategy of realpolitik committed to maintaining a world balance of power in an era of diminishing American will and capabilities; (4) the *offensive realism* of Theodore Roosevelt, imperialistic and striving for dominance; (5) the *liberal inter-*

nationalism of Woodrow Wilson and Franklin Roosevelt, championing interdependence and international institutions while relegating the use of force to a last and eventually a past resort; and (6) the *conservative internationalism* of Thomas Jefferson, James K. Polk, Harry Truman, and Ronald Reagan, envisioning force, the balance of power, and cooperation among sister democratic republics as a requirement for maintaining democratic freedom.[3]

The Obama Doctrine also falls well outside Stephen Sestanovich's compelling but oversimplified cycle of commitment and underperformance, which, he argues, has characterized American foreign policy for seven decades. Sestanovich reduces (to excess) Mead's and Nau's more elaborate classification of presidents to a stark dichotomy between maximalists who overreact to global challenges and retrenchers who underreact.[4]

Although the Obama Doctrine intersects with various points of these alternative foreign policy traditions and presidential administrations, it substantially diverges from others. Obama's inclination to downplay ideology, democracy promotion, and regime type while finding regional surrogates for American power aligns with the realism of Richard Nixon and Henry Kissinger, but Colin Dueck rightly identifies Obama as more of an "accomodationist" than any American presidential realist or retrencher.[5] Obama seeks a more permanent reconciliation with American authoritarian adversaries than just a U.S. respite from global responsibilities in the aftermath of what he considers an ill-advised Iraq war. Nixon and Kissinger ascribed far greater significance to the ubiquity and dangers of conflict among great powers than the Obama Doctrine does. Their version of declinism anticipated a return to a global version of the nineteenth-century European balance of power, whereby the United States would assume Britain's role as the ultimate balancer. Nixon and Kissinger derided the potentialities of multilateralism and soft power, for which Obama radiates indomitable enthusiasm.[6]

Obama's foreign policy tends to be far more conciliatory than Nixon's and Kissinger's détente at its softest. Nixon and his successor, Gerald Ford, strenuously opposed the phenomenon of Eurocommunism, that is, communist political parties in Western Europe taking over by means of the ballot box. In Latin America, which Nixon and Kissinger considered part of the U.S. sphere of influence, they cheered the Chilean military's overthrow of Salvador Allende's Marxist regime. In the Middle East, Nixon

International Relations Theories

	REALISM			MULTILATERALISM	
NEOREALISM (Structural Realism)	CLASSICAL REALISM	MORAL DEMOCRATIC REALISM	MUSCULAR MULTILATERALISM	SOFT MULTILATERALISM
Offensive | Defensive					
Neorealism	Classical Realism	MDR	Muscular	Soft
No objective moral standards	Variable credence to objective moral standards (weak to nonexistent)	Calculation of regime type is **critical**	Relative degree of confidence in international institutions (UN, NATO)	Variable credence to regime type (some to minimal)
Hard power	Hard power	Hard power: necessary but not sufficient	Regime type is important	Smart power/soft power
Regime type is unimportant	Variable credence to regime type (some to minimal)	Human nature must be considered		Strong belief in and reliance on international institutions (UN, NATO)
Restraint/light footprint abroad		Distribution of power		
Declinist (O)				
No American exceptionalism (O)				
Examples: John Mearsheimer (O), Stephen M. Walt (D) Christopher Layne	Examples: Henry Kissinger, James Baker, George Kennan, Hans Morgenthau, Andrew Bacevich, E. H. Carr	Examples: Ronald Reagan, Harry Truman, Scoop Jackson, George W. Bush, Winston Churchill, Reinhold Niebuhr, George Weigel, Charles Krauthammer, Victor Davis Hanson	Examples: Tony Blair, Robert Cooper	Examples: Bill and Hillary Clinton, Joseph Nye Jr., Robert Keohane
Fareed Zakaria – bridges the spectrum between neorealism and classical realism				

and Kissinger practiced hard-headed détente, substantially reducing the Soviet Union's influence and increasing American entanglement in the region, notwithstanding their unsuccessful efforts to rely on the shah of Iran as a regional surrogate. Nixon even put American nuclear forces on high alert during the Yom Kippur War of 1973 to deter the Soviet Union from intervening militarily to rescue Egypt's beleaguered Third Army, which the Israel Defense Force had cut off on the Sinai Peninsula. Thereafter, Henry Kissinger brokered a series of ceasefire arrangements between Israel and rival Arab armies that culminated in Egypt's abandoning its quasi alliance with the Soviet Union and shifting to the American camp.[7]

Although Nixon and Obama both ended American participation in controversial wars, the similarity ends there. Obama's prompt and unconditional exit strategy in Iraq more closely resembled the position of Nixon's antiwar critics than Nixon's prolonged and costly phased withdrawal of American forces from Vietnam, punctuated by tactical escalations such as incursions into Cambodia, the mining of Haiphong Harbor, and several ferocious bombing campaigns.[8]

Nor is Fareed Zakaria correct to draw a close analogy between Obama's foreign policy and the "disciplined" leadership of President Dwight D. Eisenhower.[9] Eisenhower qualifies more as a consolidator of Truman's policy of vigilant containment rather than Stephen Stestanovich's categorization of him as a retrencher—much less a conciliator of Obama's variety. Fighting off the isolationist Old Guard in the Republican Party, Eisenhower largely followed Truman's policy of containment, which committed the United States to muscular internationalism, especially in the world's major geopolitical power centers of Western Europe, East Asia, and the Middle East. Ultimately, Eisenhower ended the war in Korea, but he did not leave America's South Korean ally on its own afterward. In contrast to Obama in the withdrawal from Iraq, Eisenhower kept thousands of American troops in South Korea. American military forces remain there to this day, defending it. Furthermore, Eisenhower significantly extended American security commitments and political engagement in the Middle East. In 1958, for example, the United States joined the military committee of the Central Eastern Treaty Organization (CENTO), an alliance unsuccessfully modeled on NATO and designed to deter Soviet aggression in the Middle East.[10]

Despite Eisenhower's warnings about the military industrial complex and the deleterious effects of excessive defense spending on the domestic economy his administration averaged a higher rate of defense spending as a percentage of GDP than any other twentieth-century president during peacetime. This contrasts with a sharp decline in defense spending under Obama. Eisenhower increased America's reliance on nuclear weapons, the very weapons that Obama has determined to end. Finally, Eisenhower escalated the scope, intensity, and ambitions of covert operations as a centerpiece of national security policy.[11] After leaving office, Eisenhower became even more hawkish. He advised incoming President John F. Kennedy that Laos was the key to Southeast Asia, possibly requiring the direct intervention of American combat troops. He also criticized as too passive President Kennedy's acquiescence toward the Soviet Union's building the Berlin Wall in August 1961.[12]

Although sharing Jefferson's reluctance to use force and his preference for relying alternatively on diplomacy or economic sanctions, Obama also does not amount to an isolationist of any sort, defined traditionally as avoiding entanglements entailing the cost or risk of war outside the Western Hemisphere. Obama conceives of America's vital interest and responsibilities more expansively than Jefferson's isolationism, Washington's contingent advocacy of non-entanglement, or Jackson's assertive, nationalistic version. Obama also has expressed major qualms—to say the least—about any nineteenth-century notion of American exceptionalism that acclaims the United States as an empire of liberty, bound and entitled to become a vast continental republic.

Among post–World War II presidents, Obama's foreign policy doctrine most resembles the outlook predominating in the first three years of the Carter administration. Initially, President Carter based his grand strategy on the assumption that the Soviet Union would emulate American restraint and concessions. In his May 1977 speech at Notre Dame University, Carter dismissed what he called "our inordinate fear of Communism." His admiring biographer Peter Bourne saluted this statement as Carter's renunciation "of the fundamental pillars on which American foreign policy had been based since World War II."[13] With the conspicuous exception of Zbigniew Brzezinski, Carter's national security adviser, the preponderance of Carter's major foreign policy advisers came from the New Politics wing of the Democratic Party, more fearful of "the arrogance of American power" than the danger of Soviet expansionism.

Cyrus Vance, Carter's secretary of state until April 1980, even believed that Carter and Soviet Premier Leonid Brezhnev held "similar dreams and aspirations about fundamental issues." Like President Obama in his early support of the Muslim Brotherhood in Egypt during the formative days of the so-called Arab Spring, the Carter administration for a long while discounted the threat of radical Islam in Iran. Andrew Young, Carter's ambassador to the United Nations, went so far as to call the fanatical and virulently anti-American Ayatollah Khomeini a saint.[14]

Despite graduating from the Naval Academy, then serving in the navy as a nuclear engineer, Carter depreciated the utility of military power in the nuclear age. Carter chose as his first nuclear arms control negotiator Paul Warnke—long known for holding the United States responsible for initiating and escalating the nuclear arms race, thus giving the Soviet Union no choice but to reciprocate. Accordingly, Carter strove to achieve large reductions in Soviet and American nuclear arsenals not just by formal arms control treaties, but also by practicing forbearance in arms building, which he counted on the Soviet Union to imitate. The Carter Administration thus delayed the development and deployment of the Trident submarine, cruise missile, and MX intercontinental ballistic missile; shut down the Minuteman ICBM production sites; canceled enhanced radiation weapons, sometimes called neutron bombs; and canceled the B-1 intercontinental strategic bomber—all programs his predecessors had considered vital to maintaining the strategic balance. Like Putin with Obama's reset, the Soviet Union confounded the Carter administration's sanguine expectations by continuing its massive, comprehensive military buildup.[15]

Obama's staunch commitment to multilateralism also mirrors Carter's. Like Obama in Iraq, Carter also tried to reduce America's military commitments abroad. Carter advocated, though Congress thwarted, the withdrawal of American combat troops from South Korea. Like Obama, Carter also anguished about the use of force, employing it rarely, for limited goals, usually with limited means, and typically only as a last resort. In contrast to Obama's, however, Carter's foreign policy became decidedly more hawkish during his final year of office. Carter boosted defense spending significantly in 1980 in an unsuccessful attempt to blunt the withering critique of his successful challenger, the Republican Ronald Reagan, who preached peace through strength and castigated Carter's détente with the

Soviet Union as rank appeasement. Carter proceeded with the MX missile he had delayed, approved military aid for the mujahideen in Afghanistan, imposed a grain embargo on the Soviet Union, boycotted the 1980 Summer Olympics, and established a rapid deployment force.[16]

The born-again hawkishness of Carter during the early stages of the 1980 presidential campaign differed strikingly from his previous foreign policy but also from his ardently dovish inclinations since leaving office—the latter closer to Obama's own proclivities. Carter vigorously opposed the Reagan administration's defense buildup and confrontational policies toward the Soviet Union. In the following years he would oppose, with no less ardor, American participation in the first war with Iraq in 1990–1991, the Bush Doctrine, and the American invasion of Iraq in 2003.[17] For better or worse, Obama has yet to demonstrate any of Carter's inclination to reset his policies on the basis of political expedience or a change in circumstances. Instead, Obama has adhered firmly during his rockier second term to the main staples of his doctrine: multilateralism, retrenchment, engagement with adversaries, and restraint.

Although President Obama's foreign policy aligns in many important ways with President Clinton's, noteworthy differences exist, though not nearly as fundamental as those between Obama and Reagan. Their differences in degree became more pronounced during President Clinton's second term, when he increasingly rejected multilateralism and championed the idea of America as the indispensable nation in world politics.

Start with the similarities. Both Clinton (by personal experience) and Obama (by second-generation conviction) had strong affiliations with the antiwar left of the Democratic Party, which considered the Vietnam War an emblematic mistake of the Cold War liberalism it repudiated in favor of the "New Politics." Both men came to office preferring to give priority to domestic rather than foreign affairs. Both devoted considerable time and energy to securing a comprehensive settlement between Israel and the Palestinians, which proved beyond their reach. Both emphasized soft power and nontraditional security concerns such as climate change and failed states. Both prescribed mainly engagement with, rather than containment of, the People's Republic of China (PRC), though Clinton's decisiveness during the Taiwan Strait crisis considerably exceeded Obama's largely passive, primarily rhetorical reaction to illegal Chinese assertions of no-fly zones and exclusive sovereignty over large swaths of the western

Pacific. In March 1996 Clinton ordered two American carrier groups into the Taiwan Strait, the largest demonstration of American military power in Asia since the Vietnam War. Sino-American tensions reached this boiling point after months of Chinese provocation, as they conducted multiple missile tests over the strait in protest of the United States' allowing Taiwan's President Lee Teng-hui to speak at his alma mater, Cornell University. The PRC aimed ultimately to intimidate Taiwanese voters into rejecting a pro-independence candidate, which it assumed Lee Teng-hui to be.[18]

In contrast to President George W. Bush, who committed the United States to facilitating democratic India's emergence as a great and nuclear power, Obama and Clinton pressed for blanket nuclear nonproliferation, punishing violators regardless of the internal character of their regime. Clinton imposed sanctions on India in 1998 for conducting nuclear tests in violation of the Nuclear Non-Proliferation Treaty (NPT). Clinton and Obama shared avidity for arms control not only by treaty but also by example. Like Obama with Iran, Clinton negotiated with a rogue North Korean regime that ostensibly agreed in 1994 to halt its nuclear weapons program and permit inspections in exchange for U.S. assistance.[19]

Like Clinton, Obama has stoutly resisted Republican entreaties for a more robust, comprehensive strategic defense program, which he views as potentially destabilizing and technically infeasible. The Clinton administration also flirted with the ideas of declinism and retrenchment, which would be prominent in the thinking of President Obama and his senior national security officials. In 1993 Undersecretary of State Peter Tarnoff ignited a political firestorm by depicting the United States as a dangerously overextended declining power, its resources and leverage diminishing—statements that President Clinton controverted convincingly, at least by his second term.[20]

These similarities do not efface the marked difference in degree between Clinton and Obama, dormant but real, from the beginning. For one thing, Clinton operated in a far less favorable environment for progressive liberalism than Obama. Clinton was in some ways the Democratic equivalent of Eisenhower in the reverse—a Democratic president governing in the age of Reagan in which the so-called Reagan Democrats constituted the swing vote of American presidential politics.[21] Democrats had lost five of the six previous presidential elections because substantial numbers of traditionally Democratic white southern voters and white northern working-class voters defected to support Republican presidential candidates. Growing up in the South, then serving as governor of Arkansas, Clinton understood better than most liberals how fundamentally the Democratic Party's leftward shift since the late 1960s on moral, cultural, and foreign policy issues had alienated the Reagan Democrats. Clinton sought assiduously to fashion himself as a more centrist "New Democrat." In 1990–1991 Clinton chaired the Democratic Leadership Council, an organization espousing a more hawkish foreign policy and pro-market neoliberal domestic policy than progressive Democrats. In 1992 Clinton campaigned against George H. W. Bush as the tougher of the two on China's violations of human rights and more willing to intervene militarily in the Balkans as the former state of Yugoslavia fragmented into violent parts. Speaking in Milwaukee in October 1992, Clinton pledged to make the promotion of democracy and American values the cornerstones of his foreign policy.[22]

Clinton reverted to his more progressive instincts during the first two years of his presidency. His ambitious, controversial, and unsuccessful endeavor to enact health-care reform, however, precipitated a political backlash that altered the trajectory of his presidency. In 1994 the Republicans captured both houses of Congress. Thereafter, Clinton's foreign and domestic policies, based on the interplay between his political calculation and evolving convictions, moved steadily to the center. The UN's impotence in the face of civil war in Somalia, genocide in Rwanda, ethnic cleansing in Bosnia, and Saddam's serial defiance of UN resolutions in Iraq sobered Clinton's keenness for multilateralism as a substitute for American power. After the UN peacekeepers stood by haplessly during the summer of 1995 while Serbians murdered seven thousand Muslim men in Srebrenica, Clinton decided to ignore, rather than defer to, the UN. Clinton led a NATO intervention with Operation Deliberate Force, defeating the Bosnian Serbs, ending the war, and establishing a peace under the Dayton Accords that still endures. In 1999 Clinton and America's NATO allies again bypassed the United Nations to wage war in Kosovo, which Serbian atrocities had precipitated.[23]

Clinton's second-term policy toward Iraq illuminates, in high relief, his increasing variance from Obama's dispositions. After Saddam banished UN arms inspectors in 1998, Clinton and British Prime Minister

Tony Blair acted as a duo of the willing, commencing a bombing campaign against Iraq while the UN Security Council remained in gridlock. Clinton's explanation for the strikes, his portrayal of the Iraq threat, and his remedy for it would bear a ring more familiar to George W. Bush than to Barack Obama:

> Saddam Hussein must not be allowed to threaten his neighbors or the world with nuclear arms, poison gas or biological weapons. . . . I have no doubt today, that left unchecked, Saddam Hussein will use these terrible weapons again. . . . The situation presents a clear and present danger to the stability of the Persian Gulf and the safety of people everywhere. The international community gave Saddam one last chance to resume cooperation with the weapons inspectors. Saddam has failed to seize that chance. . . . The best way to end that threat once and for all is a new Iraqi government—a government ready to live in peace with its neighbors, a government that respects the right of its people. . . . The costs of action must be weighed against the price of inaction. If Saddam defies the world and we fail to respond, we will face a far greater threat in the future. Saddam will strike again at his neighbors. He will make war on his own people. And mark my words, he will develop weapons of mass destruction. He will deploy them, and he will use them.[24]

Clinton also attributed appreciably more positive and negative significance to regime type than Obama does. In contrast to Obama, Clinton evolved into an ardent proponent of the United States' spreading the democratic peace. Clinton, Madeleine Albright, his secretary of state during his second term, and Anthony Lake, his national security adviser during the first term, all believed in "the muscular use of American power to help spread democracy in parts of the world where indigenous reformers were looking for support as they challenged oppressive regimes." The Clinton administration pushed hard for the enlargement of NATO not only to consolidate the Cold War victory, but also to construct a wider, open, peaceful, and democratic Europe on a more durable foundation. As Derek Chollet and James Goldgeier incisively put it, "Clinton and his team saw an expanded NATO—with new missions and new members—

as the engine to create a Europe peaceful, undivided, and democratic." The Clinton administration gave precedence to NATO expansion at the expense of placating Russian sensibilities when the two came in conflict.[25]

Conversely, Obama has lacked either the ideological inclination or political motivation to move to the center, as Clinton largely had done— at least through the midterm elections of 2014, which may precipitate a major reset of the Obama Doctrine that is based on a combination of smashing Republican victories and deteriorating international conditions. Despite Clinton's electoral success, Obama and the Democratic left generally never relinquished their serious misgivings about Bill Clinton's strategy of triangulating between liberals and conservatives. Progressives feared that triangulation could eventually result in fatally compromising the party's core principles. Obama also shared no philosophical or temperamental affinity with the Reagan Democrats the way Clinton did. By 2008, moreover, Barack Obama had the luxury of conceding this constituency to the Republicans. His two successful presidential campaigns against hawkish Republican opponents heralded to liberal and even some conservative commentators the emergence of a liberal coalition of Hispanics, women, and other minorities as the swing vote in presidential politics, supplanting the Reagan Democrats. Obama thus assembled and inspired a political base highly supportive of his agenda of expanding the prerogatives of government at home and diminishing America's footprint abroad.[26]

The emergence and political demise of Senator Joseph Lieberman, Democrat of Connecticut, as a plausible national Democratic candidate encapsulates the seismic leftward shift of the Democratic Party and national security that Obama's election heralded. In 2000 Al Gore—one of the five Democratic senators voting in favor of the first Iraq war—chose Lieberman—the quintessential Harry Truman/Scoop Jackson Cold War liberal—as his running mate. By 2006 Lieberman, who remained a vocal supporter of the second Iraq war after most liberals defected, lost the Connecticut Democratic Party primary; he won reelection as an independent instead. By 2008 he had become a pariah among Democrats for giving a speech at the Republican National Convention endorsing Obama's opponent, Senator John McCain.[27] By 2012 Lieberman had decided to retire rather than run again because his plunging approval rating doomed any plausible chance of winning. Lieberman's views on national security and foreign policy did not change one bit. He did not leave the party; the party left him—for Obama's progressivism on foreign and domestic affairs.

The convergence of changing demographics and rising disillusionment with President Bush's 2003 invasion of Iraq put a strong political wind at Obama's back that was opposite to what Clinton faced. According to a Pew Foundation poll released in April 2014, the majority of Americans said, "The United States should mind its own business internationally."[28] According to an earlier Pew Foundation survey released the previous December, an increasing number of Americans were likewise more skeptical about the ability and desirability of the United States to retain its role as a global leader.[29] These impressionistic and shifting attitudes hardly determine policy or make the Obama Doctrine inevitable. The post-2008 political climate, however, does afford a conviction politician, such as Obama, more leeway to make the most of his stalwart commitment to conciliation, multilateralism, and retrenchment as an alternative to more powerful and expansive grand strategies. Obama's Democratic base in particular has moved sharply to the left of what was the party's center of gravity during the Clinton years.[30]

The Obama Doctrine emanates from a set of principles and assumptions conflicting most fundamentally with the grand strategies of Harry Truman, Ronald Reagan, and George W. Bush for the first five years of his presidency, before mounting domestic opposition powerfully constrained Bush's discretion to pursue more robust policies toward Iran, Iraq, and Putin's Russia.

Unlike Obama, Truman presided over a vast increase in America's global responsibilities and the military power to underwrite it, for which he saw no prudential alternative. Like George F. Kennan, Truman emphasized geopolitics as the measure of ranking threats and interests. Truman believed that the United States could not be secure if a single heartland power came to dominate the world's major power centers: Europe, East Asia, and the Middle East. Truman looked on the Soviet Union as an adversary with the potential intentions and capability to achieve such dominance.[31] Truman, however, rejected the realist Kennan's more modest conception of containment, his discounting of American exceptionalism, and his tendency to treat all regimes essentially alike. By Kennan's reckoning, the United States should have aimed at nothing more than keeping Germany and Japan—centers of industrial capability—out of Soviet hands. Kennan disapproved of Truman's Mutual Defense Treaty of 1952 with a democratic Japan, Truman's decision to create NATO, and Truman's intention of a liberal democratic West Germany within NATO, which would culminate under Eisenhower—all of which Kennan considered an unduly provocative overreaction to the Soviet threat. Kennan would have even tolerated a communist West Germany and Japan, a tolerance based on his realist assumption that such entities would balance against the Soviet Union regardless of their ideology or domestic structure.[32]

Truman conceived of America's interest more broadly than as just containing the Soviet Union. He aimed to establish stable liberal democracies in Western Europe and Japan in the belief that stable liberal democracies make better allies, do not fight one another, and would preclude the recurrence of rivalries that had resulted in two cataclysmic wars. Elsewhere, the Truman administration was inclined to view pro-American authoritarian regimes as less evil than communist totalitarian regimes, absent a viable democratic alternative. Truman thus conceived of the Cold War as a moral as well as geopolitical struggle.[33] He frequently proclaimed confidence "in the eventual triumph of the moral order based on liberal values" over "Soviet totalitarianism," which he denounced as an implacable "enemy of human freedom."[34] Truman deemed the character of the Soviet regime and its animating ideology to be sources of the Soviet Union's unquenchable animosity toward the United States, requiring robust and global American political, military, and economic deterrence. Elizabeth Edwards Spalding, his finest intellectual biographer, and Alonzo Hamby, his finest political biographer, have chronicled how Truman's long-harbored and deep anticommunist and anti-Soviet attitude informed his views on foreign policy and national security: "I've no faith in any totalitarian state, be it Russian, German, Spanish, Argentinian, Dago, or Japanese. They all start out with the wrong premise—that lies are justified and that the old . . . formula, the end justifies the means, is right and necessary to maintain the power of government. I do not agree, nor do I believe that either formula can help humanity to the long hoped for millennium. Honest Communism, as set out in the 'Acts of the Apostles,' would work. But Russian Godless Pervert Systems won't work."[35]

Ultimately, Truman's evolving views crystallized into the antithesis of the Obama Doctrine. In 1950 Truman signed NSC 68, outlined by the National Security Council in April of that year. The directive dictated the main lines of American foreign and defense policy for the remainder of the Truman administration. Its logic and policy prescriptions also resonated powerfully in the Reagan administration. In the short term, NSC 68 called for tripling the defense budget as necessary but not sufficient to thwart "the Soviet Union's grand geopolitical design to achieve dominance of the Eurasian landmass." In the long term, NSC 68 called for fostering "fundamental changes in the nature of the Soviet system," that is, regime change:

> In summary, we must, by means of a rapid and sustained build-up of the political, economic, and military strength of the free world and by means of an affirmative program intended to wrest the initiative from the Soviet Union, confront it with convincing evidence of the determination and the ability of the free world to frustrate the Kremlin design of a world dominated by its will. Such evidence is the only means short of war which eventually may force the Kremlin to abandon its present course of action and to negotiate acceptable agreements on issues of major importance. The whole success of the proposed program hangs ultimately on recognition by this Government, the American people, and all free people, that the Cold War is in fact a real war in which the survival of the free world is at stake. . . . The prosecution of the program will require of us all the ingenuity, sacrifice, and unity demanded by the vital importance of the issue and the tenacity to persevere until our national objectives have been attained.[36]

NSC 68's demands for American perseverance extended to the bloody conflict in Korea, where American combat deaths would exceed by a factor of more than six the combined totals of two American wars in Iraq. Even after Chinese intervention in November 1950 escalated the cost and risk of the American commitment, Truman acted in precisely the opposite fashion President Obama did in Iraq. The United States fought doggedly to restore and maintain the status quo ante bellum—a Korea divided at the thirty-eighth parallel. Despite ravaging Truman's popularity, the Korean War and the permanent American military presence that ensued there ended up accomplishing substantially more than it appeared to at the time—demonstrating to allies American reliability and tenacity, and providing the basis for South Korea's evolution into a stable, prosperous democracy in contrast with the impoverished, repressive tyranny to the north.

The Obama Doctrine also clashes ineluctably with the former Truman Democrat Ronald Reagan's foreign and defense policies. Like President Truman and the great Soviet dissidents, Reagan argued that the root cause of the Soviet Union's implacable aggression lay in the internal structure of the Soviet regime and its malevolent ideology. The Soviet Union would remain an existential danger so long as it remained a totalitarian state. Unlike Obama, Reagan also believed there were no substitutes for American military and economic preponderance—surrogates, soft power, or multilateral institutions—to protect vital U.S. interests in geopolitically crucial regimes. Unlike Obama, who has sought to expand government power domestically and retrench internationally, Reagan sought to reduce government at home and reassert American power abroad. He rejected the prevailing sentiment of his day that American decline made substantial military and strategic retrenchment inevitable. As Reagan saw it, America's best days lay ahead so long as the United States reasserted its global leadership, restored its military primacy, and unleashed the dynamism of the private sector through a combination of deep tax cuts and substantial deregulation. Reagan's National Security Decision Directive 75 (NSDD 75)—the distilled essence of his grand strategy—enunciated his ultimate objective as transforming the Soviet regime he considered the root cause of the Cold War. Reagan left office in January 1989 with a long-menacing, belligerent evil empire fatally on the ropes, primed to unravel during the administration of George Herbert Walker Bush.[37]

Reagan also defined the objective of American grand strategy not just negatively, as resisting totalitarian tyranny, but positively, as promoting freedom, prosperity, and democratic institutions when he deemed it possible and prudent. Ronald Reagan's ideals—America's dedication to liberty—and his notion of geopolitical self-interest compelled the United States to subvert the Soviet regime. Elsewhere, Reagan always preferred a liberal democratic outcome. Like Jeane Kirkpatrick, his first ambassador to the United Nations, he would settle for the lesser evil of an authoritarian pro-American regime, such as Hosni Mubarak's in Egypt, when he deemed the likely alternative a totalitarian enemy of the United States.[38] Contrast that with Obama's de-emphasis on regime type while engaging adversaries such as revolutionary Iran or the administration's initially benign assessment of the virulently anti-American Muslim Brotherhood in Egypt.[39]

Later chapters will revisit aspects of Reagan's foreign policy record, arguing that a grand strategy anchored in moral democratic realism constitutes a vastly more prudent framework than President Obama's. It will suffice here to mention some emblematic examples that highlight the wide gulf separating Reagan's policies and priorities from Obama's. Recall that Reagan inherited a set of economic and foreign policy problems no less daunting than those Obama faced after the financial crisis of 2008. By the final year of the Carter administration, the economy had deteriorated steadily and alarmingly: inflation reached 12 percent annually and interest rates soared to 21 percent. Defense spending had dropped to 4.8 percent of the GDP, less than half of the percentage that presidents from Truman through Johnson had spent. The Arab oil embargo of 1973, oil shocks of 1978–1979, huge increases in domestic spending, and proliferating government regulation had conspired to generate and perpetuate stagflation—high inflation coupled with low growth. By 1980 American prestige internationally had plummeted to near Cold War lows. The 444-day Iranian hostage crisis and the failure of Carter's rescue mission distilled the perception of that decline to its essence. Worse, the rising power and assertiveness of the Soviet Union appeared to compound the severity and consequences of all these problems. Freedom was in retreat, collectivism on the rise.

Yet Reagan did the opposite of what Obama is doing now. Instead of raising taxes and increasing regulation, Reagan cut both. Instead of shrinking the defense budget, he nearly doubled it, embarking on the most massive peacetime buildup in American history. Instead of retrenching strategically, Reagan reasserted American power and championed a hearty version of American exceptionalism, as the United States deeply engaged in vital geopolitical regions.

Reagan also pursued the shared goals of reducing and eliminating nuclear weapons by means that are precisely opposite to those Obama is using now. Whereas Obama stresses the potential of forbearance and negotiation, Reagan considered American military preponderance the most reliable safeguard of the national interest and the most dependable means to induce hostile states to disarm.[40] Reagan applied and sustained relentless economic, political, and military pressure on the Soviet Union to convince Soviet leaders they could no longer compete with the United States. This pressure did not relent even after Mikhail Gorbachev took power and even though Reagan considered him a different type of Soviet leader. Reagan refused to abandon the Strategic Defense Initiative (SDI) or the Zero Option, calling for the elimination of all intermediate-range nuclear weapons in Europe. Throughout the Reagan presidency, American defense spending continued to rise, peaking at 6.6 percent of GDP—double the percentage to which defense spending will eventually fall under Obama's plan. Obama also recoils from Reagan's optimistic estimation of and categorical commitment to strategic defense as an essential hedge against cheating, even in a world of fewer or especially zero nuclear weapons.

Contrast, finally, the purposes and content of Obama's public diplomacy with Reagan's. Typically, Obama employs public diplomacy to bridge differences, to apologize for past excesses of American foreign policy, or to rebut what he regards as extravagant claims of American exceptionalism verging on hubristic triumphalism. Typically, Reagan employed public diplomacy to wage war against the legitimacy of the Soviet regime or to propound a glowing exposition of American exceptionalism that acknowledges our vices but highlights our virtues. Examples abound: Reagan's constant refrain about the evil essence of Soviet communism; his unapologetic defense of freedom as a universal aspiration embodied in the Declaration of Independence; his famous exhortation for Gorbachev to "tear down" the Berlin Wall.[41] Reagan's speech to the National Association of Evangelicals on March 8, 1983, incorporates and conveys with gusto all his trademark themes, jarring to the sensibilities of an Obama more ambivalent about America's uniqueness or benevolence:

> There is sin and evil in the world, and we're enjoined by Scripture and the Lord Jesus to oppose it with all our might. Our nation, too, has a legacy of evil with which it must deal. The glory of this land has been its capacity for transcending the moral evils of our past. For example, the long struggle of minority citizens for equal rights, once a source of disunity and civil war, is now

a point of pride for all Americans. . . . There is no room for racism, anti-Semitism, or other forms of ethnic and racial hatred in this country. . . . But whatever sad episodes exist in our past, any objective observer must hold a positive view of American history, a history that has been the story of hopes fulfilled, and dreams made into reality. Especially in this century, America has kept alight the torch of freedom, but not just for ourselves but for millions of others around the world. And this brings me to my final point today. . . . As good Marxist-Leninists, the Soviet leaders have openly and publicly declared that the only morality they recognize is that which will further their cause, which is world revolution. . . . But if history teaches anything, it teaches that simple-minded appeasement or wishful thinking about our adversaries is folly. It means betrayal of our past, the squandering of our freedom. . . . I believe we shall rise to the challenge. I believe that communism is another sad, bizarre chapter in human history whose last pages even now are being written. I believe this because the source of our strength in the quest for human freedom is not material, but spiritual. And because it knows no limitation, it must terrify and ultimately triumph over those who would enslave their fellow man. For in the words of Isaiah: "He giveth power to the faint; and to them that have no might He increased strength. . . . But they that wait upon the Lord shall renew their strength; they shall mount up with wings as eagles; they shall run and not be weary."[42]

The wide divergence between the Obama and Bush doctrines essentially parallels the Obama-Reagan divide. Straining to distance Reagan's legacy from the Iraq war that began in 2003, some commentators have attempted to draw untenable distinctions between George W. Bush and Reagan that cannot withstand scrutiny. George W. Bush largely qualifies as a moral democratic realist in the Truman-Reagan tradition despite the legitimate debate that will continue for a long time to come over the wisdom of the Iraq war, how the United States waged it, and when the United States left it. Unlike Obama, Reagan and Bush largely agreed on the first principles of American foreign policy, including democratic regime change as a prudent aim when the regime of America's adversary constituted the root cause of the conflict, such as Nazi Germany during World War II and the Soviet Union during the Cold War.

George Shultz—Reagan's longest-serving secretary of state, whom Reagan identified as his most important foreign policy adviser—authoritatively sums up the essential similarity linking George W. Bush, Reagan, and mainstream neoconservatives whom Obama disdains:

> I don't know how you define "neoconservatism" . . . but I think it's associated with trying to spread open systems and democracy. I recall President Reagan's Westminster speech in 1982—that communism would be consigned to the "ash heap of history" and freedom was the path ahead. And what happened? Between 1980 and 1990, the number of countries that were classified as "free" or "mostly free" increased by about 50%. Open political and economic systems have been gaining ground and there's good reason for it. They work better. . . . I'm in favor of vision. Ronald Reagan had vision.[43]

As Daniel Henninger observes, too, George W. Bush did not originate the doctrine of preemption that Barack Obama opposes nearly categorically. It was George Shultz who first made the case for including preemption in our repertoire of options against certain types of threats emanating from certain types of actors.[44] Like Winston Churchill—the man he credited for doing more than "any man to preserve civilization during its hour of greatest trial"—Reagan also endorsed the preemptive use of force as the most prudent option in certain circumstances, for the reason his hero Churchill conveys: "If you will not fight when your victory is sure and not too costly . . . you may come to a moment when you will have to fight with the odds against you and only a precarious chance for survival."[45] Reagan would have deplored President Obama's more relaxed view of Islamic radicalism, nuclear proliferation in the Middle East, and the danger of a nuclear Iran in particular. "I do not think you can overstate the importance that the rise of Islamic fundamentalism will have to the rest of the world in the century ahead," Reagan wrote in his memoirs.[46] Although Reagan abstained from the unbridled democratic globalism of some but hardly all neoconservative proponents of the Bush Doctrine, Reagan found much that was congenial in the neoconservativism that Obama on the left and Rand Paul on the libertarian right continue to excoriate.[47] Reagan, neoconservative admirers of Bush, Bush himself, and hawks of all varieties stoutly oppose as dangerous and unwise strategic retrenchment or cutting defense spending significantly. On the contrary, Reagan shared with hawks of all varieties a fervent belief in the indispensability of American military preeminence, including a generous margin to spare to defeat and deter global threats to America's vital interests.[48]

Reagan shared with Bush and his neoconservative admirers, too, a passionate support for Israel. As Reagan put it, "The Holocaust, I believe, left America with a moral responsibility to ensure that what had happened to the Jews under Hitler never happens again. . . . My dedication to the preservation of Israel was as strong when I left office as when I arrived there, even though the tiny ally, with whom we shared democracy and many other values, was a source of great concern for me while I was President."[49] Bush's reset of America's military, political, and economic relationship with India also reflected his Reaganite embrace of the democratic peace argument as well as geopolitical calculation to counter the rising power of an authoritarian China. Conversely, Obama accords far less importance to either the geopolitical or regime type rationale impelling Bush to initiate and cultivate a strategic partnership between the United States and India.

Look instead to Rand Paul, Republican of Kentucky, as the figure in contemporary American politics who champions a foreign policy and national security strategy most closely aligned with the main tenets of the Obama Doctrine. Paul has revived a tradition of minimalism, a reluctance to use force, and a nonideological, narrow definition of the national interest that the Republican Party abandoned after Dwight D. Eisenhower defeated Senator Robert Taft, Republican of Ohio, for the party's presidential nomination in 1952. Notwithstanding Paul's untenable designation of himself as a Reaganite, his views on foreign and defense policy have more in common with President Obama's than the robust internationalism emblematic of Truman, Reagan, and George W. Bush. Like Obama, Paul calls for deep cuts to America's "bloated Defense Department" and devolution of America's global commitments. "A less aggressive foreign policy along with an audit of the Pentagon could save tens of billions of dollars each year without sacrificing our defense," Paul told

CNN in 2012.[50] On the National Security Agency's surveillance program and the use of drones, Paul is even more dovish than Obama. He led the filibuster against the administration's use of drones. He denounced NSA spying that has continued under Obama as unconstitutional and likened the national security leaker Edward Snowden to Martin Luther King Jr.[51]

Paul venerates George F. Kennan, who disdained Reagan, reviled American exceptionalism in foreign affairs, and opposed Truman's version of vigilant containment in favor of a more modest, less ideological, primarily diplomatic rather than military version. Paul has vigorously defended the logic and practice of Obama's foreign policy against the administration's hawkish critics. Paul acclaimed—as "exactly what we need to resolve the standoff with Iran and North Korea"—the agreement that Vladimir Putin brokered between the Obama administration and Bashir al-Assad in Syria, which invested the United States with the responsibility to divest al-Assad of chemical weapons. Paul has endorsed Obama's "restrained" and "measured" response to China's prodigious military buildup, its growing assertiveness, and Putin's swelling ambitions, including those in Ukraine. Paul has chosen as one of his principal foreign policy advisers the highly controversial Dimitri Simes, who has deep ties to the Putin regime. Unlike Obama, Simes defends Putin's tough stance in Syria and Ukraine. Like Obama, he advocates engagement and restraint rather than robust deterrence of Russia.[52]

More averse to using force than any post–World War II president, including even Obama and Carter, Paul categorically opposes it, except as a last resort, whereas Obama establishes a formidable burden of proof to justify force unilaterally, decisively, and sooner rather than later.[53]

Paul discounts the danger of a nuclear Iran or Islamic radicalism, opposed the Iraq war, and supported Obama's determination to end American involvement expeditiously. Paul blames the surge in violence tearing Iraq and the greater Middle East asunder on Dick Cheney and George W. Bush rather than Obama's complete withdrawal of all American combat troops from Iraq in 2011. Paul applauds the Obama administration's unwillingness to use force or reengage America substantially to quell the ferocious insurgency.[54] Paul opposes using force in either Iraq or Syria to defeat the fanatical Islamic State of Iraq and Syria (ISIS). In this case, he espouses a position even more dovish than Obama's while opposing the neo-Reaganite mainstream of the Republican Party.[55] Paul approves, too, of President Obama's decision to normalize relations with Cuba, which the dominant internationalist wing of the Republican Party deplores.[56]

Granted, Paul has made a concerted effort to rebrand himself as distinct from his father, Ron Paul, who—like Pat Buchanan and Charles Lindbergh before him—still considers American intervention in World War II a mistake.[57] As David Adesnik shows, however, Paul's reading list for students on his own website undermines that claim: no books on Ronald Reagan or the fall of the Soviet Union, and many favorites from left- and right-wing isolationists and moral relativists such as Chalmers Johnson's screed *Blowback*.[58] A Rand Paul presidency would probably reinforce, rather than reverse, the strong gravitational pull the Obama Doctrine has established away from full-bodied internationalism as Reagan, Truman, or George W. Bush conceived and practiced it.

No historical analogy, American foreign policy tradition, or unalloyed international relations theory encapsulates the essence of President Obama's grand strategy. The Obama Doctrine reflects, instead, the president's original and largely coherent synthesis that draws on multiple sources and experiences. The next three chapters will turn from the realm of theory to the implementation and consequences of the Obama Doctrine.

4

The Obama Doctrine's Reset with Russia and Europe

For all nations, even an immensely powerful United States, resources are finite. The concept of geopolitics as Halford Mackinder and Nicholas Spykman conceived it remains essential for ranking interests, threats, priorities, and opportunities. In his seminal *Geographical Pivot of History,* published in 1904, Mackinder warned that any single power controlling Eurasia, "the World Island," would have resources vast enough to dominate the world, including the United States.[1] Writing in 1942, Spykman inverted Mackinder's dictum, which stressed the advantage of controlling the Heartland (the core lands of Eurasia). Instead, Spykman considered controlling the Rimland—the coastal land circling Eurasia—as the prime imperative for a maritime power such as the United States.[2] Yet both these formulations lead to the same conclusion, which the history of American foreign relations has vindicated. The United States has a vital and enduring interest in preventing a hostile hegemon from dominating any or all of the world's major power centers—Europe, East Asia, and the Middle East. During the twentieth century, the United States rightly fought two world wars to prevent Germany from achieving such dominance. During the Cold War, American statesmen based their successful strategy of containment largely, though not exclusively, on similar geopolitical calculations: namely, that the United States could not be secure if an ideologically hostile and militarily powerful Soviet Union came to dominate the European continent.[3]

Henry Kissinger encapsulates why geopolitical imperatives have not lost their salience for American national security in the twenty-first century: "Geopolitically, America is an island off the shores of a large landmass of Eurasia, where resources and population far exceed those of the United States. The domination by a single power of either of Eurasia's two principal spheres—Europe or Asia—remains a good definition of strategic danger for America. . . . For such a grouping would have the capacity to outstrip America economically and, in the end, militarily."[4] Asia has eclipsed Europe—paramount between 1500 and 2000—as the more important of these two spheres. The domination by a single hostile power of the Middle East also remains "a good definition of strategic danger" for America.[5] Such a hegemon would have the potential to combine the power emanating from controlling the Middle East's oil reserves with radicalism seething in the region and the proliferation of weapons of mass destruction (WMD).

So no metric should prove more crucial than whether the Obama Doctrine has well or ill served American interests in the world's most important geopolitical regions.[6] This chapter examines the record of the Obama Doctrine in Europe. The following two chapters examine the Obama Doctrine's record in the Middle East and in Asia.

President Obama envisaged his policy of "resetting" relations with Russia as the centerpiece of the Obama Doctrine's strategy for reframing U.S. relations with Europe. Despite encountering formidable and mounting obstacles, President Obama has invested great time and energy trying to engage rather than deter increasingly authoritarian and assertive Russia— still the greatest threat to America's vital interest of keeping Europe stable, open, democratic, and cooperative.

Russian-American relations had slowly but steadily deteriorated since their peak of cooperation during the 1990s before Obama announced his "reset" in the summer of 2009. President Boris Yeltsin pursued a pro-Western policy of greater freedom at home and more conciliatory Russian foreign policy abroad. He acquiesced—albeit begrudgingly on occasion—to NATO expansion into Eastern Europe, which enlarged and consolidated the democratic zone of peace. The more open, democratic, and free-market-oriented Russia of the Yeltsin years reduced defense spending drastically and ended Russian and Soviet presence in East Central Europe. Although resenting NATO's 1999 decision to wage war without UN approval against Russia's traditional ally in Serbia for systematic Serbian atrocities perpetrated in Kosovo, Yeltsin established and provisionally sustained the most democratic and pro-Western regime in Russian history. As Leon Aron—Yeltsin's finest biographer—notes, Russia "restored to their original occupied nations . . . lands acquired and held during two-and-a-half centuries of imperial conquests, from Peter the Great to Brezhnev. Russia returned to its seventeenth-century borders."[7] Yeltsin's Russia concluded with Ukraine a landmark 1991 Treaty of Friendship, Cooperation, and Partnership, committing the two nations to respect each other's territorial integrity and the inviolability of existing borders. On December 5, 1994, Yeltsin's Russia, Ukraine, the United States, and Great Britain also signed the Budapest Memorandums, guaranteeing the independence and sovereignty of the existing borders of Ukraine in return for Ukraine's giving up thousands of nuclear warheads left there after the disintegration of the Soviet Union.[8]

The rise and ascendency of Vladimir Putin in Russian politics mark a major negative watershed in the downward spiral of Russian-American relations that President Obama inherited in January 2009. Putin largely reversed the trajectory of Russian foreign and domestic policy under Yeltsin. After becoming president of Russia in 2000, Putin acted expeditiously and ruthlessly to subdue Chechen rebels, whom he considered terrorists illegitimately seeking independence from Moscow. Putin that year launched what is known as the Second War in Chechnya—a federal republic of Moscow located in the North Caucasus—in response to a series of apartment bombings in Moscow and other Russian cities that killed hundreds. Although Chechen separatists had indeed resorted to terrorism previously, questions linger about who deserves the blame. John Dunlop, a senior fellow at the Hoover Institution at Stanford, makes a compelling case in his fine book on the subject that Russian authorities were complicit in these attacks, which Putin used as a pretext for waging a remorseless war.[9]

Thereafter, Putin put Russia on the path of greater authoritarianism at home and assertiveness abroad. Although initially supporting the U.S. war on terror and continuing to facilitate American military operations in Afghanistan, Putin assailed the Bush administration for fighting the second Iraq war. Putin objected likewise to the administration of George W. Bush abrogating the ABM Treaty of 1972 so the United States could more effectively and energetically pursue ballistic missile defense. Like his Soviet predecessors, Putin fears that Russia lacks the technical capability to compete with a determined United States in the realm of missile defense. Putin vehemently opposed President George W. Bush's missile defense plan to deploy two-stage Ground-Based Midcourse Defense (GMD) interceptors in Poland and highly capable X-Band Radar in the Czech Republic, though this plan originated to counter a potential missile threat from Iran rather than Russia's ballistic missile force.[10]

Meanwhile, Putin increased Russian support for virulently anti-American regimes in the Middle East: Bashar al-Assad's brutal dictatorship in Syria and an incendiary, anti-Semitic Islamist theocracy in Iran that appears to this writer to be intent on crossing the nuclear threshold. Putin turned sharply away from Yeltsin's more conciliatory policy toward Ukraine. He reacted angrily to the 2004 Orange Revolution in Ukraine, which peacefully replaced the fraudulently elected pro-Russian President Viktor Yanukovych with the genuine winner, the ardently pro-Western Viktor Yushchenko. Putin accused the United States and the European Union of fomenting the protests that brought Yushchenko to power.[11] In his annual address to the Federal Assembly of the Russian Federation on April 25, 2005, Putin alarmingly and appallingly called "the collapse of the Soviet Union . . . a major geopolitical disaster of the century. . . . Tens of millions of our co-citizens and compatriots found themselves outside Russian territory. Moreover, the epidemic of disintegration infected Russia itself."[12]

On February 10, 2007, Putin delivered his most important, widely disseminated, and emblematic pre-Obama foreign policy speech at the Munich Conference on Security Policy. Although deeming "President Bush . . . a decent person," Putin railed against what he calls American domination in international politics. He warned of the danger of a unipolar world, "in which there is one master, one sovereign. And at the end of the day this is pernicious not only for all those within the system, but also for the sovereign itself because it destroys itself from within. And this certainly has nothing in common with democracy. . . . What is even more important is that the model itself is flawed because at its basis there is and can be no moral foundations for modern civilisation." Putin accused the United States of "an almost uncontained hyper use of force—military force—in international relations, force that is plunging the world into an abyss of permanent conflicts." He singled out the United States for displaying "a greater and greater disdain for the basic principles of international law." According to Putin, the United States "has overstepped its national borders in every way. This is visible in the economic, political, cultural and educational policies it imposes on other nations. Well, who likes this? Who is happy about this?" He reprised his standard complaints about NATO expansion, saying that it "does not have any relation with the modernisation of the Alliance itself or with ensuring security in Europe." Putin fumed, "We have the right to ask: against whom is this expansion intended?"[13]

Putin's speech elicited sharp criticism in some quarters, especially from Senator John McCain, who linked swelling Russian assertiveness abroad with increasing authoritarianism at home. McCain rebutted Putin, asking, "Will Russia's autocratic turn become more pronounced, its foreign policy more opposed to the principles of Western democracies and its energy policies used as a tool of intimidation? Moscow must understand that it cannot enjoy a genuine partnership with the West so long as its actions, at home and abroad, conflict fundamentally with the core values of the Euro-Atlantic democracies."[14] Russian-American relations reached their post–Cold War, pre-Obama low point in the summer of 2008, when the Soviet Union intervened militarily in the former Soviet Republic of Georgia following the election of a pro-American president eager to join NATO. Putin invoked, as a pretext, alleged Georgian attacks on ethnic Russian populations within the Georgian provinces of South Ossetia and Abkhazia. Although the Bush administration condemned Russian aggression rhetorically, the United States did little materially to punish Putin for it.[15]

Obama came to office espousing a far more benign view of Russian intentions than the increasingly wary President Bush maintained by the end of his administration. Obama envisioned Russia at its worst as "a part-time spoiler" rather than a formidable geopolitical adversary.[16] He considered great-power rivalry as an archaic relic of the past, rendered largely moot by the enlightened norms of the international community. He believed that Russian-American interests aligned more fundamentally than they clashed, especially in the areas of arms control, nonproliferation, disarmament, curbing Iran's nuclear ambitions, and stabilizing the Middle East. In large measure, Obama attributed the deterioration of

Russian-American relations during the previous eight years to the Bush administration's belligerence and bumptiousness rather than the internal dynamics of Russia's increasingly authoritarian regime and the swelling ambitions it encouraged. The Obama administration assiduously courted Dmitry Medvedev, president of Russia from 2008 until Putin's return in 2012. Facing a constitutionally mandated term limit, Putin served as prime minister in the interim while ruling Russia de facto. Hillary Clinton explained the administration's logic in her memoirs: "Medvedev surprised many by bringing a new tone to the Kremlin. He seemed more open to dissenting views at home, more conciliatory abroad, and more interested in diversifying Russia's economy beyond gas, oil, and other commodities."[17] Eventually, the administration acknowledged its error in overestimating Medvedev's authority and independence. Instead of liberalizing, Putin continued to strengthen his grip on power and eliminate any potential rivals. That, however, did not diminish the president's sturdy confidence in the potential for cooperating with Russia. Like his realist and neorealist admirers, Obama assumed that the character of the Russian regime has little bearing on how Russia conducts its foreign policy, assesses its interests, and calculates risk. So Obama worried less about what Russia's growing authoritarian trend meant for the reset than did his hawkish critics or even his own secretary of state.

President Obama's first encounter with Medvedev at the 2009 Group of 20 summit meeting encouraged his lofty expectations for the reset that his more skeptical secretary of state, warier of Putin's inclinations and influence, did not entirely share. As Peter Baker describes it in the *New York Times,* "The two sat down and found they had much in common—both were new-generation leaders, trained in law, unburdened by the past, who saw themselves more as pragmatists than ideologues. And while it was clear Mr. Putin, then serving as the prime minister, was still the paramount figure, Mr. Obama resolved to build up Mr. Medvedev in hopes that he would eventually emerge as the real power."[18]

President Obama laid out his concept and rationale for establishing a better relationship with Russia in a July 7, 2009, graduation address to the New Economic School in Moscow. Obama rejected "old assumptions . . . old ways of thinking; a conception of power that is rooted in the past rather than the future." Obama rejected "the 20th century view that the United States and Russia are destined to be antagonists, and that a strong Russia or a strong America can only assert themselves in opposition to one another." He further rejected "a 19th century view that we are destined to vie for spheres of influence, and that great powers must forge competing blocs to balance one another." Instead, Obama asserted that in the twenty-first century, "a great power does not show strength by dominating or demonizing other countries." Obama pronounced that "the days when empires could treat sovereign states as pieces on a chess board" were over. He reiterated the message from his 2009 Cairo speech, saying, "Given our independence, any world order that tries to elevate one nation or one group of people over another will inevitably fail. The pursuit of power is no longer a zero-sum game. . . . That's why I have called a 'reset' in relations between the United States and Russia . . . a sustained effort among the American and Russian people to identify mutual interests, and expand dialogue and cooperation that can pave the way to progress."[19]

Obama professed his trust in the "extraordinary potential for increased cooperation between Americans and Russians" and his belief that "on the fundamental issues that will shape this century, Americans and Russians share common interests." First, both nations have "an interest in reversing the spread of nuclear weapons and preventing their use. . . . That's why we should be united in opposing North Korea's efforts to become a nuclear power, and opposing Iran's efforts to acquire a nuclear weapon." Second, both nations have "a critical national interest . . . in isolating and defeating violent extremists" such as al-Qaeda and its affiliates.[20]

No doubt the reset reaped some benefits for the United States. It facilitated significantly the American war effort in Afghanistan. As Obama's former secretary of defense Robert Gates argues persuasively, Russia simplified America's logistical difficulties considerably by permitting the United States to convey forces destined for Afghanistan through Russian territory.[21] The Obama administration also hailed the reset more controversially for securing Russian cooperation at the UN to impose tougher sanctions on Iran that purportedly brought Iran to the bargaining table over its nuclear program. Without U.S.–Russian cooperation, so this argument runs, Russia would more likely have employed its veto on the Security Council to thwart strong collective action, as Putin was inclined to do during a more truculent Bush administration. Russia still participates as a member of the P5+1 (also including China, the United Kingdom, France, the United States, and Germany), negotiating with Iran in the hope of inducing the Iranian regime not to cross the nuclear weapons threshold. Hillary Clinton's litany of the reset's successes also includes imposing sanctions on North Korea, expanding counterterrorism operations, and bringing Russia into the World Trade Organization.[22]

The reset also yielded the New Strategic Arms Reduction Treaty (New START) between the United States and Russia, signed in April 2010 and effective until 2021. By a margin of 71 to 26, the Senate ratified New START in December 2010. New START reduces to 1,550 the number of nuclear warheads and bombs for each side. It limits each side to no more than 800 deployed and nondeployed land-based intercontinental ballistic missiles (ICBMs) and submarine-launched ballistic missiles (SLBM). Within those limits, New START establishes a sub-ceiling for each side of no more than 700 deployed ICBMs, deployed SLBMs, and deployed heavy bombers equipped to deliver nuclear weapons. New START does not inhibit the Obama administration's current or planned missile defense programs directed at Iran and North Korea. It does prohibit the conversion of ICBM and SLBM launchers into launchers for ballistic missile defense.[23]

Obama acclaimed New START as a landmark achievement, thanking his "friend and partner, Dmitry Medvedev," with whom he had "developed a very effective . . . relationship built on candor, cooperation, and mutual respect."[24] He envisioned New START as just the beginning of working further with Medvedev on "big issues" of mutual concern:

> I also came to office committed to "resetting" relations between the United States and Russia, and I know that President Medvedev shared that commitment. . . . Together, we've . . . proven the benefits of cooperation. Today is an important milestone for nuclear security and non-proliferation, and for U.S.-Russia relations. . . . This day demonstrates the determination of the United States and Russia—the two nations that hold over 90 percent of the world's nuclear weapons—to pursue responsible global leadership. . . . We hope to pursue discussions with Russia on reducing both our strategic and tactical weapons, including nondeployed weapons. President Medvedev and I have agreed to expand our discussions on missile defense. . . . When nations and peoples allow themselves to be defined by their differences, the

gulf between them widens. When we fail to pursue peace, then it stays forever beyond our grasp. . . . The pursuit of peace and calm and cooperation among nations is the work of both leaders and peoples in the 21st century. For we must be as persistent and passionate in the pursuit of progress as any who would stand in our way.[25]

According to the administration's defenders, whose ranks include some prominent past and present Republican officials, New START strengthened strategic stability and improved relations between Moscow and Washington. John Kerry, who was then chairman of the Senate Foreign Relations Committee, argued, too, that ratification would "show the international community that we are honoring our commitments on nonproliferation."[26] According to critics, New START highly favored Moscow, as it required the United States to build down its arsenal of missiles while allowing the Russians—substantially under the limits—to build up theirs. Critics also charged that Russia could use the language of the legally nonbinding preamble on the interrelationship between offensive and defensive systems as a pretext to abrogate the treaty if it believes that the United States has significantly increased its missile defense capability. Writing in the *Washington Post,* former Massachusetts Governor Mitt Romney labeled New START "Obama's worst foreign-policy mistake" for these reasons.[27]

From the vantage point of 2011, though not in hindsight, the reset appeared to yield another success that year when the Arab Spring triggered the outbreak of civil war in Libya. President Obama persuaded Medvedev not to veto in the United Nations Security Council the allied bombing campaign against the Libyan dictator Muammar al-Gaddafi, which Obama portrayed as limited and merely humanitarian. The reset reached its apotheosis in March 2012, when an open microphone caught President Obama telling Medvedev, in reference to missile defense: "Let me get reelected first, then I'll have a better chance of making something happen. On all these issues, but particularly missile defense, this, this can be solved, but it's important for him [Putin] to give me space. . . . This is my last election. After my election I have more flexibility." Medvedev replied to the president: "I understand. I will transmit this information to Vladimir.[28]

The president's statement reignited the controversy over his September 2009 decision to cancel President George W. Bush's proposed antiballistic missile shield in Europe and substitute slower interceptors aimed at countering Iran's short- and intermediate-range missiles. Despite the Bush administration's denials, the Russians had complained vociferously that Bush's plan aimed to counter Russian missiles and undermine the Russian nuclear deterrent. Instead, President Obama proposed a four-phase plan, starting in Phase I with the deployment of SM-3 interceptor missiles at sea in waters adjacent to Europe and culminating in Phase IV with the deployment of interceptors in Europe that possibly would have the capability to target long-range intercontinental ballistic missiles that are part of the Russian nuclear arsenal.[29] Senator John McCain, Governor Mitt Romney, former Vice President Dick Cheney, and other hawkish Republicans pilloried Obama's cancellation of Bush's plan as a cave-in to Russian pressure that constituted appeasement.[30] The administration insisted that the reset had no connection with the decision. The president and Secretary of Defense Robert Gates defended the administration's alternative as a smarter, swifter, and more effective counter to the changing threat from Iran.[31]

Russia reacted favorably. Medvedev welcomed Obama's cancellation of Bush's plan. Putin hailed the decision as "correct and brave."[32] In March 2013 the administration canceled Phase IV of its plan, to which the Russians had continued to object fiercely and cite as an impediment to future arms control agreements. Again, Secretary of Defense Chuck Hagel denied that the desire to assuage Russian concerns prompted its abandonment, though administration officials mentioned the possibility of "side benefits that accrue with Russia."[33] Hawkish Republicans such as Senator Kelly Ayotte, Republican of New Hampshire, criticized the decision as an ill-advised concession to Russia, viewing it through the lens of what Obama told Medvedev in March 2012—that he could be more forthcoming during his second term.[34]

Although the debate about Obama's motivation for canceling continues, the results speak for themselves: the Obama administration has scaled back missile defense sharply in all dimensions, pleasing Putin and distressing Republicans. The administration cut the budget for missile defense significantly. If sequestration remains in effect, the cuts become even deeper. The administration has de-emphasized space-based and boost-phase defense and defense against long-range missiles. It has reduced by more than 20 percent the assets Congress authorized to fund the mission defense cooperation program with Israel, including the Iron Dome system.[35] Nor, to date, has the crisis unfolding in Ukraine impelled President Obama to reverse his modest plans for missile defense, which many see as part of his unrelenting efforts to salvage the reset with Russia. The president has resisted all calls from conservative hawks on Capitol Hill and in the punditry for accelerating his missile defense plans across the board, including Europe. The administration has not contemplated expanding ballistic missile defense to protect the United States and American allies from Russia's ballistic missiles. Instead, the president's defense policy aims to preserve the existing strategic-nuclear balance between the United States and Russia.[36]

If Obama had any misgivings about the efficacy of the reset with Russia, he concealed them masterfully during the 2012 presidential campaign. Obama chastised Mitt Romney in the third presidential debate for calling Russia America's number one geopolitical threat: "Governor Romney, I'm glad that you recognize that Al Qaida is a threat, because a few months ago when you were asked what's the biggest geopolitical threat facing America, you said Russia, not Al Qaida; you said Russia, in the 1980s, they're now calling to ask for their foreign policy back because, you know, the Cold War's been over for 20 years."[37]

Yet the perception had increasingly crystalized outside the Obama administration that the reset with Russia had failed even before Russia's invasion and annexation of Crimea in March 2014 doomed it. Even some prominent former members of President Obama's national security team readily acknowledged the policy failure, though Obama and his current secretary of state, John Kerry, continue to cling tenaciously to the hope the reset can endure this time of troubles with Russia. "For those who expected the reset to reopen a new era of goodwill between Russia and the United States, it proved a bitter disappointment," former Secretary of State Hillary Clinton lamented in her memoirs.[38] "There's this cycle of initial enthusiasm . . . that gives way to reality," mused Robert Gates, Obama's first secretary of defense.[39] Writing in the *New York Times* on September 2, 2013, Peter Baker—typically sympathetic to the Obama administration—described the reset with Russia as "a case study in how the heady idealism of Mr. Obama's first term has given way to the disillusionment of his second."[40] What went wrong and why?

For starters, the Obama Doctrine unwisely discounted the importance of regime type, ideology, traditional geopolitical rivalry, and American hard power. President Obama fundamentally misjudged the character of Russia's increasingly nasty, authoritarian, and assertive regime, the grandiosity of Russia's swelling ambitions, and the inability of democratic Europe to counter them without strong American leadership stressing muscular deterrence rather than conciliatory engagement.

With the few exceptions noted above, Russian behavior has confounded the optimistic assumptions on which the administration has predicated the reset. Putin has banned Americans from adopting Russian children and given asylum to the national security leaker Edward Snowden. The 2011 allied bombing campaign in Libya, which the administration considered a success of the reset, incensed Putin, who believed the Obama administration had double-crossed him when the mission expanded to removing Gaddafi—a traditional Russian ally—from power. Putin and Medvedev accused NATO of overstepping the mandate of the UN resolution authorizing a limited humanitarian bombing campaign.[41]

Russia vowed, accordingly, to block any Western military action against Bashar al-Assad's murderous dictatorship in Syria, another traditional Russian ally. Throughout the escalating Syrian civil war (a topic of extensive discussion in the next chapter), the Russians have unswervingly supported Assad and shielded him from the consequences of using chemical weapons against his own population, in defiance of President Obama's red line. Putin well served his interest of reasserting Russian influence in the Middle East at America's expense by brokering an international agreement in September 2013 that purportedly put Syrian chemical weapons under UN control, where Russia can exercise its veto on the Security Council to protect its Syrian client.[42] The Syrians accepted the proposal precisely because of the unlikelihood of its effective enforcement. The Russians successfully insisted that the UN chemical weapons agreement to divest Syria of its arsenal not include a use-of-force clause in the event of Syrian noncompliance.[43] After President Obama announced his decision on September 10, 2013, to defer military action against Syria in favor of diplomatic options, Putin responded brusquely and provocatively. His editorial in the *New York Times* the following day assailed the United States for intervening in other countries and imposing its will by brute force. Putin ridiculed the notion of American exceptionalism, while mendaciously posing as champion of the very international standards Russia has defied routinely and systematically in Chechnya, Crimea, Ukraine, Central Europe, and the Middle East.[44]

Since September 2013, Assad has consolidated his hold on power, ignoring multiple U.S. and EU calls to step down. Putin continues to render Assad critical assistance, bolstering his regime. Russia has blocked multiple resolutions at the UN that would have condemned or punished the Assad regime. Putin has defied President Obama and the NATO alliance by sending more and deadlier arms to Assad, including modern aircraft and missiles. "Russia is now doing everything to ensure that Assad wins convincingly," according to Alexei Malashenko, a Middle East expert at the Moscow Carnegie Center. "If Russia can show it's capable of carrying out its own foreign policy, regardless of America's wishes, it will be a major achievement for Putin."[45]

Notwithstanding the administration's claims to the contrary, Russia has more hindered than helped U.S. efforts to prevent the revolutionary theocracy in Iran—another traditional Russian ally—from eventually building nuclear weapons. Expect Putin to invoke the Syrian precedent, making any future military action against Iran's nuclear program contingent on the UN's approval. Essentially, this means no action, given the gridlock organic to the UN Security Council, guaranteed in this case by a certain veto by Russia as one of the five permanent members.

As President Obama shrinks the American defense budget, Putin has made restoring Russian military might a top priority. Nikolas N. Gvosdev—formerly editor of the *National Interest* and currently a professor of national security studies at the U.S. Naval War College in Newport, Rhode Island—instructs that "Russia is now engaged in its largest military buildup since the collapse of the Soviet Union more than two decades ago, with major increases in defense spending budgeted each year to 2020. Putin has pushed for this program even over the objections of some within the Kremlin who worried about costs and the possible negative impact on Russian prosperity."[46] His plan calls for Russia to spend $755 billion dollars over the next decade to field a military of one million active-duty personal armed with 2,300 new tanks, 1,200 new military aircraft and helicopters, "fifty new surface ships and twenty-eight submarines, with one hundred new satellites designed to augment Russia's communications, command and control capabilities."[47] Putin intends for Russia to possess a modernized nuclear triad (ICBMs, SLBMs, and intercontinental strategic bombers capable of delivering nuclear weapons), a formidable blue-water navy, state-of-the art space and cyber forces, and a strong land army. Under Putin, Russia has become correspondingly more brazen in conducting military exercises designed to intimidate NATO, particularly the Eastern European members, from resisting Russian ambitions in Central Europe, including Ukraine. The Russian military held Zapad ("West") exercises in 2009 and 2013, employing tactics and capabilities necessary to invade the Baltic States, cutting them off from Poland. The 2009 exercise culminated in a mock nuclear attack on Poland. On Good Friday 2013, the Russian military provoked alarm and outrage in non-NATO Sweden by simulating a nuclear attack on two Swedish military targets.[48]

Ultimately, Russia's comparatively small, stagnant, and enormously corrupt economy may not be able to afford a buildup of this magnitude. In the event that Putin consummates his plans, even the substantially downsized U.S. military Obama has in mind will stay number one overall for decades. The defense analyst Ariel Cohen warns, however, that the margin of U.S. military superiority is rapidly and significantly declining as Russia and China strengthen their militaries prodigiously while U.S. defense capabilities continue to erode under President Obama.[49] According to the National Defense Panel's report on the 2014 Quadrennial Defense Review (QDR), the recent Russian military buildup and mounting assertiveness "call into question the 2014 QDR's conclusion . . . that Europe is a net producer of security."[50] Consequently, "Europe will require more attention and a higher sense of priority from U.S. defense planners."[51] The panel's report identifies four specific challenges U.S. defense planners must address:

1. Russia's increasing use of rapidly mobile and well-equipped special operations forces with coordinated political warfare and cyberspace capabilities to create new "facts on the ground," particularly in areas of the former Soviet Union;
2. Lack of adequate defense capability in major NATO countries and continued lack of investment in defense modernization, including that in forces that can be projected within the region and beyond;
3. An intelligence, surveillance, and reconnaissance infrastructure in

Eastern Europe that is insufficient to provide strategic and operational warning; and
4. Reduced U.S. forces permanently stationed or rotationally deployed in Europe and available for rapid response to crisis as well as regular training and exercises with allies.[52]

Putin aims for no less than a Russian military commensurate with his ambitions of ending American unipolarity, preserving the authoritarian basis of his regime, restoring Russian preeminence in East Central Europe, and making Russia a global power again. Putin's nineteenth-century outlook refutes the core assumption of the Obama Doctrine—shared by most Western European democracies—that Russia no longer poses a major geopolitical threat.[53]

Since 2010, Putin has pushed what the *New York Times* favorably describes as Obama's "considerable patience" on arms control with Russia. Putin has foiled an exuberant Obama's long-cherished goal of achieving deeper cuts in nuclear arms as a follow-on to the New START treaty of 2010.[54] Russia also has violated the treaty banning medium-range nuclear missiles that Ronald Reagan and Mikhail Gorbachev concluded in 1987 (the INF Treaty) by testing ground-launch cruise missiles that the treaty proscribes. The administration termed as "serious" Russian noncompliance with the INF Treaty. According to administration officials, the Russians may have begun testing prohibited ground-launch cruise missiles as early as 2008.[55]

Since Putin's return to the presidency, Russian policy toward the resource-rich Arctic has become more expansive and confrontational. Russia has staked wide territorial claims to the Arctic Basin that Canada, Norway, and the United States contest.[56] Putin has reasserted Russia's controversial claim to own the Lomonosov Ridge, an undersea mountain range between Ellesmere Island, the most northerly point of land in Canada, and Russia's eastern Siberian coast. Putin has called for enhancing Russia's infrastructure and military capabilities in the region, which he deems critical to Russia's strategic interests.[57]

Putin also has exploited Europe's heavy reliance on Russian oil and natural gas to intimidate its neighbors and inhibit a strong EU resistance to Russian assertiveness. Russia supplies Ukraine with over 50 percent and the EU with 30 percent of their natural gas. Even before the crisis in

Ukraine erupted in 2013, Russia wielded energy as a weapon to coerce it. Russia cut supplies to Ukraine in 2006 and 2009 in disagreements over politics, prices, and payments.[58] Nor is Ukraine the only Russian neighbor to face such coercion. Russia also has threatened Belarus, Lithuania, Moldova, Georgia, and Azerbaijan with price rises and embargoes for "flirting with" pro-Western policies. According to Keith Johnson, who covers the geopolitics of energy for *Foreign Policy,* Russia eagerly uses "energy exports as a weapon, cutting off gas supplies at one time or another more than 40 times" over the past twenty years.[59] Putin counts, too, on the EU's significant, though diminishing, dependence on Russian energy to limit its response during a crisis. The *Wall Street Journal* wonders likewise: "How tough will Europe get if Russia threatens to choke off its energy?"[60] The unfolding crisis in Ukraine may provide the definitive answer to that question.

Rand's experts F. Stephen Larrabee and Peter A. Wilson, writing in the *National Interest,* understate masterfully that Putin's annexation of Crimea "challenges two basic assumptions on which U.S. policy toward Europe in the post–Cold War era has been based: (1) that Europe is essentially stable and secure, freeing the United States to focus its attention on other areas, particularly Asia and the Middle East, and (2) that Russia has become a potential partner rather than an adversary."[61] To put it plainly, Putin's systematic and relentless campaign to undermine Ukraine's independence delivered a knockout blow to Obama's reset, notwithstanding the untenable claims of Professor Stephen Cohen of New York University and the isolationist Pat Buchanan, who blame the United States for Russian aggression. Cohen argues, "We have been crossing [Putin's] red lines ever since we began to move NATO toward Russia in the 1990s. Clinton began it. Bush continued it. Obama rhetorically has continued it. The ultimate red line, and unlike perhaps Obama, Putin really believes in red lines, was Ukraine. . . . For him, and we can argue whether it is or isn't, it was a direct threat to Russian national security in the form of Crimea. And so he reacted."[62] Katrina vanden Heuvel and Cohen dubiously stipulate Putin's good faith in repeatedly requesting a ceasefire and negotiations while unfairly maligning the Ukrainian government for rejecting them.[63] Although not blaming the Ukrainian crisis solely on the United States, the defensive neorealist Stephen Walt argues that the United States must make some effort to empathize with Russia, saying,

" 'They, the Russians, have a view of how we got into this and what's at stake and we're not showing any sort of empathy for what they are doing—we don't have to like what they've done but we at least ought to be trying to understand what their view of it is.' " Walt considers it desirable and possible to establish Ukraine as a buffer state between East and West.[64] An undaunted believer in the reset who denies any link between Russia's external behavior and the internal character of its regime, Walt urges the Obama administration not to let relations "deteriorate" so that the United States and Russia "cannot agree on key issues such as Iran, Syria, and China."[65]

Commentators across the spectrum excoriated Cohen's and vanden Heuvel's defenses of Putin as factually challenged and "outrageous."[66] Nor are Walt's ambivalent position and policy prescriptions considerably more plausible than Cohen's. For all its current problems, NATO expansion not only extended and consolidated the democratic peace in Europe without menacing Russia's legitimate national interest. The existence of NATO also raises the barrier to Putin's illegitimate quest to reverse the outcome of the Cold War: reassert Russian hegemony in Central Europe, make Russia the dominant power in Eurasia, and create an environment conducive to sustaining Russian autocracy. As Hillary Clinton observes, NATO membership gives European people and leaders "greater confidence about their future in light of the ambitions of Russia's President Vladimir Putin. They understand that Putin's claim that NATO's open door is a threat to Russia reflects his refusal to accept the idea that Russia's relations with the West could be based on partnership and mutual interests, as Boris Yeltsin and Mikhail Gorbachev believed. . . . Ponder how much more difficult it would be to contain further Russian aggression if Eastern and Central European nations were not now NATO's allies."[67] Robert Kagan rightly calls Russia "a prime example of how a nation's governance at home shapes its relations with the rest of the world." He goes on to say:

> A democratizing Russia, and even Gorbachev's democratizing Soviet Union, took a fairly benign view of NATO and tended to have good relations with neighbors that were treading the same path toward democracy. But today Putin regards NATO as a hostile entity, calls its enlargement a "serious provocation" and asks "against whom is the expansion intended?" Yet NATO is no

more aggressive or provocative toward Moscow today than it was during Gorbachev's time. If anything, it is even less so, NATO has become more benign as Russia has become more aggressive. . . . Russia and China are promoting an international order that places a high value on national sovereignty and can protect autocratic governments from foreign interference. . . . The color revolutions worried Putin not only because they checked his regional ambitions, but because he feared that the examples of Ukraine and Georgia could be repeated in Russia."[68]

Even at its worst—for example, the seizure of Crimea and the ongoing threats against Ukraine—Putin's Russia is no clone of Nazi Germany or the Soviet Union. His authoritarian Russia sorely lacks the material resources of these existentially menacing regimes. The U.S. GDP is more than 16 trillion versus Russia's 2.5 trillion. The EU's GDP slightly exceeds that of the United States. Russia thus remains at best a middle-ranking power facing a potential coalition endowed with vastly superior resources.[69] Nor does Putin espouse a messianic ideology comparable to Adolf Hitler's or Joseph Stalin's.

When Putin called the collapse of the Soviet Union a great tragedy, however, that encapsulated a divergence between Russian and American interests that was unpropitious for the reset or the optimistic premises of the Obama Doctrine impelling it. In his 1997 book, *The Grand Chessboard,* Zbigniew Brzezinski foresaw why Putin would regard Russian domination of Ukraine as pivotal for achieving his grand design: "Ukraine, a new and important space on the Eurasian chessboard, is a geopolitical pivot because its very existence as an independent country helps to transform Russia. Without Ukraine, Russia ceases to be a Eurasian empire. . . . However, if Moscow regains control over Ukraine, with . . . major resources as well as its access to the Black Sea, Russia automatically again regains the wherewithal to become a powerful imperial state, spanning Europe and Asia."[70]

Ilan Berman explicates and elaborates on Brzezinski's profound geopolitical insight in his recent fine book, *Implosion,* a compelling portrayal of Russia's grave, long-term predicament that wealth derived from energy only masks. Without Ukraine's substantial population of Slavs, its large size, and its favorable location as a geographic pivot, Putin's authoritarian Russia faces a future even grimmer than the one Brzezinski's progno-sis portends. Its Slavic population continues to shrink precipitously while its increasingly radical and unassimilated Islamic population continues to grow prodigiously.[71] In the resource-rich but largely and increasingly depopulated Far East, Russia shares thousands of miles of border with a dynamic, heavily populated, and energy-craving China that has irreden-tist claims to the region it has deferred but not relinquished.[72]

The mounting authoritarianism and corruption of Putin's regime have made Russia's predicament vastly worse. Since Putin took power, Russians have fled the country in droves, emigrating at rates not witnessed since the early years following the Bolshevik Revolution. United Nations polls suggest that more than 40 percent of Russians would leave if they could. According to highly reputable demographers such as Nicholas Eberstadt, the population of Russia would shrink to 102 million if current trends continue, and Muslims would constitute close to half that amount. As Putin well knows, subverting Ukraine's independence would help stave off Russia's demographic decline, adding 46 million Christian Slavs to Russia's numbers. Controlling Ukraine—approximately the size of Spain and possessing a pivotal location and abundant natural resources, and agriculturally the former breadbasket of the Soviet Union—would place Russian power once again in the heart of Central Europe, imperiling the independence of Russia's neighbors in the region.[73]

Hence, Putin initiated the Ukrainian crisis and has escalated it ever since. In August 2013 Russia began to pressure, threaten, and bribe Ukrainian President Viktor Yanukovych to renege at the eleventh hour on a political and economic agreement with the European Union. That enraged most Ukrainians, who positively envisioned the EU agreement as a critical step to free the nation from Russian domination and move Ukraine into the orbit of the democratic West. Conversely, Yanukovych had long served as Putin's surrogate to restore Russian hegemony in Ukraine. In 2004 Yanukovych's attempts to rig the outcome of Ukraine's presidential election catalyzed the Orange Revolution, which resulted in the victory of his pro-democratic, pro-Western opponent, Viktor Yush-chenko. In 2010 Yanukovych defeated Yulia Tymoshenko, former prime minister and heroine of the Orange Revolution, in a close and contested election in which allegations of corruption ran high.[74]

Yanukovych then pursued a foreign policy increasingly subservient to Russia, filled his administration with Ukrainians hostile to the West, and instigated a series of show trials culminating in the imprisonment of Tymoshenko on bogus charges of profiting from illegal gas contracts. When Yanukovych signed a treaty with Russia in December 2013 to replace the defunct EU agreement, massive civil unrest ensued, forcing Yanukovych to flee. Putin refused to recognize the interim government. Instead, Russia has systematically undermined Ukraine's elections, illegally annexed the Crimea in March 2014 (violating the 1994 agreement promising to respect Ukraine's sovereignty in exchange for Ukraine's relinquishing its nuclear weapons), and crippled Ukraine's struggling economy by embargoing and raising the price of energy.[75] Putin's Russia continues periodically the formation of massed troops on the border of eastern Ukraine to intimidate the legitimate government of Ukraine. Publicly, Putin did not oppose the Ukrainian elections of May 25, 2014, which resulted in Petro Poroshenko's becoming president. Privately, Russia has supplied pro-Russian separatists in eastern Ukraine who are his fifth column with heavy equipment, missiles, tanks, and financial support. If Putin respected rather than menaced Ukraine's sovereignty, the raging violence there would largely cease. Whoever fired the Russian SA-11 missile that brought down the Malaysian airline flying over eastern Ukraine on July 17, 2014, Putin bears ultimate responsibility—having provided the missiles, training, political support, and sanctuary.[76] The violence has continued ever since, as Russian intimidation mounts. According to the BBC, nearly one thousand eastern Ukrainians died in the eight weeks following the purported ceasefire, known as the Minsk Protocol, which began in September 2014.[77]

Though Putin's Russia falls far short of Nazi Germany's malevolent intentions and the capabilities to realize them, both regimes played a weak hand in a similar fashion. The strategy, tactics, and consequences of Putin's dismemberment of Ukraine resemble Hitler's diabolically successful strategy employed against the stronger but vacillating Western democracies during the 1930s: (1) use your ethnic diaspora to foment strife in neighboring states; (2) disguise your intentions, proceeding incrementally; (3) exploit the guilt, gullibility, moral confusion, and war-weariness of your adversary; (4) pause and dissemble between each act of aggression; and (5) periodically initiate a peace offensive, tranquilizing public opinion.[78]

Several commentators and statesmen have likened Putin's speech on

March 18, 2014, to both chambers of the Russian Federation, justifying the annexation of Crimea, to Hitler's speeches.[79] As Zbigniew Brzezinski observed, "Those words spoken by Putin are terribly reminiscent of what Hitler was saying about Austria before the Anschluss [the occupation and annexation of Austria into Nazi Germany in 1938], which was then followed by the Sudetenland [areas of other countries inhabited mostly by German speakers], and we know the rest of the history. And that could be very serious in Europe. Either we can be passive in the face of a calamitous explosion or maybe the Ukrainians will fall apart and simply there will be a repetition of what happened in Crimea."[80] Putin mendaciously attributed the political demise of his surrogate—former Ukrainian President Yanukovych—to "Nationalists, Neo-Nazis, Russophobes, and anti-Semites" who "resorted to terror, murder, and riots. . . . They continue to set the tone in Ukraine to this day."[81] Putin falsely equated his annexation of Crimea without legitimate provocation to NATO's 1999 intervention in Kosovo to stop the Serbian dictator Slobodan Milosevic from slaughtering Muslim Kosovars.[82]

Like the remilitarization of the Rhineland and Hitler's other serial acts of aggression during the 1930s, Putin's invasion of Crimea violated freely negotiated treaties and international law. Like Hitler in the Rhineland, Putin will not stop at dismembering Ukraine unless the West rouses itself vigilantly to deter him.

The German remilitarization of the Rhineland on March 7, 1936, marked the last chance to topple the Nazi regime without the cost or risk of a major European war.[83] Hitler conceded, "The 48 hours after the March into the Rhineland were the most nerve-wracking of my life. If the French had marched into the Rhineland, we would have had to withdraw with our tail between our legs, for the military resources at our disposal would have been inadequate for moderate resistance."[84] Marinating, however, in denial and wishful thinking, Western powers refused to rearm, reevaluate their relaxed view of Hitler's intentions, or draw clear, credible lines against future Nazi aggression.

Likewise, the subjugation of Ukraine as a Russian vassal state today would transform the European balance of power adversely to the United States, invigorating Putin's grandiose ambitions to reverse the outcome of the Cold War and creating a new lease on life. In the short term, Putin aims to humiliate NATO, demonstrate its impotence, and convince Russia's neighbors that the Russian army can intervene anywhere in the region without fear of reprisal. Ultimately, Putin inclines to expand and repress rather than retrench and reform.[85] The United States, therefore, has a vital strategic interest in preserving the independence and territorial integrity of a pro-Western Ukraine. Fareed Zakaria—usually wary of intervention and one of Obama's most eloquent defenders—agrees, calling Ukraine "the most important post-Soviet country Russia seeks to dominate politically. . . . The crisis in Ukraine . . . involves a great global power, Russia, and thus can and will have far-reaching consequences. And it involves a great global principle: whether national boundaries can be changed by brute force. If it becomes acceptable to do so, what will happen in Asia, where there are dozens of contested boundaries—and several great powers that want to remake them? . . . On Ukraine, Obama must lead from the front."[86] As F. Stephen Larrabee and Peter A. Wilson trenchantly put it, "A pro-Western Ukraine closely tied to Europe would alter the strategic balance in Central Europe and pose a significant obstacle to Putin's goal of reestablishing Russia as a Eurasian power."[87]

The outcome of the struggle in Ukraine has a profound significance for the United States, not just geopolitically but morally. No people have suffered from Soviet tyranny and Russian oppression longer or more grievously than Ukrainians. Adding insult to injury, Putin still laments the demise of the Soviet Union and denies that one of his heroes (Stalin) perpetrated the Holodomor, a campaign of deliberately starving to death millions of Ukrainian peasants during Soviet collectivization of Ukrainian agriculture during the 1930s. This monstrous crime approaches the magnitude of the Holocaust.[88] According to highly esteemed Pew Foundation polls, most Ukrainians want Ukraine to remain a free, independent, unified state. That includes the majority of Russian speakers and the majorities in the eastern as well as the western parts of Ukraine. These polls also register a strong negative sentiment toward Russia's role in Ukraine.[89]

Who knows for sure whether a more muscular and credible American deterrent than Obama's reset would have dissuaded Putin from subverting Ukraine's independence? In 2008 a less conciliatory Bush administration did not deter or significantly punish Putin's aggression in Georgia—a less significant country than Ukraine, more remote geographically from America's European NATO allies. Yet international politics deals in probabilities, not certainties. A robust American response imposing significant costs and risks would steeply raise the odds against future Russian aggression directed at American allies in East Central Europe terrified of being Putin's next target.

Though Hillary Clinton implausibly exonerates the reset along with the Obama Doctrine for emboldening Putin and other tyrants, she now advocates a "new" and tougher "course" that essentially repudiates their conciliatory premises in all but name: "Putin sees geopolitics as a zero-sum-game in which, if someone is winning, then someone else has to be losing. . . . Strength and resolve were the only language Putin would understand."[90] Clinton admits, however, "that not everybody in the White House agreed with my relatively harsh analysis."[91] Count the president and his current secretary of state among those she has yet to convince about the imperative of "resetting" the "reset" toward Putin.

Since August 2013 the president has responded to mounting Russian predations in Ukraine slowly, reluctantly, incrementally, and only as a last resort when forbearance utterly fails. The administration has confined itself almost exclusively to calibrated economic sanctions and diplomacy rather than military measures geared to bolster deterrence against further Russian aggression in Ukraine and beyond. Even in the economic realm, the Obama administration and the EU before the March 2014 invasion of Crimea did little more than impose negligible, narrowly targeted, ineffectual sanctions on noncrucial sectors of the Russian economy and on some of Putin's close associates, though not on Putin himself. "Mr. Obama sees Ukraine's crisis as a problem to be managed, ideally with a minimum of violence or geopolitical upheaval," according to Peter Baker, writing in the *New York Times* six months after Putin initiated it.[92] Speaking on *Meet the Press* on March 2, 2014, a perplexed Secretary of State John Kerry said Russia, in its annexation of Crimea, was "really engaging in activity that is completely contradictory to the standards that most of us are trying to operate by in the 21st century. . . . It's certainly not behaving like a G8 country."[93] Even so, the Obama administration continued to believe that limited sanctions and negotiations would suffice. On April 17, 2014, Kerry hailed an agreement he negotiated with Russia in Geneva to calm rising tensions between Putin's fifth column of Russian separatists in eastern Ukraine and the central government in Kiev. Again, Putin ran roughshod over it. A week later an exasperated Kerry assailed Russia for "launching a full-throated effort to actively sabotage the democratic process" in Ukraine.[94] Yet the administration responded with only modest and reversible sanctions on seventeen banks, energy companies, investment accounts, and other firms that Putin and several of his advisers control. According to a *New York Times* report, Russia's security markets recovered swiftly after an initial loss once President Obama revealed the limited scope of the sanctions—excluding any large publicly listed Russian companies.[95] "The goal here is not to go after Mr. Putin personally," President Obama explained. "The goal is to change his calculus . . . to encourage him to actually walk the walk and not just talk the talk when it comes to diplomatically resolving the crisis in Ukraine."[96]

For a long while, the president and the EU had resisted imposing broad and tough sanctions on Russia's energy and banking sectors—the only type that could truly inflict significant hardship on the Russian economy over the long term. Finally, Obama and the EU resorted to stronger measures in response to the July 17, 2014, atrocity of Putin's surrogates in eastern Ukraine downing a Malaysian commercial airliner with a Russian missile. On July 29, 2014, the United States and the EU announced stiffer (though still not comprehensive) sanctions on Russia, including an arms embargo, curbs on the capacity of Russian banks to raise capital, and restrictions on Russia's ability to develop its energy resources.[97] The president stated emphatically, however, "No, it's not a new Cold War."[98] Nor would Obama long consider sterner measures that critics of the administration's restraint toward Putin have championed: providing military aid to the Ukrainian government; substantially increasing America's military presence in Eastern Europe; abrogating the New START treaty; reversing his decision to cancel the deployment of missile defense in Poland, Hungary, and the Czech Republic; substantially raising rather than reducing U.S. defense spending; treating Putin as an adversary rather than a partner, not only in Europe, but in the Middle East; and imposing comprehensive sanctions on Russia's banking and energy sector, with no loopholes or exceptions.[99] Instead, Obama pledged "to engage" Putin and seek a "diplomatic solution" to the Ukrainian crisis.[100] "It didn't have to come to this. It does not have to be this way," the president still insists. "There continues to be a better choice—the choice of de-escalation."[101] In an exclusive interview with the commentator Thomas Friedman in August 2014, Obama acknowledged that his sanctions may not succeed in taming Putin. Putin "could invade Ukraine at any time." That would make "trying to find our way back to a cooperative functioning relationship with Russia during the remainder of my term . . . much more difficult."[102]

Meanwhile, tensions between Russia and NATO continue to mount as Putin persists in defying sanctions with impunity while intensifying Russian pressure on the legitimate Ukrainian government. After a snap election of the Ukrainian Parliament on October 26, 2014, which the *Washington Post* described as full and fair, and which yielded a convincing pro-Western majority, the Russians significantly increased their military activity.[103] NATO intercepted at least nineteen Russian aircraft flying close to European aircraft. American officials have interpreted these demonstrations as a show of force by the Putin government.[104] The venerable Russia expert Paul Goble explains Putin's current strategy as, first, sowing panic among Ukrainians and the West and then waiting; second, invading when both the West and the Ukrainians are off-balance; and third, repeating the process. Without sterner resistance from the Obama administration and NATO, Goble predicts regretfully that this "recipe" will succeed: "Putin has a longer time horizon than do either Ukrainians or Western governments. He doesn't have to achieve all his goals all at once, whereas they want a resolution extremely quickly. By sowing panic, he is promoting his program."[105]

Alas, the Obama administration's current trajectory will probably encourage rather than discourage Putin from thinking he can get away with it. True, history brims with examples of presidents substantially recasting their foreign policies in the face of changing circumstances. Think of Carter's final year after the Soviet invasion of Afghanistan in December 1979 or Reagan modifying some of his tactics, though not his ultimate objective, with the advent of Gorbachev in the Soviet Union. Yet Obama's six years in office have made at least this clear: his ingrained view of the world will make it especially difficult for him to admit that the premises of the Obama Doctrine invite danger and compound risk rather than forestall them. That does not bode well for American foreign policy in any region, including Europe. As Michael Rubin concludes in his fine book *Dancing with the Devil,* engagement rarely works with regimes such as Putin's Russia.[106]

The crisis in Ukraine also has exposed the illusion of the Obama Doctrine and the president's initially rapturous admirers in Western Europe that the United States can lead from behind while Europe fills the void. Neither NATO nor the EU can substitute adequately for American military power and resolve. On the one hand, the history of Western Europe and East Asia since World War II has robustly confirmed the postulate of democratic peace theory that stable liberal democracies do not fight one another.[107] Stable liberal democracies have fewer and less serious disagreements with each other than with other types of regimes. When disagreements arise, stable liberal democracies will resolve them diplomatically—not by war or the threat of force between them. The Obama Doctrine's unwise neglect of regime type as a critical variable has impelled the president to underestimate the moral and geopolitical logic of heavily favoring stable liberal democratic allies over authoritarian adversaries such as Putin's Russia when the two come in conflict. The United States has a vital interest in expanding and sustaining the democratic zone of peace in Europe. Stable liberal democracies make better allies and unlikely adversaries. On the other hand, stable liberal democracies will not always cooperate or share a common perception of threat and interest, especially without strong leadership forging an effective coalition to fit the mission.

Neither the dynamics of the European balance of power nor international institutions such as the EU, the League of Nations, or the UN can compensate adequately for American power and resolve. Since 1914 Europe has failed to balance successfully against hegemonic threats arising from Kaiser Wilhelm's authoritarian Germany, Adolf Hitler's totalitarian Nazi Germany, or a totalitarian Soviet Union until American power proved decisive to defeat them. Since the collapse of the Soviet Union in 1991, democratic Europe's collective response to radical Islamism from abroad and within also does not inspire great confidence in Europe's capacity to address this challenge without the active engagement and support of American power.[108]

Fareed Zakaria has called the European Union the world's "great no-show" in the Ukrainian crisis, its most powerful members proving so far even more reluctant than the Obama administration to respond vigilantly toward Putin for a synergy of reasons.[109] The great military historian and national commentator Victor Davis Hanson also raises compelling doubts about whether the NATO alliance can overcome the existential predicament the Ukrainian crisis has catalyzed. Alas, the EU and NATO constitute substantially less than the sum of their parts.

First, these entities suffer from what economists term the collective action problem. NATO and the EU both consist of twenty-eight members with divergent interests and assessments of threat difficult to translate into a strong, coherent response without a dominant power such as the United States taking the initiative to forge an effective coalition of the willing. Consequently, Obama's strategy of "leading from behind" multilaterally makes American policy toward Putin hostage to the lowest common denominator of an EU consensus that rarely materializes. As Hanson observes, too, NATO has members such as Turkey, which is under an increasingly Islamist, anti-American, antidemocratic, pro-Iranian prime minister, Recep Tayyip Erdogan, "whose politics and policies are becoming antithetical to the original idea of defending the liberal values of democratic Western Europe."[110]

Second, as Raphael S. Cohen and Gabriel M. Scheinmann emphasize, "Most European militaries are in a pitiful state of decline"; only Greece, Estonia, and the United Kingdom spend NATO's goal of 2 percent of GDP on defense.[111] That holds especially true for Germany, by far the most powerful Continental European member of the EU and NATO. Since the end of the Cold War, German defense spending has dwindled from 3 percent of GDP to just 1.2 percent. Current plans call for shrinking the German army—numbering only 185,000—even further. German military procurement stresses paratroopers and helicopters for theaters such as Kosovo rather than tanks, military aircraft, and artillery suited for deterring Putin in East Central Europe. Even with the Russian military modernizing considerably, the legacy of World War II still operates a powerful constraint on Germany's building a military commensurate with its economic clout.[112]

Nor, despite having a GDP slightly in excess of the United States', will the EU members probably reverse these negative trends in defense spending. Whether the common European currency will even survive the endemic fiscal crisis in Greece and southern Europe remains an open question.[113] Even if the EU muddles through, economic stagnation, demographic decline, rising unassimilated Islamic populations in many Western European democracies, high taxes, mounting debt, stifling regulations, and the fiscal unsustainability of Western European social democracy will conspire to thwart the EU or NATO from adequately replacing U.S. military power. Europe's share of global GDP has declined ten points since the high point of the late 1970s.[114] Most EU members—except the more free-market-oriented exceptions in Eastern Europe such as Poland—have experienced little or no growth for more than a decade.[115]

Third, the lure of commerce and the high demand for Russian energy delay, dilute, and limit European sanctions on Russia. Although Robert Samuelson convincingly considers the danger of a Russian gas embargo as a "highly overrated . . . bluff," Putin's not-so-veiled threat has a chastening effect on many Western European statesmen.[116] Germany's deep commercial ties with Russia and the perception, if not the reality, of its dependence on Russian natural gas reinforce Germany's inclinations to conciliate rather than confront Russia. Although the ardently pro-American German Chancellor Angela Merkel prefers for Germany to remain firmly rooted in the Western alliance, the German public has become more ambivalent. Some 56 percent of Germans named the United States as the country with which Germany should cooperate in the future, while 53 percent named Russia.[117]

In May 2014 the French government announced it would proceed with the sale of two assault ships to Russia, despite the Russian annexation of Crimea and despite American objections.[118] In September the French government only conditionally reversed course, suspending the delivery of these ships.[119] Even the more stalwart British resisted stiff sanctions on Putin until the downing of the Malaysian airliner prompted Prime Minster David Cameron's government to reconsider. The British government is reluctant to jeopardize Russian cash flowing into London banks and high-end real estate. Italy—Russia's fourth-largest trading partner, mired in an economic slump—remains especially wobbly on sanctions. Notwithstanding the burst of Western European indignation, it remains unclear whether the Malaysian Airlines atrocity truly marks a turning point in Europe's willingness to impose and sustain powerful sanctions that could badly damage critical sectors of the Russian economy.[120]

President Obama's relationship with America's democratic allies in Europe has turned out to be far more fractious than he or the preponderance of Western Europeans rapturous about his election ever imagined. On July 24, 2008, an estimated two hundred thousand Germans and the Western European press greeted Obama's speech in Berlin with jubilation. "The loudest applause came when Obama, however subtly, offered himself as the coming antidote to all that Germans, Europeans, indeed most non-Americans, have disliked about the Bush Era," the *Guardian* exulted. "This is an anti-Bush rally," a man in the crowd said approvingly.[121] Obama pledged his commitment to cultivating a partnership with Europe in which allies "listen to each other, learn from each other and, most of all, trust each other."[122] By the time Obama returned to Berlin five years later, in June 2013, he received a more sober and critical welcome. "It is his actions, more so than his rhetoric, which have been the most underwhelming since his election," a local journalist, Aubrey Bloomfield, opined. "People are increasingly jaded after five years of broken promises and action falling behind rhetoric, and this was evident in Berlin."[123]

The growing disillusionment with Obama in Europe stems in part from the perception that the president's engagement of adversaries often comes at the expense of traditional democratic allies of the United States. As Kori Schake, a fellow at the Hoover Institution, put it in *Foreign Policy*, "The United States has become an exasperating ally, and even countries that are inclined to support us are hedging [their bets against us] because of the Obama administration's conduct. Neither our threats nor our assurances are believed. Clawing back that credibility will be an expensive undertaking."[124]

Start with the Eastern European members of NATO. Whatever the motivation for the decision, the administration's cancellation of Bush's missile defense program for Poland, Hungary, and the Czech Republic demoralized and antagonized the very constituency in Europe most sympathetic to America's legitimate national interest on a wide range of fundamental issues: deterring an authoritarian Russia seeking to impose its dominance across East Central Europe; keeping the EU inclusive and pro-American rather than restrictive and anti-American, as France since de Gaulle has envisaged it; and acting decisively with coalitions of the willing rather than deferring to a typically gridlocked UN or flaccid EU consensus. Poland's President Bronislaw Komorowski accused Obama of betraying Poland by canceling the missile defense system that President George W. Bush had promised.[125] The hero of Solidarity and Poland's former president, Lech Walesa, named Obama the world leader "who has disillusioned him the most" by abnegating America's role as the world's sole superpower.[126] In 2012 Walesa endorsed Obama's Republican opponent, Mitt Romney, saying, "We are awaiting a president who understands that . . . a strong America had always provided a balance of power to the world."[127]

The president's June 2014 trip to Europe failed utterly in its intended purpose of reassuring Eastern European allies of America's commitment to their security. As James Rubin commented in the *New York Times,* Eastern European allies criticized as inadequate Obama's verbal assurances, a modest program of $1 billion for military exercises, and a token increase of fewer than one thousand U.S. military personnel in the region.[128] The Polish foreign policy expert Krzysztof Kubiak—affiliated with the Institute of Security and International Affairs at the University of Lower Silesia—dismissed Obama's plan as a "smokescreen. . . . The only way for the United States to prove their full commitment to Poland's and the region's safety is to move one of their large military installations from one of the old NATO members to Poland."[129] The president returned to Washington with the governments of Latvia, Lithuania, and Estonia more doubtful than ever that "America would really risk a war with Russia to defend them."[130] After Obama's June 2014 trip, Poland's Foreign Minister Radoslaw Sikorski—ardently pro-American and a steadfast supporter of NATO—despaired in leaked, secretly recorded conversations that "the Polish-American alliance is worth nothing. It is therefore harmful, because it gives Poland a false sense of security."[131]

Likewise, the liberal *New York Times* opinion writer Roger Cohen labels the current state of German-American relations the worst since World War II.[132] The Obama administration contributed considerably to this downward spiral. In 2009 the president offended many Germans by skipping the twentieth anniversary celebration of the fall of the Berlin Wall.[133] In the fall of 2013 the administration provoked outrage in Germany with revelations of NSA spying on Chancellor Angela Merkel, one of the most pro-American leaders in the nation's history.[134] In July 2014 German-American relations sank even lower when the German government requested the top representative of America's Secret Service in Germany to leave the country. Clemens Binninger, a member of Merkel's Christian Democrats chairing the Intelligence Oversight Committee in the Bundestag, explained that the Obama administration's "failure to cooperate on resolving various [spying] allegations" prompted this dramatic action usually reserved for adversaries rather than allies.[135]

The Obama administration has also frayed the special relationship with Great Britain—the bedrock of American alliances since President Franklin Roosevelt and British Prime Minister Winston Churchill forged it in the early days of World War II. Multiple administration officials have even denied the very existence of a special relationship.[136] Reversing Ronald Reagan's unwavering support for British Prime Minister Margaret Thatcher during the Falklands War of 1982, Obama has declared himself neutral in the dispute between the United Kingdom and Argentina. Various Obama administration State Department spokesmen have revealed the president's pro-Argentinian tilt, referring to the islands as the Malvinas rather than the Falklands.[137] Without consulting its staunchest ally, the administration also gave the Russians secret information on the British nuclear deterrent to entice them to sign the New START treaty.[138]

Granted, the president hardly bears exclusive responsibility for the fluctuating tensions between the United States and its European democratic allies inherent in the structure, psychology, and history of the relationship. Even during the Cold War, the United States disagreed sharply and frequently on security issues, especially in the Middle East, where the United States before President Obama became steadily more pro-Israel while Western Europe moved in the opposite, pro-Arab direction. During the Yom Kippur War of 1973, virtually every one of America's NATO allies denied the United States overflight rights to resupply Israel until the Nixon administration and Congress enticed Portugal financially to allow American cargo aircraft to use the Azores. In 1966 Charles de Gaulle provoked a veritable crisis in the Western alliance by withdrawing France from NATO on the basis of his increasingly benign assessment of the Soviet Union, his mounting distrust of the United States, and his conception of French grandeur. Likewise, the Reagan administration and Western Europe clashed regularly: over the gravity of the Soviet threat and how to respond to it; over the deployment of Euromissiles, the nuclear freeze movement, and the Strategic Defense Initiative; over the Polish government's repression of the labor movement Solidarity and the imposition of severe sanctions on the Soviet regime for instigating it; and over Reagan's unabashedly anticommunist rhetoric. In 1986 the French refusal to grant the U.S. overflight rights nearly derailed a massive American air strike on Libya in response to Libyan-sponsored discotheque bombings in West Germany.[139]

The variance between Western Europe's and America's view of the world has enlarged since the end of the Cold War, having peaked during the presidency of George W. Bush. As Robert Kagan famously put it in *Of Paradise and Power:*

> Europe is turning away from power, or to put it a little differently, it is moving beyond power into a self-contained world of laws and rules and transnational negotiation and cooperation. It is entering a post-historical paradise of peace and relative prosperity, the realization of Immanuel Kant's "perpetual peace." Meanwhile, the United States remains mired in history, exercising power in an anarchic Hobbesian world where international laws and rules are unreliable, and where true security and the defense and promotion of a liberal order still depend on the possession and use of military might. That is why on major strategic and international questions today, Americans are from Mars and Europeans are from Venus. They agree on little and understand one another less and less. And this state of affairs is not transitory—the product of one American election or one catastrophic event. The reasons for the transatlantic divide are deep, long in development, and likely to endure. When it comes to setting national priorities, determining threats, defining challenges, and fashioning and implementing foreign and defense policies, the United States and Europe have parted ways.[140]

Kagan's dichotomy is illuminating and original, though problematic. It best explains the antipathy of Continental Western Europe toward a Bush Doctrine, the American war in Iraq, President Bush's unbridled belief in American exceptionalism, and his Texas demeanor, so grating to the sensibilities of elite secular opinion. Even for the Bush presidency, however, Kagan's dichotomy requires substantial qualification. Eastern European allies freed from Soviet tyranny view power more like America than Western Europe, whereas Great Britain, with a long "special relationship" with the United States, stands somewhere in between. Moreover, Kagan's dichotomy cannot explain satisfactorily why relations between the United States and democratic Europe have become fraught with difficulty under Obama. Paradoxically, today's transatlantic predicament arises not from the Obama Doctrine's rejection of but from its embrace of

Western Europe's discomfort with power politics, devaluation of military force, reliance on multilateralism, and confidence in international law.

Since Obama became president, Europeans have rediscovered the hard way that American retrenchment and conciliation of adversaries menaces rather than enhances their security. Whatever partial and contingent success transnational institutions such as the EU have achieved in promoting Europe's tranquility depends primarily on the clarity, capability, credibility, and commitment of American power that the Obama Doctrine imperils. During the Cold War, American security guarantees proved indispensable in integrating a democratic Germany into the Western alliance and alleviating the historic fears of Germany's neighbors that German revival would threaten the security of Europe.[141] Now, neither NATO nor the EU can substitute for a dearth of American power and leadership on which their efficacy and Europe's security still depend.

The Obama Doctrine risks creating a power vacuum in Central Europe, which Vladimir Putin's authoritarian Russia relishes the opportunity to fill, at the expense of freedom and prosperity in the region. The unfolding crisis in Ukraine offers perhaps only a chilling preview of what the Obama Doctrine may finally unleash. Count on Putin to reprise the salami-slicing strategy he employed in Ukraine in many other areas across East Central Europe that Russia still covets—including Moldova, the Baltics, and Belarus—where sizable Russian minorities provide the pretext.

Lord Hastings Lionel Ismay, NATO's first secretary general, quipped that the alliance's goal was "to keep the Russians out, the Americans in, and the Germans down."[142] That remains no less true today, with emendations. The United States needs a muscular presence in Europe to keep Putin's authoritarian Russia out, Germany firmly anchored in the democratic West, and East Central Europe democratic and free from the ravages of Russian imperialism. In many ways, Putin's regime resembles the Soviet Union in his calculation of cost and risk rather than a Nazi regime bent on war and hence undeterrable. The audacity of Putin's Russia and the Soviet Union compensates for their daunting internal weaknesses. By the early 1980s, a corrupt, repressive, expansionist, militaristic, economically stagnant Soviet Union became increasingly vulnerable to sustained pressure, which President Ronald Reagan intensified comprehensively and decisively. The restoration of American military and economic power under Reagan gave the Soviet Union little choice but to take a risk on a reformer such as Mikhail Gorbachev. Gorbachev recognized that the Soviet Union could not compete against a self-confident United States unless it liberalized at home and pursued more conciliatory policies abroad. Now Putin's demographically declining, economically languishing, intellectually stifling regime confronts a set of stark choices similar to the Soviet Union's during the 1980s. By pursuing a version of Ronald Reagan's strategy of vigilance—economically, politically, and militarily—the West would improve dramatically the chances of the Russian regime's eventually choosing benign reform rather than imperial expansion in a dangerous, desperate attempt to avert collapse.[143]

Yet President Obama continues to do the opposite. David J. Kramer, president of Freedom House, explains compellingly why continuing Obama's strategy of engagement will make matters worse:

> Over the past several months, President Obama and his Western colleagues have engaged with Vladimir Putin on numerous occasions to try to resolve the crisis in Ukraine. Obama and Putin have spoken nine times and met briefly in France in June; German Chancellor Angela Merkel has spoken to Putin on close to 40 occasions and met him in France as well as in Brazil during the World Cup. The problem is not lack of dialogue with Putin. The problem is the leader in the Kremlin who seeks to destabilize his neighbors and prevent them from democratizing and integrating more closely with the West at the same time he cracks down in ugly ways inside his own country. Were Ukraine, Georgia, Moldova, and other countries in the region to succeed, their progress would pose a serious challenge to the thoroughly corrupt, authoritarian system. . . . Putin is willing to do whatever it takes to stay in power, including, it appears, invading Ukraine under the phony pretext of "humanitarian intervention." . . . This makes Putin, and now even Russia, a serious threat. To deal with this challenge requires even tougher sanctions . . . and the provision of military assistance by which Ukraine and other neighbors—and not just NATO members—can defend themselves. The last thing we need is a renewed search for accommodation with Putin.[144]

Ultimately, the reset with Russia that is organic to the Obama Doctrine has enabled Putin's enormous arrogance and grandiose ambitions, while nourishing doubt in the minds of America's democratic allies in Europe about American reliability and resolve. Consequently, President Obama will leave office with Europe less secure and America's deterrent less credible than before, barring an about-face by the administration to "reset the reset" after the midterm elections of November 2014.

5

The Obama Doctrine Meets
the Middle East
and Afghanistan

In the Middle East, President Obama has remained largely faithful (critics say excessively so) to the main staples of the Obama Doctrine. He has emphasized engaging with former adversaries, namely Iran, while pressuring Israel—America's only democratic ally in the region—to a degree that contrasts starkly with the policies of his two predecessors. In keeping with his propensity to rely more on diplomacy than on military power, Obama has made strategic withdrawal, rather than winning the wars he inherited in Afghanistan and Iraq, his priority. The rationale for the trajectory of the war that the administration has belatedly waged against ISIS reflects likewise the president's deep ambivalence about using force decisively. Although it remains to be seen, legitimate doubts arise about whether Obama's self-imposed restrictions against using force and his emphasis on sustaining a coalition rather than fashioning a coalition to fit the mission (i.e., leading from behind) will suffice to succeed against an adversary as implacable as ISIS. Meanwhile, President Obama's pursuit of a nuclear deal with Iran—which has intensified since the midterm elections of 2014—suggests that engagement rather than deterrence remains his preferred strategy in the region.

The Middle East ranks below Europe and East Asia in geopolitical significance for the United States. Oil is the only critical resource the Middle

East possesses in abundance. None of the major and at best middle-ranking powers or terrorist entities inhabiting the region can conceivably threaten the United States existentially the way Nazi Germany or the Soviet Union did during the twentieth century. American decision makers should focus primarily on vast power shifts in East Asia and Europe, where an authoritarian China and Russia lurk as potential hegemons.

Even so, the United States rightly deemed it vital during the Cold War to prevent either the Soviet Union or a hostile regional power from directly or indirectly dominating the Middle East's vast oil reserves, on which the United States, its allies, and the world largely depended. Since the Johnson administration, the security of democratic Israel also has loomed large in America's moral, geopolitical, and domestic calculations. No American president until George W. Bush ascribed much importance to promoting democracy in an Islamic Middle East, where few viable democratic alternatives existed, with the partial exception of Cold War Turkey, which oscillated between an open society and authoritarianism. Unlike Western Europe, Japan, the Philippines, Taiwan, and South Korea, where American ideals and self-interest largely coincided, the United States practiced the ethic of the lesser moral and geopolitical evil in the Islamic Middle East. Typically, that entailed cooperating with pro-American, anti-Soviet authoritarian regimes in the region: secular dictatorships such as Iran under the shah, Egypt under Anwar Sadat and Hosni Mubarak, and conservative Sunni monarchies such as Saudi Arabia and Jordan.

As Robert Blackwill and Meghan O'Sullivan observe, the energy revolution taking place in the United States has diminished further the geopolitical importance of the Middle East since its zenith during the 1970s when a Saudi-led Organization of the Petroleum Exporting Countries (OPEC) wielded formidable power and influence over the supply and price of oil. Newly available techniques and technologies such as horizontal drilling and fracking have enabled the United States cost effectively to extract natural gas and petroleum from vast U.S. reserves of oil shale—a process heretofore commercially cost-prohibitive. Since 2007, U.S. domestic production of natural gas and petroleum has increased 50 percent as a consequence. This energy revolution hugely benefits the United States geopolitically as well as economically, while eroding the influence of Middle Eastern energy producers, often unstable, mercurial, or hostile to the United States.[1]

Although decreasing American reliance on energy imports enhances U.S. leverage and discretion, the United States still has vital interests in the Middle East, which demand American leadership and resources: deterring radical rogue regimes, especially those possessing weapons of mass destruction; thwarting terrorist entities such as ISIS that are menacing to Americans everywhere; preventing a revolutionary Iran from crossing the nuclear threshold and triggering a nuclear arms race in the world's most volatile region; ensuring the supply and reliable flow of Middle Eastern energy still important for sustaining stable energy markets and global economic growth; and protecting democratic allies such as Israel from annihilation.

Keep this caveat at the forefront when examining the Obama Doctrine's record in the Middle East and Afghanistan: the chaos, instability, Islamist extremism, rising sectarianism, Sunni-Shiite split, Arab-Israeli dispute, terrorism, nuclear proliferation, and endemic violence rife in the region did not begin with Obama. Nor will these problems vanish with Obama's departure. Indigenous sources and dynamics account significantly, though not exclusively, for the most serious conflicts afflicting the Middle East and Afghanistan. Even the wisest of presidents operates in the Middle East with especially powerful constraints on his range of choices and capacity to shape events felicitously. President Obama also inherited two controversial wars figuring prominently in his presidential campaign of 2008: a conditionally but largely improving situation in Iraq, notwithstanding his categorical opposition to the war and vow to end it; and a deteriorating situation in Afghanistan, which he pledged to reverse.[2]

Yet Obama came to office supremely confident in his ability to extricate the United States from Iraq expeditiously and without severe repercussions, to engage adversaries whose animosity he blamed largely on his predecessor, to achieve a two-state solution between Israel and the Palestinians, and to convince Iran without war to abandon its nuclear ambitions through a combination of conciliation, diplomacy, and economic sanctions rather than force. Obama assumed, too, that the United States could substantially and safely retrench militarily from the region while devoting more resources to nation building at home and pivoting to Asia with a shrinking defense budget to underwrite it.[3]

Obama viewed American prospects in the Middle East not only with optimism, but also through the lens of his intense skepticism about the ability of military intervention to solve conflicts and his deep reluctance to use force. His experiences in Iraq, Afghanistan, and Libya have amplified that skepticism and reluctance. Moreover, Obama has discounted the threat of Islamism, downplayed the importance of regime type for identifying friends and foes in the region, and defined the threat of terrorism narrowly to al-Qaeda rather than broadly, like George W. Bush, to encompass rogue regimes such as Iran.[4]

In contrast to Bush after 9/11, the Obama administration has assigned low priority to promoting democracy in the Middle East.[5] The president has foresworn categorically the legitimacy of imposing regime change by force in a plethora of major speeches before the UN and in the region. Obama gave that theme full vent in his landmark Cairo address in 2009, which admirers such as David Brooks of the *New York Times* acclaimed for having "blended idealism with cunning," and detractors such as Victor Davis Hanson assailed for exaggerating the historic contributions of Muslims and the deficiencies of American foreign policy.[6] President Obama has deviated from his characteristic aversion to promoting democracy in the Middle East only twice. Both occurred in the early phase of the Arab Spring, in 2011: leading a multilateral coalition from behind in the Libyan civil war, which resulted in the ouster of the dictator Muammar Gaddafi; and encouraging the Egyptian dictator Hosni Mubarak to abdicate, which led initially to the election of the virulently anti-Semitic, anti-American, antidemocratic Muslim Brotherhood, but ended with a coup imposing military rule.[7]

Like the failed reset with Russia, however, events in the Middle East have demolished the Obama Doctrine's lofty expectations that the United States could achieve more by doing less, by engaging with adversaries, by distancing the United States from traditional democratic allies, and by diminishing American military power in the region. Turkey has become increasingly repressive, Islamist, and hostile to the United States, rather than turning out to be the close partner Obama had envisaged. Iraq has imploded since President Obama categorically removed all American troops in 2011. Nor does the downward spiral in Iraq bode well for the outcome of the Obama administration's impending withdrawal of all American forces from Afghanistan.

Except in Tunisia, Arab Spring has become Arab winter, as violence surges and freedom is in retreat. Obama's leading from behind in Libya now appears more of a failure than a success, as disorder and sectarian strife beset that tormented country. The ferocious civil war raging in Syria that began in 2011 has metastasized into a bloody regional sectarian struggle between increasingly extremist Sunni and Shiite coalitions. The death toll has exceeded two hundred thousand; many of the victims are innocent civilians, and no end of the slaughter is in sight. The Syrian conflict has spawned radical entities such as the Islamic State in Iraq and Syria (ISIS), more venomous and dangerous than al-Qaeda, which also is still alive and well despite the Obama administration's well-executed mission to hunt and kill Osama bin Laden in his sanctuary in Pakistan.[8] The Arab-Israeli peace process, in which the Obama administration invested so much time, energy, and prestige, yielded nothing but intractability from the start. By the fall of 2014, the prospects for any agreement between Israel and the Palestinians lay in ruins, especially in the aftermath of democratic Israel's robust military reprisal in Gaza against the terrorist and rejectionist Hamas. Meanwhile, a militant revolutionary Iran has moved closer to crossing the nuclear threshold. President Obama's deliberate and sustained attempts to conciliate the Islamic world and praise Islam's accomplishments have generated absolutely no improvement in America's standing in the Arab and Muslim world. On the contrary, support for the United States in several Middle Eastern countries has declined to levels below even that during George W. Bush's final year of office.[9]

What happened? Were any or all of these outcomes beyond our control? Did Obama's foreign policy ameliorate or exacerbate these problems and dangers? What accounts for the huge and growing gap between the Obama Doctrine's "delivery" and "promise" in the Middle East?[10]

Take the case of Turkey. In a 2012 interview with Fareed Zakaria, editor-at-large of *Time* magazine, President Obama hailed Turkish Prime Minister Recep Tayyip Erdogan as one of the few world leaders with whom he has "forged" close personal "bonds of trust."[11] In April 2009 Obama addressed the Turkish Parliament during his first visit to a major Muslim country, praising Erdogan effusively and pledging America's "strong and enduring friendship." Obama expected that "Turkey and the United States" would "stand together—and work together—to overcome the challenges of our time."[12] The president has courted Turkey assiduously ever since.

Yet the president's rosy belief in the harmony of Turkish-American interests bears little resemblance to reality. Turkey no longer remains the secular, imperfect, but comparatively decent quasi democracy it was during the Cold War through 2003. Under Prime Minister Erdogan and his Justice and Development Party (AKP), Turkey has become increasingly anti-Western, anti-American, anti-Semitic, and antidemocratic. Although Michael Rubin of the American Enterprise Institute may exaggerate when he calls Turkey "an Islamist Republic in all but name," Erdogan has indeed moved the regime in an Islamist direction.[13]

Erdogan has mounted a sustained assault on secularism in government, education, and civil society. He has eviscerated the independence of the Turkish judiciary, curtailed freedom of the press, and demonized his secular political opposition. In 2008 his government staged a show trial, indicting eighty-six Turkish leaders for plotting to restore secular government. In the summer of 2013, Turkish police used tear gas and water cannons to intimidate tens of thousands of Turks who took to the streets protesting the corruption and repressiveness of the government. Erdogan blamed the protests on foreign influences, especially Israel.[14] According to the Committee to Protect Journalists reports for 2012 and 2013, Turkey incarcerates more journalists than any other country.[15] The widely respected Freedom House has downgraded Turkey's ranking in the category of respecting civil liberties from three to four on a scale of one to seven, because of the thousands held in detention without trial.[16]

Correspondingly, Erdogan has reoriented Turkish foreign policy away from cooperation with the West to a more assertive, neo-Ottoman, Islamist direction, which includes extravagant ambitions redolent of an increasingly autocratic Putin.[17] In the spring of 2013, Erdogan proclaimed that the AKP "signals" the birth of global Turkish power and the mission for a new world order. "This is the centenary of our exit from the Middle East," he said. "Whatever we lost between 1911 and 1923, whatever lands we withdrew from, from 2011 to 2023 we shall once again meet our brothers in those lands."[18] Erdogan has worked energetically against American interests throughout the Middle East, exacerbating rather than ameliorating the region's multiple major conflicts.[19] Erdogan has sabotaged the Obama administration's strenuous efforts to achieve harmony between Israel and its neighbors, repudiating Turkey's previous policy of maintaining good relations in favor of cultivating the most radical elements in the region. As Erdogan has consolidated his power, his anti-Semitic diatribes have intensified and multiplied. Erdogan has repeatedly called Israel the greatest threat to Middle East peace.[20] Meanwhile, he has facilitated the rise of radical Islamist entities such as ISIS through a combination of actively supporting the most radical factions of the Syrian rebels fighting Bashar al-Assad, only loosely enforcing security athwart the nine-hundred-mile Turkish-Syrian border, and woefully underestimating ISIS's threat to his own country, which Erdogan has only belatedly acknowledged but done little to combat.[21]

Likewise, Erdogan fervently supported the short-lived, implacably anti-American, anti-Western, anti-Semitic Muslim Brotherhood regime in Egypt under Mohamed Morsi, and he decried the popularly supported military intervention that supplanted it. The analyst Mohammad Abdel Kader of the Al Arabiya Institute for Studies called Erdogan's Turkey "the regional hub for the Muslim Brotherhood's international organization," including the Brotherhood's Palestinian wing, Hamas in Gaza.[22] In 2010 Erdogan's government conspired with Hamas to provoke the Gaza flotilla raid: the Israeli Defense Force boarded six so-called humanitarian vessels running an Israeli blockade that even the typically anti-Israel UN deemed legal. The IDF killed eight armed Turkish activists on the one ship that resisted, triggering Erdogan's outrage and the expulsion of the Israeli ambassador. Israeli Prime Minister Benjamin Netanyahu reluctantly acceded to President Obama's pressure to apologize—to no avail. Erdogan has rebuffed all efforts at reconciliation with Israel, linking Zionism with fascism and deploring Jewish self-determination as a crime against humanity.[23] In July 2014 Erdogan likened Israel's war in Gaza that Hamas instigated to the Holocaust. "What is the difference between what Nazis and Hitler did and what this Israeli administration is doing now?"[24]

Erdogan's Turkey has become a serious problem, not just for Israel but for the United States. Although Turkish leaders have stated consistently and publicly that Turkey will not accept Iran's possessing nuclear weapons, Turkish state banks and other Turkish enterprises have evaded and undermined the sanctions regime in Iran, with the complicity of the government.[25] On October 16, 2013, moreover, David Ignatius reported in the *Washington Post* that Turkey had disclosed the identity of ten Iranians who had been meeting with agents of the Mossad. U.S. intelligence officials confirm this betrayal of vital American interests.[26] The loss of this significant intelligence makes even more difficult the daunting task of detecting and deterring Iran's clandestine nuclear weapons program.[27] Ignatius's revelation followed a report in the October 12, 2013, *Wall Street Journal* that Hakan Fidan, Turkey's intelligence chief, passed to Iran sensitive intelligence that the United States and Israel had collected. Like Erdogan, Fidan has supported jihadists and Muslim Brotherhood elements across the Muslim Middle East, including initially entities such as ISIS in Syria. This unsavory and ill-advised propensity to patronize the most radical elements of the Syrian opposition collides with the Obama administration's own enunciated policy of distinguishing between moderate and radical factions among the Syrian rebels.[28] Though opinions vary on the degree of Turkish culpability for enabling ISIS, the Erdogan government is guilty of negligence and miscalculation at a minimum— probably even worse, at least until recently.[29] As late as the American midterm elections in the fall of 2014, Turkey continued to complicate the Obama administration's fight against ISIS by vacillating about whether to give the United States permission to use Turkish military bases for operations. Erdogan insists that toppling the Assad government in Syria should take precedence over President Obama's declared policy of defeating ISIS.[30] After months of negotiations, Turkey and the United States finally reached an agreement in February 2015 to arm the Syrian rebels while theoretically closing Turkey's borders to ISIS. Whether this agreement will translate into effective action or amounts merely to rhetoric masking the reality of Turkish noncooperation remains an open question. On the basis of past experience, the burden should lie on the optimists who believe Erdogan is genuine rather than duplicitous.[31]

Indeed, the nonpartisan experts Blaise Misztal, Halil Karaveli, and Svante Cornell predict that no foreign policy reset in Turkey is likely since President Erdogan became Turkey's first popularly elected president in August 2014, extending his dominance of Turkish politics for at least another five years.[32] So the United States should expect Turkish-American relations to become more fractious, given the anti-Western Islamist trajectory and dispositions of the AKP. As Daniel Pipes has observed, Erdogan's ascending to the presidency and his handpicked successor, Ahmet Davutoglu, replacing him as prime minister portends "nothing good" for Turkey and its foreign policy.[33] Turkey will probably continue gravitating away from the NATO alliance of democracies and toward flirting with Shanghai Cooperation Organization, which its leaders Russia and China envisage as a counterweight to NATO. Ankara's embrace of the Muslim Brotherhood and Islamist extremists in the Syrian civil war will continue to antagonize more moderate Sunni regimes in Egypt, Saudi Arabia, and Jordan, which are traditionally less hostile to the United States. Davutoglu's enthusiasm for Hamas will continue to facilitate Hamas's poisoning even a remote chance for achieving the Obama administration's professed goal of a genuine two-state solution that recognizes Israel's right to exist within secure boundaries while establishing a Palestinian state.[34] The terrifying rampage of ISIS in Iraq and Syria has failed to ameliorate the seething animosity between Turkey and its sizable Kurdish minority. In October 2014 Kurdistan's Worker's Party (PKK) threatened to resume its insurgency against Turkey because of Turkish inaction while ISIS lay siege to the Kurdish town of Kobani in Syria. Ergodan considers the PKK as dangerous as ISIS.[35]

Alarmingly, Pipes also classifies Erdogan and Davutoglu as more Islamist than neo-Ottoman in their foreign policy outlook. Behlul Ozkan, a Fletcher School–educated professor of political science at Marmara University in Turkey and a former student of Davutoglu, agrees that Davutoglu is "an 'Islamist ideologue' whose grandiose ambitions clash with reality and whose vision of pan-Islamic 'lebensraum' ('living space')—is underpinned more by power than by ethics."[36] Ozkan finds especially troubling Davutoglu's worldview, revealed in the more than three hundred articles and essays he published during the 1990s:

> The neo-Ottomanist label that is frequently attributed to Davutoglu is misleading. He criticizes neo-Ottomanism in his articles for being too Western-oriented. Davutoglu is a pan-Islamist. He is deeply influenced by Islam, yet he also uses Islam to achieve his foreign policy goals. He believes in a Sunni Muslim hegemonic order led by Turkey that would encompass the Middle East, the Caucasus and Central Asia, and include Albania and Bosnia as well. And I say Sunni because Iran is not part of this envisaged world. He argues that Turkey cannot be confined to its present-day borders. Should it continue to cling to its post–Cold War policy of preserving the status quo, Turkey will be destroyed. He

believes that the nation-states that were formed in 1918 were arti-ficial. But he does not idealize post-nation-state systems such as the European Union. To the contrary, he wants to go back in time to an order based on Islamic unity, on which Turkey expands its power not through military power but by creating spheres of influence. But this is a fantasy that has no academic basis.[37]

President Obama's misplaced admiration for Erdogan thus ill serves America's interests throughout the Middle East. As was the case with the failure of the administration's reset toward Russia, the source of Obama's misdiagnosis of Turkey under Erdogan lies in the Obama Doctrine's dan-gerous denial of the inextricable links among regime type, ideology, for-eign policy ambitions, and calculations of risk. Misztal, Karaveli, and Cornell convey concisely the dynamics and implications of those links, which any sound American strategy must take into account:

> Turkey's foreign policy posture away from the west . . . was never independent of internal dynamics. Indeed, it was driven by the Islamist ideology of the AKP, its pursuit of economic clout and business interests across the region, and domestic political con-cerns, primarily the Kurdish issue. Ankara attempted to estab-lish Turkish regional hegemony first by pursuing a policy of "zero problems with neighbors" resting greatly on pan-Islamic soli-darity, and then pursuing an interventionist Sunni policy when it appeared that the seemingly imminent fall of Assad in Syria, along with the rise of the Muslim Brotherhood in Egypt and Syria, could bring about a regional order in line with the ideologi-cal preferences of the AKP.[38]

The Obama Doctrine's strong disposition for retrenchment and against the use of military force also has contributed mightily to the unfolding disintegration of Iraq and the rise of ISIS to fill the vacuum that Ameri-can military withdrawal has wrought. The Obama administration and its prominent defenders, such as the commentators Fareed Zakaria and Leslie Gelb, have blamed this impending disaster on President George W. Bush and Iraq's problematic former prime minister Nouri al-Maliki.[39] Gelb writes off Iraq as Vietnam 2.0, calling it an ill-advised intervention on behalf of a government not worth the fight.[40] During his press conference of August 9, 2014, President Obama exonerated himself completely, claiming that pulling out all American ground troops in Iraq was not his decision, but Iraq's. Nor does Obama still believe that it would have made any positive difference if the administration had left troops in Iraq: "The only difference would be we'd have a bunch of troops on the ground that would be vulnerable. And however many troops we had, we would have to now be reinforcing, I'd have to be protecting them, and we'd have a much bigger job. And probably, we would end up having to go up again in terms of the number of ground troops to make sure that those forces were not vulnerable."[41]

Yet Gelb's Vietnam analogy and Obama's blatant revisionism cannot withstand scrutiny. By 2008 the Bush administration had largely recovered from its serious mistakes dealing with an Iraqi insurgence that had erupted after the conclusion of the stunningly successful conventional war phase of the second Iraq war. General David Petraeus's brilliant execution of Present Bush's strategy that Senator Obama categorically opposed achieved significant progress establishing the conditions for the emergence of a stable, self-sustaining Iraq that would be decent to its people and its neighbors. Petraeus warned, however, that successfully finishing the mission required a long-term American military presence to curb Maliki's worst sectarian instincts, reconcile Shia and Sunni factions, and provide a bulwark against Iranian intimidation and subversion.[42]

In 2011, instead, President Obama declared the Iraq war ended and American military withdrawal complete. Obama boasted of leaving behind a stable, secure Iraq—an optimistic assessment of the situation that Vice President Biden presaged in an interview with Larry King in early 2010:

> I am very optimistic about—about Iraq. I mean, this could be one of the great achievements of this administration. You're going to see 90,000 American troops come marching home by the end of the summer. You're going to see a stable government in Iraq that is actually moving toward a representative government. I spent— I've been there 17 times now. I go about every two months— three months. I know every one of the major players in all the segments of that society. It's impressed me. I've been impressed

how they have been deciding to use the political process rather than guns to settle their differences.[43]

Alas, the situation in Iraq began to deteriorate badly immediately after the American withdrawal. Maliki became steadily more arbitrary, authoritarian, sectarian, and reliant on Iran. Violence erupted, killing more than 5,300 Iraqis in 2013 and spiraling higher in 2014, and the prognosis is grim. When the United States withdrew at the end of 2011, militant groups had receded, the monthly death tolls at the "dozens rather than the hundreds." By 2014 radical and ferocious entities such as ISIS had intensified their campaign of attack; there was inadequate American power in place to assist, and the Iraqi government had fragmented into warring factions. Maliki's felicitous resignation, making way for his successor, Haider al-Abadi, to replace him, constitutes a necessary but insufficient condition for assembling a decent, inclusive government capable of keeping Iraq together and effectively countering ISIS. Writing the closest approximation to an authoritative account in the *New Yorker*, Dexter Filkins cites the overhasty American withdrawal in 2011 as one of the major reasons for the stunning and predictable collapse of Iraq:

> By 2011, by any reasonable measure, the Americans had made a lot of headway but were not finished with the job. For many months, the Obama and Maliki governments talked about keeping a residual force of American troops in Iraq, which would act largely to train Iraq's Army and to provide intelligence against Sunni insurgents. (It would almost certainly have barred them from fighting.) Those were important reasons to stay, but the most important went largely unstated: it was to continue to act as a restraint on Maliki's sectarian impulses, at least until the Iraqi political system was strong enough to contain him on its own. The negotiations between Obama and Maliki fell apart, in no small measure because of a lack of engagement by the White House. Today, many Iraqis, including some close to Maliki, say that a small force of American soldiers—working in non-combat roles—would have provided a crucial stabilizing factor that is now missing from Iraq. . . . President Obama wanted the Americans to come home, and Maliki didn't particularly want them to stay.[44]

Leon Panetta corroborates Filkins's account:

Privately, the various leadership factions in Iraq all confided they wanted some U.S. forces to remain as a bulwark against sectarian violence. But none was willing to take that position publicly. . . . We had leverage. . . . My fear, as I voiced to the President and others, was that if the country split apart or slid back into the pervasive violence that we'd experienced in the years immediately following the U.S. invasion, it could become a new haven for terrorists to plot attacks on the United States. . . . The deal never materialized. . . . Those on our side of the debate viewed the White House as so eager to rid itself of Iraq it was willing to withdraw rather than lock in arrangements that would preserve our influence and interests. . . . To this day, I believe that a small, focused U.S. troop presence could have effectively advised the Iraqi military on how to deal with Al Qaeda's resurgence and the sectarian violence that has engulfed the country.[45]

Senator John McCain assails the Obama administration's withdrawal even more strongly, calling for the resignation of President Obama's national security team for failing to keep Iraq secure. "Could all this have been avoided? The answer is absolutely yes," he seethed.[46] McCain also argues that the administration will make the same mistake if it follows through on its plan to withdraw from Afghanistan unconditionally. Writing in the more tranquil year of 2012, even Indyk, Lieberthal, and O'Hanlon—authors of the finest favorable book on Obama's foreign policy—then described the withdrawal of all combat troops as "a reasonable gamble."[47] It hardly looks that way now.[48]

As the conservative commentator Andrew McCarthy observes, Obama does not bear sole responsibility for the implosion of Iraq.[49] The Bush administration negotiated the original Status of Forces Agreement, which called for full withdrawal of American combat troops by 2011, though it planned to modify the agreement to leave a force of 20,000 that American military commanders had requested.[50] Maliki loudly and publicly exhorted the United States to go home. Even so, the leaders of all Iraqi political parties confided privately to American commanders their desire for several thousand America military personnel to remain. The president made only a perfunctory effort to assert America's considerable leverage to attain a Status of Forces Agreement that would have prolonged an American military presence indefinitely, though at much lower levels. During the negotiations in 2011, Obama scotched a possible compromise he later accepted in 2014 for the deployment of 800 American troops, refusing to accept the sufficiency—even temporarily—of Maliki's verbal assurance on immunity for U.S. troops from Iraqi prosecution. Instead, Obama insisted on a deal breaker—given the prevailing political climate of Iraq—that the Iraqi Parliament ratify that immunity.[51]

The *New Yorker's* Filkins depicts Obama as "ambivalent about retaining even a small force in Iraq" under any circumstances. "The American attitude was: Let's get out of here as quickly as possible," recalled Sami al-Askari, an Iraqi member of Parliament.[52] Furthermore, the president's own words belie his claim that he did not eagerly pull all troops out of Iraq in 2011. Obama trumpeted in dozens of speeches and appearances—including his second inaugural address in 2013—how his administration had ended the war. During the fourth and final presidential debate in October 2012, Obama acclaimed his withdrawal of all troops from Iraq and blasted his Republican challenger, Mitt Romney, for favoring a Status of Forces Agreement that would have sustained an American military presence:

> Mr. Romney: With regards to Iraq, you and I agreed I believe that there should be a status of forces agreement. Did you . . .
> President Obama: That's not true.
> Mr. Romney: Oh you didn't? You didn't want a status of . . . ?
> President Obama: What I would not have done was left 10,000 troops in Iraq that would tie us down. And that certainly would not help us in the Middle East.[53]

In April 2014 Ben Rhodes, the U.S. deputy national security adviser, reaffirmed that Obama still considered the full withdrawal the correct decision: "There is a risk in overstating the difference that American troops could make in the internal politics of Iraq. Having troops there did not allow us to dictate sectarian alliances. Iraqis are going to respond to their own political imperatives."[54]

This chapter will return to the subject of ISIS and Iraq while later examining Obama's reaction to the raging civil war in Syria that has morphed into a full-blown sectarian war. Whether the Obama administration has the foresight and fortitude to salvage the situation in Iraq remains to be seen. It suffices to say here that four years of savage and intensifying conflict have eradicated any effective Iraqi control over the three-hundred-mile border it shares with Syria, mostly desert. The radicalization of the Syrian opposition has spilled into Iraq and come at the expense of moderates of both countries.[55]

In Afghanistan, too, the president has made withdrawal rather than victory the goal. After months of agonizing and fractious debate, the president approved in 2009 a smaller surge than his campaign had promised or the U.S. military had advised, though it was larger than his most dovish advisers wanted, including Biden, who categorically opposed a significant increase of American combat troops in Afghanistan, even for a scaled-back mission of achieving stability rather than defeating the Taliban. Obama also undermined the efficacy of his surge of 30,000 American troops by proclaiming simultaneously that "after 18 months our troops will begin to come home."[56] In 2011 Obama accelerated the rate of drawing down American troops far more greatly and unconditionally than his secretary of defense or commanders considered prudent.[57] In May 2014 the president announced that the United States would withdraw all combat troops from Afghanistan by 2016, despite the recommendations of American military advisers that the United States should leave a residual force of at least 10,000 combat troops beyond that self-imposed deadline that hawkish critics charged risked engulfing Afghanistan with the same violence and instability as Iraq.[58] The president has conditioned leaving even a residual force of 9,800 noncombat troops in Afghanistan indefinitely on a long-term security agreement with Afghanistan that outgoing Afghani Prime Minister Hamid Karzai—deeply distrustful of the president—for months refused to sign. In the fall of 2014 Karzai's successor, Ashraf Ghani, calculated differently, signing a bilateral security agreement with the United States.[59]

The marked deterioration in the United States' relationship with Pakistan further diminishes the precarious prospects of a stable Afghani government's surviving, especially after the American troops depart. Fault the Pakistanis in this instance—not the Obama administration—for the increasing lack of cooperation between the two countries. The Pakistani military—never firmly pro-American even in the best of days—increasingly views the United States as a threat. Islamic radicalism has swelled in Pakistan, impelling the regime to hedge its bets in the war on terror. Although helping the United States in some ways—"such as providing supply lines through Pakistan"—the Pakistanis also provided sanctuary for terrorists—including the Taliban and other extremists. The Pakistanis exhibited gross negligence at best in failing to discover Osama bin Laden hiding for years in their country until President Obama ordered the brilliantly planned and executed operation killing him. The Obama administration's hundreds of drone attacks against terrorist sanctuaries in Pakistan have further enraged Pakistani public opinion—already strongly anti-American when Obama became president.[60] Pakistan was "really no ally," lamented Secretary of Defense Robert Gates.[61] Neither the Obama administration's offer of greater economic aid and strategic partnership nor periodically calling out Pakistan for its double-dealing worked to reverse the downward spiral in relations. Instead, cultivating a strategic partnership with a decent, democratic India has the added benefit of offering the least bad choice for containing the considerable danger of radicalism and instability wracking a Pakistani regime possessing nuclear weapons. For a variety of reasons discussed in the following chapter, however, the Obama administration, until recently, has assigned low priority to Indian-American relations. Meanwhile, Pakistan probably will collaborate with, rather than resist, the Taliban in Afghanistan, which bodes ill for any moderate Afghani regime's enduring without an American military presence.[62]

Undaunted, Obama has proclaimed it is "time to turn the page" on the decade in which so much of our foreign policy was focused on Iraq and Afghanistan, despite conceding that American withdrawal may jeopardize the conditional but significant progress in security achieved after a decade of U.S. involvement: "We have to recognize Afghanistan will not be a perfect place, and it is not America's responsibility to make it one. The future of Afghanistan must be decided by Afghans."[63] Obama's former secretary of defense Robert Gates has scathingly criticized the president for not believing "in his own strategy" and not considering the Afghan "war to be his. For him it was all about getting out."[64] Gates complained that "President Obama . . . whose commitment to the strategy was essential to success" was "skeptical if not downright convinced it would fail. (Bush had seemed to believe wholeheartedly that the Iraq surge would work.)"[65] Gates concluded, "President Obama simply wanted the 'bad' war in Iraq to be ended, and once in office, the U.S. role in Afghanistan—the so-called good war—be limited in scope and duration. His fundamental problem in Afghanistan was that his political and philosophical preferences . . . conflicted with his own pro-war public rhetoric, . . . the nearly unanimous recommendations of his senior civilian and military advisers at State and Defense, and the realities on the ground in Afghanistan."[66]

The Obama administration also has misread the dynamics of the Arab Spring—the cataclysmic wave of violence, protests, coups, and civil wars beginning in Tunisia in September 2010, then rolling across the Arab Middle East, toppling regimes in Libya, Egypt, and Yemen, while igniting a ferocious civil war in Syria and widespread protests elsewhere in the region. Initially, the president viewed these convulsions with caution and ambivalence. In behavior consistent with his reset toward Russia, Obama spent his first two years in office strongly depreciating the importance of ideology, regime type, and human rights in the Middle East. Obama renounced Bush's notion of an "axis of evil" and his advocacy of democratic regime change as the remedy for the region's strife. In May 2009 Obama ignored the pro-Western Iranian opposition's abortive Green Revolution in favor of engaging an implacably anti-American Islamist regime in (non-Arab) Iran that was on the verge of achieving a nuclear breakout capability. The administration also trod lightly with authoritarian Egypt, Saudi Arabia, and Jordan for their deficiencies in human rights, criticizing them rarely, gently, and elliptically. Obama's landmark speeches in Ankara and Cairo flattered the contributions of Islam profusely while remaining silent about Islamist radicalism as even a source of concern.

In the summer of 2010, however, the president moved tentatively, though not permanently, in the direction of weighing the risk of supporting what he called "increasingly unpopular and repressive regimes" versus "a strong push from the United States for reform." In a glowing account of the president's handling of the Arab Spring and leading from behind in Libya, Ryan Lizza quotes a private memorandum in which Obama observed, "Increased repression could threaten the political and economic stability of some of our allies. . . . Moreover, our regional and international credibility will be undermined if we are seen or perceived to be backing repressive regimes and ignoring the rights and aspirations of citizens." Even so, the president maintained his strict limits on what the United States would countenance to influence the outcome of reform in the Middle East, especially if it entailed any American military involvement in the region.[67]

The collapse of President Hosni Mubarak's regime in Egypt months later confronted the Obama administration with an agonizing dilemma that would have vexed any president. On the one hand, Mubarak had long served as a fairly reliable ally by the standards of the Islamic Middle East—a secular leader supporting the peace treaty with Israel and opposing Iran's acquiring nuclear weapons. On the other hand, the octogenarian Mubarak had become increasingly corrupt and intent on transforming Egypt into a "dynastic state" by contriving to anoint his son, Gamal, as his successor. Hundreds of thousands of Egyptians filled Tahrir Square in February 2011, demanding Mubarak relinquish power. Soon after giving Mubarak a vote of confidence, the Obama administration reversed course, rightly calculating that it was impossible to save Mubarak in the face of overwhelming popular will.

So President Obama called for Mubarak to go, but he lacked a sound plan for either Egypt or the region. As he had in regard to Turkey and Iran, Obama failed to recognize the danger and malevolence of Islamism in Egypt, instead welcoming the election of the Muslim Brotherhood and pronouncing President Mohamed Morsi a legitimate democrat. The administration assumed falsely that the pragmatism of the Muslim Brotherhood would outweigh its ideology in governing Egypt. Vali Nasr draws a parallel between the administration's expectation that the Muslim Brotherhood would stay the course with democracy and the misplaced enthusiasm the Western media displayed between 1977 and 1979:

> You will not find much concern for theocracy there; any such talk was quickly drowned by giddy and often Pollyannaish expectations of democracy's imminent triumph. But Iran's democrats, as attractive as they may have been, lacked the capabilities of the clerics and communists. The Pahlavi monarchy's swift demise caught the democrats unprepared . . . and gave the upper hand to the architects of a new dictatorship. . . . The protests of Egypt

captivated the world, but Egyptian liberal democrats are no more likely to win in the future than were their Iranian counterparts back in 1979. The Shah's rapid collapse benefited not democracy but theocracy. Given the decades-long surge of the Muslim Brotherhood, there is a strong chance that the same will happen in Egypt.[68]

Unfortunately, Morsi proved true to the Muslim Brotherhood's founders. He and his followers sought to crush any opposition and impose strict religious Sharia law on the entire populace, including the large Coptic Christian minority, which the Brotherhood treated brutally. The incompetence, repressiveness, and intolerance organic to the virulently anti-American, anti-Semitic Muslim Brotherhood impelled Egyptians to repent of their choice quickly. After more than 14 million people took to the streets in the summer of 2013 to demand Morsi's removal, Egypt's General Abdel Fattah el-Sisi staged a successful coup. The Obama administration's flirtations with Morsi not only distressed Israel, but also antagonized Saudi Arabia, which considers the Muslim Brotherhood a "dangerous rival" and its main ally—Erdogan's Turkey—a threat to "Saudi primacy."[69]

In October 2013 the administration made a bad situation worse by suspending a substantial amount of the $1.2 billion in annual aid to Egypt in reprisal for the military's ouster of Morsi and its severe crackdown on the Muslim Brotherhood. Between July and October 2013, more than one thousand people died in street clashes between the military and Muslim Brotherhood demonstrators protesting the military coup. The Egyptian military ignored the Obama administration's multiple warnings not to stage the coup in the first place and to crack down on the Brotherhood thereafter. The military-backed government imposed martial law and systematically suppressed the Islamist opposition.[70]

Yet suspending aid to Egypt subverted, rather than served, America's moral and strategic interests. The Egyptian military coup did not depose a legitimate, stable, liberal democratic regime, but a fanatical, anti-American Islamist dictatorship in the making. No decent, democratic alternative exists in Egypt at present. The unsavory choice in Egypt lies between the greater and lesser evil: a virulently anti-American, anti-Semitic Sunni version of the Shiite ayatollas running the revolutionary theocracy in Iran, and a less anti-American dictatorship committed to upholding the cold but invaluable peace between Egypt and Israel that has endured since Egyptian President Anwar Sadat and Israeli Prime Minister Menachem Begin signed the Camp David Accords in 1978. Suspending aid to Egypt sent the perverse signal that the Obama administration prefers the Muslim Brotherhood and Islamists over the Egyptian military and traditional Sunni regimes. It also will reduce American influence in Egypt, encouraging the generals to look elsewhere for support.[71]

Writing in the *Daily Caller,* the commentator Clifford Smith recommended sagely envisaging the Egyptian conundrum through the prism of Jeane Kirkpatrick's famous essay "Dictatorships and Double Standards," published in 1979.[72] Kirkpatrick supported the goal of spreading stable liberal democracy for moral and geopolitical reasons. What she criticized was the Carter administration's pressuring America's less repressive right-wing allies and destabilizing them, while conciliating totalitarian enemies of the United States such as the Soviet Union. That ill-conceived strategy multiplied America's adversaries and demoralized democratic allies. Kirkpatrick advocated, conversely, that the United States back pro-American authoritarian allies when the only other viable contenders are more repressive, aggressive, anti-American regimes.[73]

The record of the Cold War largely vindicated the prudence of her outlook and policy prescriptions. Compare, for example, the advent of freedom and democracy in formerly authoritarian South Korea, Taiwan, and Chile with the persistence of tyranny in communist North Korea, Cuba, and China. Nor, given totalitarian communism's incapacity to reform, could the Cold War truly end until the Soviet Union collapsed. Now support for the military-backed authoritarian regime in Egypt at least offers the potential for allowing benign evolutionary democratic reform. Aid to Egypt bolsters, rather than threatens, the peace between Egypt and Israel—one of the few remaining bright spots for American policy in the Middle East. By suspending aid to the Egyptian military, the Obama administration has lowered the barrier to the greater evil: a destitute, rancorous, radical Islamist Egypt hostile to the legacy of Sadat.

Nor did what one Obama adviser favorably call "leading from behind" in Libya herald a more humble, more effective, more legitimate way of war "at odds with the John Wayne expectation for what America is in the world."[74] On the contrary, Libya has descended into a protracted, increasingly violent sectarian chaos since the 2011 multilateral military intervention that resulted in the overthrow and death of Muammar al-Gaddafi. The implosion of Libya culminated in the September 11, 2012, attack on the American consulate in Benghazi—when four Americans, including the ambassador, were killed—which an obtuse White House in denial about Islamism reflexively blamed on an anti-Islamic YouTube video rather than on terrorists timing their premeditated murder for the anniversary of 9/11.[75]

The author James Mann astutely sums up the Libyan campaign—the first war President Obama initiated—as the apotheosis of Obama's view of the world:

> It demonstrated for the first time that he was willing to put American military power to work on behalf of humanitarian goals, in a way that the realists he admired would not. Above all, it showed the Obama administration's intense commitment to multilateralism. The president approved the use of military force only after the urging of America's closest allies and only after getting formal approval from the Arab League. Moreover, Obama's multilateralism was of a new strain. It went well beyond previous versions, in which the United States simply consulted with its allies. This time, the United States started the military campaign and stepped aside while the allies took over. It was an approach virtually without precedent since World War II. In the Obamian view, the United States should preserve its leadership role in the world in the coming decades, but it could only do so by . . . acknowledging the limits of its power and the greater need to share the costs and responsibilities of a military campaign. . . . America would go along, so long as it did not have to carry the military burden on its own.[76]

Count this writer among the detractors of Obama's worldview, exemplified in the Libyan campaign that Mann largely admires and Ryan Lizza fulsomely praises. No one should regret the demise of Gaddafi, a brutal tyrant and energetic sponsor of terrorism during the 1980s, whom Ronald Reagan called a madman. Unlike the nuclear threat of Iran, however, or at least debatably the metastasizing conflagration in Syria (an Iranian surrogate), the civil war in Libya involved no vital interest of the United States. Gaddafi dismantled his nuclear program in 2003 and no longer posed a regional threat. Furthermore, the intervention in Libya failed even as a humanitarian intervention that plausibly may have justified it despite the absence of a compelling geopolitical rationale. The premature exit from Libya, emblematic of Obama's ill-advised strategy toward Iraq and Afghanistan, contributed mightily to its implosion. In an August 2014 interview with Tom Friedman, the president admitted as much without grasping the damning implications of his propensity to let his strict, self-imposed limits on means dictate his ends, regardless of the consequences. "I absolutely believed that [the overthrow of Gaddafi] was the right thing to do, but . . . we [and] our European partners underestimated the need to come in full force. . . . There has to be a much more aggressive effort to rebuild societies."[77] Why doesn't this "lesson" apply to Iraq, Afghanistan, and Syria? The president offered no answer to this troubling question that his own assessment raised.

The Libyan campaign also fostered the dangerous illusion that Obama's intense multilateralism can typically substitute for American hard power and the will to use it, alone or with narrow coalitions of the willing if necessary. For all its problems and, at best, ambiguous outcome, Libya offered the rare best-case scenario for the type of multilateral intervention President Obama wrongly regards as more the norm than the exception. The dismal history of UN collective security since 1945 attests eloquently to the futility of making the United Nations or even an alliance such as NATO, rooted in freedom and shared values, the arbiter of legitimacy for when and how the United States uses force. Gridlock inheres in the logic and the structure of the UN Security Council, where each of the five permanent members—the United States, Russia, China, France, and Great Britain—possesses a veto to thwart any collective UN action it opposes in the realm of international security.[78]

Since 1945 the frequency and magnitude of the UN's failures have dwarfed its rare and evanescent successes: Korea in 1950 and the Iraq war of 1990–1991, which the Security Council approved unanimously. The United States succeeded in enlisting the authority of the Security Council in resisting North Korean aggression against South Korea only because the Soviet Union was boycotting for the UN's refusal to recognize the People's Republic of China as the legitimate representative of China. Thereafter, Soviet-American rivalry produced gridlock in the Security Council, marginalizing the UN in all great-power conflicts that dominated the remainder of the Cold War. Even without the Soviet-American impasse, gridlock remains the default position for most great-power conflicts that have emerged since the end of the Cold War. The United States succeeded in enlisting the authority of the Security Council in reversing Saddam Hussein's 1990 invasion of Kuwait thanks only to a felicitous convergence of events that seldom occurs in international politics. Iraq had committed a brazen act of aggression against a sovereign state. The impending disintegration of the Soviet Union, the lingering international fallout from the Chinese massacre of students in Tiananmen Square in 1989, and French reluctance to alienate the United States with German unification looming gave leaders in all three of these countries more incentive than usual to maintain Washington's goodwill.[79]

Since the first Iraq war, the UN Security Council has reverted to gridlock as the norm. UN intervention in Bosnia in the 1990s was too weak to succeed, but large enough to curtail effective action until larger, stronger NATO forces replaced hapless UN contingents. The UN intervention in Somalia ended in debacle after the firefight in Mogadishu in 1993. The UN did nothing to prevent the 1994 genocide in Rwanda or massacres in Sudan a decade later. In 1999 the US and its NATO allies—including France—bypassed a gridlocked UN Security Council to wage war against Serbia for atrocities in Kosovo. The UN Security Council vacillated for more than a decade while Saddam Hussein defied seventeen UN resolutions with impunity.[80]

On President Obama's watch, the UN Security Council has never taken decisive action in response to any major conflict, with the partial and ambiguous exception of Libya, where the situation continues to deteriorate. Russia and China sorely regret their acquiescence to the intervention, pledging to exercise their vetoes on the Security Council to prevent Libya from serving as a precedent. Both nations charged the Obama administration with deception, portraying the UN intervention merely as humanitarian, its limited goal to protect civilians from slaughter rather than entailing the more ambitious goal of regime change it turned out to be.[81] The propensity to gridlock that is organic to the UN also inheres to a lesser but still significant degree in the NATO alliance of twenty-eight nations, making NATO consensus too unreliable as a prerequisite for decisive American action. So it reflects a triumph of hope over experience to suggest that the Obama administration can replicate the Libyan model successfully elsewhere.

Even for Libya—the rare best-case scenario when consensus exists and allies make a substantially greater contribution than usual—leading from behind proved more rhetorical than real: the United States still shouldered the preponderance of the military burden.[82] The Obama administration also set a terrible precedent by dismissing the need for congressional approval for U.S. military intervention in Libya while giving greater credence to the approval of the UN, NATO, and, astonishingly, the Arab League. This provocative disregard for the Article I authority of Congress and deference to "the international community" is not only constitutionally dubious, but also politically unwise. Domestic support will erode sooner rather than later for controversial military interventions that Americans' elected representatives have not approved.

The Obama administration's intense multilateralism and aversion to force have turned out badly for Syria, where no good options exist. What began as an internal civil war has expanded into a regional conflict, pitting Iran and it surrogate, Hezbollah, against a Sunni coalition increasingly dependent on radical Islamists such as ISIS. The death toll as of August 2014 reached 191,000, and there is no end to the carnage in sight.[83] At every major turn, however, the administration has miscalculated, making a bad situation worse. The president started off assuming falsely that the United States could profitably engage Syria despite the Assad family's long record of repression and unbridled hostility toward the United States. Secretary of State John Kerry also implied that the murderous Bashar al-Assad was a reformer with whom the United States could do business, a delusion he shared with his predecessor, Hillary Clinton.[84] As the Syrian civil war escalated in scope and ferocity, the president issued a red line against Assad's use of chemical weapons but flinched when the Syrian dictator crossed it. Instead, the United States and Russia agreed on September 13, 2013, on the transfer of Syrian chemical weapons to international control. Though President Obama still touts this Russian-American agreement as a major success, Putin emerged as the real victor, at America's expense. Furthermore, Assad consolidated his grip on power, reaping a reward rather than a penalty for using chemical weapons.[85] Testifying before the

House Intelligence Committee on February 4, 2014, Obama's director of national intelligence conceded that Assad has grown stronger "by virtue of his agreement to remove the chemical weapons."[86]

The Russian-American accord culminated several wrenching months of President Obama's irresolution and serial retreats. First, the United States announced it would launch strikes to punish Assad for using chemical weapons. Secretary of State Kerry undercut the threat, calling the contemplated strikes "unbelievably small."[87] After claiming the authority to act unilaterally as commander in chief, the president backed away, delaying any strikes pending his unavailing search to secure congressional approval and the support of allies. Ultimately, the president managed to assemble a grand coalition of two—the United States and intrepid France—compared to the thirty-seven nations that joined the United States in 2003 to fight the second Iraq war under the predecessor he routinely excoriated for unilateralism. In Congress, the president spared himself almost certain defeat, accepting Vladimir Putin's diplomatic alternative to military action.[88]

It reflects wishful thinking in the extreme to count on the UN's reliably verifying and enforcing the U.S.-Russian agreement to control Syrian chemical weapons. How can UN inspectors possibly discover, in a timely fashion, the bulk of Syrian President Bashar al-Assad's large and widely disbursed chemical weapons stockpile amid a bloody, intensifying civil war that has become regional? What, in Assad's long record of brutality and duplicity, inspires legitimate confidence in his willingness to cooperate with UN inspectors? Deferring to Russian objections, the Obama administration also abandoned its preliminary demand that the UN resolution codifying the agreement on chemical weapons provide for the option of using force for noncompliance. Nor, as a practical matter, could the UN use force even if the agreement theoretically invested it with that authority. No doubt Russia will veto any Security Council resolution calling for military strikes against Assad, no matter how compelling the evidence indicating noncompliance.[89]

The administration's retreat from its red line resonated negatively beyond Syria, undermining the credibility of Obama's pivot to Asia, his serial warnings to Putin, and his countless assurances that he would not tolerate a nuclear Iran. By focusing almost exclusively on the risks of action, the president underestimated the risk of inaction in Syria and the dynamism of the terrorist entities the conflagration unleashed. Hillary Clinton, the former secretary of state, speculated that arming the Syrian rebels in 2012 may have forestalled the rise of ISIS, now on the rampage in Syria and Iraq. Until his belated about-face on September 11, 2014, President Obama had long and stoutly resisted arming the rebels despite the urgings of Secretary Clinton, his former secretary of defense Leon Panetta, his former chairman of the Joint Chiefs of Staff Martin Dempsey, and his more hawkish critics such as Senator John McCain.[90] Panetta reiterated in a September 2014 CBS interview with the reporter Scott Pelley on *60 Minutes* that the president defied the advice of his entire national security team, who "unanimously" exhorted him "to do more to support rebels . . . fighting against Bashar al-Assad" at the beginning of the Syrian civil war.[91]

The scholar and commentator Marc Lynch doubts cogently whether offering more support for the Syrian rebels sooner would have been as decisive as critics of the president imply. "Syria's combination of a weak, fragmented collage of rebel organizations with a divided competitive array of external sponsors" offered the "worst profile possible for effective external support."[92] Even so, critics can assert with greater plausibility that the president's reluctance to arm the rebels harmed the never robust chances for a moderate opposition emerging as an alternative to Assad. Also, the president himself seems to have repudiated his previous position and Lynch's on the futility of arming the rebels. On September 10, 2014, President Obama pledged to arm moderate elements of the Syrian opposition, an option he had disparaged just a month before in an interview with Tom Friedman of the *New York Times,* calling "the notion" that arming Syrian rebels would have made a difference merely a "fantasy."[93]

Although arming the rebels sooner may not have stopped the rise of ISIS in Syria, Obama's premature withdrawal of American troops bears a large share of the responsibility for ISIS's filling the vacuum in Iraq. President George W. Bush predicted prophetically the horrors such a premature withdrawal would unleash, announcing his Iraqi surge on January 10, 2007:

> The consequences of failure are clear. Radical Islamic extremists would grow in strength and gain new recruits. They would be in a better position to topple moderate governments, create chaos

in the region and use oil revenues to fund their ambitions. Iran would be emboldened in its pursuit of nuclear weapons. Our enemies would have a safe haven from which to plan and launch attacks on the American people. . . . [Iran and Syria] are allowing terrorists and insurgents to use their territory to move in and out of Iraq. Iran is providing material support for attacks on American troops. We will disrupt the attacks on our forces. We will interrupt the flow of support from Iran and Syria. And we will seek out and destroy the networks providing advanced weaponry and training to our enemies in Iraq.[94]

ISIS has become one of the most feared and ferocious terrorist entities in the world, routinely beheading, crucifying, and amputating the limbs of its mounting victims. ISIS now controls a nation-size area encompassing substantial parts of Iraq and Syria. Iraq will not survive ISIS's onslaught unless the United States promptly and decisively takes the lead to defeat it. ISIS also intends to bring the fight to the United States. Director of National Intelligence James Clapper has estimated that there are more than seven thousand foreigners fighting alongside radical jihadists, many of whom possess passports from Western nations.[95] ISIS also controls seven oil fields and two refineries in eastern Syria and northern Iraq. According to K. T. McFarland, assistant secretary of defense under Ronald Reagan, ISIS sells 40,000 barrels of oil a day on the black market, generating approximately $2 million a day, and has a potential to double that to 80,000 barrels a day.[96] That makes ISIS rich, its military well provisioned, and its capacity to bribe enormous. ISIS has set its sights, too, on the oil fields of southern Iraq, which produce 3 million barrels a day, and eventually the grand prize of Saudi Arabia's 10 million barrels a day. The economic analyst Stuart Varney warns that killing ISIS is a financial necessity because "the price and supply of oil for the world is at stake," noting that oil consumers already are paying a premium for the ISIS threat.[97]

As the commentator Richard Grenell observes, however, the president has a long history of underestimating the threat of ISIS.[98] The president rebuffed several Iraqi pleas in 2013 to "strike Islamic State terrorists with drones," according to Marc A. Thiessen, a defense analyst at the American Enterprise Institute.[99] President Obama described ISIS to David Remnick in a January 2014 interview: "If a jayvee team puts on Lakers uniforms that doesn't make them Kobe Bryant."[100] James Clapper, whom President Obama appointed director of national intelligence, conceded that the United States underestimated ISIS: "What we didn't do was predict the will to fight. . . . We underestimated ISIL (the Islamic State) and overestimated the fighting capability of the Iraqi Army. . . . I didn't see the collapse of the Iraqi security forces in the north coming."[101]

The savage beheadings of the American journalists James Foley and Steven Sotloff stunned the leading officials of Obama's dovish national security team out of their complacency. Secretary of Defense Chuck Hagel called ISIS a greater threat than al-Qaeda: "They are an imminent threat to every interest we have, whether in Iraq or anywhere else."[102] General Martin Dempsey called ISIS an organization that "has an apocalyptic end-of-days strategic vision that will eventually have to be defeated."[103] Vice President Joe Biden—typically at the forefront of advocating military restraint—vowed to "follow ISIS to the gates of hell until they are brought to justice."[104] The president initially responded more equivocally than his advisers and an enraged American public heavily in favor of more decisive action, especially after the beheading of their fellow Americans. On August 28, 2014, Obama admitted, shockingly, that "we don't have a strategy yet" to deal with ISIS, despite having months while the threat gathered to devise one.[105]

Whatever the motivation for his epiphany just days later, the president's address on September 10, 2014, marked a major, though contingent, step toward the more hawkish position of his advisers and Republican critics such as Senator John McCain and former Vice President Dick Cheney. The president declared unambiguously that the United States must destroy ISIS rather than merely manage it, as he had said previously. He prepared the American people for a campaign of long duration, outlining a four-part plan entailing strategic airstrikes against ISIS in Iraq and Syria and arming and providing logistical support for local forces on the ground, including "moderate elements" of the Syrian opposition. In this address the president also categorically rejected any alliance of convenience to combat ISIS with the murderous Assad regime in Syria. Obama's tone conveyed substantially more resolution than his startling previous revelation that the administration as yet had not devised a strategy and his initial assurance that the United States could settle for reducing ISIS to a "manageable problem" rather than defeating it.[106]

Yet what President Obama said and did not say in his ISIS address raises serious questions about his determination to achieve victory and his conception of it. Start with the president's emblematic denial of the Islamist dimension of the threat. He has yet to grasp the critical distinction between Islam as a *religion,* with which the United States has no quarrel, and Islamism as an *ideology* demanding man's complete subservience and adherence to strict religious law. The Islamism that ISIS exemplifies constitutes the moral and geopolitical equivalent of fascism, which the United States must unremittingly oppose in all its manifestations. The president's wishful thinking about radical Islamists accounts for many of his most egregious foreign policy miscalculations in the Middle East: initially embracing the Muslim Brotherhood in Egypt; envisaging the increasingly Islamist president of Turkey, Recep Erdogan, as a partner for peace rather than an adversary; shielding the fanatical Islamist Hamas in Gaza from the full and well-earned brunt of Israel's reprisal for firing thousands of missiles into the Jewish state, with the aim of killing civilians—a solicitude for Hamas that also antagonized the military government in Egypt and the Saudi Arabians, who loathed it; and engaging the rabidly anti-American theocracy in Iran.[107]

Nor does the president's emphasis in his ISIS address on what the United States will *not* do inspire the maximum confidence in his ability or resolution to defeat ISIS decisively. The president conceives of his strategy toward ISIS as an analogue to what we have pursued against Yemen and Somalia for years. Yet Yemen and Somalia remain hotbeds of terrorism despite U.S. airstrikes that have killed several high-level leaders and operatives. ISIS is, moreover, a more formidable enemy that will require considerably more exertion to defeat than terrorism emanating from these two countries.[108]

Even more problematic, the president has ruled out American forces' having any "combat mission—we will not get dragged into another ground war in Iraq."[109] Instead, the administration intends to rely exclusively on the Iraqi military, the Kurds, and the moderate Syrian opposition to defeat ISIS.[110] Is it really prudent to rule out the more decisive use of American military power, given the magnitude of the danger and the ferocity of the opponent? Can an Iraqi army that has performed badly in the past successfully divest ISIS of the seven oil fields and two refineries in northern Iraq and eastern Syria essential for financing its bestial and relentless campaign? Would achieving that vital objective require American Special Forces at a minimum? Will a broad and effective international coalition as yet unspecified really materialize? Or is Jeff Shesol, writing in the *New Yorker,* right to mock Obama's purported coalition as "willing and unable?"[111] What has so suddenly and drastically changed in the president's thinking to explain his heretofore nonexistent confidence in the Syrian opposition he derided only weeks before as "former doctors, farmers, pharmacologists, and so forth" incapable of standing up to Assad to now serve as effective substitutes for American ground forces? Will Obama truly employ air power swiftly, massively, and simultaneously to pulverize ISIS's logistical tail in Syria, eviscerate ISIS's combat capabilities in Iraq, and deny ISIS the freedom of movement on which its rampage depends?

Michael O'Hanlon, a Brookings policy expert, considers the president's plan logically sound, though he concedes the United States will need "quite probably, its boots on the ground" to succeed ultimately.[112] Robin Simcox, a research fellow at the Henry M. Jackson Society in London, predicts that no strategy to defeat ISIS and restore order in Iraq can succeed without American Special Forces, combat troops, and a long-term American military presence.[113] Although conceding it "would entail some risk," the sober and highly esteemed Middle Eastern expert Kenneth Pollack believes that the Obama plan may provide the template for turning the Syrian opposition into a real fighting force, not only to stop ISIS but to defeat Assad in Syria.[114] Writing in the *New York Times,* Anne Barnard and David Kirkpatrick have described as merely "tepid" Arab support for the U.S. fight against ISIS on which the president counts heavily to substitute for American ground forces. Neither Jordan nor Egypt will join the coalition.[115] Even in Iraq, where the threat of ISIS is gravest, the Obama plan has elicited only mixed reaction.

Weighing in on the president's ISIS strategy, Obama's former secretary of state Robert Gates said the United States cannot succeed against ISIS without U.S. ground troops and warns of the danger of the president's continuing to insist otherwise. "The reality is, they're not gonna be able to be successful against ISIS strictly from the air, or strictly depending on the Iraqi forces, or the Peshmerga, [or] the Sunni tribes acting on their own. So there will be boots on the ground if there's to be any hope of success in the strategy. . . . And I think that by continuing to repeat that [there won't be boots on the ground], the president, in effect, traps himself."[116]

So what happens if the combination of American airpower and logistical support for local forces on the ground without an exemplary record of success does not suffice? Will the president reconsider his self-imposed limits and do what it takes to win against a danger he himself deemed grave? Or will the president make withdrawal rather than victory the priority, reprising his mistakes in Iraq and Afghanistan, striking another hard blow to America's reputation for reliability, and emboldening aggressors not just in the Middle East?

The president's greater hawkishness toward ISIS comes late and coincides with plummeting poll numbers indicating a huge majority of Americans consider him woefully weak in the realm of national security and responding to foreign dangers. A September 2014 NBC/*Wall Street Journal* poll echoed the findings of other major reputable pollsters: Republicans enjoy an eighteen-point advantage on which party deals best with foreign policy and a whopping thirty-eight-point advantage on which party best ensures the national defense; 47 percent consider America less safe than it was before the 9/11 attack thirteen years earlier.[117] For all its tougher rhetoric, the president's ISIS speech still raises legitimate apprehensions that the president could revert to his deep aversion to using force decisively should the public mood shift. The president has yet to convince that he truly understands the enemy.

Perhaps President Obama's ISIS strategy will succeed without augmentation. Perhaps the conflict will validate precluding American ground troops to accomplish it. Perhaps Obama will succeed in assembling an effective coalition that now numbers ten compared to the coalition of thirty-seven George W. Bush assembled for the second Iraq war—a coalition Obama vilified as insufficiently broad, the exemplar of his predecessor's pugnacious unilateralism. Perhaps the president's ISIS speech heralds the beginning of his evolution away from the minimalist and conciliatory tenets of an Obama Doctrine that he theretofore tenaciously held. Perhaps the president's reset on ISIS will induce greater strategic clarity and resolution. Perhaps the president will not flinch this time from enforcing his red line—even if the going gets tough—as he did with Assad in Syria and Putin in Ukraine. Otherwise, the United States and our allies may pay a stiff price, especially with the revolutionary, implacably anti-American regime of Iran taking measure of the administration's resolve.

Henry Kissinger rightly identifies revolutionary Iran as an even bigger problem than ISIS: "There has come into being a kind of a Shia belt from Tehran through Baghdad to Beirut. And this gives Iran the opportunity to reconstruct the ancient Persian Empire—this time under the Shia label. . . . ISIS is a group of adventurers with a very aggressive ideology. But they have to conquer more and more territory before they can become a geo-strategic, permanent reality. I think a conflict with ISIS—important as it is—is more manageable than a confrontation with Iran."[118] With mounting frequency and intensity, Iran has fomented tension throughout the region directly and through its surrogates: Assad in Syria, Hezbollah in Lebanon, and Hamas in Gaza. Iranian leaders have threatened repeatedly to annihilate Israel. The pace and purpose of Iran's nuclear program has generated increasing alarm, particularly in Israel but also rhetorically at least in the Obama administration. Though actively discouraging Israel from taking preemptive action and viewing American military strikes as an absolutely last resort, President Obama has pronounced it unacceptable on many occasions for Iran to acquire nuclear weapons. "I do not bluff," President Obama told interviewer Jeffrey Goldberg. "When the United States says it is unacceptable for Iran to have nuclear weapons, we mean what we say."[119]

As Kenneth Pollack explains in his fine *Unthinkable: Iran, the Bomb, and American Strategy,* the Obama administration has predicated its "Dual Track policy" toward Iran on the controversial assumption that genuine differences exist between moderates and radicals over the relative importance of the Iranian nuclear program. Obama disdained President Bush's designation of Iran as a rogue regime and foreswore his objective of regime change to address the root cause of the problem. Obama proclaimed himself "not big on extremism" as an explanation for how the Iranian leaders calculated risk, ends, and means.[120] Instead, Obama believed the Iranian regime was strategic, not compulsive, and would respond constructively to engagement and incentives. The administration's version of a carrot-and-stick approach toward Iran offered rewards—primarily economic but also relief from diplomatic isolation—if the Iranian regime agreed to compromise on its nuclear program, and punishments—primarily stiffer sanctions—if not.[121]

President Obama's dual-track policy unfolded in three phases. Phase One—running until the end of 2009—relied almost exclusively on carrots rather than sticks: engaging the Iranian leaders, including the virulently anti-Semitic Iranian President Mahmoud Ahmadinejad; indicating his administration had no goal of overthrowing the Iranian regime; apologizing for American involvement in the 1953 coup deposing Iranian President Mohammad Mosaddegh; offering the prospect of long-term reconciliation; and barely condemning Iran's brutal repression of the May 2009 Green Revolution, an uprising that protested election fraud and the regime's systematic violations of human rights. Unidentified senior administration officials told Pollack that "they were not going to make a bunch of empty statements on human rights abuses and so jeopardize engagement and a deal on the nuclear issue."[122]

Phase Two began in late 2009—after months of engagement yielded more Iranian defiance—and culminated in August 2012 with the P5+1 countries (the five permanent members of the UN Security Council—the United States, Great Britain, Russia, China, and France—plus Germany) recommending and the United Nations imposing stiff sanctions on Iran. Sanctions followed a series of unsuccessful meetings between the P5+1 and Iranian representatives in Geneva and Vienna. In this case, the Obama administration succeeded in deftly forging a broad coalition—including Saudi Arabia, India, Japan, and China—all of whom had done almost nothing but offer verbal protest of Iran's nuclear program during the administration of the more belligerent George W. Bush. Pollack also attributes much of the willingness of theretofore reluctant nations to impose unprecedentedly comprehensive sanctions to the fear of Israeli military action otherwise. "Had it not been for Israelis repeatedly sounding the alarm . . . the Iranians probably would have crossed the nuclear threshold long ago."[123]

Although the UN sanctions forced Iran to pay a substantially higher price for noncompliance, the Iranians continued to move steadily toward a nuclear breakout capability of perhaps as little as six months or even less, according to some reputable estimates rendered in the fall of 2013. The term *breakout capability* refers to the time it would take to enrich enough uranium for a nuclear weapon. In September 2013 the Obama administration inaugurated Phase Three of its dual-track policy, reverting to Phase One's heavy reliance on engagement and inducement to mitigate Phase Two's stress on punishment. The Obama administration's renewed optimism about a nuclear deal with Iran soared with the June 15, 2013, election of Hassan Rouhani as president of Iran, reputedly a moderate and centrist seeking a diplomatic rapprochement with the West. Rouhani's skillful public relations offensive and a late September 2013 telephone conversation with the president during the Iranian leader's visit to the United States amplified the Obama administration's favorable impression that Iran had finally become serious about negotiating about rather than shielding its nuclear program from scrutiny. Rouhani elicited rapturous reaction to his often-repeated claim that Iran would never build nuclear weapons.[124]

Addressing the United Nations on September 24, 2013, Obama resolved to focus the remainder of his presidency on improving relations with Iran and achieving an agreement between Israel and the Palestinians as the top priorities of his administration. All other issues in the Middle East would recede in importance, according to Susan Rice, the president's national security adviser. The tone and substance of Obama's address not only again repudiated President Bush's freedom agenda, but also heralded the president's renunciation of the ephemerally more expansive vision he had tentatively offered at the crest of the administration's optimism about the trajectory of the Arab Spring.[125] The president stressed engagement, discounted ideology and regime type as positive or negative variables, and envisaged a more modest role for the United States in the Middle East— all trademarks of the Obama Doctrine before and after the minor deviation of pressing for Mubarak's exit in Egypt and intervening to oust Gaddafi in Libya.[126] Accordingly, President Obama welcomed signs of a "more moderate course" from Iran under Rouhani, while stressing that Iran had to match "conciliatory words" with deeds. "The roadblocks may prove to be too great but I firmly believe the diplomatic path must be tested," Obama declared.[127]

On November 25, 2013, the P5+1 powers and Iran forged an interim agreement, freezing Iran's nuclear program for six months, starting Monday, January 20, 2014, in exchange for relief from crippling Western sanctions. Iran agreed in theory to neutralize its stockpile of weapons-grade uranium and freeze construction on its uncompleted heavy-water reactor in Arak, which, once completed, will be capable of producing two plutonium bombs a year. The accord also calls for regular international inspections at Iran's two major uranium enrichment sites. The P5+1 also abandoned their previous demand of categorically denying Iran the right to enrich uranium, which was codified in multiple UN resolutions. According to the terms of the interim agreement, the permanent agreement that Obama hopes will follow will constrain but not abolish that right, which would be based on Iran's practical needs.[128]

The Obama administration and its defenders praised the interim agreement for constraining Iran's nuclear activities while providing time and the impetus for negotiating a comprehensive agreement to stop Iran from crossing the nuclear weapons threshold.[129] Kenneth Pollack called it "only a small step in the right direction," less bad than the alternative of preemption.[130] Hawkish Republicans and Israeli Prime Minister Netanyahu assailed not only the provisions of the interim agreement, but the process of negotiations with a "rogue regime" such as Iran for anesthetizing the West to Iran's "relentless strategy to advance its nuclear weapons objectives."[131] Critics—this writer included—offered five principal objections to the interim accord in particular and reaching a nuclear deal with Iran in general.[132]

First, even in the "remote chance" of Iranian compliance, the agreement leaves Iran's nuclear infrastructure in place. Iran does not have to dismantle any of its 19,000 nuclear centrifuges used to generate weapons-grade uranium. Nor do the Iranians have to dismantle any of their weapons-grade nuclear reactors. Under the interim accord, Iran still retains the enrichment capability to develop nuclear weapons expeditiously. The accord also imposes no limits on Iran's ballistic missile program or other systems capable of delivering nuclear weapons.

Second, Iran's long record of dissimulation about its nuclear program casts doubt on the verifiability and enforcement of the interim accord. Iran has hundreds of nuclear sites, many of which remain hidden and undetected. The closed nature of Iran's regime makes detection difficult, especially if the leadership takes measures to evade compliance.[133]

Third, easing sanctions bolsters a terrible and aggressive regime, the root cause of the Iranian danger. Under the interim accord, Iran's regime received an immediate infusion of $7 billion.[134] A comprehensive accord would lift sanctions entirely, depriving the United States permanently of a significant source of leverage to constrain revolutionary Iran. Russia and China almost certainly would veto any American attempt in the Security Council to reimpose sanctions, no matter what Iran does.

Fourth, the dismal history of negotiating with revolutionary Iran inspires little confidence the president will succeed in talking President Rouhani into renouncing Iran's nuclear weapons program and its hegemonic ambitions. Negotiations are usually justified, sometimes even with mortal enemies.[135] Despite his view of the Soviet Union as an evil empire bent on world domination, Reagan used talks wisely to reduce the danger of war by miscalculation and to undermine the Soviet regime. Yet Reagan's success offers cold comfort in regard to Obama's talks with Iran. Reagan negotiated from a position of strength amid renewed prosperity that his policies had unleashed and the most comprehensive American military buildup in peacetime history. Conversely, Obama negotiates with a weaker hand, having slashed the defense budget, pressed for devolution of America's strategic responsibilities, and flinched on enforcing red lines against Assad and Putin. Unlike Reagan in his approach toward the Soviet Union, Obama has repeatedly pledged to Iran he has no intention of pushing for regime change.[136]

Fifth, the interim agreement raises the already formidable barriers to Israel's undertaking preemptive action to defend itself against an Iranian regime that has routinely called for Israel's annihilation. Any Israeli strike during the negotiations would incur the wrath not only of the UN, but also of the Obama administration, which has put more pressure on Israel than on Iran.[137]

Critics also reject the foundational premise of the administration's quest to negotiate with Iran; namely, that Rouhani is a moderate who wants and can deliver a nuclear deal mutually beneficial to the legitimate interests of Iran and the United States. Michael Rubin of the American Enterprise Institute, the author of a compelling study on the danger of negotiating with rogue regimes, and the Iran expert Reuel Marc Gerecht argue that Rouhani masquerades as a moderate to tranquilize Western opinion.[138] In a series of major essays, Gerecht has detailed thoroughly Rouhani's long history of unswerving loyalty to the fanatically anti-American Ayatollahs Khomeini and Khamenei, which makes the Iranian president an unlikely candidate to become the Iranian Gorbachev.[139] In January 2014 Rouhani boasted on Twitter that "world powers surrendered to Iranian national will" by agreeing to the interim accord. Rouhani declared victory likewise in an interview the same month: "No facility will be closed; enrichment will continue, and qualitative and nuclear research will be expanded. All research into a new generation of centrifuges will continue."[140]

This writer dissents from the thoughtful position of Kenneth Pollack—President Obama's ablest, though qualified, defender on the subject of Iran—who makes an elegant case for containment as the least bad alternative even if Iran crosses the nuclear threshold. On the contrary, this writer considers a nuclear Iran by far the worst alternative. Nor does this writer accept Pollack's assessment that "Rouhani is sincere in his desire for a nuclear deal."[141] Yet even Pollack warns that any credible strategy of containment will require far more vigilance than the administration has demonstrated: "Given President Obama's constant rhetoric about getting America out of wars in the Middle East, his precipitous withdrawal of U.S. troops from Iraq, his impending drawdown in Afghanistan, and his reluctance to commit U.S. forces elsewhere in the Middle East, the Iranians have concluded that, even in the event of a terrorist attack on American soil, the Obama administration would not respond with force and . . . they may be right in their assessment."[142]

Instead, Pollack advocates promoting regime change in Iran, waging ideological battle, keeping robust conventional military capabilities in the Gulf, and actively building missile defenses—all of which run counter to the president's convictions.[143] Echoing the concerns of the administration's critics, Pollack also identifies as the biggest diplomatic obstacle facing the United States in the event of a comprehensive agreement with Iran as "getting the United Nations Security Council (and the European Union) to reimpose sanctions if Iran were to ever restart its prohibited nuclear programs—especially if the evidence of cheating was ambiguous." Pollack recommends merely suspending rather than lifting sanctions so the United States and its allies can swiftly reimpose them in the event of Iranian noncompliance.[144]

Meanwhile, the P5+1 and Iran may be on the verge of reaching a permanent accord bound to provoke fierce opposition from Republicans now in control of the Congress, as well as from Israel and America's Sunni allies in the Middle East, such as Saudi Arabia. When the interim agreement expired in June 2014, Iran agreed to extend the deadline until

November 24 in exchange for additional sanctions relief. National Public Radio reported in late September 2014 that substantial differences remained between the two sides on how much uranium enrichment Iran will be permitted; the possible nuclear dimensions to Iran's weapons research; the status of the underground Fordow Fuel Enrichment Plant (FFEP), near the holy city of Qom; the controversial heavy-water facility near Arak, capable of producing weapons-grade plutonium; and the number of centrifuges—now totaling 19,000—Iran would retain.[145] In April 2014 Secretary of State John Kerry testified at a Senate hearing that Iran could produce enough fissile material for a nuclear bomb in two months. "We're operating with a time period for a so-called 'breakout' of about two months."[146] On September 5, 2014, the International Atomic Energy Agency issued a troubling report concluding Iran had failed to satisfy the confidence-building measures of the interim accord that its nuclear activities were purely peaceful. The Iranian government also has increasingly resisted scrutiny of its nuclear program, in violation of the letter and the spirit of the interim accord.[147]

Even so, the administration remains eager to conclude a deal. The *Wall Street Journal* reported in November 2014 that President Obama had written secretly to Iran's Supreme Leader Ayatollah Ali Khamenei the previous month, describing "their shared interest" in fighting ISIS and stressing the imperative of reaching a comprehensive agreement with the P5+1 powers on the future of Iran's nuclear program in exchange for lifting sanctions. The president's letter also assured the Iranians that U.S. military operations in Syria would not target Iran's ally Bashar al-Assad.[148] As Michael Doran and Max Boot observe, President Obama has staked his foreign policy on the bold gamble that the United States not only can tame Iranian ambitions through a comprehensive arms accord, but also can make Iran a partner rather than an adversary in regional security. Yet the situation will probably get worse rather than better if the administration persists on that perilous course for the reasons Doran and Boot trenchantly articulate, writing in the *New York Times*:

> If Iran is allowed to maintain its nuclear program with international blessing . . . Saudi Arabia has made clear that it is prepared to build its own bomb, while Israel has threatened to launch a unilateral strike on Iranian nuclear facilities. Mr. Obama's hope of

using an opening to Iran to stabilize the Middle East will almost certainly backfire. Before long, America is likely to be forced into its traditional, post-1979 role as the leader of a coalition to counter Iranian designs. The place to begin is in Syria, which is now ground zero in the struggle between the two regional blocs. Trying to draw the Iranians into a negotiated solution will almost certainly mean keeping Mr. Assad in power. That, in turn, will only play into the hands of Sunni extremists.[149]

Naturally, some prominent scholars and statesmen dismiss Doran and Boot's concerns as overwrought. The neorealists Kenneth Waltz and Stephen Walt, as well as the Iran scholar Paul Pillar, all insist that the United States could live tolerably even with a nuclear Iran—a position that even the Obama administration publicly rejects, though it may privately come to embrace it if the use of force emerges as the only plausible alternative for stopping it. According to Waltz and Walt, all states behave similarly and rationally in international politics regardless of their regime types or the propensities of their individual leaders. Hence, both assure us that the logic of nuclear deterrence applies to the Islamic Republic of Iran in the same way it operated between the ideologically discordant United States and Soviet Union during the Cold War.[150] Pillar argues, too, that "more than three decades of history demonstrate that the Islamic Republic's rulers, like most rulers elsewhere, are overwhelmingly concerned with preserving their regime and their power—in this life, not some future one. . . . The principles of deterrence are not invalid just because the party to be deterred wears a turban and a beard."[151]

Yet the case for Doran and Boot's alarming scenario is far more compelling than for the benign one proposed by Waltz, Walt, and Pillar. A long litany of historical examples demolishes both Waltz's and Walt's notion that all states pursue the same types of foreign policies. Would a nuclear-armed Iran pose no greater cause for alarm than, say, a nuclear-armed, democratic Denmark, Canada, or Finland? Nor do all evil, insatiable, expansionist regimes and tyrannies calculate risks in the same way. Harry Truman, Ronald Reagan, and Winston Churchill drew a wise and critical distinction between the Soviet and Nazi regimes not on the basis of morals or the scale of their objectives, but on their capacity to be deterred. Whereas Hitler was determined to fight a war sooner rather than later, war with the Soviet Union was not inevitable. Marxist ideology counseled tactical flexibility in pursuit of unlimited objectives. Nor was the Soviet Union all that cautious during the Cold War. The world avoided the stark choice between nuclear war and surrender not because both sides possessed nuclear weapons, but because the United States did. No Soviet regime would have practiced the forbearance the United States did when it possessed unassailable nuclear superiority between 1945 and 1965.

Neither the United States nor the Soviet Union had incentive to strike first, because each side deployed thousands of warheads in multiple modes, many invulnerable to preemptive attack. Both sides thus retained an assured second-strike capability. Even the most devastating surprise attack would leave the victims with ample numbers of nuclear warheads with which to retaliate and inflict unacceptable damage. Iran would become a nuclear power, however, in an environment radically different from the Cold War. A nuclear Iran would not only pose an existential threat to Israel, but would also probably precipitate a nuclear arms race among a plethora of authoritarian Middle Eastern regimes, including Saudi Arabia, Turkey, and Egypt. So credit the Obama administration for at least worrying about the consequences of a nuclear Iran. The president's problem lies instead with his fundamentally misguided strategy of pursuing a grand bargain along the lines of President Nixon's historic opening to China in 1972 with an organically hostile, repressive, and expansionist Iranian regime.[152]

The Obama administration also misjudged the dynamics and equities of the conflict between Israel and the Palestinians, vastly overrating the potential to reach a legitimate agreement to achieve a durable peace accord between them. "Nowhere in Obama's foreign policy," writes the normally admiring trio of Indyk, Lieberthal, and O'Hanlon, "has the gap been wider between promise and delivery than in the Middle East."[153] Instead, the 2014 war in Gaza should put in hibernation for a long time to come the fleeting chances of an agreement between Israel and the Palestinians. Relations between the United States and Israel have become significantly more fractious during the Obama administration, though cooperation continues unabated in many realms, including security and provision of generous sums of American aid. A clash of personalities and perspectives accounts for the mounting discord between the United States and Israel. In contrast to his warm relations with the Islamist president of Turkey and his solicitude for many of America's adversaries, President Obama actively dislikes Israeli Prime Minister Benjamin Netanyahu, complaining in November 2011 to then-President Nicholas Sarkozy of France over an open microphone, "I have to deal with him every day."[154] During the 2014 war in Gaza, the president became "enraged" at the Israeli government's actions and treatment of Secretary of State John Kerry—an antipathy Obama has never expressed toward authoritarian adversaries such as Putin, Chinese leadership, the mullahs in Tehran, or Israel's neighbors bent on eradicating it.[155] The president and Prime Minister Netanyahu also have profoundly different views about Israeli settlements, the danger of Iran and what to do about the Iranian nuclear program, the civil war in Syria, and whether the Palestinian Authority on the West Bank truly seeks a two-state solution compatible with Israel's legitimate security interests. The president believes genuinely that it would well serve American and Israeli interests to create a continuous Palestinian state whereby Jerusalem is divided and Israel is confined to its pre-1967 borders, with only minor adjustments, whereas a long line of Israeli statesmen—including Prime Minister Netanyahu—warn that fully relinquishing territories conquered in the Six-Day War of June 1967 would relegate Israel to Auschwitz borders, rendering it ripe for destruction.[156]

Given the multiple and escalating crises roiling the Middle East—the tumult of the Arab Spring, the Syrian civil war, the gathering danger of a nuclear Iran, the escalating provocations from the fanatical Hamas leadership running Gaza, the implosion of Iraq, and the rampage of ISIS—Indyk, Lieberthal, and O'Hanlon make a vital point even critics of the president must weigh heavily: even the wisest and most skillful statesmanship probably would not "have overcome the considerable obstacles" to reconcile Israel and the Palestinians. Yet the president and Secretary of State Kerry also unduly minimized these obstacles while obsessively pursuing negotiations between the Israelis and Palestinians in unpropitious circumstances almost certain to yield no agreement or a bad one. Moreover, even Indyk, Lieberthal, and O'Hanlon criticize the president for "compounding the difficulties rather than ameliorating them" in the way Obama went about it.[157]

The failure of President Obama's approach stems primarily, however, from his badly flawed "theory of the case." He and Secretary of State Kerry assume dubiously that an inherently moderate Palestinian Authority genuinely wishes to achieve a two-state solution that accepts Israel's right to exist as a Jewish state within defensible boundaries. Both Obama and Kerry consider Israeli settlements and demands for a united Jerusalem under exclusive Israeli sovereignty rather than Palestinian intransigence as the prime obstacles to peace. Accordingly, the president has pressured Israel consistently to make concessions to facilitate a peace agreement with the Palestinians that the Netanyahu government deems undesirable and politically impossible. Netanyahu took great offense at Obama's demand in May 2009 for a complete settlement freeze, including one in East Jerusalem, and his designation of the settlements as "illegitimate"—an important negative shift well beyond the boundaries set by any previous U.S. president. Israelis resented and feared Obama's assiduous courtship of the Arab world and deliberate efforts to "distance the United States from Israel." Obama countered that his outreach to the Muslim community is designed precisely to "reduce the antagonisms and the dangers posed by a hostile Muslim world to Israel and the West."[158]

During his second term, the president intensified his ill-fated efforts to broker an agreement between Israel and the Palestinians. Secretary of State John Kerry launched a restart of the negotiations on July 29, 2013, imposing an April deadline to reach a final status agreement to the Israeli-Palestinian conflict. Again, Israel incurred the preponderance of the administration's displeasure for the impasse. In a February 2014 interview with Jeffrey Goldberg, the president warned of Israel's bleak future if Prime Minster Netanyahu rejects a U.S.-drafted framework for peace with the Palestinians. He reiterated that Israel should accept a "contiguous sovereign Palestinian state"—a requirement that would sever a geographically tiny, existentially vulnerable Israel, making it almost impossible to defend. His distaste for Netanyahu contrasts starkly with his favorable impression of Palestinian leaders. He has complimented the Palestinian Authority's President Mahmoud Abbas for being "sincere about his willingness to recognize . . . Israel's legitimate security needs [and] to shun violence."[159]

Yet neither an authoritarian Abbas nor Hamas (the odious equivalent of ISIS) recognizes Israel's right to exist as a Jewish state with defensible boundaries. The Palestinian Authority has refused to abandon its insistence on the so-called right of return, a refusal based on an unprecedentedly porous definition of who qualifies as a refugee. Israel, home to more than 850,000 refugees from the Muslim Middle East, would commit demographic suicide were it to capitulate to that fraudulent demand seeking the elimination of Israel through diplomacy rather than a war the Palestinian Authority would decisively lose.[160] Unlike President George W. Bush, who denounced the Trojan horse of the right of return, President Obama has remained silent, implying he agrees with it.[161]

Ultimately, the Obama administration may have dangerously conflated the Palestinian Authority's willingness to negotiate with a commitment to achieving a genuine peace. In April 2014 Kerry's ill-fated reset came to a crashing halt when Palestinian Fatah and Hamas decided to form a unity government. Benjamin Netanyahu's Security Cabinet responded by cutting off peace talks, which Obama and Kerry expected to conclude with a final agreement by April 29. The administration violated any reasonable standard of prudence pursuing this ill-fated, ill-conceived peace initiative facing such intractable conditions.[162] Even stipulating the possible but questionable premise that Abbas seeks a two-state solution rather than Israel's demise, the administration also could not point to any plausible basis for agreement on key issues such as Israel's borders or the status of Jerusalem, especially with the Middle East ablaze in violence and radicalism, which make Israel even more reluctant than usual to incur existential risks.[163]

The Gaza conflict in the summer of 2014 "had a very negative impact" on the Israeli-American relationship, according to Martin Indyk. "There's a lot of strain in the relationship now. The personal relationship between the president and the prime minister has been fraught for some time and it's become more complicated by recent events."[164] Major Israeli leaders and the Israeli press across the political spectrum viewed the Gaza conflict as the logical outcome of the administration's flawed approach. The Gaza war broke as Israeli distrust of Kerry was already intense and rising. Just six weeks earlier, Kerry had generated a firestorm for intimating that Israel would become an apartheid state if it did not accept a framework for a peace settlement it deemed dangerous for Israel's security.[165] Israelis accused Kerry of obstinately pressing for an early ceasefire that would work to Hamas's advantage by denying Israel a decisive victory. Conversely, President Obama pressed for an immediate ceasefire because of "the bombing of U.N. compounds and the loss of innocent life, particularly children," which the administration blamed on Israeli excess rather than Hamas's deliberately eliciting that result by embedding its fighters among civilians.[166]

However admirable the president's concern for protecting civilian lives, the administration blundered in pursuing a premature Gaza ceasefire, undermining America's interests while exasperating Israel, Egypt, Saudi Arabia, and some moderate Palestinians. The liberal and highly respected commentator David Ignatius distills the essence of the administration's error, emblematic of the president's misunderstanding of the Israeli-Palestinian dispute and obtuseness to the malevolence of Islamic radicalism: "Kerry's error has been to put so much emphasis on achieving a quick halt to the bloodshed that he has solidified the role of Hamas, the intractable, unpopular Islamist group that leads Gaza, along with the two hard-line Islamist nations that are its key supporters, Qatar and Turkey. In the process, he has undercut not simply the Israelis but also the Egyptians and the Fatah movement that runs the Palestinian Authority, all of which want to see an end to Hamas rule in Gaza."[167]

Hamas is the Palestinian equivalent of ISIS. The cost and risks of war probably will increase sharply unless Israel defeats Hamas decisively. An Israeli victory entails destroying the extensive network of tunnels that would give Hamas the ability to launch devastating coordinated attacks within Israel. It entails crippling the capacity of Hamas to launch hundreds of missiles into Israeli territory, targeting civilians. The United States has a strong interest in actively encouraging rather than impeding Israel's achieving such a decisive victory. As Walter Russell Mead observes, Saudi Arabia, Egypt, and moderate Sunni states in the region hope that Israel crushes "the Muslim Brotherhood–affiliated Hamas" to strike a blow against Islamic radicalism also menacing their regimes.[168] The Obama administration's push for a premature ceasefire crystalizes the growing perception in these countries that the current administration neither cares about nor understands their interests. The president has already alienated the Saudis and Egyptians in particular by courting the radical Iranian regime to negotiate a nuclear deal, initially supporting the Muslim Brotherhood government of Mohamed Morsi, and long withholding aid to the Syrian rebels fighting the Iranian surrogate Bashar al-Assad. By failing to encourage an Israeli victory, President Obama lost a precious opportunity to boost the battered confidence of moderate Sunni regimes in his strategic judgment.[169]

The administration's admirable desire to stop the killing of innocents does not trump the moral and strategic equities of the Gaza conflict. Hamas initiated the latest cycle of violence, murdering three Israeli teenagers on Israeli soil. Israel had no choice but to respond robustly to that intolerable provocation. Israel is free, prosperous, and ardently pro-American, whereas Hamas is a repressive, aggressive, virulently anti-American Islamist theocracy aligned with revolutionary Iran and Hezbollah in Lebanon. Few entities have displayed such utter disregard for their own population as Hamas, which has routinely used its civilians as human shields. The editorial board of the venerable *Washington Post* has condemned the "depravity of Hamas's strategy" of baiting Israel to kill civilians by placing them in tunnels and other military infrastructure, then blaming Israel for the casualties to delegitimize it in the eyes of the "international community."[170]

The Obama administration's push for a premature ceasefire in Gaza also defies the hard lessons of history, which indicate that the most just and durable periods of peace occur when wars have decisive outcomes. Conversely, stopping the fighting too soon often increases the cost and risk of war later. These hard lessons run counter to the inclinations of progressives—such as President Obama—to stress forbearance, calibration, and restraint in the employment of force. Like Saddam Hussein in the Iraq war of 1990–1991, Hamas calculates it wins by surviving. Hamas seeks not only to delegitimize Israel but also to discredit any moderate Palestinian alternative. Hamas's "depraved" strategy has already reaped rewards, unleashing a virulent and ugly wave of anti-Semitism in Western Europe and the Islamic world. Pressure has intensified on Israel to end its blockade of Gaza that Hamas's implacable aggression has vindicated. As Michael Oren has warned, saving Hamas from the consequences of its actions would merely repeat the mistakes of Israel's previous battle with terrorists in Lebanon in 2006 and Gaza in 2008 and 2012. Israel won tactical victories but suffered strategic defeats because of the less-than-decisive outcomes that allowed Hamas and Hezbollah to survive.[171]

Relations between President Obama and Israeli Prime Minister Netanyahu plunged to new lows when Jeffrey Goldberg—a commentator to whom the president has confided frequently—quoted one leading administration official calling Netanyahu a "chickenshit" prime minister concerned only with his political survival and another official calling the prime minister "a coward."[172] White House efforts to distance the president from this latest expression of the administration's disdain for Netanyahu brought no respite to the raging controversy. Prime Minister Netanyahu lashed back that he was unfairly attacked for vigilantly defending Israel's legitimate interests. The administration's incendiary remarks about Netanyahu became public amid intensifying disagreement between the two countries over Israel's settlement policies, negotiations with the Palestinians, and the possibly impending nuclear deal with Iran. The president objected vehemently to Netanyahu's decision to build 1,060 housing units in Jewish neighborhoods—the legality of which no previous administration has disputed. As a signal of the administration's displeasure, Secretary of State Kerry, National Security Adviser Susan Rice, and other leading officials refused to meet with Israeli Defense Minister Moshe Ya'alon during his fall 2014 visit to Washington.[173] Ya'alon has well earned his reputation as being one of Kerry's sternest critics, pillorying the secretary of state for the way he initiated, conducted, and persisted in peace negotiations with the Palestinians that the Netanyahu government deemed futile and harmful.

Netanyahu also opposes as naive and existentially threatening to Israel what he surmises are the main features of the impending American-Iranian nuclear deal. Expect relations between the Obama administration and the Netanyahu government to worsen considerably in the aftermath of the midterm elections of 2014.[174] Freed from electoral constraints, the president will have more latitude to defy the strong pro-Israel sentiment in the Republican Party, the Congress, and much of the American public in pursuit of his "theory of the case" on the Palestinian issue and Iran.[175]

Invariably, premature ceasefires in Gaza, premature withdrawals from Iraq, the illusion of arms control with Iran, undermining democratic friends while conciliating repressive foes, and anything short of victory in the administration's belated war against ISIS will incite the worst instincts in a region teeming with radical entities and rogue regimes hostile to America's interests. Any plausible hope for salvaging the administration's unavailing Middle Eastern policy depends on the president's ceasing to do most of what he has done so far. Perhaps future historians will cite the war against ISIS as Obama's liminal moment for repudiating an Obama Doctrine that has aggravated rather than ameliorated the problems besetting a conflict-ridden but still vital region. If, instead, the president doubles down on the Obama Doctrine, the United States and our allies should prepare for more unwelcome consequences in the Middle East and beyond. A nuclear deal that leaves Iran on the doorstep of a nuclear breakout capability will swamp any positive benefit the administration hopes to derive in the region from combatting ISIS. For our Middle Eastern allies rightly consider Iran the greater danger.

6

The Obama Doctrine's Asian Pivot

Like those dealing with Europe and the Middle East, President Obama's Asia policy has de-emphasized traditional geopolitical rivalry, elevated climate change as a priority rather than a peripheral security issue, and emphasized diplomacy rather than hard power in fashioning an Asia pivot that remains more rhetoric than reality. A combination of China's prodigious military buildup and America's precipitous build-down has increased the apprehension of traditional American democratic allies in East Asia (and a potentially new one, democratic India). Concern mounts that the United States might revert to offshore balancing rather than credibly deter an increasingly powerful, ambitious, and arrogant Chinese authoritarian regime that is perhaps seeking hegemony rather than equilibrium.

This is perilous. Asia has eclipsed Europe as the world's foremost center of power. Some 3.8 billion people—over half of the world's population—live in Asia, also the fastest-growing region economically and militarily. By 2025 Asia probably will generate half of the world's output of goods and services. So the United States must prevent hostile powers from dominating this opulent and dynamic region for the same reasons, largely, though not exclusively, that dictated American intervention in both world wars to defeat Germany and the policy of containment to thwart the Soviet Union's hegemonic ambitions during the Cold War. As Aaron Friedberg observes, control of East Asia by a potentially hostile power "could give it preferred access to, if not full command over, the region's vast industrial, financial, natural, and technological resources." Such an Asian hegemon would inevitably possess the secure and broad base to "project power into other regions, much as the United States was able to do from the Western Hemisphere throughout the twentieth century."[1]

Two other complementary objectives should also direct U.S. grand strategy toward this increasingly vital region. First, the United States should continue to cultivate and defend stable liberal democracy in Asia when possible and prudent for the same reasons that spurred America's most successful Cold War presidents to emphasize regime type and ideology in discerning friends, foes, threats, and opportunities. Stable liberal democracies do not fight one another, make more reliable allies, and have fewer fundamental clashes of interest with each other than with tyrannies, especially revolutionary or revisionist totalitarian regimes animated by messianic ideologies. Second, the United States should foster conditions in Asia conducive to American trade and investment. Asia ranks as America's largest trading partner in goods: combined U.S. exports and imports totaled nearly $1.5 trillion for 2013—though the United States, as usual, ran a large deficit (nearly $500 billion).[2]

The "Asian pivot" that Secretary of State Hillary Clinton unveiled in October 2011 signifies the Obama administration's recognition that "the Asia-Pacific has become a key driver of global politics" for the twenty-first century:

> It boasts almost half the world's population. It includes many of the key engines of the global economy, as well as the largest emitters of greenhouse gases. It is home to several of our key allies and important emerging powers like China, India, and Indonesia. . . . U.S. commitment there is essential. . . . Harnessing Asia's growth and dynamism is central to American economic and strategic interests and a key priority for President Obama. Open markets in Asia provide the United States with unprecedented opportunities for investment, trade, and access to cutting-edge technology. Our economic recovery at home will depend on exports and the ability of American firms to tap into the vast and growing consumer base of Asia. Strategically, maintaining peace across the Asia-Pacific is increasingly crucial to global progress, whether through defending freedom of navigation in the South China Sea, countering the

proliferation efforts of North Korea, or ensuring transparency in the military activities of the region's key players.[3]

No doubt, constructively managing the rise of a dynamic but highly authoritarian China poses the most daunting challenge for the United States in this most vital of regions. China already has the world's second-largest economy. After 1978, when Deng Xiaoping began loosening the Communist Party's control of the economy, permitting a broader though constrained role for the market, GDP growth averaged more than 9 percent annually for the next three decades, elevating more than 500 million people out of poverty. China's economy grew by 7.3 percent in 2014, more than twice the U.S. growth rate of nearly 3 percent.[4] Some analysts predict China will supplant the United States as the world's number one economic power, extrapolating from China's prodigious growth rate during the past three decades, as well as perceived long-term structural challenges facing the U.S. economy and the lingering effects of the 2008 financial crisis that China, unlike the United States, weathered largely unscathed.[5] Adjusted for purchasing power, the Chinese economy surpassed the U.S. economy in 2014 to become the world's largest. Yet the United States still retains a healthy lead in aggregate unadjusted GDP. Even by the most optimistic estimates, China will not catch the United States in unadjusted GDP for a long while. U.S. per-capita GDP is also five times larger than China's, though China's has nearly doubled since 2009.[6] In 2014 China became the world's largest trading nation. China is the U.S.'s number two trading partner, behind only Canada. China owns $1.2 trillion in U.S. bills, notes, and bonds—8 percent of publicly held U.S. debt. China's heavy dependence on access to U.S. markets partially offsets but does not neutralize this potentially significant source of Chinese leverage over the U.S. economy.[7]

Josef Joffe argues more optimistically, on the basis of the lessons of history and the particulars of Chinese politics, that China's economic growth will level out as "youthful exuberance" gives way to maturity, just as Japan, West Germany, Korea, and Taiwan in the twentieth century failed to sustain the rapid pace of the early decades of their economic miracles.[8] Despite the sluggish growth of the Obama years and massive structural deficits arising from burgeoning entitlement programs, the United States will remain number one by Joffe's reckoning because of the inherent strengths of America's free-market system, healthy demographics, huge potential reserves of energy, and a vastly superior educational system grounded in freedom of inquiry—all of which an authoritarian, aging China, where the state controls and commands the preponderance of the economy, sorely lacks. According to the demographer Nicholas Eberstadt, "China's demographic future remains dire, not just because of the One Child Policy's ill effects."[9] The looming problems include a "shrinking pool of working-age men and women and a rapidly aging population that will slow economic growth, perhaps severely."[10] Nor, as Joffe rightly notes, does authoritarian modernization typically end well, especially without political liberalization, which the Communist Party of China ferociously resists. A despotic system such as China's "eventually freezes up and then turns upon itself, devouring the seeds of spectacular growth and finally producing stagnation."[11]

Though Joffe comes closer to the mark than declinists counting on China's supplanting the United States, Charles Krauthammer wisely rejects the notion of inevitability from any quarter. Krauthammer calls decline for America today a choice, "not a condition." Unlike Britain and Europe in their largely unavoidable decline after World War II, the United States is "in the position of deciding whether to abdicate or retain its dominance. Decline—or continued ascendancy—is in our hands."[12] Whether the United States experiences relative economic decline or renewal hinges largely on the outcome of the clash between two rival conceptions of political economy dividing the Democratic Party under Obama and the mainstream of the Republican Party.

The Obama administration, in word and deed, has sought to move the relationship between government and the individual substantially in the direction of a European social democracy. President Obama has succeeded greatly in his ambition to expand the size, scope, cost, responsibilities and prerogatives of government, more heavily regulating the private sector and raising taxes on Americans in the ranks of the upper middle class and above. As part of his agenda to address what he considers a paramount threat of global warming, President Obama aspires to impose cap-and-trade legislation (though he has not yet achieved significant restraints on the use of hydrocarbon fuels) that limits greenhouse gas emissions, as well as international treaties, thereby establishing a global system that makes advanced economies bear the lion's share of the burden for reducing emissions. President Obama champions substantially reducing the size of the American military, not only as a virtue, but as a necessity to protect his ambitious domestic agenda from the pressure the cascading federal debt has generated. Although conceding that the American economy has not fully recovered from the financial crisis of 2008, defenders of the president, such as the economic and political commentator Paul Krugman, argue that the Obama stimulus and his expansion of government have helped mitigate the worst of the slump, while achieving greater social justice. "Obama has done more to limit inequality than he gets credit for," says Krugman. "The rich are paying higher taxes. . . . Meanwhile, the financial aid in Obamacare—expanded Medicaid subsidies to help lower-income households pay insurance premiums—goes disproportionately to less-well-off Americans. . . . The extent of his partial success ranges from the pretty good to the not-so-bad. . . . Health reform looks pretty good. . . . Financial reform is . . . not so bad. . . . There's a lot more protection against runaway finance than anyone except angry Wall Streeters seems to realize. . . . As far as climate policy goes, there's reason for hope."[13]

Conservative critics blame President Obama's sweeping domestic agenda for creating massive debt, impeding growth, raising tax burdens, robbing national defense to pay for it, and discouraging wealth creation. By their reckoning, the president risks making an eminently avoidable American decline a self-fulfilling prophecy, putting the United States on a path to become a Western European–style social democracy at the very moment when that model has proved unsustainable even there. Their program for American economic renewal on which the robustness of American hard power depends represents the antithesis of President Obama's scheme: lowering taxes; unleashing the market; curbing government regulation; encouraging the exploration and exploitation of huge new national gas and petroleum reserves on the North American continent; building the Alaskan and Canadian pipelines; fracking untapped sites in North Dakota; exploring for energy and drilling off the American coastlines; putting Obamacare on the path of ultimate extinction; and significantly increasing the defense budget to at least 4 percent and up to 5 percent of the GDP—a figure low by Cold War standards and easily affordable so long as the United States curbs its vastly greater and voraciously growing domestic spending. George Shultz, President Reagan's secretary of state for seven years and President Nixon's secretary of the treasury, spells out the essence of this neo-Reaganite agenda in an August 6, 2014, editorial in the *Wall Street Journal:* (1) lower marginal tax rates substantially and eliminate many deductions on a revenue-neutral basis; (2) lower corporate tax rates substantially so that American multinationals have a powerful incentive to return and reinvest the $1.95 trillion accumulated outside the United States; (3) simplify and reduce proliferating and labyrinthine regulations stifling economic growth; (4) establish a transparent rules-based monetary policy by taking the mystery out of the Federal Reserve, requiring it to explain policy publicly, using cost-benefit thinking in the explanation; (5) control domestic spending—particularly entitlement spending, which is the major source of budget deficits—by changing wage indexing to price indexing while raising the retirement age; (6) encourage market-based reforms to health care such as high-deductible catastrophic health insurance for the young and health savings accounts for most Americans; (7) eliminate the sequester rules and spend what it takes to maintain American military preeminence.[14]

Whatever side has the better argument on the merits (count this writer in the ranks of the neo-Reaganites), American voters will decide ultimately whether the Obama Doctrine's political economy or the neo-Reaganite alternative prevails politically, and there are profound implications for American hard power and influence abroad. Even if the United States retains its preeminence, as Josef Joffe predicts it will, a rapidly industrializing and economically booming China, with a large though eventually dwindling labor force, still lurks as a formidable potential competitor for the United States—unprecedentedly so in the economic realm.

China also has become the world's second-largest military power, wielding a sophisticated and growing array of capabilities that will increasingly call into question American military preeminence in the western Pacific. Over the past two decades, China's defense spending has increased by double digits annually. The 2014 Chinese defense budget rose by a hefty 12.2 percent, equaling roughly $132 billion in U.S. dollars.[15] The United States will spend $496 billion dollars on defense for fiscal year 2015, more than three times China's defense spending. Overall, U.S defense spending accounts for approximately 37 percent of total global military spending. Yet the size of the American defense budget and U.S. military forces has shrunk significantly under the Obama presidency—a downward trend that sequestration has accelerated, limiting the

Asian pivot largely to realms of diplomacy and soft power, notwithstanding the administration's rhetoric to the contrary.

Despite the substantially larger size of the U.S. defense budget, Chinese expenditure gets more value for the dollar because of considerably higher costs in the United States for personnel and weapons.[16] China has also enjoyed the advantage, until recently, of having the luxury of concentrating its defense efforts almost exclusively on Asia. Conversely, the United States has global responsibilities that diffuse American military power to multiple theaters, especially Europe and the Middle East. The PRC's voracious and increasing demand for imported energy—including Saudi Arabian oil—will erode this Chinese advantage in years to come. The imperative of securing its energy supply has spurred the PRC, already moving in that direction for a host of reasons, to develop a blue-water navy capable of keeping vital waterways such as the Strait of Malacca open to Chinese commerce. More than 30 percent of global trade and more than 50 percent of China's oil passes on ships through the Malacca Strait, the narrow waterway connecting the China Sea and the India Ocean and the shortest maritime route from East Asia to the Persian Gulf. China's dependence on foreign oil will probably grow. By 2030 China may import 80 percent of the oil it consumes.[17] China already has launched one aircraft carrier, and it plans to build additional modern carriers. According to the defense analysts Bryan McGrath and Seth Cropsey, China's plan to build aircraft carriers aims not to contest the U.S. Navy directly, but to undermine the credibility of American alliances and security commitments throughout East Asia: "Creating uncertainty and doubt in the minds of regional governments that the United States can continue to assure their security is at the heart of China's desire to see the U.S. diminished in the region."[18] Andrew Krepinevich, president of the Center for Strategic and Budgetary Assessments, compares what China calls a "peaceful rise" strategy to the Soviet Union's attempt to "Finlandize" Europe during the Cold War: "If the military balance shifted in Moscow's favor, America's European allies might conclude that Moscow could not be resisted and would fall under Soviet sway. All of Europe would then share the fate of Finland, which had remained nominally independent after World War II but abided by foreign-policy rules set by the Soviets." Krepinevich warns that American allies and friends in Asia may have no choice but to follow Finland's Cold

War example should the U.S. military advantage over China continue to diminish precipitously.[19]

As James Holmes observes, the Chinese Navy continues to enhance its strategic footprint in the Indian Ocean, pursuing a string-of-pearls strategy along its southern rimland, investing in "seaport development at sites such as Gwadar in Southern Pakistan," and courting South Asian governments to obtain port access for Chinese naval and commercial vessels.[20] Indian strategists fear that China intends to develop an array of naval bases in Cambodia, Thailand, Myanmar, Sri Lanka, Pakistan, and Bangladesh to project power throughout South Asia and into the Middle East, threatening India's naval primacy in its own backyard.[21]

The bipartisan and highly regarded National Defense Panel Review of the 2014 Quadrennial Defense Review considers the "scale and sophistication of China's military buildup over the past twenty years . . . of great concern." By 2020 the Chinese Navy will total nearly 350 ships, compared to fewer than 279 ships for the U.S. Navy under the Obama administration's shipbuilding plan—a cut of more than 10 percent from the 313 the president's chief of Naval Operations deemed the bare minimum to meet U.S. security commitments, including those in the Pacific. China has deployed a large and diverse force of conventional ballistic missiles and land- and air-and-sea-based cruise missiles capable of striking American bases and naval vessels beyond Guam.[22] China continues strenuously to upgrade its impressive cyber war capability and its capacity to degrade and destroy America's space assets, on which American maritime supremacy depends. China continues likewise to upgrade its deployed nuclear arsenal, planning in the next five years to double the number of land-launched and sea-launched nuclear ballistic missiles capable of striking targets in the United States.[23]

Although the this country retains a major advantage in submarines of all varieties, the Chinese will soon surpass the United States in number of conventional attack submarines and narrow the qualitative gap. The Obama administration plans to diminish from fifty-five to forty-one the U.S. attack submarine fleet, perhaps the most effective hedge against China's anti-access strategy, which aims to keep the U.S. Navy out of range of Asia. As Seth Cropsey notes, "a robust attack submarine fleet" constitutes "a highly persuasive deterrent against conflict itself." Attack submarines are difficult to detect and able to inflict major damage on the enemy's fleet. "Their cruise missiles can destroy targets ashore," such as China's land-based anti-ship ballistic missiles.[24] Meanwhile, China plans to introduce new types of diesel and nuclear submarines to its fleet; it is currently operating with forty-five submarines in six different classes.[25] U.S. naval planners worry plenty about the Type 095 guided-missile attack submarine China is planning to construct over the next decade. These submarines will possess a land-attack as well as anti-ship capability that enables them to strike U.S. bases across the region and surface ships thousands of miles out to sea in the Pacific.[26] The Chinese possess more than two thousand modern, highly capable fighter aircraft, plan to deploy two new types of fighters by the end of the decade, and have developed a stealth fighter; a stealth bomber is soon to follow. The Chinese plan to expand, improve, and increase their already formidable and diverse missile inventory on land and at sea.[27]

China's well-conceived anti-access and area-denial strategy (A2/AD) has already rendered precarious the ability of America's surface fleet—particularly the aircraft carrier task force central to the projection of American power—to survive in the waters off Taiwan and the East and South China Seas. The comparatively short range of American carrier aircraft means that the United States may find it prohibitive to bring airpower to bear in these vital regions now that aircraft carriers can no longer operate safely within their range. In the not-so-distant future, the increasing range, numbers, and sophistication of the next generation of China's long-range anti-ship and anti-defense missiles may imperil the survivability of the American surface fleet for thousands of miles across the Pacific beyond Asia's shores. Mounting a credible defense of Taiwan in the event of Chinese attack will become increasingly prohibitive well within a decade.[28]

The National Defense Panel Review warns, "The balance of power in the Western Pacific is changing in a way unfavorable to the United States, and . . . China's rapid military modernization is creating a challenging context for U.S. military posture, planning, and modernization." Although believing that "the United States should seek to expand and deepen cooperation with China when it can," the National Defense Panel Review concludes soberly that

China's renewed nationalism and increasingly assertive unilateral actions, especially in the cyber and maritime domains, constitute a growing threat to the international order. Government sanctioned computer hacking and blatant industrial espionage coupled with a pattern of piracy and counterfeiting of U.S. intellectual property are disturbing examples of disregard for the open network of rules-based trade and commerce. Moreover, China pursues semi-mercantilist trade practices, arbitrarily manipulates the value of its currency, and abuses the privileges of WTO membership. In addition, China's increasingly assertive behavior over territorial disputes in the East and South China Seas . . . suggest[s] that the United States must prepare to deal with an increasingly powerful and more assertive China with which it will have serious differences in the security domain. China's assertive behavior presents the most serious long-term threat to stability and to the security of U.S. allies and partners in the region.[29]

Scholars and statesmen with a more benign view of China's intentions discount the negative transformative potential of the Chinese military buildup and downplay concerns that a newly assertive China has become a destabilizing force. According to Boston College Professor Robert Ross, even President Obama's largely nonmilitary version of an Asian pivot unnecessarily and dangerously

compounds Beijing's insecurities and will only feed China's aggressiveness, undermine regional stability, and decrease the possibility of cooperation. . . . Instead of inflating estimates of Chinese power . . . the United States should recognize China's underlying weakness and its own enduring strengths. The right China policy would assuage, not exploit, Beijing's anxieties, while protecting U.S. interests in the region. . . . Because the U.S. Navy will continue to dominate Asia's seas, the United States can reassure its allies of its resolve to counterbalance China while still quietly disengaging from maritime disputes and reducing its presence on China's land borders.[30]

Yet Ross takes for granted what the National Defense Review and naval experts consider in peril with greater convincingness—the permanence of U.S. maritime supremacy in the Pacific in light of current trends.[31] Contrary to what Ross suggests, American disengagement from maritime disputes in the East and South China Sea would erode rather than bolster the already shaky confidence of our Asian allies in American capability and fortitude to foil what they construe as China's swelling ambitions at their expense. Japan, the Philippines, Vietnam, India, and South Korea yearn for more rather than less American muscle in the region as a counterweight to China.[32]

Whether the internal character of the Chinese regime substantially affects China's external behavior is a contentious question with profound implications for U.S. foreign policy that this chapter will discuss presently. As he does Russia and the Middle East, President Obama views the region through the prism of the spiral model, which stresses the danger of overreacting to threats, rather than the deterrence model, which stresses the danger of insufficient vigilance.[33] President Obama has minimized the importance of regime type and human rights record in crafting his policies toward Asia in general and China in particular. His Asian pivot has not altered that appreciably. Most analysts agree, however, that China has sorely disappointed the expectations of those who had hoped that economic prosperity would inspire political liberalization, as it did for the East Asian Dragons. Although substantially less controlling than at the high point of Mao's totalitarianism, the Chinese Communist Party and the state continue to dominate the economy directly and through the ownership of more than 80 percent of China's ostensibly non-state-owned enterprises. The size and resources of the state-owned enterprises dwarf the non-state sector, the latter's share shrinking steadily from a low base.[34] Over the twenty-year history of the Heritage Foundation's Index of Economic Freedom, China has scored consistently at the lower boundaries of the "Mostly Unfree" category, including 2015, when China ranked 139th in freedom of 186 globally and 30th of 42 in the Asia-Pacific region.[35]

Although Deng Xiaoping and his successors have mitigated the worst features of Mao's horrific totalitarianism, responsible for killing millions and impoverishing the country for decades, the current Chinese regime remains highly repressive by all measures; the media are heavily censured and the ruling Communist Party is virulently intolerant of religious freedom, any form of organized dissent, and independent political parties. The Communist Party totally controls the judiciary, remaining above the law rather than subject to it. The *hukou* system (China's household registration mechanism) still in place limits the ability of China's 600 million rural residents and migrant workers to access many urban services, including education. In 2014 China ranked as usual near the bottom of Freedom House's scale measuring political freedom around the world; a score of 1 is the best and 7 the worst. The PRC scored 6.5 overall ("Not Free" status)—6.0 on civil liberties, and 7.0 on political rights.[36]

China has moved backward on political freedom and human rights since Xi Jinping became China's top leader in 2013. In April 2013 the General Office of the Communist Party's Central Committee issued Document No. 9, exhorting Communist Party cadres to eradicate subversive Western ideas that threaten the party's monopoly of power. The seven perils included: "1. Promoting Western Constitutional Democracy . . . 2. Promoting 'universal values' in an attempt to weaken the theoretical foundations of the Party's leadership . . . 3. Promoting civil society in an attempt to dismantle the ruling party's social foundation . . . 4. Promoting Neoliberalism [thus advocating privatization of China's state-owned industries] . . . 5. Promoting the West's idea of journalism . . . 6. Promoting historical nihilism, trying to undermine the history of the CCP and of New China . . . [and] 7. Questioning . . . the socialist nature of socialism with Chinese characteristics."[37] Writing in the *New York Times,* Chris Buckley described Document No. 9 as bearing "the unmistakable imprimatur of Xi Jinping," who has "signaled a shift to a more . . . traditional leftist stance with his 'rectification' campaign to ensure discipline and conspicuous attempts to defend the legacy of Mao Zedong."[38] China shows no signs, for example, of relenting on its campaign to roll back Hong Kong's political, press, and religious freedoms and to control the election of Hong Kong's chief executive—in violation of the 1984 Sino-British Joint Declaration that Hong Kong would rule its city with a high degree of autonomy.[39] The Communist Party has suppressed the massive student-led demonstrations protesting the CCP's determination to extinguish Hong Kong's freedoms. As Jeff Bader—an expert on China, formerly the Obama administration's top official, now at the Brookings Institution and staunch advocate of Sino-American engagement—observed regarding the implications of the Hong Kong protests:

> We have to focus on reality, not purely idealism. The reality is Beijing is quite intractable. They have a different sensibility and

perception. . . . They see Chinese stability, as well as the leadership of the party, at stake. These are issues on which there is almost no room for compromise. There is fragility in China and the belief among the leadership that if something happens in Hong Kong there will be a contagious effect on the mainland that might prove irresistible. This underlies what they do. . . . So none of us should delude ourselves that there could be a change of heart or softness coming from China just around the corner. They're going to hold their line. . . . Beijing is not going to lose. They're just not willing to, and they have the power to make that will stick. . . . For the party, these events probably makes [sic] them more determined to assert and maintain control. It shows them the risk of relaxing control.[40]

David Shambaugh, director of the China policy program at George Washington University and long a believer that China seeks a stability that is compatible with Western interests, has labeled China's political repression right now as the "harshest" since the Tiananmen Square massacre of 1989. According to Shambaugh, "The situation has gone from bad to worse from Hu Jintao to Xi Jinping."[41] Carl Minzner, an associate professor at Fordham Law School specializing in Chinese law and politics, argues that China's era of reform under the rule of the Communist Party has ended. Though an "excessive, unchecked power in the hands of a few has fueled a viral growth of a long list of social and economic problems," party leaders since 1989 have "systematically stymied the gradual evolution of positive local experiments with the kinds of institutions—an independent judiciary, meaningful legislatures, bottom-up electoral participation—that might help seriously curtail these problems." Instead, Minzner explains, China's leaders have resorted to the "tactics drawn from the 1950s and '60s—ones being used now: party rectification movements, politicized anticorruption purges, televised self-confessions by social media celebrities, foreign corporate investigators and alleged terrorists. And this is dangerous."[42]

President Obama thus has sought to implement the Obama Doctrine in Asia in the context of a larger ongoing debate over the nature of China's rise and the most prudent strategy for dealing with it constructively in a manner consistent with America's national interest. An overwhelming majority of scholars, commentators, and statesmen agree on the need for sustaining a strong American presence in East Asia; neorealist academic proponents of "offshore balancing" are the conspicuous exception. According to the offshore balancers, the United States can reduce its military forces largely outside Europe, East Asia, and the Middle East, relying instead on regional powers to check one another, and intervene in Eurasia only as a last resort to prevent a hegemon from establishing a position menacing to U.S. interests.[43] John Mearsheimer and Stephen M. Walt cite America's strategy in the 1930s as a successful example of offshore balancing, preferable to America's successful postwar strategy of maintaining a robust forward presence in vital geopolitical regions.[44]

Yet offshore balancing—really a version of pre–World War I and interwar isolationism thinly disguised—vastly increased the terrible cost of defeating Germany in both world wars, catastrophic conflicts that a robust forward American presence might have averted in the first place.[45] As Robert Haddick observes, offshore balancing has typically increased the likelihood that the United States would have to intervene under unfavorable circumstances.[46] American statesmen since World War II have rejected offshore balancing, which produced such horrific results when it was employed during the first half of the twentieth century.[47] The success of the strategy of vigilantly containing the Soviet Union vindicated their superior judgment. Proponents of offshore balancing underplay the felicitous stabilizing role that a strong U.S. forward presence has played in Eurasia and the destabilizing consequences of U.S. withdrawal. Moreover, the proliferation of nuclear weapons and missiles virtually precludes the United States from recovering successfully from the miscalculations that made the outcome of both world wars of the twentieth century staggeringly bloody and perilously close-run things. If a hegemon achieves dominance in Eurasia in today's military/strategic environment, no reenactment of D-Day to liberate Europe or facsimile of island-hopping campaigns to defeat Japan can succeed to reverse that outcome the way American armed forces did after intervening—dreadfully unprepared and nearly too late—in World War II.

The danger of offshore balancing looms even larger for East Asia than for Europe or the Middle East. Unlike Europe west of Russia, where strong regional institutions buttress the zone of democratic peace, Asia remains highly competitive, nationalistic, contentious, and ideologically diverse. Nor can regional institutions such as the Association of Southeast Asian Nations (ASEAN) or the Asia-Pacific Economic Cooperation (APEC) match the influence or exert the mollifying effect on rivalry of the EU. Geopolitically, China towers above any of the best middle-ranking powers aspiring for hegemony in the Middle East. No regional substitutes for American power will suffice to forge an effective balancing coalition should China embark on an expansionist course. Although Japan and India logically constitute the cornerstones of any American alliance system in East Asia, these fellow stable liberal democracies lack the combination of resources and political will to counter China successfully without the active backing and participation of the United States.

Consensus exists across the political spectrum not just on the need for a forward American presence in Asia, but also on the necessity and desirability of trading actively with China. China's membership in the WTO has sapped U.S. leverage to link trade to other aspects of Chinese foreign policy. As even those most wary of Chinese intentions admit, trading actively with China may eventually facilitate reforming and taming the ambitions of the regime by fostering the emergence of a Chinese entrepreneurial middle class demanding commensurate political right. Even the sternest of hard-liners on China do not envisaged the regime as a revolutionary threat tantamount to Nazi Germany or the Soviet Union. Nor do the most unabashed enthusiasts of engagement with China advocate counting on soft power alone to underwrite a constructive Sino-American relationship or stability in Asia at large.[48]

Instead, the debate over whether the Obama Doctrine or a more vigilant alternative is the best practicable strategy for dealing with China centers on these interrelated questions: Are the policy injunctions derived from the spiral or deterrent model a more reliable guide for crafting a prudent strategy toward China? Is China a strategic partner, a competitor, or a hybrid of both? Is China's "peaceful rise" merely a tactic, as Robert Sutter worries, or a permanent strategy, as Robert Ross more optimistically suggests?[49] What link exists, if any, among the internal dynamics of the Chinese regime, its external aspirations, and its calculation of risk? Is China a status quo power seeking stability, or a revisionist power seeking hegemony in the mold of an authoritarian Wilhelmine Germany? How much deterring does China prudently require? What configuration should deterrence prudently take? Or will robust deterrence trigger a spiral, making Chinese enmity a self-fulfilling prophecy?

The sinologist David Shambaugh distorts more than clarifies by identifying three distinct schools of thought on the question of the prospect for China's rise and its implications for the United States: (1) international relations realists—pessimistic that China's rise inevitably and unacceptably challenges the United States and that the two are locked in a zero-sum contest for regional and global hegemony; (2) liberal multilateralists—optimistic in the capacity of the existing liberal order to defang China's rise through enmeshing it in an indelible web of institutions and procedures; and (3) constructivists—also optimistic about "inculcating the norms of international behavior into Chinese society and individuals."[50]

Actually, opinion on China can be divided more neatly into two contending camps. Multilateralists, constructivists (really liberals emphasizing norms rather than institution), most neorealists, and classical realists are inclined to view China as a power with aims and ambitions compatible with the legitimate interests of the United States. This camp, urging moderation and restraint toward China, advocates greater emphasis on engagement with China rather than deterrence, especially in the form of hard power. By the logic of these engagers, the United States and China can achieve a durable non-zero-sum-game equilibrium in East Asia by fostering trade and immersing both countries in the norms and practices of international institutions and "the international community." Liberal and realist proponents of engagement disagree about whether the external behavior of the Chinese regime affects the PRC's external goals and behavior. Unlike the realists, liberals such as former President Bill Clinton accept that a more open, democratic China would be a more benign China to its citizens and its neighbors, and they assume engagement will facilitate that end better and more safely than more confrontational alternatives. Or as Clinton put it: "Will we do more to advance the cause of human rights if China is isolated or if our nations are engaged in a growing web of political and economic cooperation and contacts? I am persuaded that the best path for advancing freedom in China is for the United States to intensify and broaden its engagement with that nation."[51]

The esteemed academic liberal multilateralist G. John Ikenberry dismisses the notion that China has become a dangerous geopolitical foe the

United States must confront. As he sees it, China is not a full-scale revisionist power but a "spoiler" at best, while being "deeply integrated into the world economy and its governing institutions. . . . China, despite its rapid ascent, has no ambitious global agenda. . . . In the age of liberal order, revisionist struggles are a fool's errand. Indeed, China and Russia know this."[52] Writing in the realist tradition, the sinologist Avery Goldstein depicts China's grand strategy as aiming mainly to sustain a peaceful setting for the country's rise to the ranks of a great power.[53] What unites the realist and liberal wings of these pro-engagement, soft-deterrence advocates is their belief in the spiral model of conflict. Like President Obama, this group fears the consequences of overreacting rather than underreacting to China's rise. Consequently, this group opposes American military programs that degrade China's nuclear or conventional deterrent, a strong democratic alliance system to contain or encircle China, or any encouragement whatsoever of Taiwan's declaring independence.[54]

Conversely, the camp urging greater vigilance—the deterrence model—views China as engaging in a contest for supremacy in Asia that the United States must stoutly resist. This camp (composed primarily of moral democratic realists) ascribes China's hegemonic ambitions to the nature of its authoritarian, repressive regime. Ross Terrill locates the wellspring of "Chinese Imperialism" in a policy he calls a hybrid of Chinese nationalism and Western Marxism.[55] Wilhelmine Germany is, according to the sinologist Arthur Waldron, the best if imperfect analogy for thinking about a rising, authoritarian China: a powerful, belligerent, revisionist state seeking its place in the sun in a way menacing to the legitimate interests of other great powers and featuring an authoritarian government pitted against a dynamic society.[56] Terrill, Waldron, Aaron Friedberg, Michael Pillsbury, and other advocates of greater vigilance toward China do not propose economically quarantining China.[57] Nor does this group consider war with China as inevitable. Though viewing China as dangerously revisionist, moral democratic realists consider China eminently deterrable, well within the bounds of plausible American capabilities so long as the United States maintains its military preeminence and radiates the requisite resolve.[58]

Though not discounting the possibility of China's evolving in a more benign direction, moral democratic realists expect that engagement without robust deterrence will reinforce rather than undermine the current regime as it implacably strives to stay in power by substituting for genuine reform a policy of national prestige abroad and repression at home. This group foresees the Chinese regime's eventually facing a crisis of legitimacy arising from the inherent contradictions between sustaining prosperity and maintaining the Communist Party's monopoly on political power.[59] In these circumstances, moral democratic realists warn, an authoritarian China may find even more tempting the option of provoking dangerous foreign crises and intensifying its quest for hegemony in East Asia, unless the United States and its democratic allies—particularly India and Japan—sustain a clear, credible, and capable deterrence to such a dangerous course. The massive protests in Hong Kong in October 2014 underscored the enduring salience of the chilling scenario Arthur Waldron laid out a decade ago:

> Beijing has carried out *none* of the difficult reforms Moscow managed . . . even before the Communist system imploded once and for all. How likely can it be that the People's Republic will expire quietly, with little bloodshed and with a reasonably smooth institutional transition? By contrast, how likely is it that its demise will be accompanied instead by a violent death-rattle, in the form of massacres and/or flailing-out abroad? That rival factions will descend into civil war? That the army and security apparatus will attempt to restore order by means of a coup against the party and by installing a regime of repression at home and xenophobia abroad—that is, Chinese fascism?[60]

Moral democratic realists prescribe a mixed strategy—continuing to engage China economically while containing Chinese military power and expansionism vigilantly—aiming in the long run for Chinese political liberalization leading to true democracy. Militarily, this entails maintaining unassailable American military preeminence in air, sea, and space, including the Western Pacific.[61] Politically, this entails active U.S. participation and backing for democratic allies in Asia, especially India and Japan, whose values are congenial to the United States and who are expressing mounting alarm about China's swelling assertiveness. Many moral democratic realists also exhort the United States to encourage—energetically—progress in Chinese observance of human rights, the deepening of Chinese democracy, and the emergence of pluralism. In their eyes, peace with an authoritarian communist Chinese regime will never be secure.[62] Aaron Friedberg speculates that the United States would probably accept a democratic China "as a preponderant player in East Asia." Until then he advises American policy makers to "maintain a favorable balance of power in the region."[63]

The classical realist Robert Kaplan and offensive neorealist John Mearsheimer stand as outliers among the hard-liners for their discounting the importance of China's regime in their analysis. Both take a somber view of Chinese intentions that is based largely on Robert Gilpin's theory of hegemonic war—an elaboration of Thucydides' explanation of the Peloponnesian War between Athens and Sparta.[64] According to Mearsheimer, either a democratic or authoritarian China is unlikely to be tranquil because China "will attempt to dominate Asia the way the United States dominates the Western Hemisphere." Correspondingly, the United States will strive mightily to prevent China from achieving hegemony, which would result in "an intense security competition with considerable potential for war."[65] According to Kaplan, the geography of East Asia will encourage the growth of Sino-American naval rivalry rather "than the growth of armies as in continental Europe at the beginning of the last century."[66] Kaplan likened China's undeclared strategy to a twenty-first-century version of the Melian Dialogue. "As Thucydides writes, 'the strong do what they can and the weak suffer what they must.' Thus, the Melians give in without violence . . . in other words, power politics, almost mathematical in its abstraction, without war."[67]

President Obama entered office convinced of the prime importance of Asia for America's long-term prosperity and security. His administration assigned high priority to deepening American engagement in the region, including more active participation in regional organizations such as ASEAN and APEC, as well as meaningful involvement in the East Asian Summit (EAS). With the noteworthy exception of Myanmar, where Secretary of State Hillary Clinton took the lead in pushing for reform, the president and his spokesperson largely downplayed human rights and the internal characteristics of Asian regimes. The Obama administration also "did not focus on the balance of power or realpolitik," according to Jeffrey Bader, Obama's former senior director of East Asian affairs at the National Security Council.[68] Nor did the president and his chief spokespersons envisage a relationship with China as a zero-sum game.

On the contrary, the president adopted a welcoming approach to China's emergence, influence, and expanded role. Obama was initially optimistic about the prospects for working cooperatively with China on what he defined early in his administration as the major issues affecting Sino-American relations: alleviating the effects of the financial crisis of 2008, which China largely escaped; negotiating a climate change treaty; and curbing nuclear proliferation, especially in North Korea and Iran. Obama assumed generally that major international issues required China's active cooperation or at least neutrality if they are going to be addressed constructively.[69] The president's views about Asia, the rise of China, and its implications for the United States put him firmly in the camp of the spiral model—that is, those worried more about overreacting than underreacting militarily to China's rise. This frame of mind has largely prevailed even after Secretary of State Clinton's formal announcement of the Asian pivot in November 2011 moved the administration toward rhetorically, though less substantively, supplementing engagement with a modest dose of calibrated balancing.

The Obama administration's Asia policy has evolved through two phases. Engaging China dominated the first phase, which also relegated matters of hard power, and security relationships with democratic allies such as India and Japan, to more secondary concerns.[70] Secretary of State Clinton's first trip to China, in February 2009, set the tone and highlighted the priorities for the Obama administration's initial policies toward China. Addressing the Asia Society in New York City on the eve of her departure to Asia, Clinton drew what Mark Landler, writing in the *New York Times,* called "a clear line between the Obama administration's approach [toward China] and that of the Bush White House, which viewed China more as a rival than a partner." Contrary to those who believe that "China on the rise is by definition an adversary," the Obama administration believes that "the United States and China benefit from, and contribute to, each other's successes."[71] Shortly before reaching Beijing, Clinton insisted that the United States would not permit disagreements on human rights to interfere with Chinese-American engagement on climate change, the global financial crisis, or security threats. "We have to continue to press them. . . . But we pretty much know what they're going to say," she said. "Pressing on those issues can't interfere with the global economic crisis, the global climate change crisis and the security crises."[72]

The United States and China achieved only modest and evanescent success early on, forging common policies to address economic concerns. Although China in 2009 backed the administration's exhortation for large national stimulus packages within the G-20, Western Europe rebuffed the president's entreaties. China also rebuffed the Obama administration's strenuous efforts to reach a comprehensive global agreement limiting greenhouse gases. Although China has overtaken the United States as the largest emitter of greenhouse gases, China insisted on being categorized as an Annex II developing country with no formal obligations rather than an Annex I country largely accountable over the long term for greenhouse gas emissions and thus bearing a larger and legally binding responsibility for them. Paradoxically, Chinese recalcitrance delighted conservative hawks in this instance, demolishing whatever limited chance the administration had of convincing a Democrat-controlled Senate to pass a cap-and-trade system the Obama administration deemed necessary and desirable for American compliance with Copenhagen's costly and highly controversial scheme for regulation of emissions.[73]

The Obama administration promotes China's consistent criticism of Iranian defiance on its nuclear program as a major triumph of the president's policy of engagement.[74] The Chinese also have participated actively in the ongoing P5+1 negotiations with Iran, trying to reach an accord that would prevent the Iranians from developing and possessing nuclear weapons. The Obama administration has enjoyed, at best, mixed success in enlisting China's support in managing the threat of North Korea's nuclear program and constraining the North Korean regime's truculence more generally. Initially critical of North Korea's testing of long-range ballistic missiles, China declined to implement UN sanctions on the regime. As Obama sympathizers Indyk, Lieberthal, and O'Hanlon observe, "North Korea will remain a source of tension. . . . China is not prepared to get tough enough with North Korea to help bring that [nuclear] program to a halt."[75] Although China does not want North Korea to have nuclear weapons, the Chinese do not want the North Korean regime to collapse under the weight of international pressure.

Ultimately, North Korea has proved no less vexing to President Obama than to his predecessor, who also had little success contending with this brutal, dying, but dangerous regime on nuclear as well as non-nuclear issues. In 2009 North Korea exacerbated tensions with the United

States by imprisoning two American journalists—Laura Ling and Eunice Lee—who strayed inadvertently into North Korean territory. It took the intercession of former President Bill Clinton, traveling to North Korea with the approval of the Obama administration, to secure their release.[76] In 2010 North Korea provoked two major confrontations with the United States and South Korea: the March torpedoing and sinking of a South Korean naval vessel, the *Cheonan,* off the west coast of South Korea near Baengnyeong, killing forty-six seamen; and the November bombing of the South Korean island of Yeonping, killing four people.[77] Yet China provided cover for the North Korean regime on both occasions, refusing to condemn the attacks and blocking the UN from imposing any sanctions. Evidently, the PRC values the survival of the North Korean regime more than improving relations with South Korea, which China deeply antagonized by running interference for Pyongyang at Seoul's expense.[78]

Although according highest priority to engaging China, the president achieved some notable successes during the first phase of his Asia policy, bolstering U.S. relations with South Korea and Japan. The president pledged, in response to North Korean shelling of Baengnyeong, that the United States would defend South Korea from North Korean aggression. He referred to South Korea as "one of our most important allies" and a "cornerstone of U.S. security in the Pacific region."[79] Despite Beijing's objections, the United States and South Korea conducted joint naval exercises in November 2010 to deter further North Korean attacks as a signal to China.[80] The United States and South Korea also signed a free trade agreement in December 2010, which both countries ratified in the fall of 2011.[81] The administration also deftly managed a tense period in U.S.–Japanese relations that began in September 2009 when Yukio Hatoyama became the first prime minister from the modern Democratic Party of Japan (DJP). Hatoyama proposed to move Japanese foreign policy in a more Asia-centric, pro-Chinese direction and to downgrade Japan's long-standing ties with the United States, including the mutual defense treaty. Embracing Hatoyama in public, Obama insisted in private that Japan and the United States must subordinate their dispute about the future configuration of U.S. bases in Okinawa to the imperative of reaffirming the centrality of the U.S.–Japanese alliance for Asian security. Japan's flirtation with neutralism ended in May 2010, when a combination of Hatoyama's domestic failures and the unpopularity of his strategy of rebalancing

Japanese foreign policy impelled him to resign. His successor, Naoto Kan, pronounced the U.S.-Japanese alliance the pillar of Japan's foreign policy.[82] The Obama administration's prompt and generous response to the 2011 Tohoku earthquake and tsunami engendered considerable goodwill in Japan. Operation Tomodachi—one of the largest relief efforts of recent years, involving twenty U.S. Navy ships, including the USS *Ronald Reagan* aircraft carrier—delivered massive quantities of supplies to the Japanese government and rendered extensive technical assistance to prevent meltdowns of damaged Japanese nuclear reactors.[83]

The first phase of Obama's Asian policy also witnessed more active American involvement in regional organizations such as ASEAN. President Obama stressed the benefits of closer ties with Indonesia—the country with the world's largest Muslim population—as part of his outreach to the Islamic world and in affirmation of Indonesia's rising importance. According to the National Security Council, the size of Indonesia's economy will surpass those of most European nations by the 2020s.[84] In November 2010 President Obama visited Indonesia—where he lived from age ten to sixteen—and signed a Comprehensive Treaty of Partnership with the country's president at the time, Susilo Bambang Yudhoyono, which provided U.S. aid in exchange for scholarships, university partnerships programs, and climate change and clean energy programs. Yet Indonesia's rising economic nationalism, dislike of American foreign policy in the Middle East, and ambivalence about abandoning its traditional nonaligned status remain obstacles to achieving stronger military and political ties.[85]

President Obama's strategy of engaging China while emphasizing American soft power elsewhere in Asia yielded few tangible successes but no major catastrophes during the first year of his presidency. The following year, 2010, however, witnessed a marked rise in Chinese assertiveness toward its maritime neighbors and the United States—assertiveness that has broadened and intensified ever since. China's burgeoning military capabilities and its swelling, legally untenable claims to vast areas of disputed territorial seas have increasingly antagonized and alarmed China's neighbors while threatening freedom of navigation and the United States' ability to project power into the region. America's principal allies in the region—particularly Japan and the Philippines—increasingly worry that Obama's unremitting efforts to shrink the U.S. military and defense budget and curtail the employment of American hard power will create a power vacuum in the Pacific that China, whose aspirations they view as hegemonic, will inevitably fill without more muscular American deterrence than Obama has countenanced. The administration's proclamation of the Asia pivot in the fall of 2011 reflected these major trends and developments, which shook but did not shatter the president's sanguine but contentious assumption about the large degree of convergence between China's and the U.S's interests, regardless of the internal character of the Chinese regime.

Much of the pivot to Asia and the Pacific builds on the policies the president initiated in his first year of office, which entailed mainly diplomacy, rhetorical reassurance, and soft power. Although the Asia pivot has some new aspects in the military realm—increasing the number of U.S. forces allocated to the Pacific (from 50 to 60 percent), deploying and rotating troops and equipment to Australia and New Zealand, and consummating agreements that permit the U.S. Navy access to former American bases in the Philippines—the continuities between Obama's pre- and post-Asian pivot policies loom larger than the discontinuities.

The Asian pivot remains a work in progress, according to its defenders, or amorphous and lacking substance, according to its detractors. So any judgments about its merits fall into the categories of speculative, conditional, preliminary, and controversial. Nevertheless, the following observations stay well within the bounds of the plausible, sometimes verging on the reliable.

First, the Asian pivot has not restrained in the least China's increasing arrogance on display in the South China Sea, arguably the most geopolitically crucial juncture of the non-Western world, for reasons Robert Kaplan articulates splendidly:

> The South China Sea . . . is as central to Asia as the Mediterranean is to Europe. Here is the heart of Eurasia's navigable rimland, punctuated by the Malacca, Sunda, Lombbok, and Makassar straits. More than half the world's annual merchant fleet tonnage passes through these choke points, and a third of all maritime traffic worldwide. . . . Roughly two thirds of South Korea's energy supplies, nearly 60 percent of Japan's and Taiwan's energy supplies, and 80 percent of China's crude oil imports come through

the South China Sea. . . . In addition . . . , the South China Sea has a proven oil reserve of seven billion barrels, and an estimated 900 trillion cubic feet of natural gas. . . . Some Chinese observers have called the South China Sea "the second Persian Gulf." . . . China is desperate for new energy. . . . If one assumes that the Persian Gulf and Northeast Asia are the two critical areas of the non-Western world that the United States should not let another great power dominate, consider the energy-rich South China Sea . . . the third.[86]

On the contrary, China's actions as well as the rationale for claims in the South China Sea have catalyzed and crystallized the perception—particularly since late 2013—that China seeks a dominance over the South China Sea that is incompatible with the legitimate interests of its maritime neighbors and of the United States. China has asserted sovereignty over the entire South China Sea on the basis of a nine-dash line that is invalid under international law, particularly the United Nations Convention on the Law of the Sea (UNCLOS). In 2011 China proceeded to escalate a series of long-running disputes: with Vietnam regarding sovereignty over the Paracel Islands, located in the South China Sea two hundred miles off the coast of Vietnam; with the Philippines, Vietnam, Brunei, and Malaysia over the Spratly Islands, an area estimated to hold huge oil and natural gas reserves; and with the Philippines over the Scarborough Shoal, a chain of reefs about 123 miles west of Subic Bay, off the Philippine island of Luzon. The Chinese have used various methods to enforce these claims, including troops, civilian ships, naval vessels to blockade access, and construction of facilities. Nor have the Chinese confined their assertiveness to their weaker maritime neighbors in the area. On December 5, 2013, Chinese naval vessels provoked a confrontation with the U.S. Navy in the international waters of the South China Sea, warning the USS *Cowpens,* a guided-missile cruiser, to halt its course and then attempting to block its path.[87]

Second, China's increasingly brazen territorial assertions have escalated tensions in Northeast Asia as well as Southeast Asia. In November 2013 China declared an East China Sea Air Defense Identification Zone (ADIZ) that encompassed most of the East China Sea. The ADIZ requires all non-Chinese military and civilian aircraft to identify themselves and their missions to Chinese authorities before entering the zone. China's claimed ADIZ spans half of Japan's claimed ADIZ, including the Senkaku Islands. Japan and China have long disputed sovereignty over these islands for strategic, symbolic, and economic reasons. Prodigious amounts of natural gas and oil deposits may lie under the Senkakus' territorial waters. According to Robert Haddick, China is aggressively employing a salami-slicing or cabbage strategy in pursuit of hegemony in Western Pacific:

> This practice, known as salami-slicing, involves the slow accumulation of small changes, none of which in isolation amounts to a casus belli, but which add up over time to a substantial change in the strategic picture. By using salami-slicing tactics in the East and South China Seas, China does not have to choose between trade with the rest of the world and the achievement of an expanded security perimeter in the Western Pacific at the expense of China's neighbors. Given enough time, and continued confusion by the United States and its allies on how to respond, China is on course to eventually achieve them both. . . . Chinese leaders would not be funding exponential increases in air, naval, and missile power if they did not have a strategy they believed would work. China's actions are evidence that its leaders believe China will achieve escalation dominance in the Western Pacific in due course. If that's what they believe, U.S. and allied deterrence is not persuasive under current circumstances.[88]

According to Michael Pillsbury, China is pursuing "a marathon strategy," derived from the lessons of the Warring States period of Chinese history, to supplant the United States as the world's most dominant power. The main elements of this marathon strategy include inducing complacency to avoid alerting your opponent, manipulating your opponent's advisers, being patient to achieve victory, stealing your opponent's ideals and technology for strategic purposes, recognizing that the hegemon will take extreme action to retain its dominant position, and waiting for the maximum opportunity to strike.[89]

Third, the Obama administration's muted reactions to Chinese provocations in the East and South China Seas have failed to reassure American allies in the region of the president's resolve to deter China robustly. The Chinese declaration of the ADIZ infuriated Japanese Prime Minister Shinzo Abe, who called it a profoundly dangerous act. The Philippines, South Korea, and Taiwan also declared the ADIZ a violation of international law, vowing to disregard it. All four of these democratic allies implored the United States to resist agreement with China's declaration. Initially, President Obama obliged, vowing that the United States would not comply with the ADIZ. In defiance, he ordered two unarmed American B-52 bombers to fly into the zone without providing notification. Yet the administration backed off almost immediately. The Federal Aviation Administration ordered American commercial airliners to comply with the Chinese ADIZ. The State Department directed U.S. aircraft carriers to abide by it. Secretary of Defense Chuck Hagel and General Martin Dempsey refrained from categorizing the ADIZ as dangerous or destabilizing. Visiting Beijing in December 2013, Vice President Biden softened unequivocal condemnation of the ADIZ.[90]

The Obama administration's about-face eroded the fragile confidence among America's democratic Asian allies in the content and credibility of the Asian pivot. At a January 2014 conference in Davos, Switzerland, Japanese Prime Minister Abe compared the mounting rivalry between China and Japan to the escalating tensions between Germany and Great Britain before World War I.[91] In February 2014 Philippines President Benigno S. Aquino III urged neighboring nations to display greater firmness in resisting China's assertions in the Pacific. Aquino compared the West's lack of resolve—including the Obama administration's—to appeasement of Nazi Germany at democratic Czechoslovakia's expense, culminating in the ignominious capitulation to Hitler's demands at Munich in September 1938 that rendered the Czech state indefensible.[92] Add authoritarian Vietnam to the growing list of China's neighbors worried about China, doubtful of the Obama administration's strategic clarity, and pressing for closer ties with its former enemy. Though Vietnam is wary of any formal treaty arrangement, its capacity to resist becoming a Chinese vassal state depends on the United States' ability and willingness to project power in the Pacific, which a combination of the Chinese military buildup, geographical propinquity, and the determination of the Obama administration to shrink the U.S. military have eroded.[93]

Facing intense pressure from these dismayed allies to take a firmer line, the Obama administration in early 2014 sharpened its rhetorical attacks on China's territorial claims in the South and East China Seas. The administration blamed China for the escalating tensions and warned vaguely of unspecified changes in America's military posture in the region should China persist.[94] Yet the president continues to envisage the pivot to Asia essentially as a political rather than military endeavor, according to both defenders and detractors of his policy. The administration has focused mainly on economics and diplomacy: deepening American economic involvement in the region; negotiating a Trans-Pacific Partnership Agreement (TPP), which would create a free-trade zone among twelve nations, and encouraging Japan to join it; signing a ten-year agreement with the Philippines in April 2014 that allows for a rotating American military presence but no bases; and rhetorically reaffirming American security commitments in the region, pledging to defend Asian allies such as Japan and South Korea from any attack while reaching out diplomatically to other major countries in the region, such as Indonesia.[95]

Nor has the president or his leading national security officials modified their view of China as more a potential partner with whom the United States can do business than an emerging adversary requiring a more vigilant American strategy and more robust military capabilities to underwrite it. Notwithstanding the surging consternation of America's Asian allies about Chinese capabilities, behavior, and intentions, the president has defined as one of the Asian pivot's chief objectives building a stable, productive, constructive relationship with an authoritarian China. "We welcome China's peaceful rise," the president responded at an April 2014 press conference in Manila to skeptics raising questions about whether the Obama Doctrine was sufficiently robust in light of Putin's aggression in Ukraine, turmoil in the Middle East, and China's swelling arrogance. "We have a constructive relationship with China," he added. "There are a whole range of issues on the international stage in which cooperation between the U.S. and China are vital. So our goal is not to counter China. Our goal is not to contain China." A clearly exasperated president bristled at the suggestion of any contradiction between the Obama Doctrine's reluctance to employ force and the corollary determination to downsize the American military, on the one hand, and the strength of American alliances in Asia, on the other: "Typically, criticism of our foreign policy has been directed at the failure to use military force. . . . Why is it that everybody is so eager to use military force after we've just gone through a decade of war at enormous costs to our troops and our budget? . . . My job as Commander-in-Chief is to deploy military force as a last resort, and to deploy it wisely." At the same time, President Obama insists "unequivocally" and beyond "dispute" that "our alliances in the Asia Pacific have never been stronger. . . . Our relationships with ASEAN countries in Southeast Asia have never been stronger."[96]

Yet America's Asian allies have a more ominous perception of the existing state of affairs and trends in the region than President Obama's glowing assessment implies. A Pew Foundation survey conducted between March and June 2014 reports that "large majorities in many Asian countries fear that China's territorial ambitions could lead to war."[97] Those fears run especially high in the Philippines (93 percent), Japan (85 percent), and Vietnam (84 percent). The Pew survey also found only 7 percent of Japanese have a favorable view of China, compared with 66 percent who are favorable toward the United States; only 31 percent of Indians have a favorable view of China, compared with 55 percent for the United States; and only 16 percent of Vietnamese have a favorable view of China, compared with 76 percent for the United States. In Asia, China is more favorably viewed than the United States only in Thailand and the Islamic countries of Indonesia, Malaysia, Bangladesh, and Pakistan, despite the Obama administration's zealous courtship of the Islamic world, which has also yielded no improvement in American popularity throughout the Middle East.[98]

Since Obama's pivot, Asia has continued to undergo the world's fastest military buildup, in part because of growing apprehensions about Chinese ambitions and doubts about American determination to counter them. Every country in Southeast Asia has initiated a major military buildup. Since 2012 India has raised defense spending by more than 10 percent annually, whereas the government of the Philippines nearly doubled its spending in 2011, and its defense spending has been steadily on the rise ever since.[99] India has accelerated plans to build a new base on its east coast and the pace of its shipbuilding program—including a nuclear aircraft carrier, five or six ballistic-missile programs, and other warships—to counter the prodigious growth of China's naval presence in the Indian Ocean.[100]

Since 2006 South Korea has doubled its military budget, building advanced submarines and destroyers and purchasing advanced F-15K fighters and AWACS (Airborne Warning and Control System) surveillance aircraft from the United States.[101] Japanese Prime Minister Abe continues to fulfill his pledge to reverse the decline in Japanese defense spending, submitting a record military budget request that increases military spending for the third straight year. The Japanese military buildup—including drones, stealth fighters, and a new Japanese submarine—reflects Japan's intensifying military rivalry with China. As the 2014 Defense of Japan White Paper observes:

> China has been sustaining large increases in its defense spending and broadly and rapidly reinforcing its military forces, mainly its nuclear and missile force as well as its Navy and Air Force. As part of such efforts . . . China is strengthening its so-called "A2/AD" capabilities . . . working to improve joint operational capabilities, enhance capabilities for extended-range power projection, conduct practical exercises, cultivate and acquire highly-capable personnel for administering operations of informatized forces, and improve the foundation of its domestic defense industry. Furthermore, China has been rapidly expanding and intensifying its activities in the seas and airspace, including the East China Sea and South China Sea. In particular, China has adopted so-called assertive measures, including attempts to alter the status quo by coercive measures, in response to issues involving conflicting maritime interests. Japan has great concern over such Chinese military activities . . . together with the lack of transparency in its military affairs and security issues, and needs to pay utmost attention to them. These activities also raise security concerns for the region and the international community.[102]

As the *Economist* reports, "underlying" Japan's defense "spending boost is a deeper concern than Chinese expansion: American decline." Shigeru Ishiba, secretary general of the Liberal Democratic Party (LDP), explained earlier in 2014 that "China's defense spending will continue its double-digit growth, enhancing its relative strength and reducing America's power."[103] Yet neither Japan alone, nor Japan in combination with other Asian powers, can match China's growing military might or counter

China's stronger offensive military capabilities. To grasp the point, consider that "China spends more on its military than Japan, South Korea, Taiwan and Vietnam combined."[104]

Nor has all gone smoothly even with President Obama's soft-power outreach to Asia's multilateral organizations. The president subverted one of his main priorities by canceling an Asia trip in October 2013 because of a government shutdown. He thus missed the Asia-Pacific Economic Cooperation meeting in Indonesia and the meeting of ASEAN while Chinese influence in the region surged. Chinese President Xi Jinping attended both summits, thereby highlighting Obama's absence. Lamenting the president's cancellation, Sadanand Dhume, a resident fellow at the American Enterprise Institute and a *Wall Street Journal* columnist, assailed the administration for "presiding over arguably the fastest dilution of American influence [in Asia] since the end of the Vietnam war."[105] Jane Perlez offered an equally unflattering assessment in the *New York Times:* "With the cancellation of the visits, the much-promoted but already anemic American 'pivot' to Asia was further undercut, leaving regional allies increasingly doubtful the United States will be a viable counterbalance to a rising China."[106] Rizal Sukma, executive director of the Center for Strategic and International Studies in Jakarta, called Indonesia's attitude toward China in the wake of the Obama cancellation "a display of growing comfort amid persistent ambiguity." Sukma explains Indonesia as anxious about China's long-term intentions in East Asia, but doubtful "regarding America's ability to sustain the pivot strategy, with the huge cuts in the defense budget over the next five years."[107]

Fourth, Indonesian doubts about Obama's Asian pivot not only echo the concerns of America's East Asian allies, but also point to the pivot's gravest flaw—the growing deficiency of American hard power to underwrite it. No Asian trip, multilateral forum, or invocation of American smart power can substitute for that. President Obama's rhetoric to the contrary notwithstanding, the administration's current and long-term defense plans since the Asian pivot continue to broaden the gap between what the United States will have in air, sea, and space capabilities and what the military needs to maintain American dominance in the Pacific. Most of the substantive moves the administration has announced it has taken or will take—such as the planned deployment of an additional 2,500 marines to Australia—are modest and symbolic. Essentially, the

Obama strategy entails allocating a larger share (an increase of 20 percent to 60 percent of all overseas forces) to the Pacific of a smaller and still shrinking military. Furthermore, this proportional though not necessarily absolute increase remains, to date, mainly rhetorical and hypothetical rather than real because of a combination of the administration's steep reductions in the defense budget, Putin's ongoing challenge to European stability, and a resumption of U.S. fighting in the Middle East against ISIS that the administration did not anticipate.[108] In March 2014 Katrina McFarland, the Obama administration's assistant secretary of defense for military acquisition, conceded, "Right now, the pivot is being looked at again, because candidly it can't happen," owing to budget pressure.[109]

The Obama administration's current defense budget and future plans cannot field an effective counter to China's large and increasingly expanding A2/AD capabilities, which threaten to Finlandize East Asia. The American military will possess inadequate numbers and capabilities to fulfill its current air-sea battle (ASB) operational concept, which aims to ensure American military preeminence in the Western Pacific and entails the capabilities to preempt a sizable portion of China's A2/AD capability, including Chinese cruise and ballistic anti-ship missiles deployed on the Chinese mainland.[110] ASB will require substantially more than what the Obama administration has in hand and in mind: more submarines, long-range bombers, ballistic and cruise missiles; more surface vessels and unmanned vehicles; a more energetic strategic and theater missile defense program; and better protection for American command control, communication, and intelligence, including protection of American satellites from China's aggressive antisatellite program. Even a more modest strategy that aims merely to deny the Chinese Navy the ability to operate in the Western Pacific—more risky because it affords less credible protection to American allies in the region—will require more robust capabilities than what the administration's shrinking defense budget will provide.[111]

The Obama Doctrine has continued to diminish the already precarious credibility of American alliances in Asia, as it has in Europe and the Middle East. Chuck Hagel, Obama's dovish secretary of defense, conceded in February 2014 that the Asian pivot has not altered this adverse trend: "We are entering an era where American dominance on the seas, in the skies and in space can no longer be taken for granted."[112] Admiral Jonathan Greenert, until recently President Obama's chief of naval operations, also told Congress in March 2014 of his worries about the ability of the United States to keep up with Chinese military growth. Likewise, Greenert cautioned that he is "very concerned" about "our ability to project power in an area against an advanced adversary with those advanced capabilities. We're slipping behind."[113] Michael Pillsbury warns ominously, too:

> From now through 2030, the Chinese will have more than $1 trillion available to spend on new weapons for their navy and air force, according to a study conducted for the Pentagon by the RAND Corporation. This, combined with U.S. trends, which are headed in the other direction . . . paints a picture of near parity, if not outright Chinese military superiority, by midcentury. The future military balance of power is slowly shifting, from a ten-to-one U.S. superiority, toward equality, and then eventually to Chinese superiority. Congressional testimony in December 2013 revealed that the U.S. Navy's shipbuilding budget may be as low as $15 billion annually for the next thirty years, while the price of each new navy ship will escalate. Our only chance to remain dominant will be to develop superior technology and counter-measures . . . such as the Defense Department's new doctrine of AirSea Battle, which combines naval and air assets to defend against adversaries intent on denying freedom of navigation.[114]

The deteriorating military balance in East Asia raises the probabilities and risks of states to bandwagon rather than balance against China, lowering the barrier to aggression throughout the region; or our democratic allies' fear of China without a reliable American anchor may even ignite a regional nuclear arms race, in which Japan and South Korea join India and China as nuclear powers. As Robert Kaplan warns, even a "multipolar Asia in military terms would be a Chinese-dominated Asia. . . . Because China is not a half a world away from the region, but in fact constitutes the region's geographic, demographic, and economic organizing principle, Chinese dominance would naturally be more overwhelming than the American variety. That is to say nothing about China's own authoritarian system, which . . . is . . . less benign than the American model of government, which, in turn, partly determines the American style of empire."[115]

Fifth, the Obama administration has only belatedly and tentatively begun to court a decent, democratic India—an unwisely low priority for the first five years of an administration purportedly attempting to craft a credible Asian pivot. "We can't get any attention from this administration," a senior Indian diplomatic official commented to the *New York Times* reporter Gardiner Harris in March 2014. "They're busy with Russia, Syria, the Middle East and Iran. But in the current circumstances, it is vital that they also pay attention to the India relationship soon, since the current drift could get much worse."[116] This neglect of India ranks high on the list of the Obama administration's foreign policy mistakes. India shares with the United States a compelling interest regarding two of the major foreign policy challenges for the early twenty-first century: managing the rise of China in a constructive direction, credibly deterring a still authoritarian Chinese regime from achieving hegemony in Asia; and defeating Islamic radicalism. No nation other than democratic Israel has lost more to terrorism. No nation besides the United States has a greater incentive to prevail over Islamic extremism than India. As Robert D. Blackwill, America's ambassador to India from 2001 to 2003, instructively put it: "Consider the key countries of the world, which share with us these vital interests, and the willingness to do something about threats to these interests in an unambiguous way over the long term—for their own reasons India may lead the list."[117]

India is a potentially powerful as well as philosophically congenial ally for the United States as well as Japan—a cornerstone for any plausible arrangement raising the barriers to Chinese expansionism in East Asia, which is incompatible with the legitimate interests of American allies in the region. With the world's fourth-largest economy, India will soon surpass Japan as the third largest. The administration of George W. Bush prudently committed the United States to assisting India in becoming a great power—a goal consistent with the logic of his administration's Asian pivot, which envisaged China as a strategic competitor and democratic India and Japan as reliable strategic partners. Reversing the policy of the Clinton administration, categorically opposed to nuclear proliferation, President Bush welcomed India's nuclear weapons program, grounded in the sharp distinction he drew generally between dictatorships and democracies. The Bush administration even went so far as to provide the Indian government with civilian nuclear technology to facilitate it.[118]

Yet relations between the United States and India have largely languished on President Obama's watch until recently. India and the United States have disagreed about how to respond to major diplomatic issues, including the crisis in Ukraine and whether to investigate the Sri Lankan government's alleged atrocities committed during the final phase of its civil war. The December 2013 arrest of an Indian diplomat in New York for alleged fraud and mistreatment of a domestic worker also precipitated an imbroglio that damaged Indian-American relations for months thereafter. The Indian government and population chafed at what it considered American arrogance in arresting and deporting a public official, while the administration pushed back for what it considered India's callous indifference to American laws protecting the most vulnerable from exploitation.[119]

As Walter Russell Mead observes, India's serious post-2009 economic downturn also contributed to the deterioration in relations between the United States and India during the Obama presidency. The Congress Party, which dominated Indian politics from its independence until its crushing loss to the Bharatiya Janata Party (BJP) in May 2014, had steadily reverted to the failed paternalistic and land policies of the past. Consequently, economic growth slowed. Deficits mounted. The Indian currency depreciated sharply. The Indian stock market became more volatile, the government more protectionist. In these circumstances, an increasingly frustrated Obama administration complained about the legitimacy of India's refusal to open its markets. The Indian government has obstructed, for example, the creation of a level playing field for foreign investment in India's civil nuclear industry—especially galling to the United States, whose support was essential for India's securing access to critical nuclear fuel and technology in the first place.[120] Yet the Obama administration also deserves considerable blame for the frosty state of Indian and American relations, just beginning to thaw. President Obama's defining engagement with China as the administration's paramount priority, shrinking the American military, and retrenching globally have fostered doubts about the credibility of the strategic pivot to Asia. Nor do the administration's policies and priorities reassure Indian statesmen that the president comprehends India's critical role as a crucial democratic counterweight to Chinese ambitions.

The BJP's assumption of power on May 26, 2014, under Prime Minister Narendra Modi offers the Obama administration a monumental opportunity to take a significant step in the right direction. Assiduously cultivating a relationship with Modi would inject a heavy dose of strategic and moral clarity into a heretofore underwhelming Asian pivot bereft of adequate resources or reliable criteria for identifying friends, foes, threats, and opportunities. The United States and our East Asian allies—particularly democratic Japan—should celebrate the outcome of the watershed landslide election that brought Modi to power. The huge margin of the BJP's victory in May 2014 marks a seismic rejection of the Congress Party's policy of redistribution at home and neutralism abroad, which is inextricably linked with the legacy of the Gandhi family. Since 1947 these policies have stifled India's economic growth and inhibited its emergence as a major economic power.[121]

Modi—an outsider of humble origin—campaigned on principles that Ronald Reagan and Margaret Thatcher would have appreciated. "When I say good governance, I believe that there should be minimum government and maximum government, because to run such a huge country, there are so many traditions, rules, regulations, hierarchies, all these things are there that become obstacles in their way," Modi told the Council on Foreign Relations in New York on September 29, 2014. "And the government's own order becomes obstacles sometimes, problems sometimes." Modi champions a pro-business, pro-market agenda, emphasizing incentives for wealth creation as the wellsprings of social mobility and economic dynamism. Modi advocates investing significantly more to improve India's primitive infrastructure while significantly lowering the burden of government regulation and taxation. Modi proclaims himself dedicated to upholding India's democratic institutions and a strict constructionist of India's constitution.[122] His exemplary record as chief minister of Gujarat bodes well for his performance as prime minister. Under Modi, Gujarat's 10 percent annual growth rate exceeded China's, whereas India's overall growth rate had fallen to 5 percent since 2008. Gujarat also boasts India's lowest unemployment rates.[123] Modi's trinity of less government, less regulation, and less taxation transformed Gujarat into an exciting place for investment. In anticipation of Modi's victory, the Indian stock market soared, reaching a record high on March 16, 2014.[124]

Modi's foreign policy and national security strategy mesh nicely with the logic of a more robust Asian pivot necessary to reassure American allies and vindicate American interests in the region. Although envisioning Pakistan as the most immediate threat, Indian strategists increasingly consider China the paramount long-term strategic threat. Modi promises to continue raising Indian defense spending substantially, starting with a 14 percent increase in 2014.[125] Modi has criticized China's expansionist mindset, calls for India to take a more assertive leadership role to counter it, and anticipates taking cooperation with Japan to new heights. Modi will probably deepen India's emerging strategic, economic, and military cooperation with Israel that the end of the Cold War and the rise of Islamic radicalism catalyzed. Reassuringly, Modi has pledged his fealty to the foreign policy legacy of former BJP Prime Minister Atal Bihari Vajpayee, who cultivated partnerships with the United States and Israel, as well as diplomatic engagement with India's longtime rival Pakistan—now no longer even a semi-reliable friend of the United States. In addition, the United States can rely heavily on India to contain an increasingly volatile, anti-American Pakistan more and more susceptible to Islamist impulses.[126]

Despite his convincing mandate and enormous popularity at the polls, Modi will have to overcome a plethora of obstacles to achieving his plans for bold tax, land, and labor reforms. Ellen Barry, writing in the *New York Times,* identifies some of the most daunting among them. Modi's BJP does not control the upper house of India's parliament. Count, too, on the intensely statist national bureaucracy fiercely resisting Modi's agenda. In India's federal system, state leaders—many hostile to Modi's program—wield considerable influence over many important areas of policy. Some 500 million Indians still live in poverty. Modi has raised high expectations difficult to fulfill.[127] Modi also remains a highly controversial figure in Indian politics.[128] Many liberals, leftists, and Islamists still blame him for failing to quell the 2002 Gujarat riots, which killed hundreds of people (mostly Muslim). India's Supreme Court cleared Modi of any complicity in the rioting. Further, the Gujarat state court declined to prosecute because there was insufficient evidence. In 2005, however, the U.S. State Department denied Modi a visa on the basis of these serious but still unproven allegations.[129]

President Obama sensibly reversed the ban, paving the way for Modi's September 2014 visit to the United States, which included a two-hour meeting between the two at the White House. The prime minister and the president agreed in theory to seek closer defense and national security ties, though the talks achieved no significant breakthroughs, and differences persist.[130] The day before Obama and Modi's White House meeting, Richard N. Haass, president of the Council on Foreign Relations, aptly summed up the current state of the bilateral U.S.–India relationship as "potentially one of the most important for the United States." Haass qualified his statement with the word *potentially* because "we are not yet there. Our relationship is underdeveloped in terms of trade and investment, energy security, and strategic cooperation on both regional issues, including South and East Asia, as well as transnational issues, including terrorism and climate change. And the challenge and the opportunity for both countries . . . is to translate all this potential into reality."[131] It is hazardous to predict confidently where the U.S.–Indian relationship goes from here. Will the Obama administration build on and sustain—not only rhetorically but tangibly—its long overdue focus on a long-neglected India? Or does the president view his reset with India as entailing primarily diplomacy and soft power? Will multiple crises abroad and Obama's still-zealous desire to engage China despite mounting difficulties continue to distract and inhibit the president from seizing this opportunity to forge a vibrant partnership with a decent, democratic India that shares our interests and values? No measure besides reinvigorating American defense and bolstering America's alliance with Japan would do more to serve American interests in Asia rightly understood than broadening and deepening the U.S.–Indian relationship across the board, including militarily.[132]

Since the midterm elections of 2014, the president has intensified his welcome but still-tentative overtures to India. His visit to India in January 2015 not only yielded an important deal furthering India's nuclear program, but also revealed a surprising rapport between the president and Modi that may bode well for both countries.[133] Yet neither the atmospherics of the president's salutary overtures to India nor the administration's rhetoric compensates for the adverse trends in the military balance that have led an increasing number of Asian countries to dismiss the Asian pivot "as hot air." The president still refuses to accept that China may be a revisionist power requiring robust deterrence rather than the forbearance that still dominates the administration's policies with only marginal qualifications. Meanwhile, the U.S. military continues to diminish while the Chinese military continues to grow. The president remains eager and optimistic about working with Beijing on a number of his priorities—

from climate change to limiting Iran's nuclear program. The president continues to downplay human rights in his dealing with China and fails to draw any link between China's increasing repressiveness at home and assertiveness abroad.[134] President Obama did not allow China's crackdown on pro-democracy protesters in Taiwan to interfere with the business of the annual APEC conference meeting in Beijing in November 2014. "We have principles and values we want to promote, but we're not looking to inject the United States into the middle of this," a senior administration official confided to the *New York Times* correspondent Mark Landler.[135]

The tone and results of Obama's meetings with Chinese officials at APEC indicate that Obama has not modified his agenda of stressing progress on climate change and improving relations with China even after the rebuke of the midterm elections at home, in which Democrats lost both houses of Congress. On November 12, 2014, President Obama and China's Premier Xi Ping announced substantial new agreements to curb greenhouse gas emissions, whereby the United States will have to reduce carbon emissions to between 26 and 28 percent below 2005 levels. Likewise, China pledged to reach its peak year of emissions by 2030 and to expand its share of total energy consumption coming from zero-emission sources to 20 percent by then.[136] The two countries also reached agreements to notify each other of any military exercises and to adhere scrupulously to rules of engagement should their forces cross paths on land and in the air.[137] What the Obama administration deemed significant progress reflects the high priority the president still accords to cooperating with, rather than confronting, China, despite mounting difficulties in the relationship. In his meetings with Xi Ping, the president once more downplayed China's relentless military buildup, growing assertiveness in its disputes with maritime neighbors, and increasing repression at home, including attempts at quelling pro-democracy movements in Hong Kong. "They are trying to put the relationship on a positive trajectory for the next couple of years," speculated Jeff Bader.[138]

As he has regarding Europe and the Middle East, President Obama has gambled that a combination of American soft power, engagement diplomatically, and retrenchment militarily can vindicate American ideals and self-interest at lower cost and risk than more muscular alternatives. Yet neither an emerging India—still way to the rear of China economically and militarily—nor any other combination of Asian powers can substitute for American military preeminence in the Pacific. Despite the president's denials, concern continues to soar in Asia that declining American power, credibility, and commitment will leave the way open for Beijing to exercise dominance over the region. Roger Cohen opines in the *New York Times* chillingly but compellingly, "No global city can prosper in an environment where stability appears less certain and freedom in danger of curtailment. That is one reason why America's commitment to Asia matters as China rises—and doubts about America stir unease."[139] Alas, President Obama's highly charged rhetoric seems to have fostered both doubt and unease. Cohen continues, "The 'pivot to Asia,' like the Syrian 'red line,' like 'Assad must go,' betrayed a common theme: words without meaning from an American president, commitments without follow-up, phrases without plans. In Asia, as in Europe, these things get noted."[140]

Conclusion

This book makes the case that the Obama administration's grand strategy reflects a clear, coherent, consistent doctrine. What this writer calls the *Obama Doctrine* is a synthesis of various elements of classical realism, neorealism, and liberal multilateralism; it appropriates the most problematic features of these paradigms without their countervailing virtues. Like neorealism, the Obama Doctrine underplays the importance of ideology and regime type in determining friends, foes, threats, and opportunities. This conceptual error accounts largely for the administration's serial miscalculations dealing with Putin's authoritarian Russia, an authoritarian, revisionist China, and radical Islamist regimes and entities in the Middle East, such as a revolutionary Shiite Iranian regime, the Muslim Brotherhood, Hamas, Hezbollah, and ISIS. It accounts likewise for the administration's propensity imprudently to subordinate the concerns of liberal democratic allies such as the Eastern European members of NATO, Japan, Colombia, and Israel in favor of engagement with authoritarian rivals or competitors of the United States. Like liberal multilateralism, the Obama Doctrine overrates the efficacy of international institutions as arbiters of legitimacy, while unduly discounting the imperatives of traditional geopolitics and benefits of American military preeminence the administration's improvident defense policies have dangerously undermined. The president's aversion to risk often magnifies dangers because he focuses almost exclusively on the cost of action, oblivious to the often greater cost of inaction.

The Obama Doctrine also reflects an inordinately pessimistic projection of America's relative decline that neither the rise of other powers nor America's prospects make desirable or inevitable. Historically, the free market, favorable demographics, an abundance of untapped energy, limited government, and the creativity of the American people have served as the wellspring for American political and economic renewal that has repeatedly proved the pessimists wrong. Today the United States and its democratic allies possess the resources to maintain a preponderance of power in the world's most important geopolitical regions—even in East Asia, where an authoritarian China, still growing prodigiously, economically and militarily, confronts the United States with its toughest long-term challenge for the twenty-first century. Together, the United States, Japan, India, and South Korea can afford, by a wide margin, to craft and sustain a muscular deterrent to an authoritarian China's potentially hegemonic ambitions. Such deterrence is achievable especially if China's growth slows through a combination of its entering a more mature stage of development, the stifling effect of the Communist Party's determination to maintain absolute power, and the inherent unsustainability of dynamism in the long run of a closed society. Denying China an outlet for its expansionism militarily, while engaging Beijing economically, may eventually catalyze the domestic reforms that will liberalize the regime, tame its ambitions, and make it a more benign neighbor in Asia. Thwarting rather than enabling Russian expansionism with misguided resets based on false assumptions would reassure America's European allies while increasing pressure on an authoritarian Russia to reform benignly or collapse ignominiously. Defeating rather than propitiating radical Islam constitutes a necessary, though not sufficient, condition for tranquilizing the toxic political culture of the Islamic Middle East—the root cause of the most pernicious dangers emanating from that strife-ridden region.

The Obama Doctrine's near categorical imperative of using force only discretely, incrementally, multilaterally, and as a last resort reflects the president's deep aversion to risk and a corresponding desire to constrain what he considers to be the dangers arising from the arrogance of American power. Yet the history of American diplomacy and the troubling record of the Obama administration's foreign policy tell us that the greater risk lies in diminishing our strategic profile, making withdrawal rather than victory the priority, and allowing American hard power to wane. As Samuel Huntington observes, a significant correlation exists between "the rise and fall of American power in the world and the rise and fall of liberty and democracy in the world. That correlation also exists for the rise and fall of American prosperity since the 1930s."[1] Witness the corresponding expansion of American power, freedom, and prosperity after World War II. Witness the same felicitous outcome for the 1980s and 1990s.[2] Contrast these positive correlations with freedom in retreat, collectivism on the rise, and the U.S. economy in dire straits during the isolationism and depression of the 1930s. Contrast these positive correlations likewise with the stagflation, the surge in Soviet expansionism, and the perception of American decline that characterized the era of détente and retrenchment of the 1970s amid the lacerating debate over the meaning and outcome of the Vietnam War.

So Obama's ambition to narrow American interests and diminish American military power will probably compound the very costs and risks the Obama Doctrine strives to minimize. As Josef Joffe observes, the Obama doctrine is

> neither isolationism nor interventionism, exceptionalism or universalism, nationalism or institutionalism. It is the politics of reticence abroad coupled with the expansion of the "social state," as the Europeans call it, at home. In matters military, defense budgets are declining in ways not seen since demobilization after V-J day. The use of force has shifted from massive deployment to over-the-horizon balancing and to pinpoint attacks exploiting the economy and safety of high-precision standoff weapons. This is not "Europeanization," but a distinct turn from "exceptionalism" and reflexive entanglement in the travails of the world. . . . Yet a world in which the United States turned inward would be far less predictable and a less safe one. . . . How would the world fare if the global commons were run by China or Russia, illiberal giants both?[3]

Instead, the moral democratic realism most characteristic of Harry Truman and Ronald Reagan, adapted to the conditions of the twenty-first century, furnishes the most prudent template for American grand strategy, vastly superior to the Obama Doctrine and other contending alternatives: namely, the various forms of realism depreciating ideology and regime type; the untenable neo-isolationism of offshore balancing; or a liberal multilateralism depreciating the importance of hard power and the frequent imperative in a still-dangerous world of acting decisively either unilaterally or with limited coalitions of the willing to fit the mission. After World War II, the Truman administration successfully laid out the rationale and provided the means for the policy of vigilant containment that extended the democratic zone of peace and facilitated the triumph over an existentially dangerous Soviet Empire. Likewise, the spectacular revival the United States experienced during the Reagan years demolished the gloomy conventional wisdom of the 1970s that lamented the inevitability of American decline. Ultimately, Reagan's foreign policy completed what Truman's policies, infused with moral democratic realism, had initiated. Reagan contributed mightily not only to winning the Cold War, but also to catalyzing what Samuel Huntington calls the third wave of democratic expansion globally.[4]

Revisionist scholars continue untenably to underestimate and misrepresent the enormous contributions of Truman and Reagan to the demise of the "evil empire." Strobe Talbott, a prominent journalist and author before he became deputy secretary of state during the Clinton administration, disparaged the policy of vigilant containment that Truman had initiated, and his successors until Nixon had largely sustained, as provocative and unnecessary. Or as Talbott put it, the United States won the Cold War because "it need not have been fought in the first place."[5] Likewise, according to a revisionist school of thought whose ranks include James Mann, John Patrick Diggins, Jack Matlock, Justin Vaïsse, and Beth Fischer, the Soviet Union fell for internal reasons, Soviet Premier Mikhail Gorbachev being the main hero. Revisionists consider Reagan's most important, though secondary, contribution his willingness during his second term to abandon the belligerent policies of his first.[6] According to Beth Fischer, for example, an enlightened and sensible Gorbachev induced Reagan to compromise, thus defusing the spiraling cycle of tension between the United States and the Soviet Union that Reagan's hardline policies triggered in the first place.[7] According to James Mann and Justin Vaïsse, Reagan dissociated himself from the hard-liners dominant in his first term and switched to a more realistic policy of peace.[8]

This revisionist deconstruction of Truman and Reagan cannot withstand scrutiny. The Russian archives have confirmed the prudence of Truman's assessment of the Soviet threat and his administration's robust response to it.[9] True, Ronald Reagan and British Prime Minister Margaret Thatcher recognized sooner than most hard-liners—or for that matter, most realists such as Richard Nixon and Henry Kissinger—that Gorbachev was a different type of Soviet leader. When circumstances changed during Reagan's second term, he adjusted his policies and tamed some of his rhetoric, but not the premises underlying them. Reagan responded positively to changes in the Soviet regime during Gorbachev's tenure that he believed put it on the path of ultimate extinction. Ultimately, Gorbachev agreed to end the Cold War not on the Soviet Union's terms, but on Reagan's, with the Iron Curtain down, Eastern Europe free, and a united Germany incorporated into NATO. American pressure did not abate at any point during the Reagan presidency, despite Reagan's view that engaging Gorbachev could expedite the implosion of the Soviet regime. Reagan persisted with SDI and the "zero option," calling for the elimination of all intermediate-range nuclear weapons in Europe. Gorbachev capitulated. American defense spending continued to rise steeply throughout the Reagan presidency, peaking at $302 billion (6.6 percent of the GDP) in fiscal year 1988. Even after Gorbachev came to power, the Reagan administration continued to aid freedom fighters resisting Soviet imperialism in Asia, the Middle East, and Central America. Nor did Reagan ever relent in his assault on the moral legitimacy of the Soviet regime. In June 1987, over the objection of his so-called realist advisers, he exhorted Gorbachev to tear down the Berlin Wall, assailing the wall as a fitting symbol of the regime that built it.[10]

Reagan's understanding of himself also demolishes the revisionist interpretation of his motives and policies. Summing up his foreign policy legacy to students at the University of Virginia on December 16, 1988, he welcomed improvements in Soviet-American relations but urged Americans to "keep our heads, and that means keeping our skepticism" because "fundamental differences remain." He attributed that improvement to his policy of firmness, not conciliation: "Plain talk, strong defenses, vibrant allies, and readiness to use American military power when American power was needed—helped to prompt the reappraisal that Soviet leaders have undertaken of their previous policies. Even more, Western resolve demonstrated that the hardline advocated by some within the Soviet Union would be fruitless, just as our economic successes have set a shining example."[11] Reagan contrasted his policies with the more conciliatory policies of his predecessors during the 1970s: "We need to recall that in the years of détente we tended to forget the greatest weapon the democracies have in their struggle is public candor: the truth. We must never do that again. It's not an act of belligerence to speak to the fundamental differences between totalitarianism and democracy; it's a moral imperative. . . . Throughout history, we see evidence that adversaries negotiate seriously with democratic nations when they knew the democracies harbor no illusions about those adversaries."[12]

It is hard to see, too, how Gorbachev and a policy of conciliation deserve more credit for ending the Cold War on American terms than Reagan and his policy of unremitting vigilance. Cambridge University Professor Jonathan Haslam proffers this persuasive judgment in his magisterial study of the Cold War that is based on recently released Soviet archives: "In a critical sense, whether one likes to admit it or not . . . the Carter-Reagan buildup in counterforce systems, the anticommunist zeal within Reagan's administration, and the obsession with space-based defense played a key role in the unravelling of Soviet security policy across the board."[13]

Neither Truman nor Reagan conducted an error-free foreign policy. On the contrary, both made serious mistakes. Witness the Truman administration's costly miscalculation about Chinese intervention in Korea, or Reagan's rank negligence during the Iran-Contra scandal, the worst of his administration. Other Cold War presidents in the robustly internationalist tradition made even more serious and frequent mistakes. Witness, to cite just a few examples, Eisenhower's excessive and sometimes counterproductive use of covert action or the Bay of Pigs debacle during the Kennedy administration. Witness, too, the flawed strategy implicating several administrations that culminated in the costly and lacerating defeat in Vietnam.

Even so, the successes of robust internationalism dwarf its failures. Truman's and Reagan's versions of moral democratic realism have especially great contemporary as well as historical salience. As a caveat, important changes have occurred in world politics since the end of the Cold War. Bipolarity no longer characterizes the distribution of world power. Instead, the United States has the capacity to remain the world's paramount military power for decades to come if the Americans have the political will and foresight to sustain it. The world is moving toward some form of unbalanced multipolarity economically; the United States is the first among not-so-equals, China is on our heels, India is rising, and the European Union and Japan are also in the top tier. East Asia has replaced Europe as the world's paramount geopolitical region on the basis of population, territory, economic clout, and military capabilities. The Middle East has risen in significance, though not in ranking—still behind Asia and Europe—because of the dangerous intersection of Islamic radicalism, the spread of weapons of mass destruction, and the voracious global demand for massive quantities of oil.

Nevertheless, the moral democratic realism most characteristic of Truman, Reagan, and George W. Bush—and also deeply influential in other Cold War administrations before Nixon's—yields six enduring principles that should inform any prudent alternative to a perilously imprudent Obama Doctrine at odds with American ideals and self-interest, rightly understood:

1. The United States should strive to remain the world's default power.

Good statesmen and decent states can reduce and mitigate, but never eliminate, the danger of war even in the best of times because of the ineradicable flaws in human nature. The anarchical system of international politics, where there is no monopoly on the legitimate use of violence, compounds the severity and stark consequences of violence and strife. In these ineluctable circumstances, the vindication of America's national interests hinges primarily on the robustness of American power. Coalitions of the willing can supplement but never substitute for American hard power, particularly military power. Multilateral institutions in general and the UN in particular can inhibit the necessary exercise of American power if American statesmen are unwise enough to make them the arbiters of legitimacy for when and how to use force. No nation, no alliance, no international organization can have a veto on American action, especially those, such as the United Nations, that are often organically hostile to American interests and values. A decent respect for the decent opinions of mankind does not require slavish adherence to the indecent opinions routinely emanating from the anti-American tyrannies prevalent in the UN General Assembly.[14]

2. A strong defense is the best deterrent.

The greatest dangers to the United States typically arise not from vigilance or the arrogance of American power, but from unpreparedness or an excessive reluctance to fight. Historically, retreat, retrenchment, and disarmament by example pave the road to moral and geopolitical disaster. Consequently, the United States should strive to maintain what Winston Churchill called overwhelming power, with plenty to spare for unforeseen circumstances. This posture will deter most aggressors most of the time and defeat them at the lowest possible cost and risk in cases where even the most muscular deterrent fails.[15]

President Truman tripled the defense budget during the Korean War. The Eisenhower and Kennedy administrations spent more than 8 percent of the GDP on national defense. Confronted with a large budget deficit, Reagan, unlike Obama, gave priority to his military buildup, rightly envisaging it as freedom insurance. Today the United States must replenish the military capital Ronald Reagan bequeathed to the nation, but which President Obama's plan to shrink the American military will squander. For the sake of freedom and security, the United States must remain at the cutting edge of military innovation, deployment of state-of-the-art weapons systems, and research and development, thus keeping well ahead of potential and actual adversaries waiting in the wings even in times of comparative tranquility. The root cause of U.S. budget woes lies not with defense spending but with domestic spending, particularly entitlement programs. The United States can well afford to spend 4 to 5 percent of the GDP on defense, compared to the less than 3 percent it eventually will spend if current trends initiated by Obama continue. The United States now spends only 15 percent of every federal dollar on defense, compared to 47 percent of every dollar under President John F. Kennedy and 29 percent on every federal dollar under Ronald Reagan.[16]

3. Regime type matters vitally for discerning friends, foes, threats, and opportunities.

A prudent grand strategy accords great weight to regime type and ideology in discerning friends, foes, opportunities, and perils. Not all regimes behave alike. Some are more aggressive or benign than others. Truman, Reagan, George W. Bush, and the Cold War presidents excluding Nixon and Carter distinguished sharply between stable liberal democratic regimes, on the one hand, and totalitarian regimes—often animated by messianic, malevolent ideologies—on the other. Truman, Reagan, and

George W. Bush in particular rightly considered stable liberal democracies more reliable U.S. allies, more likely to cooperate with us, and less likely to fight with one another than with other types of regimes—a conviction the historical record affirms. As Reagan himself put it regarding a decent, democratic Israel, "No conviction I've ever held has been stronger than my belief that the United States must ensure the survival of Israel. . . . My dedication to the preservation of Israel was as strong when I left the White House as when I arrived there, even though this tiny ally, with whom we shared democracy and many other values, was a source of great concern from me while I was president."[17] Truman, Reagan, and the Cold War presidents excluding Nixon and Carter believed, too, that pernicious regimes and ideologies accounted historically for the most menacing threats to the United States. Reagan in particular aimed to transform and liberalize a totalitarian Soviet regime responsible for initiating, escalating, and perpetuating the Cold War.

Today a grand strategy anchored in moral democratic realism would confront, not deny, the gathering danger of Islamic fascism—be it a revolutionary, virulently anti-American, Shiite theocracy in Iran bent on crossing the nuclear threshold; a savage and ideologically radical ISIS; the anti-American, anti-Semitic Muslim Brotherhood in Egypt; or the militant and unrelenting Hamas in Gaza. Today a grand strategy anchored in moral democratic realism would identify a still-dangerous, authoritarian, and expansionist China as a competitor requiring powerful military containment as well as economic engagement. Today a grand strategy anchored in moral democratic realism would give precedence to defending democratic friends in Eastern Europe, Great Britain, Columbia, India, Israel, Japan, and South Korea rather than resetting relations with an increasingly authoritarian Putin, aiming to reverse the outcome of the Cold War; an increasingly repressive China, striving for hegemony in East Asia; or dictatorships in the Islamic Middle East, loathing the United States for its very essence.

That does not mean the United States should court enormous risks to establish democracies everywhere, on any pretext. Truman, Reagan, Eisenhower, Kennedy, Johnson, and both Bushes never advocated that. As they well recognized, sometimes the prospects for democracy are too bleak and America's geopolitical stakes in the outcome too limited to justify active American involvement. Sometimes an authoritarian regime that is less anti-American—such as the current military dictatorship in Egypt, post-Morsi—is the lesser evil when the most likely alternative is an even more repressive regime that is intrinsically anti-American, more belligerent, and more difficult to reform.[18]

4. The United States must think geopolitically.

A grand strategy anchored in moral democratic realism and adapted to contemporary conditions ranks threats, interests, and opportunities on the basis of geopolitical criteria rather than abstract, vague, and unenforceable principles of cosmic justice. For all nations—even a nation as powerful as a United States, by no means destined to decline—resources are finite. So the United States must establish its priorities wisely. The geopolitical logic that Truman, Reagan, and the most successful Cold War presidents employed dictates that preventing a rising China from dominating in Asia has become the greatest long-term challenge for the United States. Eventually, an authoritarian China may well face the same reckoning that the Soviet Union did during the 1980s—reform the political system, collapse, or expand—because of the unlikelihood of reconciling the Chinese Communist Party's vicelike grip on power with sustaining economic dynamism in the long term. In prudent anticipation of that reckoning, the United States should have in place a credible democratic alliance system and formidable military deterrent, as Ronald Reagan did with the Soviet Union. This would increase mightily the favorable odds that China will reform rather than fight the way Gorbachev did during the 1980s.

The neoconservative disposition that Truman, Reagan, and George W. Bush would have found so congenial in many respects is more right than wrong in diagnosing the threats the United States faces and the most prudent policy prescriptions for dealing with those threats. Like neoconservatives of all varieties, Truman, Reagan, George W. Bush, and Cold War presidents excluding Nixon and Carter assailed isolationism, declinism, global retrenchment, or the fallacy of moral equivalence as geopolitically reckless and morally unsound. Yet they recoiled from the unbridled democratic globalism of some less prudent neoconservatives who risk expending precious resources and political capital on peripheral goals. Mirroring these prudential dispositions, Charles Krauthammer has warned presciently that the United States must concentrate primarily on the most important things: first, prevent hegemons from emerging in East Asia, Europe, and the Middle East; then, to the extent possible, consolidate and expand the zone of democratic peace in these major power centers where the absence of liberty could prove most perilous. Elsewhere, the United States should vigorously encourage freedom, but not by force, except in rare circumstances (such as Rwanda in 1994) when minimal force, with minimal risk, and a prompt exit strategy can avert mass murder or genocide.[19]

5. America's leaders must embrace American exceptionalism.

A prudent grand strategy requires a synergistic combination of economic prosperity at home, the robustness of American power abroad, and the continued appeal and vitality of the American way of life. The Obama Doctrine calls for making government more powerful at home while making the United States less powerful, more deferential, and more humble abroad, a strategy—redolent of Jimmy Carter's—that moral democratic realists derided as an invitation to moral, economic, and geopolitical peril that greater self-confidence and vigilance could avert.

Truman, Reagan, George W. Bush, and the Cold War presidents (excluding Carter) generally did not consider the United States a perfect nation, but a great, good, and unique one, its power indispensable for achieving any decent world order where freedom could survive and thrive. These presidents enthusiastically championed traditional notions of American exceptionalism—or what Ronald Reagan called a "shining city on a hill," despite its flaws—that today many realists, multiculturalists, and President Obama find so troubling. Moral democratic realists emphatically reject the fallacy of moral equivalence, or even worse, the tendency to blame the United States first, which President Obama has frequently exhibited, especially in his outreach to the Islamic World. Or as Ronald Reagan put it, summing up his record: "We should stop apologizing for America's legitimate national interests and start asserting them."[20] The preponderance of America's presidents since Woodrow Wilson have infused their conception of the national interests with moral content grounded in the Declaration of Independence, as well as practical content grounded in geopolitics. Beginning with George Washington, the greatest American statesmen have insisted that the United States must wage war and conduct peace in a manner consistent with American society and the principles of well-ordered liberty. The seminal exposition of Reagan's grand strategy toward the Soviet Union (NSDD 75) stipulated accordingly: "U.S. policy must have an ideological thrust which clearly affirms the superiority of the U.S. and Western values of individual dignity and freedom, a free press, free trade unions, free enterprise, and political democracy over the repressive features of Soviet Communism."[21] The virtue and necessity of defending freedom with no pale pastels applies forcibly to our times as well.

6. Different times call for different strategies to best preserve America's national interest.

Prudent statesmanship requires the capacity to discern when changing times require different measures to achieve the same goals aimed at judiciously vindicating the national interest at the lowest possible cost and risk. Strategies appropriate for one set of circumstances are often inappropriate for others. For instance, the United States could pursue a strategy of armed neutrality, or offshore balancing outside the Western Hemisphere, during the nineteenth century, when it was weak in the world of the strong and could take the effective operation of the European balance of power for granted; yet the conditions the United States faced in the twentieth century called for a more vigilant, internationalist foreign policy.

Nor did the wisest of our presidents consider a strategy of containment and deterrence appropriate in all circumstances. On the contrary, Franklin Roosevelt, Harry Truman, John Kennedy, Ronald Reagan, and George W. Bush, among others, defended the moral and practical wisdom of preemptively using force against certain types of actors, such as Nazi Germany and perhaps even a revolutionary Iranian regime bent on crossing the nuclear threshold.[22] Reagan foresaw grave danger, for example, should an Islamist Iran ever acquire nuclear weapons, a horror he warned about presciently in his memoirs. His secretary of state George Shultz originated the tenet on which the Bush Doctrine hinged: that American strategy toward rogue regimes and terrorist entities in the Middle East had to include preemption in its repertoire of options.[23] Unlike the Obama Doctrine's near categorical aversion to using force except as a last resort, a grand strategy anchored in moral democratic realism treats preemption as a prudential judgment: weighing the gravity of the danger, the probability of its realization, the availability of plausible alternative means, and the prospects of success.

A grand strategy anchored in moral democratic realism thus incorporates the transcendent noble principles of the American founding while rendering due appreciation for the perennial imperatives of power and geopolitics. Its categorical commitment to sustaining American military preeminence and championing American exceptionalism not only enhances deterrence but reduces the blood, toil, tears, and sweat of wars that the United States must fight to avert greater moral and geopolitical evils.

Conversely, the Obama Doctrine unwisely abandons the venerable tradition of muscular internationalism emblematic of Reagan, Truman, Eisenhower, Kennedy, Johnson, and both Bushes. Even the grand strategy of the Clinton administration looks robust and highly successful by comparison to Obama's, especially during President Clinton's second term, when he increasingly embraced the idea of America as the indispensable nation. Robert Kaplan sums up well the importance of American global leadership, American military primacy, and what the world stands to lose if the United States relinquishes its role as the world's default power:

> Because the United States dominates the Western Hemisphere and has power to spare to affect the balance of power in the Eastern Hemisphere, the U.S. not only keeps the peace (aside from small wars that erupt here and there), it guards the global commons, that is, the sea lines of communication that allow for international trade. Without the U.S. Navy and Air Force, globalization as we know it would be impossible. The fact that Russia is still constrained in its attempts to seriously undermine the sovereignty of states in Eastern and Central Europe; the fact that the Middle East has so far at least avoided an interstate Holocaust of sorts; the fact that India and Pakistan have not engaged in a full-scale war in decades, and have never used their nuclear weapons; the fact that North Korea merely threatens South Korea and Japan with large-scale military aggression rather than actually carrying it out, is all in large measure because of a U.S. global

security umbrella. The fact that small and embattled nations, be it Israel or Georgia, can even exist is because of what ultimately the U.S. military provides. Indeed, it is the deployment of American air and naval platforms worldwide that gives American diplomacy much of its signal heft, which it then uses to support democracy and freer societies everywhere.[24]

Without American military primacy and forward presence, the world will become a much more dangerous place; life in many places will be more nasty, more solitary, more brutish, and more short. Yet President Obama has doubled down on his gamble of abandoning America's pivotal role as the world's default power. American power and influence have eroded correspondingly, lowering the barriers to aggression in Europe, Asia, and the Middle East. The Obama Doctrine exalts restraint and multilateralism, defines American interests narrowly, and counts more on American soft power than on the hard power that the president's massive defense cuts have diminished. Since 2009 the United States and our democratic allies have experienced merely a foretaste of much worse to come unless and until the president or his successor repudiates the doctrine that has driven his grand strategy through the midterm elections of 2014, when his party suffered a resounding defeat. Aristotle held prudence—or practical wisdom—as the paramount virtue for a statesman. Prudence entails choosing right ends and the right means to achieve them.[25] Consider the Obama Doctrine a failure on both counts. The gathering dangers to the United States and the costs and risk of surmounting them will mount steeply and inexorably until the Obama administration ceases to do what it is still doing now.

Epilogue

Since the midterm elections of 2014, we have witnessed a precipitous rise in the global turmoil that the first six years of the Obama Doctrine has mightily and negatively encouraged. General Martin Dempsey, President Obama's own chairman of the Joint Chiefs of Staff until September 2015, has joined the burgeoning chorus sounding the alarm that "the global security environment" has become more dangerous.[1] Undaunted, the president remains preternaturally confident in his grand strategy, calling for engaging adversaries, distancing the United States from its most stalwart democratic friends, shrinking American hard power, and relying instead on soft power and the "international community" embodied in multilateral institutions such as the United Nations. President Obama has defiantly doubled down on these main features of the Obama Doctrine amid escalating Islamist terror, including a resurgent al-Qaeda, which the administration previously claimed to have defeated, growing strife across the Middle East and in Ukraine, and an eroding American military advantage in East Asia as China's ambitions swell and its prodigious military buildup accelerates. The administration's *National Security Strategy* issued in February 2015 constitutes a veritable Obama Doctrine 2.0: ignoring rather than heeding the existence of, much less the danger emanating from, radical Islam of any variety; rating climate change as a graver threat than China, Putin's Russia, or a revolutionary, militant, theocratic Iran; welcoming the emergence of rising powers; and boasting of the administration's success in bringing "most of our troops home" from Iraq.[2]

The president continues to expand voraciously the entitlement state while according low priority to national defense. His proposed defense budget of $534 billion for fiscal year 2016 exceeds by only $38 billion the spending caps mandated by the sequestration formula he previously championed and Congress unwisely imposed. This nominal increase falls well short of the $638 billion defense budget that the National Defense Panel recommends as the bare minimum for expediting full readiness, reversing precipitous cuts in American military forces that have occurred under the Obama administration, and significantly boosting investment in force modernization, including research and development of cutting-edge weapons systems such as missile defense—programs that have languished under President Obama.[3] According to administration officials, Obama's defense budget reflects "the fiscal reality of government austerity and the political reality of a president who pledged to end two costly and exhausting land wars. The result . . . will be a military that continues to be capable of defeating any adversary but is too small for protracted foreign occupations."[4]

Nor are even these nominal increases a sure thing. Less dovish Democrats and hawkish Republicans have expressed their considerable doubts about whether the president will truly fight hard for more defense spending under any circumstances. Wager heavily on the president's rejecting any major increase in military spending that involves curtailing his cherished domestic agenda. Wager heavily, too, on the Republicans' rejecting any major increases in taxes and domestic spending in exchange for a major boost in defense spending even were President Obama truly amenable to such a compromise.[5]

The Obama administration's defense program continues, therefore, to exacerbate the adverse trends widening the gulf between American capabilities and commitments. In East Asia, especially, the cumulative effects of Obama's shrinking defense budgets render more hollow by the day the already tenuous credibility of his Asia pivot, thereby demoralizing America's increasingly fearful allies in the region, emboldening an increasingly repressive, belligerent, expansionist Chinese regime striving for hegemony rather than stability. The Chinese also have accelerated their campaign to supplant the dollar as the world's dominant reserve currency. In April 2015 China took a major step in that direction when the European members of the International Monetary Fund (IMF) embraced China's demand to include the yuan as a unit of IMF currency.[6] Likewise, China has implacably accelerated its island-building program on disputed islands in the South China Sea, in violation of the legitimate claims of the Philippines, Vietnam, Malaysia, and Brunei.[7]

Neither the president's unexpected but welcome rapport with Indian

Prime Minister Modi, manifest during the president's January 2015 visit to India, nor his April 2015 summit with Prime Minister Abe of Japan has sufficed to reverse the Obama Doctrine's perilous trajectory, which is likely to lower the barriers to aggression in the world's most important geopolitical region for the twenty-first century. Instead, the president's 2015 *National Security Strategy* depicts India primarily as a diplomatic partner, not a potential democratic counterweight to an authoritarian and arrogant China, whose rise the administration still intends to facilitate by engagement rather than containment.[8] Alas, the April 2015 summit between Obama and Japanese Prime Minister Abe yielded nothing more than increasingly hollow American rhetorical assurances of America's ongoing commitment to Japan.[9] As Aaron Friedberg observed in May 2015, China has become "even more repressive and more nationalistic than it was only a few years ago." Meanwhile, Friedberg warns, "the Obama administration's loudly proclaimed pivot has not stopped a serious, ongoing erosion in the American position in East Asia."[10]

Nor since the midterm elections of 2014 has the Obama administration or Western Europe roused themselves to hold an increasingly brazen Putin accountable for Russia's marching uninhibited into Ukraine, intensifying pressure on the Baltic states and Moldova, and escalating military maneuvers to intimidate NATO into acquiescence.[11] In the Middle East, Putin has added injury to insult, sanctioning a deal with Iran that provides the regime Russian antiaircraft missiles, thereby raising the prospective cost and risk of any strike against the Iranian nuclear program.[12]

Even so, President Obama still refuses to arm the legitimate government of Ukraine in its epic struggle to defend itself despite mounting support even in his own dovish administration to do so. Moreover, he and his secretary of state, John Kerry, still delude themselves that diplomacy and soft power can induce Putin to relinquish his imperial ambitions. In May 2015 Kerry met with Putin in Sochi, dangling the possibility of easing sanctions on Russia in exchange for nominal Russian adherence to yet another counterfeit ceasefire (the Minsk Agreement) that will provide cover for relentless Russian aggression against the legitimate Ukrainian government.[13] As Anne Applebaum observes mordantly, the president has virtually reversed the role the United States played during the 1980s, when it revived American power, spread freedom, and broke the evil empire: "The Soviet leadership was terrified that a cowboy in the White House—

someone who was so nutty he made jokes about signing 'legislation that would outlaw Russia forever'—might just flip a switch and send a missile. Nowadays, it's we who fear the madmen in foreign capitals, while our own large nuclear arsenal goes unmentioned and unacknowledged by a Western political class that is frankly embarrassed that it still exists. And this, paradoxically, is very dangerous."[14]

Deploring the administration's naïveté and passivity on moral and strategic grounds, Senator John McCain rightly declared himself "ashamed" of President Obama for not arming Ukraine's military and for legitimizing "the dismemberment of a country in Europe. . . . Vladimir Putin wants Ukraine not to be part of Europe. And he is succeeding in doing so. He's put enormous pressure on the Baltics, not to mention Moldova and continued occupation of Georgia as well. This is really a dark chapter in the history of our [NATO] alliance."[15] Likewise, more American generals also have challenged Obama's sanguine view of Putin, joining the ranks of those such as former governor Mitt Romney who proclaim Russia to be the greatest threat to U.S. national security. Add to that list Marine Corp General Joseph Dunford, the chairman of the Joint Chiefs of Staff who succeeded Dempsey, and General Paul Selva, vice chairman of the JCS, in their confirmation hearings before Congress in July 2015.[16] Both identified Russia as a major enemy rather than the partner for peace President Obama still envisages it to be.

Since the midterm elections of 2014, the turmoil roiling the Middle East has escalated. Egyptian President Fattah el-Sisi warned in March 2015 that his country is on the brink of collapse. Though the president has finally resumed arms sales to the Egyptian military after an ill-advised embargo, President Sisi remains deeply apprehensive toward the administration's policies on a number of counts. He continues to assail the president for failing to understand either Egypt's predicament or the virulence of Islamist extremism threatening the entire region.[17] Likewise, Jordan has become increasingly apprehensive about the surge in the numbers of Hezbollah terrorists—surrogates of Iran—threatening just across the border in Syria.[18] Islamist terror is also on the rise throughout the region. Major attacks occurred during the early months of 2015 in Tunisia (which the president and others touted as the Arab Spring's great success) and Yemen (which the president lauded as the model for effective U.S. counterterrorism policy). Even so, the Obama administration continues willfully to downplay any Islamist dimension to this surge of violence or ISIS's ruthless determination to establish a militant Sunni Islamist state across wide swaths of Syria and Iraq.[19] Even Iranian-backed al-Qaeda has largely recovered from its earlier partial defeat and resumed terrorist activities across the Arabian Peninsula, including a July 2015 attack on the Turkish-Syrian border that killed more than thirty and wounded hundreds more.[20] All this belies President Obama's premature claim of its demise.[21]

As sceptics predicted, moreover, the president's calibrated and limited use of force against ISIS—restricting American troops to a support rather than combat role and relying on local forces in the region to do the fighting on the ground—has proved woefully insufficient to defeat ISIS. Worse, Iran has emerged as the chief beneficiary of this desultory strategy, filling the vacuum that the Obama administration's premature withdrawal from Iraq has created, snatching defeat from the jaws of victory. As the former army chief of staff Ray Odierno testified in his exit interview in July 2015, the Obama administration could have prevented ISIS's rise most effectively not by making a devil's bargain with Iran but by leaving 30,000 to 35,000 American troops in Iraq and remaining "engaged" there—wise recommendations the president did not follow.[22]

Instead, the administration has fecklessly encouraged Iran to take over much of the ground fighting against ISIS in Iraq, deploying advanced rockets, missiles, and artillery.[23] The Obama administration also views Syria as part of Iran's sphere of influence, thereby reneging on the president's previous vow that Assad had to go following his 2013 use of chemical weapons against his own population and crossing the president's now-vanished red line.[24] General David Petraeus offers a devastating critique of the president's determination to pursue détente with Iran in complete defiance of our compelling moral, as well as geopolitical, interests. He warns that Iran—not ISIS—is our biggest problem in the Middle East:

> The current Iranian regime is not our ally. . . . It is ultimately part of the problem, not the solution. The more the Iranians are seen to be dominating the region, the more it is going to inflame Sunni radicalism and fuel the rise of groups like the Islamic State. . . . Iranian power in the Middle East is thus a double problem. It is foremost problematic because it is deeply hostile to us and our

friends. But it is also dangerous because, the more it is felt, the more it sets off reactions that are also harmful to our interests— Sunni radicalism and, if we aren't careful, the prospect of nuclear proliferation as well.[25]

Walter Russell Mead hits the mark squarely, drawing this unfavorable comparison between Captain Ahab in Melville's *Moby-Dick* and President Obama when it comes to Obama's obsession with reaching a nuclear arms accord with Iran—the centerpiece of his ill-conceived, ill-fated policy of transforming Iran from an adversary into a strategic partner: "President Obama perseveres, convinced that everyone will thank him when the Great White Whale of Middle East policy—a lasting nuclear deal with Iran—is finally harpooned. But as the endgame draws nigh, a unified chorus of naysayers is rising in volume."[26]

The swelling ranks of these naysayers span a wide spectrum: the forty-seven Republican senators who signed Senator Tom Cotton's March 2015 Open Letter to the Iranian Congress; virtually the entire cadre of major Republican presidential candidates for 2016, save Rand Paul; some hawkish Democrats; Israeli Prime Minister Benjamin Netanyahu, who accepted, over Obama's ferocious objection, Speaker of the House John Boehner's invitation to deliver a Churchillian address warning of the perils of the impending nuclear deal with Iran; and Sunni Arab regimes such as Saudi Arabia—heartily in agreement with Netanyahu on this point and threatening to build a nuclear capability of their own in response. In May 2015 Saudi King Salman declined to attend meetings at the White House with Obama or the Camp David Summit as a signal of increasing "displeasure with the administration" over Iran and other matters, according to Helene Cooper reporting in the *New York Times*.[27]

Count this writer among the ranks of the naysayers. Charles Krauthammer rightly assails the nuclear agreement with Iran as an "epic capitulation" that makes President Obama's policies toward Cuba and Ukraine look brilliantly successful by comparison. Alas, the nuclear agreement confirms the worst fears of President Obama's critics. The administration has settled on a bad deal that will facilitate Iran's eventually crossing the nuclear threshold even in the unlikely event that the notoriously mendacious Iranian regime abides by it.[28] By the terms of the 109-page agreement, Iran will retain its basic nuclear infrastructure. After fifteen years of the agreement, all limits expire on Iran's right to produce nuclear fuel. After eight years of the agreement, all limits expire on Iran's prerogative to conduct research on advanced centrifuges. Iran will retain more than five thousand centrifuges and three hundred kilograms of low-enriched uranium. Even by the most favorable estimates, Iran's breakout time of one year will diminish steadily to zero under the fifteen-year duration of the agreement.[29]

Throughout, the Obama administration has routinely capitulated to Iran on all the major issues, abandoning its initial insistence that Iran dismantle all its enrichment facilities and terminate all activities related to building nuclear weapons. Iran will not only keep its entire nuclear infrastructure, but also receive hundreds of billions of dollars of sanctions relief for its hard-pressed economy in exchange for these counterfeit restrictions on its nuclear program. The agreement imposes no limits whatsoever on the Iranian regime's use of this huge cash infusion to intensify its relentless campaign to menace Israel and Iran's Sunni Arab neighbors. On the contrary, the agreement will lift the arms embargo on missiles in eight years, on conventional weapons in five years, and on both types of weapons even sooner once the International Atomic Energy Agency deems Iran's program entirely peaceful and the regime fully in compliance with its provisions.[30]

Even the stalwartly pro-Obama Tom Friedman, writing in the *New York Times,* concedes in his tepid defense of the agreement that "it is stunning . . . how well the Iranians, sitting alone on their side of the table, have played a weak hand against the United States, Russia, China, France, Germany and Britain on their side of the table. When the time comes, I'm hiring Ali Khamenei to sell my house. . . . When you signal to the guy on the other side of the table that you're not willing to either blow him up or blow him off—to get up and walk away—you reduce yourself to just an equal and get the best bad deal nonviolence can buy."[31]

The nuclear deal with Iran is also unverifiable. Iran still refuses to concede to the IAEA unrestricted access to any and all aspects of the Iranian nuclear program—which is critical in light of the high stakes of failing to detect violations and the Iranian regime's dismal record on transparency and compliance. It does not reassure, moreover, that Putin's Russia—of all places—will hold the bulk of Iran's enriched uranium—theoretically 98 percent of its stockpile—which Iran must divest under the agreement.

Nor is the Iran deal enforceable, even if the verification scheme operates in a timely and effective way to expose Iranian noncompliance. Consider, for example, the gridlock inherent in the so-called snap-back provision, which reimposes sanctions if an eight-nation panel agrees that Iran has violated the nuclear provisions. What is the likelihood that the panel members—Britain, China, France, Russia, Germany, the United States, and the European Union—will agree to that? The autocrats in Beijing and a virulently anti-American, dangerously expansionist Putin have consistently acted as Iran's lawyers during the negotiations, lobbying for an immediate lifting of the sanctions, which will immensely profit the Russian arms industry eager to sell to the Iranian regime hundreds of billions of dollars in weapons and secure access to Iranian oil for the voraciously energy-dependent Chinese. It beggars belief that either Putin or China's dictators will ever countenance snapping back the sanctions on Iran once the agreement improvidently lifts them.

Worst of all, the nuclear agreement with Iran distills the essence of an Obama Doctrine that has assaulted the moral legitimacy of American power and its material basis, emboldened American adversaries everywhere, and imperiled America's traditional democratic allies. Ultimately, the nuclear agreement that Obama heralds as a geopolitical triumph akin to Nixon's opening to China will have the opposite result, triggering an unbridled nuclear arms race in the world's most violent and volatile geopolitical regions. In all likelihood, the Iranian regime—like North Korea during the 1990s—will use the agreement to wage war by other means, gulling the West into a false sense of security while steadily proceeding to achieve a nuclear breakout capability.

Henry Kissinger and George Schultz predict chillingly: "America's traditional allies will conclude that the U.S. has traded temporary nuclear cooperation for acquiescence to Iranian hegemony. They will increasingly look to create their own nuclear balances and, if necessary, call in other powers to sustain their integrity. Does America still hope to arrest the region's trends toward sectarian upheaval, state collapse, and the disequilibrium of power tilting toward Tehran or do we not accept this as an irremediable aspect of the regional balance?"[32] Kissinger also assails as dangerous and false the analogy Obama and his defenders draw between their policy of rapprochement with Iran and Nixon's opening to China:

It has been argued that the new approach to U.S.–Iranian relations will develop out of the nuclear negotiations. . . . The example of America's relationship with China is often cited to this
effect, because it moved from hostility to mutual acceptance
and even cooperation in a relatively short period of time in the
1970s. . . . The comparison is not apt. China was facing forty-two
Soviet divisions on its northern border after a decade of escalating mutual hostility and Chinese internal turmoil. It had every
reason to explore an alternative international system in which to
anchor itself. No such incentive is self-evident in Iranian-Western
relations. In the past decade, Iran has witnessed the removal of
two of its most significant adversaries, the Taliban regime in
Afghanistan and Saddam Hussein's Iraq. . . . Two of its principal competitors for regional influence, Egypt and Saudi Arabia,
have been preoccupied by internal challenges even as Iran has
moved swiftly and apparently successfully to crush its internal
opposition following a 2009 pro-democracy uprising. Its leaders
have largely been welcomed into international respectability without committing to any major substantive changes in policy and
courted by Western companies for investment opportunities even
while sanctions are in place. Ironically, the rise of Sunni jihadism
along Iran's frontiers may produce second thoughts in Iran. But
it is equally plausible that Tehran regards the strategic landscape
as shifting in its favor and its revolutionary course as being vindicated. . . . Ayatollah Khamenei described the nuclear talks as part
of an eternal religious struggle in which negotiation was a form of
combat and compromise was forbidden.[33]

Recollecting his extensive April 2015 interview with President
Obama, Thomas Friedman identified engagement with former adversaries as a common denominator of the Obama Doctrine, not just with Iran
but also with other anti-American tyrannies such as Cuba, Myanmar, and
Venezuela. The president told Friedman that "engagement" with these
adversaries would serve America's interest "far better than endless sanctions and isolation."[34] Yet the mounting violence, chaos, and apprehension
among America's allies in the Middle East belie the president's optimism.
Instead, the flawed premises and faulty execution of the Obama Doctrine

have made a terrible and deteriorating situation worse. Since the president secured enough congressional support to implement his agreement with Iran, Iranian rhetoric and behavior have become increasingly provocative and belligerent, at home and in Syria.[35] Indeed, President Obama's feckless Syria policy has collapsed morally as well as geopolitically into catastrophe. Mocking the naive premises of the reset with Russia, which the president refuses to abandon, Putin has deployed Russian troops and airpower in Syria to bolster Assad, filling the vacuum that the Obama administration's precipitous strategic retreat has created. At this writing, not only have Russian planes commenced bombing the Syrian rebels, but Putin has warned the United States to keep its military aircraft out of Syrian airspace. Hundreds of thousands of Syrian refugees have fled the carnage, deluging not only the Middle East but also Western Europe, some of whom are clamoring for entry into the United States. Yet Obama persists in his failure to recognize that Russia and Iran constitute threats, not partners for peace, in Syria and elsewhere. Speaking at the United Nations General Assembly on September 27, 2015, President Obama surrealistically disparaged his critics, whose "notion of strength is . . . opposition to old enemies; perceived adversaries; a rising China; a resurgent Russia; a revolutionary Iran; or an Islam that is incompatible with peace."[36]

As the administration placates Iran, declares Cuba's tyrannical Castro no longer an enemy, takes Cuba off the terror sponsors list, and meets with Venezuela's virulently anti-American president, President Obama has ramped up his implacable campaign to put considerable distance between his administration and a decent, democratic, and unflaggingly pro-American Israel.[37] The contrast between Obama's accommodation of Iran and growing estrangement from Prime Minister Netanyahu encapsulates the perverse essence of the Obama Doctrine, which a lame-duck Obama can now indulge unconstrained by electoral calculations. Netanyahu's February 2015 speech to the U.S. Congress and his words on the campaign trail purportedly ruling out a Palestinian state stoked President Obama's deep dislike of and disagreements with Netanyahu that run back to the early days of his administration. President Obama seized on these statements as much as a pretext as a cause for considering not backing Israel at the United Nations, where Israel faces an implacable majority hostile to its very existence.[38] Senator Marco Rubio, Republican of Florida, called this unprecedented step—reflecting a blend of Obama's pique and policy preferences—a "historic and tragic mistake" that will embolden Israel's enemies and undermine America's interests.[39] Without the liberal use of the American veto, Israel's mortal enemies will ostracize the Jewish state at the UN the way the UN more legitimately succeeded during the 1980s in delegitimizing South Africa until the apartheid regime collapsed. The United States will purchase neither peace nor honor by facilitating this grossly unjust outcome, as the Obama administration is evidently preparing to do.

The United States and our democratic allies will pay dearly for the staggering toll the Obama Doctrine has taken on American credibility, capabilities, and resolve. As Senator Rubio put it in his May 13 address to the Council on Foreign Relations:

[President Obama] entered office believing America was too hard on our adversaries, too engaged in too many places. . . . He enacted hundreds of billions of dollars in defense cuts that left our Army on track to be at pre–World War Two levels, our Navy at pre–World War One levels, and our Air Force with the smallest and oldest combat force in its history. He demonstrated a disregard for our moral purpose that at times flirted with disdain. He criticized America for having arrogance and the audacity to dictate our terms to other nations. From his reset with Russia, to his open hand to Iran, to his unreciprocated opening to Cuba, he has embraced regimes that systematically oppose every principle our nation has long championed. The deterioration of our physical and ideological strength has led to a world far more dangerous than when President Obama entered office.[40]

No plausible hope exists that a president so deeply ideological as Obama will repent of and rectify his serial mistakes internationally or domestically. On the contrary, he is, in the words of Bret Stephens, the unteachable president, dogmatic in his defense of his untenable doctrine.[41] Accordingly, Obama, brimming with self-assurance, defended his most controversial policies in an extended interview with Jeffery Goldberg published in the *Atlantic* on May 21. "Look. . . . It's my name on this," the president told Goldberg, defending his nuclear deal with Iran and its dubious underlying assumptions that the Iranian regime will abide by it and calculate risk rationally.[42] Although acknowledging the virulent anti-Semitism of the Iranian regime, Obama defanged and relativized its significance: "The fact that you are anti-Semitic, or racist, doesn't preclude you from being interested in survival. It doesn't preclude you from being rational about the need to keep your economy afloat. It doesn't preclude you from making strategic decisions about how you stay in power; and so the fact that the supreme leader is anti-Semitic doesn't mean that this overrides all of his other considerations." Indeed, the president appeared to suggest nonsensically that Iranian anti-Semitism was not all that different from or more debilitating than what the United States experienced in earlier, less enlightened periods of our history: "You know, if you look at the history of anti-Semitism, Jeff, there were a whole lot of European leaders—and there were deep strains of anti-Semitism in this country." The president downplayed, too, the danger of either the Saudis or the other Gulf States responding by pursuing the nuclear option themselves. "The protection that we provide as their partner is a far greater deterrent than they could ever hope to achieve by developing their nuclear stockpile."[43]

Disregarding the compelling evidence that the administration snatched defeat from the jaws of victory by withdrawing from Iraq, the president remains adamant "on the lessons of Iraq," which he continues to invoke as justification for his categorical refusal to employ decisive force against ISIS: "I think it was a mistake for us to go in in the first place. . . . Despite that error, those sacrifices allowed the Iraqis to take back their country. That opportunity was squandered by Prime Minister Maliki and the unwillingness to reach out effectively to the Sunni and Kurdish populations. . . . I know that there are some in Republican quarters who have suggested that I've overlearned the mistake of Iraq, and that, in fact, just because the 2003 invasion did not go well doesn't argue that we shouldn't go back in. And one lesson . . . to draw from what happened is that if the Iraqis themselves are not willing or capable to arrive at the political accommodations necessary to govern, if they are not willing to fight for the security of their country, we cannot do that for them."[44]

Nor is Hillary Clinton the answer to what ails American foreign policy. On the contrary, she served loyally as Obama's first mate on the *Titanic* of his foreign policy before expediently and untenably disavowing her responsibilities for Obama's policies, which she actively supported when it counted. Secretary Clinton has remained silent on Obama's threats to Israel, his unwillingness to arm Ukraine, his program to down-size the American military, his enthusiasm for détente with Iran, and his indefatigable policy of conciliating rather than containing China.[45] Or to quote Senator Rubio's trenchant assessment of Hillary Clinton's deficiencies as a candidate for commander in chief: "We simply cannot afford to elect as our next president one of the leading agents of this administration's foreign policy . . . whose tenure as secretary of state was ineffective at best, and dangerously negligent at worst."[46]

It will take decades, as well as a series of Republican presidents in the hawkish internationalist tradition, to restore the American power and prestige that the Obama Doctrine has so imprudently squandered. The world will probably become a more dangerous place in the final months of an Obama administration obsessed with its Great White Whale of protecting the world from the arrogance of American power rather than the threats emanating from enemies who despise us for who we are, not for what we do. Senator Lindsey Graham furnishes at least some grounds for optimism, detecting that Congress has already begun to show salutary signs of forging a bipartisan foreign policy that embraces rather than recoils from discharging America's global responsibilities.[47] For the remainder of the Obama presidency, however—indeed until Americans choose their presidents more wisely—this potentially encouraging development will have limited positive effect. Americans must cling to the hope until Obama goes that there is considerable truth in the adage attributed to Otto von Bismarck: God protects children, drunkards, and the United States. For peril and woe will eventually befall the United States and our democratic allies unless Obama's successors repudiate and reverse what the imprudence of the Obama Doctrine has wrought.

Acknowledgments

I owe an enormous debt to the friends, family members, and colleagues who facilitated my writing this book. Their critical advice and support improved it immensely. Responsibility for any of the book's shortcomings belongs to me alone.

Special thanks go to Karen Elliot House, Victor Davis Hanson, Joseph Collins, and Michael G. Franc for commenting promptly, sympathetically, and incisively on the manuscript. Erin Rodewald, my intrepid research assistant, did a masterful job throughout the process, editing, researching, and offering invaluable suggestions for refining and clarifying my arguments. She displayed near saintly forbearance as she cheerfully, patiently, and expeditiously accommodated my incessant requests for more research and rapid turnarounds of multiple revisions of the manuscript.

It was a pleasure and an honor working again with the University Press of Kentucky. Special thanks go to the press's former director Steve Wrinn, its acquisitions editor Allison Webster, and its fine staff for making this project possible. Steve and Allison chose superb outside reviewers with impeccable credentials. This book benefited hugely from my reviewers' rigorous, balanced, and constructive assessment.

I also wish to acknowledge my boundless appreciation for the encouragement and joy the Boys from Hawthorne—especially Brian—have provided not only for this endeavor, but for all others. You have been my "friends now for so many years" and inspired me professionally to "be true to" my "school" so that "the bad guys know me and they leave me alone."

My family deserves the greatest thanks, starting with my parents, Morton and Dorothy Kaufman, and my sister, Dr. Julie Kaufman, for their magnanimous offer of assistance at a pivotal moment when they would have had ample justification to deny it. My parents instilled in me a passion for study, unstintingly supporting my academic endeavors for decades, including law school and graduate school in political science. My greatest thanks and appreciation go to my outstanding daughters— Caroline "Memphis Mel" Kaufman and Natalie "the Ritz" Kaufman— above all, for their love and devotion. I consider them my supreme earthly blessing not only because of the sterling content of their characters but also because of the boundless joy and laughter they continue to provide their old man. Hail Squanto.

Notes

Introduction

1. Ryan Lizza, "The Consequentialist: How the Arab Spring Remade Obama's Foreign Policy," *New Yorker,* May 2, 2011, www.newyorker.com/magazine/2011/05/02/the-consequentialist?currentPage=all.

2. Fareed Zakaria, "Stop Searching for an Obama Doctrine," *Washington Post,* July 6, 2011, www.washingtonpost.com/opinions/stop-searching-for-an-obama-doctrine/2011/07/06/gIQAQMmI1H_story.html.

3. David Remnick, "Going the Distance: On and Off the Road with Barack Obama," *New Yorker,* January 27, 2014, www.newyorker.com/magazine/2014/01/27/going-the-distance-2?currentPage=all.

4. Will Inboden, "Looking for an Obama Doctrine That Doesn't Exist," *Foreign Policy,* September 16, 2013, http://shadow.foreignpolicy.com/posts/2013/09/16/looking_for_an_obama_doctrine_that_doesnt_exist; and William C. Martel, "America's Grand Strategy Disaster," *National Interest,* June 9, 2014, http://nationalinterest.org/feature/americas-grand-strategy-disaster-10627.

5. Thomas L. Friedman, "Obama's Foreign Policy Book," *New York Times,* May 31, 2014, www.nytimes.com/2014/06/01/opinion/sunday/friedman-obamas-foreign-policy-book.html; E. J. Dionne, "Finding Strength in Restraint," *Commercial Appeal,* May 30, 2014, www.commercialappeal.com/news/e-j-dionne-why-restraint-makes-us-stronger; and Stephen Sestanovich, *Maximalist: America in the World from Truman to Obama* (New York: Alfred A. Knopf, 2014), 301–24.

6. Walter Russell Mead, "The President's Foreign Policy Paradox," *Wall Street Journal,* March, 28, 2014, http://online.wsj.com/news/articles/SB10001424052702303725404579457950519734142.

7. Dinesh D'Souza, *The Roots of Obama's Rage* (New York: Regnery Publishing, 2011); and Dinesh D'Souza, *Obama's America: Unmaking the American Dream* (New York: Regnery Publishing, 2012).

8. Bob Woodward, *Obama's Wars* (New York: Simon and Schuster, 2010); Robert M. Gates, *Duty: Memoirs of a Secretary at War* (New York: Alfred A. Knopf, 2014). For all their difference, both authors state without equivocation that President Obama largely acts as his own secretary of state and almost always gets his way within his administration. See also James Mann, *The Obamians: The Struggle inside the White House to Redefine American Power* (New York: Viking, 2012).

9. William A. Galston, "The Big 2016 Foreign Policy Debates: Rand

Paul Will Fight GOP Hawks, and Joe Biden Could Run to the Left of Hillary Clinton," *Wall Street Journal,* July 22, 2014, http://online.wsj.com/articles/william-a-galston-the-big-2016-foreign-policy-debates-1406071181.

10. Gates, *Duty,* 566–67; and Leon Panetta, with Jim Newton, *Worthy Fights: A Memoir of Leadership in War and Peace* (New York: Penguin Press, 2014), 442–43.

11. Josh Rogin, "A Foreign Policy Shakeup at the White House," *Daily Beast,* June 5, 2013, http://thekojonnamdishow.org/shows/2013-06-05/a_foreign_policy_shakeup_at_the_white_house. Rogin, senior correspondent for national security and politics, provides an assessment of the shift in the White House foreign policy team.

12. Joshua Muravchik, "In the Cold War: Kerry Froze," *Los Angeles Times,* August 10, 2004, http://articles.latimes.com/2004/aug/10/opinion/oe-muravchik10.

13. Robert Kaufman, "We Can Do Better Than Hagel," *Orange County Register,* February 20, 2013, www.ocregister.com/articles/hagel-496467-obama-president.html.

14. Robert Burns, "Obama Picks Ashton Carter to Be Next Secretary of Defense," *PBS News Hour,* December 5, 2014, www.pbs.org/newshour/rundown/ashton-carter-announced-obamas-next-secretary-defense/.

15. Samantha Power, "Force Full: Bush's Illiberal Power," *New Republic,* March 3, 2003, www.newrepublic.com/article/srebenica-liberalism-balkan-united%20nations.

16. Mark Landler, "Obama Could Replace Aides Bruised by a Cascade of Crises," *New York Times,* October 29, 2014, www.nytimes.com/2014/10/30/world/middleeast/mounting-crises-raise-questions-on-capacity-of-obamas-team.html?_r=0.

17. Josef Joffe, *The Myth of America's Decline: Politics, Economics, and a Half Century of False Prophecies* (New York: Liveright, 2014), 246–60.

18. Stephen G. Brooks, G. John Ikenberry, and William C. Wohlforth, "Lean Forward: In Defense of American Engagement," *Foreign Affairs,* January/February 2013, www.foreignaffairs.com/articles/138468/stephen-g-brooks-g-john-ikenberry-and-william-c-wohlforth/lean-forward.

19. Barack Obama, *National Security Strategy,* February 2015, www.whitehouse.gov/sites/default/files/docs/2015_national_security_strategy.pdf.

1. The Main Tenets of the Obama Doctrine

1. James T. Kloppenberg, *Reading Obama: Dreams, Hope, and the American Political Tradition* (Princeton: Princeton University Press, 2010), 221. Kloppenberg is also a man of the left, criticizing the president on rare occasions for not being progressive enough. See also David Greenberg, "Hope, Change, Nietzsche," *New Republic,* May 26, 2011, www.newrepublic.com/book/review/reading-obama-james-kloppenberg.

2. Barack Obama, *The Audacity of Hope: Thoughts on Reclaiming the American Dream* (New York: Crown, 2006), 133.

3. Barack Obama, *Dreams from My Father: A Story of Race and Inheritance* (New York: Times Books, 1995), 289.

4. Quoted in Michael Duffy and Michael Scherer, "The Role Model: What Obama Sees in Reagan," *Time*, January 27, 2011, http://content.time.com/time/magazine/article/0,9171,2044712,00.html.

5. Obama, *Audacity of Hope*, 289.

6. Barack Obama, "Breaking the Cold War Mentality," *Sundial*, March 10, 1983, 1–3.

7. Barack Obama, "Against Going to War in Iraq," speech made at the Federal Plaza in Chicago, October 2, 2002, http://obamaspeeches.com/001-2002-Speech-Against-the-Iraq-War-Obama-Speech.htm.

8. Barack Obama, "Renewing American Leadership," *Foreign Affairs*, July/August 2007, www.foreignaffairs.com/articles/62636/barack-obama/renewing-american-leadership.

9. Elisabeth Bumiller, "A Cast of 300 Advises Obama on Foreign Policy," *New York Times*, July 18, 2008, www.nytimes.com/2008/07/18/us/politics/18advisers.html?pagewanted=all&_r=0.

10. Spencer Ackerman, "The Obama Doctrine," *American Prospect*, March 19, 2008, http://prospect.org/article/obama-doctrine.

11. Barack Obama, "Obama Flashback: The Day I'm Inaugurated Muslim Hostility Will Ease," New Hampshire Public Radio, November 21, 2007, www.breitbart.com/Breitbart-TV/2012/09/14/FLASHBACK-Obama-The-Day-Im-Inaugurated-Muslim-Hostility-Will-Ease.

12. Obama, "Renewing American Leadership."

13. Ibid.

14. See Jeffrey Bloodworth, *Losing the Center: The Decline of American Liberalism, 1968–1992* (Lexington: University Press of Kentucky, 2013); and Ronald Radosh, *Divided They Fell: The Demise of the Democratic Party, 1964–1996* (New York: Free Press, 1996), for example.

15. J. William Fulbright, *The Arrogance of Power* (New York: Random House, 1966).

16. Barack Obama, "Remarks by President Obama to the Turkish Parliament," Ankara, Turkey, April 6, 2009, www.whitehouse.gov/the_press_office/Remarks-By-President-Obama-To-The-Turkish-Parliament.

17. Barack Obama, "Remarks by the President on a New Beginning," Cairo University, Cairo, Egypt, June 4, 2009, www.whitehouse.gov/the_press_office/Remarks-by-the-President-at-Cairo-University-6-04-09.

18. Barack Obama, "Remarks by the President to the United Nations General Assembly," New York, September 23, 2009, www.whitehouse.gov/the-press-office/remarks-president-united-nations-general-assembly.

19. Barack Obama, "News Conference by President Obama," Strasbourg, France, April 4, 2009, www.whitehouse.gov/the-press-office/news-conference-president-obama-4042009.

20. Ibid.

21. Barack Obama, "Remarks by President Obama in Address to the United Nations General Assembly," New York, September 24, 2013, https://www.whitehouse.gov/the-press-office/2013/09/24/remarks-president-obama-address-united-nations-general-assembly.

22. Ryan Lizza, "The Consequentialist: How the Arab Spring Remade Obama's Foreign Policy," *New Yorker,* May 2, 2011, www.newyorker.com/magazine/2011/05/02/the-consequentialist.

23. David Remnick, "Going the Distance: On and Off the Road with Barack Obama," *New Yorker,* January 27, 2014, http://www.newyorker.com/magazine/2014/01/27/going-the-distance-2?currentPage=all.

24. Ray Takeyh, "What Really Happened in Iran: The CIA, the Ouster of Mosaddeq, and the Restoration of the Shah," *Foreign Affairs,* July/August 2014, 2–3, www.foreignaffairs.com/articles/middle-east/2014-06-16/what-really-happened-iran.

25. Obama, "Remarks by the President to the UN General Assembly," September 23, 2009.

26. Lizza, "The Consequentialist: How the Arab Spring Remade Obama's Foreign Policy."

27. Barack Obama, "Remarks by the President at the United States Military Academy Commencement Ceremony," West Point, N.Y., May 28, 2014, www.whitehouse.gov/the-press-office/2014/05/28/remarks-president-united-states-military-academy-commencement-ceremony.

28. Ibid.

29. Barack Obama, "Statement by the President on ISIL," September 10, 2014, www.whitehouse.gov/the-press-office/2014/09/10/statement-president-isil-1.

30. Jeffrey Goldberg, "Obama to Israel: Time Is Running Out," *BloombergView,* March 2, 2014, www.bloombergview.com/articles/2014-03-02/obama-to-israel-time-is-running-out.

31. Editorial Board, "Trouble at the Core of U.S. Foreign Policy," *Washington Post,* September 25, 2013, www.washingtonpost.com/opinions/trouble-at-the-core-of-us-foreign-policy/2013/09/25/b7d2652a-2608-11e3-b75d-5b7f66349852_story.html; and Joshua Muravchik, "The Abandonment of Democracy," *Commentary,* July 1, 2009, www.commentarymagazine.com/article/the-abandonment-of-democracy/. For a more favorable account of Obama's commitment to democracy—a view this author rejects—see Thomas Carothers, "Democratic Policy under Obama: Revitalization or Retreat?" Carnegie Endowment for International Peace, January 11, 2012, http://carnegieendowment.org/2012/01/11/democracy-policy-under-obama-revitalization-or-retreat.

32. Obama, "Remarks by President Obama in Address to the UN General Assembly," September 24, 2013.

33. Daniel Pipes, "There Are No Moderates: Dealing with Fundamentalist Islam," *National Interest,* Fall 1995, www.danielpipes.org/274/there-are-no-moderates-dealing-with-fundamentalist-islam.

34. "Terror Act or Workplace Violence? Hasan Trial Raises Sensitive Issues," *Arizona Daily Star,* August 11, 2013, http://archive.today/sNvP8.

35. Kenneth Timmerman, "The Real Questions about Benghazi," *Washington Times,* September 19, 2013, www.washingtontimes.com/news/2013/sep/19/timmerman-the-real-questions-about-benghazi/?page=all.

36. Michael Hirsh, "The Boko Haram–Benghazi Link," *Politico Magazine,* May 12, 2014, www.politico.com/magazine/story/2014/05/the-boko-haram-benghazi-link-106583.html#.U9HSDKhvvRw.

37. Josh Rogin, "Hillary's State Department Refused to Brand Boko Haram as Terrorists," *Daily Beast,* May 7, 2014, www.thedailybeast.com/articles/2014/05/07/hillary-s-state-department-refused-to-brand-boko-haram-as-terrorists.html.

38. Matthew Yglesias, "Obama: The Vox Conversation, Part Two: Foreign Policy," *Vox,* January 23, 2015, www.vox.com/a/barack-obama-interview-vox-conversation/obama-foreign-policy-transcript.

39. Barack Obama, "Remarks by the President at the Acceptance of the Nobel Peace Prize," Oslo, Norway, December 10, 2009, www.whitehouse.gov/the-press-office/remarks-president-acceptance-nobel-peace-prize.

40. Anthony Cordesman, quoted in Kathleen Hennessey and Christi Parsons, "Obama's Mideast Airstrike Refrain: And Then What?" *Los Angeles Times,* June 19, 2014, www.latimes.com/world/middleeast/la-fg-obama-iraq-20140619-story.html#page=1.

41. Martin S. Indyk, Kenneth G. Lieberthal, and Michael E. O'Hanlon, *Bending History: Barack Obama's Foreign Policy* (Washington, D.C.: Brookings Institution Press, 2012), 70–71.

42. Julianne Smith, quoted in Hennessey and Parsons, "Obama's Mideast Airstrike Refrain."

43. Barack Obama, "Statement by the President on Syria," August 31, 2013, www.whitehouse.gov/the-press-office/2013/08/31/statement-president-syria.

44. Barack Obama, "Remarks by the President in Address to the Nation on Syria," White House, September 10, 2013, www.whitehouse.gov/the-press-office/2013/09/10/remarks-president-address-nation-syria.

45. For the most crystalline statement of the spiral model, see Robert Jervis, *Perception and Misperception in International Politics* (Princeton: Princeton University Press, 1976), 58–113. For the classic statement of the neoconservative version of the deterrence model, which this writer finds more compelling than any alternative, see Donald Kagan, *On the Origins of War and the Preservation of Peace* (New York: Doubleday, 1995).

46. Obama, "Remarks by the President at the United States Military Academy," May 28, 2014.

47. Lizza, "The Consequentialist: How the Arab Spring Remade Obama's Foreign Policy."

48. Thomas Wright, "Four Disappointments in Obama's West Point Speech," *Brookings,* May 28, 2014, www.brookings.edu/blogs/up-front/posts/2014/05/28-four-disappointments-obama-west-point-speech-wright.

49. Obama, "Remarks by the President at the United States Military Academy," May 28, 2014.

50. President of the United States, *National Security Strategy,* May 2010, www. whitehouse.gov/sites/default/files/rss_viewer/national_security_strategy.pdf, 18.

51. Ibid.

52. Obama, "Remarks by the President at the United States Military Academy," May 28, 2014.

53. Barack Obama, "Remarks by President Barack Obama in Prague as Delivered," Prague, Czech Republic, April 5, 2009, www.whitehouse.gov/the_press_office/ Remarks-By-President-Barack-Obama-In-Prague-As-Delivered.

54. Ibid.

55. *National Security Strategy,* May 2010, 47.

56. Barack Obama, "Remarks by President Obama at the League of Conservation Voters Capital Dinner," Washington, D.C., June 25, 2014, www.whitehouse.gov/ the-press-office/2014/06/25/remarks-president-league-conservation-voters-capital-dinner.

57. Dave Rochelson, "President-Elect Obama Promises 'New Chapter' on Climate Change," Change.Gov: The Office of the President Elect, November 18, 2008, http://change. gov/newsroom/entry/president_elect_obama_promises_new_chapter_on_climate_change/.

58. Heather Smith, "Obama's Green Record: Some Small Victories, One Gaping Flop," *Grist,* December 20, 2013, http://grist.org/climate-energy/obamas-green-record-some-small-victories-one-gaping-flop/.

59. Coral Davenport, "President Said to Be Planning to Use Executive Authority on Carbon Rule," *New York Times,* May 28, 2014, www.nytimes.com/2014/05/29/ us/politics/obama-to-offer-rules-to-sharply-curb-power-plants-carbon-emissions. html?_r=0.

60. Barack Obama, "Remarks by the President at the Morning Plenary Session of the United Nations Climate Change Conference," Copenhagen, Denmark, December 18, 2009, www.whitehouse.gov/the-press-office/remarks-president-morning-plenary-session-united-nations-climate-change-conference.

61. *National Security Strategy,* May 2010, 1–10.

62. Thom Shanker and Helene Cooper, "Pentagon Plans to Shrink Army to Pre–World War II Level," *New York Times,* February 23, 2014, www.nytimes. com/2014/02/24/us/politics/pentagon-plans-to-shrink-army-to-pre-world-war-ii-level.html; see also Colin Dueck, *The Obama Doctrine: American Grand Strategy Today* (New York: Oxford University Press, 2015), for a fine analysis of the Obama Doctrine, which came out after this author submitted this manuscript for review. Dueck emphasizes the domestic determinants more than this author does, whereas this book emphasizes the ideological wellspring of the Obama Doctrine from the standpoint of foreign policy. The two approaches are complementary and compatible in many respects.

63. U.S. Department of Defense, "Remarks by Secretary Hagel and Gen. Dempsey on the Fiscal Year 2015 Budget Preview in the Pentagon Briefing Room," http://archive.defense.gov/Transcripts/Transcript.aspx?TranscriptID=5377.

64. Bob Woodward, *The Price of Politics* (New York: Simon and Schuster, 2012), offers a definitive account of how the Obama administration conceived of the sequester and devised it to fall more heavily on defense than domestic spending.

65. Clark A. Murdock, Ryan Crotty, and Angela Weaver, *Building the 2021 Affordable Military* (Lanham, Md.: Rowman and Littlefield, 2014), 4.

66. Seth Cropsey, "Don't Bury the Tomahawk," *Real Clear Defense*, March 30, 2014, www.realcleardefense.com/articles/2014/03/30/dont_bury_the_tomahawk_107160-comments.html.

67. Mackenzie Eaglen, "Defense in Decline," *US News & World Report*, July 8, 2014, www.usnews.com/opinion/blogs/world-report/2014/07/08/us-cuts-defense-budget-while-russia-and-china-spend-more; and Peter Apps, "U.S. Military to Face Growing Crises, Falling Budgets," *Reuters*, July 2, 2014, www.reuters.com/article/2014/07/02/us-usa-iraq-analysis-idUSKBN0F71VM20140702.

68. U.S. Department of Defense, "Sustaining U.S. Global Leadership: Priorities for 21st Century Defense," January 2012, www.defense.gov/news/defense_strategic_guidance.pdf.

69. U.S. Department of Defense, "Remarks by Hagel and Dempsey on Fiscal Year 2015 Budget Preview."

70. Department of Defense, "Chairman's Assessment of the Quadrennial Defense Review 2014," http://archive.defense.gov/pubs/2014_Quadrennial_Defense_Review.pdf, 62.

71. David Remnick, *The Bridge: The Life and Rise of Barack Obama* (New York: Alfred A. Knopf, 2010). For a more critical account of Obama's preternatural confidence, closer to this writer's view, see Elliott Abrams, "The Citizen of the World Presidency," *Commentary*, September 1, 2013, www.commentarymagazine.com/article/the-citizen-of-the-world-presidency-1/.

72. Hillary Clinton, quoted by Glenn Kessler, "Hillary Clinton's Uncredible Statement on Syria," *Washington Post*, April 4, 2011, www.washingtonpost.com/blogs/fact-checker/post/hillary-clintons-uncredible-statement-on-syria/2011/04/01/AFWPEYaC_blog.html.

73. Barack Obama, *National Security Strategy*, February 2015, www.whitehouse.gov/sites/default/files/docs/2015_national_security_strategy.pdf.

74. Barack Obama, "Remarks by the President in State of the Union Address," January 20, 2015, www.whitehouse.gov/the-press-office/2015/01/20/remarks-president-state-union-address-january-20-2015.

2. The Obama Doctrine and International Relations Theory

1. Fareed Zakaria, "Obama the Realist," *Newsweek*, December 4, 2009, www.newsweek.com/zakaria-obama-realist-75621.

2. For the quintessential statement of classical realism, see Edward Hallett Carr, *The Twenty Years' Crisis, 1919–1939: An Introduction to the Study of International Relations* (London: Macmillan, 1940); and Hans J. Morgenthau, *Politics*

among Nations: The Struggle for Power and Peace, 6th ed., rev. Kenneth Thompson (New York: Alfred A. Knopf, 1985). For the prototypical statement of neorealism, see Kenneth N. Waltz, *Theory of International Politics* (Reading, Mass.: Addison-Wesley, 1979).

3. George F. Kennan, *American Diplomacy, 1900–1950* (Chicago: University of Chicago Press, 1951).

4. George F. Kennan, *Realities of American Foreign Policy* (Princeton: Princeton University Press, 1954), 47.

5. Robert G. Kaufman, "E. H. Carr, Winston Churchill, Reinhold Niebuhr, and Us: The Case for Principled, Prudential Democratic Realism," *Security Studies* 5, no. 2 (December 1995): 314–53. Niebuhr argued against isolationism and for the moral superiority of democratic capitalism, took Communist and Nazi ideology seriously as the wellspring of those regimes' insatiable ambitions, and defended Churchill's defense of preemption under circumstances that inspired the Bush Doctrine that Bacevich excoriates.

6. Andrew J. Bacevich, *Washington Rules: America's Path to Permanent War* (New York: Metropolitan Books 2010).

7. Andrew J. Bacevich, "The Right Choice? The Conservative Case for Barack Obama," *American Conservative,* March 24, 2008, www.theamericanconservative.com/articles/the-right-choice/.

8. Peter Beinart, "The End of American Exceptionalism," *National Journal,* February 3, 2014, www.nationaljournal.com/magazine/the-end-of-american-exceptionalism-20140203.

9. Stephen M. Walt, "The Myth of American Exceptionalism," *Foreign Policy,* October 11, 2011, www.foreignpolicy.com/articles/2011/10/11/the_myth_of_american_exceptionalism.

10. John J. Mearsheimer, "Can China Rise Peacefully?" *National Interest,* October 25, 2014, http://nationalinterest.org/commentary/can-china-rise-peacefully-10204.

11. Edward V. Gulick, *Europe's Classical Balance of Power* (1955; repr., New York: W. W. Norton, 1967) Henry A. Kissinger, *A World Restored: Metternich, Castlereagh, and the Problem of Peace, 1812–22* (Boston: Houghton Mifflin, 1957).

12. Arnold Wolfers, *Discord and Collaboration: Essays on International Politics* (Baltimore: Johns Hopkins University Press, 1962), 181–204.

13. Randall L. Schweller, *Unanswered Threats: Political Constraints on the Balance of Power* (Princeton: Princeton University Press, 2006).

14. See Stephen M. Walt, *The Origins of Alliances* (Ithaca: Cornell University Press, 1987); and John Mearsheimer, *The Tragedy of Great Power Politics* (New York: W. W. Norton, 2001), for example.

15. Hans J. Morgenthau, *Scientific Man vs. Power Politics* (Chicago: University of Chicago Press, 1946), 8.

16. Ibid.

17. Mearsheimer, "Can China Rise Peacefully?"

18. Fareed Zakaria, "Realism and Domestic Politics: A Review Essay," *International Security* 17, no. 1 (Summer 1992): 177–98.

19. Randall L. Schweller, *Maxwell's Demon and the Golden Apple: Global Discord in the New Millennium* (Baltimore: Johns Hopkins University Press, 2014), 37–38.

20. See Richard N. Haass, *Foreign Policy Begins at Home: The Case for Putting America's House in Order* (New York: Basic Books, 2013); and Andrew J. Bacevich, *The Limits of Power: The End of American Exceptionalism* (New York: Metropolitan Books, 2008), for example.

21. Christopher Layne, "From Preponderance to Offshore Balancing: America's Future Grand Strategy," *International Security* 22, no. 1 (Summer 1997): 86–124; Stephen M. Walt, *Taming American Power: The Global Response to U.S. Primacy* (New York: W. W. Norton, 2005); and John Mearsheimer, "Rebalancing the Middle East," *Newsweek,* November 28, 2008, www.newsweek.com/john-mearsheimer-rebalancing-middle-east-85225.

22. Barry R. Posen, *Restraint: A New Foundation for U.S. Grand Strategy* (Ithaca: Cornell University Press, 2014), 24–68.

23. Ibid.

24. Halford J. Mackinder, *Democratic Ideals and Reality: A Study in the Politics of Reconstruction* (New York: Henry Holt, 1919).

25. Posen, *Restraint,* 69–71.

26. Owen Harries and Tom Switzer, "Leading from Behind: Third Time a Charm?" *American Interest,* April 12, 2013, www.the-american-interest.com/articles/2013/04/12/leading-from-behind-third-time-a-charm/.

27. Barry R. Posen, "We Can Live with a Nuclear Iran," *New York Times,* February 27, 2006, www.nytimes.com/2006/02/27/opinion/27posen.html?pagewanted=all&_r=0.

28. Kenneth N. Waltz, "Why Iran Should Get the Bomb: Nuclear Balancing Would Mean Stability," *Foreign Affairs,* July/August 2012, www.foreignaffairs.com/articles/137731/kenneth-n-waltz/why-iran-should-get-the-bomb.

29. Stephen M. Walt, "What's Really at Stake in the Iranian Nuclear Deal," *Foreign Policy,* November 25, 2013, www.foreignpolicy.com/posts/2013/11/25/iran_the_us_and_the_middle_east_balance_of_power.

30. Fareed Zakaria, *The Post-American World: Release 2.0* (New York: W. W. Norton, 2011).

31. Christopher Layne, "This Time It's Real: The End of Unipolarity and the Pax Americana," *International Studies Quarterly* 56, no. 1 (2012): 203–13.

32. For the extended version of this thesis, see Paul Kennedy, *The Rise and Fall of the Great Powers: Economic Change and Military Conflict from 1500 to 2000* (New York: Random House, 1987).

33. Joseph S. Nye Jr., *Soft Power: The Means to Success in World Politics* (New York: Public Affairs, 2004); and Joseph S. Nye Jr., *The Future of Power* (New York: Public Affairs, 2011).

34. Transcript, "Senate Confirmation Hearing: Hillary Clinton," *New York Times,* January 13, 2009, www.nytimes.com/2009/01/13/us/politics/13text-clinton.html?pagewanted=all&_r=0.

35. Robert Kaplan, "Obama's Foreign Policy Record, TBD," *Real Clear World,* August 14, 2014, www.realclearworld.com/articles/2014/08/14/obamas_foreign_policy_record_tbd.html.

36. Paul Saunder, "Obama Is Not a Realist," *National Interest,* August 26, 2014, www.nationalinterest.org/feature/barack-obama-not-realist-11124; also see, contra Saunder, Stephen M. Walt, "Is Barack Obama More of a Foreign Policy Realist Than I Am?" *Foreign Policy,* August 19, 2014, www.foreignpolicy.com/articles/2014/08/19/is_barack_obamamore_of_a_realist_than_i_am_stephen_m_walt_iraq_russia_gaza.

37. For a fine rendition of Tony Blair's muscular multilateralism, see Robert Cooper, *The Breaking of Nations: Order and Chaos in the Twenty-First Century* (New York: Atlantic Monthly Press, 2004).

38. For the theoretical pedigree of Obama's hope about international institutions perpetuating order even absent a dominant power that created them, see Robert O. Keohane, *After Hegemony: Cooperation and Discord in the World Political Economy* (Princeton: Princeton University Press 1984).

39. Obama, quoted in David Brooks, "Obama, Gospel and Verse," *New York Times,* April 26, 2007, www.nytimes.com/2007/04/26/opinion/26brooks.html.

40. Andrew J. Bacevich, *American Empire: The Realities and Consequences of U.S. Diplomacy* (Cambridge: Harvard University Press, 2002).

41. Barack Obama, "Remarks by the President at the Acceptance of the Nobel Peace Prize," Oslo, Norway, December 10, 2009, www.whitehouse.gov/the-press-office/remarks-president-acceptance-nobel-peace-prize.

42. Kaufman, "E. H. Carr, Winston Churchill, Reinhold Niebuhr, and Us," provides an extended analysis.

43. Reinhold Niebuhr, "Winston Churchill and Great Britain," in *A Reinhold Niebuhr Reader,* ed. Charles E. Brown (Philadelphia: Trinity Press, 1992), 90–92.

44. Reinhold Niebuhr, *Christianity and Power Politics* (New York: Scribner's, 1940).

45. Richard Wightman Fox, *Reinhold Niebuhr: A Biography* (New York: Pantheon, 1985), 224–48.

46. Reinhold Niebuhr, *The Children of Light and the Children of Darkness: A Vindication of Democracy and a Critique of Its Traditional Defense* (New York: Scribner's, 1940), xi–xii.

47. Reinhold Niebuhr, *Moral Man and Immoral Society: A Study in Ethics and Politics* (New York: Charles Scribner's Sons, 1932), 110.

48. Gustav Niebuhr and Elisabeth Sifton, "Why Reinhold Niebuhr Supported Israel," *Huffington Post,* May 7, 2014, www.huffingtonpost.com/gustav-niebuhr/why-reinhold-niebuhr-supp_b_5280958.html; and Carys Moseley, "Reinhold Niebuhr's Approach to the State of Israel: The Ethical Promise and Theological Limits of Christian Realism," *Studies in Christian-Jewish Relations* 4, no. 1 (2009), http://ejournals.bc.edu/ojs/index.php/scjr/article/view/1517/1370.

49. Reinhold Niebuhr, "Our Stake in Israel," *New Republic,* February 3, 1957, www.newrepublic.com/book/review/our-stake-in-the-state-israel.

50. Andrew J. Bacevich, "How We Became Israel," *American Conservative*, September 10, 2012, www.theamericanconservative.com/articles/how-we-became-israel/.

51. Josef Joffe, "The Unreality of Obama's Realpolitik," *Wall Street Journal*, February 2, 2015, www.wsj.com/articles/josef-joffe-the-unreality-of-obamas-realpolitik-1422923777.

3. The Obama Doctrine and Rival Traditions of American Diplomacy

1. Walter Russell Mead, *Special Providence: American Foreign Policy and How It Changed the World* (New York: Alfred A. Knopf, 2001).

2. Robert G. Kaufman, *In Defense of the Bush Doctrine* (Lexington: University Press of Kentucky, 2007); Robert G. Kaufman, "The First Principles of Ronald Reagan's Foreign Policy," *First Principles Series Report #40*, Heritage Foundation, November 1, 2011; Charles Krauthammer, *Democratic Realism: An American Foreign Policy for a Unipolar World* (Washington, D.C.: American Enterprise Institute Press, 2004); and George Weigel, *American Interests, American Purpose: Moral Reasoning and U.S. Foreign Policy* (New York: Praeger, 1989).

3. Henry Nau, *Conservative Internationalism: Armed Diplomacy under Jefferson, Polk, Truman, and Reagan* (Princeton: Princeton University Press, 2013), 11–60.

4. Stephen Sestanovich, *Maximalist: America in the World from Truman to Obama* (New York: Alfred A. Knopf, 2014), 3–13.

5. Colin Dueck, *Hard Line: The Republican Party and U.S. Foreign Policy since World War II* (Princeton: Princeton University Press, 2010), 303.

6. Robert G. Kaufman, "The Unrealistic Realism of Richard Nixon and Henry Kissinger," in *War, Justice and Peace in American Grand Strategy: From the Founding Era to the Twenty-First Century,* ed. Bryan-Paul Frost, Paul O. Carrese, and Stephen F. Knott (Baltimore: Johns Hopkins University Press, forthcoming).

7. Robert G. Kaufman, *Henry M. Jackson: A Life in Politics* (Seattle: University of Washington Press, 2000), 242–300.

8. Henry A. Kissinger, *Diplomacy* (New York: Simon and Schuster, 1994), 674–761.

9. Fareed Zakaria, "Obama's Disciplined Leadership Is Right for Today," *Washington Post,* May 29, 2014, www.washingtonpost.com/opinions/fareed-zakaria-obamas-disciplined-leadership-is-right-for-today/2014/05/29/7b4eb460-e76d-11e3-afc6-a1dd9407abcf_story.html.

10. Dueck, *Hard Line,* 85–116.

11. John Lewis Gaddis, *Strategies of Containment: A Critical Appraisal of American National Security Policy during the Cold War* (New York: Oxford University Press, 2005), 125–96.

12. Stephen A. Ambrose, *Eisenhower: Soldier and President* (New York: Simon and Schuster, 1991), 549–70.

13. Peter C. Bourne, *Jimmy Carter: A Comprehensive Biography from Plains to Post-Presidency* (New York: Scribner's, 1997), 385–86.

14. Kaufman, *Henry M. Jackson,* 350–53.

15. Patrick Glynn, *Closing Pandora's Box: Arms Races, Arms Control, and the History of the Cold War* (New York: Basic Books, 1992), 289; and Jeffrey Herf, *War by Other Means: Soviet Power, West German Resistance, and the Battle of the Euromissiles* (New York: Free Press, 1991), 45–66.

16. Zbigniew Brzezinski, *Power and Principle: Memoirs of the National Security Advisor, 1977–1981* (New York: Farrar, Straus & Giroux, 1983), 459.

17. Douglas Brinkley, *The Unfinished Presidency: Jimmy Carter's Quest for Global Peace* (New York: Viking, 1998), 99–123, 317–46.

18. William G. Hyland, *Clinton's World: Remaking American Foreign Policy* (Westport, Conn.: Praeger, 1999), 1–30, 109–27, 155–71.

19. Brinkley, *Unfinished Presidency,* 388–411.

20. Derek Chollet and James Goldgeier, *America between the Wars: From 11/9 to 9/11; The Misunderstood Years between the Fall of the Berlin Wall and the Start of the War on Terror* (New York: Public Affairs 2008), 64–65.

21. Sean Wilentz, *The Age of Reagan: A History, 1974–2008* (New York: Harper, 2008).

22. Thomas L. Friedman, "Clinton's Foreign Policy Agenda Reaches across Broad Spectrum," *New York Times,* October 4, 1992, www.nytimes.com/1992/10/04/us/1992-campaign-issues-foreign-policy-looking-abroad-clinton-foreign-policy.html.

23. Madeleine Albright, *Madam Secretary: A Memoir* (New York: Miramax Books, 2003), 224–44, 459–545.

24. Transcript, "President Clinton Explains Iraq Strike," CNN, December 16, 1998, www.cnn.com/ALLPOLITICS/stories/1998/12/16/transcripts/clinton.html.

25. Chollet and Goldgeier, *America between the Wars,* 67–71, 135–36.

26. Ruy Teixeira and John Halpin, "The Return of the Obama Coalition," Center for American Progress, November 8, 2012, www.americanprogress.org/issues/progressive-movement/news/2012/11/08/44348/the-return-of-the-obama-coalition/, provides a penetrating, favorable analysis of Obama's coalition and how it reflects deep changes in American politics.

27. Senator Joseph Lieberman, interview by the author, January 7, 2007.

28. Andrew Kohut, "Americans: Disengaged, Feeling Less Respected, but Still See U.S. as World's Military Superpower," Pew Research Center, April 1, 2014, www.pewresearch.org/fact-tank/2014/04/01/americans-disengaged-feeling-less-respected-but-still-see-u-s-as-worlds-military-superpower/.

29. "Public Sees U.S. Power Declining as Support for Global Engagement Slips," Pew Research Center, December 3, 2013, www.people-press.org/2013/12/03/public-sees-u-s-power-declining-as-support-for-global-engagement-slips/.

30. "Partisan Polarization Surges in Bush, Obama Years: Trends in American Values: 1987–2012," Pew Research Center, June 4, 2012, www.people-press.org/2012/06/04/partisan-polarization-surges-in-bush-obama-years/.

31. Gaddis, *Strategies of Containment,* 24–124; and Eugene V. Rostow, *Toward*

Managed Peace: The National Security Interests of the United States, 1759 to the Present (New Haven: Yale University Press, 1993), 283–308.

32. Gaddis, *Strategies of Containment*, 24–124; Rostow, *Toward Managed Peace*, 283–308.

33. Elizabeth Edwards Spalding, *The First Cold Warrior: Harry Truman, Containment, and the Remaking of Liberal Internationalism* (Lexington: University Press of Kentucky, 2006), provides the best intellectual biography focusing on Truman's foreign policy.

34. Alonzo L. Hamby, *Man of the People: A Life of Harry S. Truman* (New York: Oxford University Press, 1995), 346.

35. Ibid., 313–14.

36. NSC 68, quoted in Ernest R. May, ed., *American Cold War Strategy: Interpreting NSC 68* (New York: St. Martin's, 1993), 80–81.

37. National Security Decision Directive 75 (hereafter cited as NSDD 75), "U.S. Relations with the USSR," January 17, 1983, www.reagan.utexas.edu/archives/reference/Scanned%20NSDDS/NSDD75.pdf.

38. Jeane J. Kirkpatrick, *Dictatorships and Double Standards: Rationalization and Reason in Politics* (New York: Simon and Schuster, 1982).

39. For the distilled essence of Reagan's approach, see the following sources: Ronald Reagan, *Reagan, in His Own Hand: The Writings of Ronald Reagan That Reveal His Revolutionary Vision for America,* ed. Kiron K. Skinner, Annelise Anderson, and Martin Anderson (New York: Free Press, 2001), 23–218; NSDD 75; NSSD 11-82, August 21, 1982, Ronald Reagan Presidential Library; Kaufman, "The First Principles of Ronald Reagan's Foreign Policy"; Paul Kengor, *The Crusader: Ronald Reagan and the Fall of Communism* (New York: Regan Books, 2006); and Richard Pipes, *Vixi: Memoirs of a Non-Belonger* (New Haven: Yale University Press, 2003), 125–211.

40. Paul Lettow, *Ronald Reagan and His Quest to Abolish Nuclear Weapons* (New York: Random House, 2005), is the finest book on Reagan's quest to eliminate nuclear weapons; it illustrates the stark contrast between Reagan's and Obama's approaches.

41. Ronald Reagan, "Address from the Brandenburg Gate," West Berlin, June 12, 1987, http://millercenter.org/president/speeches/speech-3415.

42. Ronald Reagan, "Remarks at the Annual Convention of the National Association of Evangelicals," Orlando, Fla., March 8, 1983, www.reagan.utexas.edu/archives/speeches/1983/30883b.htm.

43. Daniel Henninger, "Father of the Bush Doctrine: The Saturday Interview with George Shultz," *Wall Street Journal,* April 29, 2006, A8, http://online.wsj.com/news/articles/SB114626915007139434.

44. Ibid.

45. For Reagan's response to Churchill's Iron Curtain speech, see Ronald Reagan, "The Brotherhood of Man," remarks at the Westminster College Cold War Memorial, Fulton, Mo., November 19, 1990, www.pbs.org/wgbh/americanexperience/features/primary-resources/reagan-brotherhood/.

46. Ronald Reagan, *An American Life* (New York: Simon and Schuster, 1990), 409.

47. Francis Fukuyama, *America at the Crossroads: Democracy, Power, and the Neoconservative Legacy* (New Haven: Yale University Press, 2006), 205–6.

48. Kaufman, *In Defense of the Bush Doctrine,* 87–101.

49. Reagan, *An American Life,* 418.

50. Rand Paul, "Romney's Wrong on Middle East, Defense Spending," CNN, October 10, 2012, www.cnn.com/2012/10/10/opinion/rand-paul-romney-foreign-policy/.

51. Rand Paul, "Transcript of Rand Paul's Heritage Foundation Speech," News.Mic, February 6, 2013, http://mic.com/articles/25024/rand-paul-speech-full-text-transcript.

52. Alana Goodman, "Rand Paul's Russian Connection," *Washington Free Beacon,* August 20, 2014, www.freebeacon.com/politics/rand-pauls-russian-connection.

53. Rand Paul, "On Diplomacy," *National Interest,* January 16, 2014, http://nationalinterest.org/commentary/rand-paul-diplomacy-9714.

54. Rand Paul, "America Shouldn't Choose Sides in Iraq's Civil War," *Wall Street Journal,* June 19, 2014, http://online.wsj.com/articles/sen-rand-paul-america-shouldnt-choose-sides-in-iraqs-civil-war-1403219558.

55. Rand Paul, "How U.S. Interventionists Abetted the Rise of ISIS," *Wall Street Journal,* August 27, 2014, www.wsj.com/articles/rand-paul-how-u-s-interventionists-abetted-the-rise-of-isis-1409178958; for an excellent analysis of Paul's Doctrine of Retreat and its compatibility with the Obama Doctrine, see Bret Stephens, *America in Retreat: The New Isolationism and the Coming Global Disorder* (New York: Sentinel Books, 2014).

56. Reid J. Epstein, "Rand Paul Backs Obama on Cuba, Highlighting GOP Split," *Wall Street Journal,* December 18, 2014, http://blogs.wsj.com/washwire/2014/12/18/rand-paul-others-split-from-gop-on-obamas-cuba-engagement/.

57. Pat Buchanan, *Churchill, Hitler, and "the Unnecessary War": How Britain Lost Its Empire and the West Lost the World* (New York: Three Rivers Press, 2008).

58. David Adesnik, "A Revealing Reading List: Rand Paul's Book Recommendations," *Weekly Standard,* July 21, 2014, www.weeklystandard.com/articles/revealing-reading-list_796396.html; and Chalmers Johnson, *Blowback: The Costs and Consequences of American Empire* (New York: Holt, 2004).

4. The Obama Doctrine's Reset with Russia and Europe

1. Halford John Mackinder, *Democratic Ideals and Reality: A Study in the Politics of Reconstruction* (New York: Henry Holt, 1919); and Mackinder, *The Geographical Pivot of History* (N.p.: n.p., 1904).

2. Nicholas J. Spykman, *America's Strategy in World Politics: The United States and the Balance of Power* (1942; repr., New Brunswick, N.J.: Transaction Publishers, 2012).

3. John Lewis Gaddis, *Strategies of Containment: A Critical Appraisal of American National Security Policy during the Cold War* (New York: Oxford University Press, 2005).

4. Henry A. Kissinger, *Diplomacy* (New York: Simon and Schuster, 1994), 813.

5. Ibid.

6. Walter Russell Mead, "The Return of Geopolitics: The Revenge of the Revisionist Powers," *Foreign Affairs,* May/June 2014, 80–91, www.foreignaffairs.com/articles/141211/walter-russell-mead/the-return-of-geopolitics.

7. Leon Aron, *Yeltsin: A Revolutionary Life* (New York: St Martin's Press, 2000), 667–68.

8. Ibid.

9. John Dunlop, *The Moscow Bombings of September 1999: Examinations of Russian Terrorist Attacks at the Onset of Vladimir Putin's Rule* (Stuttgart, Germany: Ibidem, 2014).

10. Steven Lee Myers, "Bush and Putin Remain Apart on Missile Defense," *New York Times,* April 6, 2008, www.nytimes.com/2008/04/06/world/americas/06ihtprexy.1.11699484.html?_r=0.

11. Adrian Karatnycky, "Ukraine's Orange Revolution," *Foreign Affairs,* March/April 2005, www.foreignaffairs.com/articles/60620/adrian-karatnycky/ukraines-orange-revolution.

12. Vladimir Putin, "Address to the Federal Assembly of the Russian Federation," the Kremlin, Moscow, April 25, 2005, http://archive.kremlin.ru/eng/speeches/2005/04/25/2031_type70029type82912_87086.shtml.

13. Vladimir Putin, "Speech and the Following Discussion at the Munich Conference on Security Policy," Munich, Germany, February 10, 2007, http://archive.kremlin.ru/eng/speeches/2007/02/10/0138_type82912type82914type82917type84779_118123.shtml.

14. John McCain, quoted in Thom Shanker and Mark Landler, "Putin Says U.S. Is Undermining Global Stability," *New York Times,* February 11, 2007, www.nytimes.com/2007/02/11/world/europe/11munich.html?pagewanted=all&_r=0.

15. Steven Pifer, "George W. Bush Was Tough on Russia? Give Me a Break," Brookings, March 24, 2014, www.brookings.edu/research/opinions/2014/03/24-bush-tough-on-putin-give-me-a-break-pifer.

16. G. John Ikenberry, "The Illusion of Geopolitics: The Enduring Power of the Liberal Order," *Foreign Affairs,* May/June 2014, 80, www.foreignaffairs.com/articles/141212/g-john-ikenberry/the-illusion-of-geopolitics.

17. Hillary Rodham Clinton, *Hard Choices* (New York: Simon and Schuster, 2014), 230.

18. Peter Baker, "U.S.–Russian Ties Still Fall Short of 'Reset' Goal," *New York Times,* September 2, 2013, www.nytimes.com/2013/09/03/world/europe/us-russian-ties-still-fall-short-of-reset-goal.html?pagewanted=all.

19. Barack Obama, "Remarks by the President at the New Economic School Graduation," Moscow, Russia, July 7, 2009, www.whitehouse.gov/the-press-office/remarks-president-new-economic-school-graduation.

20. Ibid.

21. Phil Stewart, "Obama Must Carefully Calibrate Russia Response, Rhetoric: Gates," Reuters, March 2, 2014, www.reuters.com/article/2014/03/03/us-ukraine-crisis-usa-gates-idUSBREA2202Q20140303.

22. Clinton, *Hard Choices*, 235.

23. U.S. Department of State, text of the New START treaty, signed in Prague, April 8, 2010, www.state.gov/documents/organization/140035.pdf.

24. Barack Obama, "Remarks by President Obama and President Medvedev of Russia at New START Treaty Signing Ceremony and Press Conference," Prague, Czech Republic, April 8, 2010, www.whitehouse.gov/the-press-office/remarks-president-obama-and-president-medvedev-russia-new-start-treaty-signing-cere.

25. Ibid.

26. John F. Kerry, "How New-START Will Improve Our Nation's Security," *Washington Post*, July 7, 2010, www.washingtonpost.com/wp-dyn/content/article/2010/07/06/AR2010070603942.html.

27. Mitt Romney, "Obama's Worst Foreign-Policy Mistake," *Washington Post*, July 6, 2010, www.washingtonpost.com/wp-dyn/content/article/2010/07/05/AR2010070502657.html.

28. President Obama and President Medvedev, quoted in David Nakamura and Debbi Wilgoren, "Caught on Open Mike, Obama Tells Medvedev He Needs 'Space' on Missile Defense," *Washington Post*, March 26, 2012, www.washingtonpost.com/politics/obama-tells-medvedev-solution-on-missile-defense-is-unlikely-before-elections/2012/03/26/gIQASoblbS_story.html.

29. Peter Baker, "White House Scraps Bush's Approach to Missile Shield," *New York Times*, September 17, 2009, www.nytimes.com/2009/09/18/world/europe/18shield.html.

30. Quoted in Glenn Kessler, "The GOP Claim That Obama Scrapped a Missile Defense System as a 'Gift' to Putin," *Washington Post*, March 28, 2014, www.washingtonpost.com/blogs/fact-checker/wp/2014/03/28/the-gop-claim-that-obama-scrapped-a-missile-defense-system-as-a-gift-to-putin/.

31. Robert M. Gates, "A Better Missile Defense for a Safer Europe," *New York Times*, September 19, 2009, www.nytimes.com/2009/09/20/opinion/20gates.html?pagewanted=all.

32. Clifford J. Levy and Peter Baker, "Russia's Reaction on Missile Plan Leaves Iran Issue Hanging," *New York Times*, September 18, 2009, www.nytimes.com/2009/09/19/world/europe/19shield.html?pagewanted=print

33. David M. Herszenhorn and Michael R. Gordon, "U.S. Cancels Part of Missile Defense That Russia Opposed," *New York Times*, March 16, 2013, www.nytimes.com/2013/03/17/world/europe/with-eye-on-north-korea-us-cancels-missile-defense-russia-opposed.html.

34. Rachel Oswald, "GOP Applauds New Interceptors for Alaska, Accuses Obama of Secret Deal with Russia," *Global Security Newswire*, March 20, 2013, www.nti.org/gsn/article/gop-applauds-new-interceptors-alaska-accuses-obama-secret-deal-russia/.

35. Baker Spring, "Congress Must Stop Obama's Downward Spiral of Missile Defense," *Heritage Foundation Research Report*, May 20, 2013, www.heritage.org/research/reports/2013/05/congress-must-stop-obamas-downward-spiral-of-missile-defense.

36. Gordon Lubold, "Will Putin Push Obama to Reset His Missile Plans for Eastern Europe?" *Foreign Policy*, April 23, 2014, http://foreignpolicy.com/2014/04/23/will-putin-push-obama-to-reset-his-missile-defense-plans-for-eastern-europe/.

37. Commission on Presidential Debates, Transcript, "President Barack Obama and Former Gov. Mitt Romney, R-Mass., Participate in a Candidates Debate," Lynn University, Boca Raton, Fla., October 22, 2012, http://debates.org/index.php?page=october-22-2012-the-third-obama-romney-presidential-debate.

38. Clinton, *Hard Choices*, 206.

39. Robert M. Gates, quoted in Baker, "U.S.–Russian Ties Still Fall Short of 'Reset' Goal."

40. Ibid.

41. Patrick Goodenough, "Russia, Angry about Libya, Won't Support Resolution on Syria," CNSNews.com, May 19, 2011, http://cnsnews.com/news/article/russia-angry-about-libya-won-t-support-resolution-syria.

42. Fiona Hill, "Putin Scores on Syria: How He Got the Upper Hand—and How He Will Use It," *Foreign Affairs*, September 11, 2013, www.foreignaffairs.com/articles/139905/fiona-hill/putin-scores-on-syria.

43. "Russia Opposes Use of Force in Syria Resolution," *Huffington Post*, September 17, 2013, www.huffingtonpost.com/2013/09/17/russia-syria-resolution-use-of-force_n_3940204.html.

44. Vladimir V. Putin, "A Plea for Caution from Russia," *New York Times*, September 11, 2013, www.nytimes.com/2013/09/12/opinion/putin-plea-for-caution-from-russia-on-syria.html?pagewanted=all.

45. Alexei Malashenko, quoted in Henry Meyer, Stepan Kravchenko, and Donna Abu-Nasr, "Putin Defies Obama in Syria as Arms Fuel Assad Resurgence," *Bloomberg*, April 3, 2014, www.bloomberg.com/news/print/2014-04-02/putin-defies-obama-in-syria-as-arms-fuel-assad-resurgence.html.

46. Nikolas K. Gvosdev, "The Bear Awakens: Russia's Military Is Back," *National Interest*, November 12, 2014, http://nationalinterest.org/commentary/russias-military-back-9181.

47. Ibid.

48. Edward Lucas, *The New Cold War: Putin's Russia and the Threat to the West*, rev. ed. (New York: Palgrave Macmillan, 2014), 1–15.

49. Ariel Cohen, "A U.S. Response to Russia's Military Modernization," *Heritage Foundation Backgrounder #2901*, May 29, 2014, www.heritage.org/research/reports/2014/05/a-us-response-to-russias-military-modernization.

50. National Defense Panel, "Ensuring a Strong U.S. Defense for the Future," National Defense Panel Review of the 2014 Quadrennial Defense Review, July 31, 2014, www.usip.org/sites/default/files/Ensuring-a-Strong-U.S.-Defense-for-the-Future-NDP-Review-of-the-QDR_0.pdf, 7.

51. Ibid., 19.

52. Ibid.

53. Gvosdev, "The Bear Awakens."

54. Michael R. Gordon, "U.S. Says Russia Tested Missile, Despite Treaty," *New York Times,* January 29, 2014, www.nytimes.com/2014/01/30/world/europe/us-says-russia-tested-missile-despite-treaty.html?_r=0.

55. Michael R. Gordon, "U.S. Says Russia Tested Cruise Missile, Violating Treaty," *New York Times,* July 28, 2014, www.nytimes.com/2014/07/29/world/europe/us-says-russia-tested-cruise-missile-in-violation-of-treaty.html.

56. Dylan C. Robinson, "Far North Turf War: Who Really Rules the Arctic?" *Metronews,* March 23, 2014, http://metronews.ca/news/world/980914/the-far-north-turf-war-who-really-rules-the-arctic/.

57. "Canada to Claim North Pole as Its Own," *Guardian,* December 9, 2013, www.theguardian.com/world/2013/dec/10/canada-north-pole-claim.

58. Steven Mufson, "Shifting Energy Trends Blunt Russia's Natural-Gas Weapon," *Washington Post,* March 1, 2014, www.washingtonpost.com/business/economy/shifting-energy-trends-blunt-russias-natural-gas-weapon/2014/02/28/7d090062-9ef7-11e3-a050-dc3322a94fa7_story.html.

59. Keith Johnson, "Why Russia's Putin Won't Use Energy as a Weapon," *Portland Press Herald,* March 4, 2014, www.pressherald.com/2014/03/04/why_russia_s_putin_won_t_use_energy_as_a_weapon__commentary/.

60. John Bussey, "U.S. Can Use Energy as a Weapon against Putin," *Wall Street Journal,* March 4, 2014, http://online.wsj.com/news/articles/SB10001424052702304585004579419672311009300#printMode.

61. F. Stephen Larrabee and Peter A. Wilson, "Calling Putin's Bluff," *National Interest,* April 12, 2014, http://nationalinterest.org/commentary/calling-putins-bluff-10233.

62. Stephen Cohen, "Stephen Cohen Blames U.S. for Russian Aggression: 'We Crossed His Red Line,'" *Real Clear Politics Video,* 00:42, March 4, 2014, www.realclearpolitics.com/video/2014/03/04/stephen_cohen_blames_us_for_russian_aggression_we_crossed_his_red_line.html. See also Stephen F. Cohen, "Distorting Russia: How the American Media Misrepresent Putin, Sochi and Ukraine," *Nation,* February 12, 2014, www.thenation.com/article/178344/distorting-russia#; Stephen F. Cohen, "The Silence of American Hawks about Kiev's Atrocities," *Nation,* June 30, 2014, www.thenation.com/article/180466/silence-american-hawks-about-kievs-atrocities; and Patrick J. Buchanan, "A GOP Ultimatum to Vlad: Where Do We Come Off Telling the Russians What Kind of Government They May Have?" July 29, 2014, http://buchanan.org/blog/gop-ultimatum-vlad-6757.

63. Katrina vanden Heuvel and Stephen F. Cohen, "Why Is Washington Risking War with Russia?" *Nation,* July 30, 2014, www.thenation.com/article/180825/why-washington-risking-war-russia.

64. Philip Hamilton, "Professor Stephen Walt on the Crisis in Ukraine," *Boston Global Forum,* March 2014, www.bostonglobalforum.org/2014/03/professor-stephen-walt-on-the-crisis-in-ukraine/.

65. Ibid.

66. Cathy Young, "Putin's Pal," *Slate,* July 24, 2014, www.slate.com/articles/news_and_politics/foreigners/2014/07/stephen_cohen_vladimir_putin_s_apologist_the_nation_just_published_the_most.html.

67. Clinton, *Hard Choices,* 212.

68. Robert Kagan, *The Return of History and the End of Dreams* (New York: Alfred A. Knopf, 2008), 61, 63, 68.

69. "World Economic Outlook, April 2014," International Monetary Fund, www.imf.org/external/Pubs/ft/weo/2014/01/pdf/text.pdf.

70. Zbigniew Brzezinski, *The Grand Chessboard: American Primacy and Its Geostrategic Imperatives* (New York: Basic Books, 1997), 98–99.

71. Nicholas Eberstadt, "The Dying Bear: Russia's Demographic Disaster," *Foreign Affairs,* November/December 2011, www.foreignaffairs.com/articles/136511/nicholas-eberstadt/the-dying-bear; and Nick Eberstadt and Apoorva Shah, "No Amount of 'Reset' Can Avert Looming Russian Disaster," *American Enterprise Institute Ideas,* July 8, 2009, www.aei-ideas.org/2009/07/no-amount-of-reset-can-avert-the-looming-russian-disaster/.

72. Ilan Berman, *Implosion: The End of Russia and What It Means for America* (Washington, D.C.: Regnery, 2013), 1–41.

73. Ibid., 43–123.

74. Gideon Rose, *Crisis in Ukraine* (New York: Council on Foreign Relations, 2014).

75. Jeffrey Mankoff, "Russia's Latest Land Grab: How Putin Won Crimea and Lost Ukraine," *Foreign Affairs,* May/June 2014, 60–68, www.foreignaffairs.com/articles/141210/jeffrey-mankoff/russias-latest-land-grab.

76. Michael Birnbaum and Karen DeYoung, "Russia Supplied Missile Launchers to Separatists, U.S. Official Says," *Washington Post,* July 19, 2014, www.washingtonpost.com/world/europe/ukranian-officials-accuse-rebel-militias-of-moving-bodies-tampering-with-evidence/2014/07/19/bef07204-0f1c-11e4-b8e5-d0de80767fc2_story.html.

77. "Almost 1,000 Dead since East Ukraine Truce—UN," *BBC News Europe,* November 20, 2014, www.bbc.com/news/world-europe-30126207.

78. Walter Russell Mead, "Putin: The Mask Comes Off, but Will Anybody Care? *American Interest,* March 15, 2014, www.the-american-interest.com/wrm/2014/03/15/putin-the-mask-comes-off-but-will-anybody-care/; Robert G. Kaufman, "Is Ukraine Putin's Rhineland?" *Orange County Register,* April 27, 2014, www.ocregister.com/articles/hitler-611410-rhineland-putin.html.

79. "Putin's Words over Crimea 'Terribly Reminiscent of Hitler,'" *Euronews,* March 20, 2014, www.euronewscom/2014/03/20putins-words-over-crimea-terribly-reminiscent-of-hitler/.

80. Ibid.

81. Vladimir Putin, "Address by President of the Russian Federation," the Kremlin, Moscow, March 18, 2014, http://eng.kremlin.ru/news/6889.

82. Ibid.

83. Williamson Murray, *The Change in the European Balance of Power, 1938–1939: The Path to Ruin* (Princeton: Princeton University Press, 1984), is the definitive book on how Hitler's Rhineland gambit began a process of transforming the European balance of power to the detriment of the Western democracies.

84. Adolph Hitler, quoted in Alan Bullock, *Hitler: A Study in Tyranny*, rev. ed. (New York: Harper and Row, 1962), 135.

85. Leon Aron, "How to Understand Putin's Ukraine Strategy," CNN, March 1, 2014, http://globalpublicsquare.blogs.cnn.com/2014/03/01/how-to-understand-putins-ukraine-strategy/comment-page-1/. For an earlier, well-respected, more benign assessment of Putin as opportunist—an assessment that recent events render less plausible—see Jeffrey Mankoff, *Russian Foreign Policy: The Return of Great Power Politics*, 2nd ed. (Lanham, Md.: Rowman and Littlefield, 2011).

86. Fareed Zakaria, "On Ukraine, Obama Must Lead from the Front," *Washington Post*, March 13, 2014, www.washingtonpost.com/opinions/fareed-zakaria-on-ukraine-obama-must-lead-from-the-front/2014/03/13/10b9359a-aaea-11e3-af5f-4c56b834c4bf_story.html.

87. Larrabee and Wilson, "Calling Putin's Bluff."

88. Robert Conquest, *Harvest of Sorrow: Soviet Collectivization and the Terror-Famine* (New York: Oxford University Press, 1986); and Timothy Snyder, *Bloodlands: Europe between Hitler and Stalin* (New York: Basic Books, 2010), 21–118.

89. "Despite Concerns about Governance, Ukrainians Want to Remain One Country," Pew Research Global Attitudes Project, May 8, 2014, www.pewglobal.org/2014/05/08/despite-concerns-about-governance-ukrainians-want-to-remain-one-country/.

90. Clinton, *Hard Choices*, 227.

91. Ibid., 244.

92. Peter Baker, "Wary Stance from Obama on Ukraine," *New York Times*, February 24, 2014, www.nytimes.com/2014/02/25/world/europe/wary-stance-from-obama.html?_r=0.

93. John Kerry, "Interview with David Gregory," *Meet the Press*, March 2, 2014, www.state.gov/secretary/remarks/2014/03/222721.htm.

94. "Ukraine Crisis: John Kerry Issues Blunt Warning to Russia as Deadly Clashes at Slaviansk Raise Tensions," *ABC News*, April 24, 2014, www.abc.net.au/news/2014-04-25/ukrainian-clashes-raise-tensions-as-russia-begins-military-dril/5410730.

95. Peter Baker, "U.S. Expands Sanctions, Adding Holdings of Russians in Putin's Financial Circle," *New York Times*, April 28, 2014, www.nytimes.com/2014/04/29/world/asia/obama-sanctions-russia.html.

96. Ibid.

97. Griff Witte and Karen DeYoung, "Obama Announces Expanded Sanctions against Russia as EU Aligns," *Washington Post*, July 29, 2014, www.washingtonpost.com/world/europe/europe-agrees-to-sweeping-new-sanctions-against-russia/2014/07/29/97db98e2-e28d-43f8-a2b6-8816f9ce49ec_story.html.

98. Barack Obama, "Statement by the President on Ukraine," July 29, 2014, www.whitehouse.gov/the-press-office/2014/07/29/statement-president-ukraine.

99. See, e.g., Robert G. Kaufman, "What Reagan Would Have Done about the Malaysian Airliner," *Daily Caller*, July 21, 2014, www.dailycaller.com/2014/07/21/what-reagan-would-have-done-about-the-malaysian-airliner/.

100. Obama, "Statement by the President on Ukraine."

101. Witte and DeYoung, "Obama Announces Expanded Sanctions."

102. Thomas L. Friedman, "Obama on the World," *New York Times*, August 8, 2014, www.nytimes.com/2014/08/09/opinion/president-obama-thomas-l-friedman-iraq-and-world-affairs.html.

103. Yurly Gorodnichenko, Dmytro Goriunov, and Tymofiy Mylovanov, "Fraud in the Ukrainian Election? Not This Time," *Washington Post*, November 4, 2014, www.washingtonpost.com/blogs/monkey-cage/wp/2014/11/04/fraud-in-the-ukrainian-election-not-this-time/.

104. Michael Birnbaum, "NATO Says Russian Jets, Bombers Circle Europe in Unusual Incidents," *Washington Post*, October 29, 2014, www.washingtonpost.com/world/europe/nato-says-russian-jets-bombers-circle-europe-in-unusual-incidents/2014/10/29/6098d964-5f97-11e4-827b-2d813561bdfd_story.html.

105. Paul Goble, "Putin's Strategy in Ukraine—Sow Panic, Provoke, Invade and Then Repeat the Process, *Interpreter*, November 3, 2014, www.interpretermag.com/putins-strategy-in-ukraine-sow-panic-provoke-invade-and-then-repeat-the-process/.

106. Michael J. Rubin, *Dancing with the Devil: The Perils of Engaging Rogue Regimes* (New York: Encounter Books, 2014).

107. The literature for democratic peace theory is vast, the evidence confirming it overwhelming. See, for example, Michael W. Doyle, "Liberalism and World Politics," *American Political Science Review* 80, no. 4 (December 1986): 1151–69. For an unsuccessful neorealist attempt to invalidate the democratic peace argument and its implications, see Stephen M. Walt, "Never Say Never: Wishful Thinking on Democracy and War," *Foreign Affairs*, January/February 1999, 146–51, www.foreignaffairs.com/articles/54641/stephen-m-walt/never-say-never-wishful-thinking-on-democracy-and-war.

108. For a brilliantly concise account of Europe's lamentable record and consequences of appeasing radical Islamists, see George Weigel, *The Cube and the Cathedral* (New York: Basic Books, 2006).

109. Fareed Zakaria, "The E.U. is the World's Great No-Show," *Washington Post*, July 24, 2014, www.washingtonpost.com/opinions/fareed-zakaria-the-european-union-is-the-worlds-great-no-show/2014/07/24/f92ee906-1367-11e4-8936-26932bcfd6ed_story.html.

110. Victor Davis Hanson, "The End of NATO?" *National Review*, August 7, 2014, www.nationalreview.com/article/384766/end-nato-victor-davis-hanson.

111. Raphael S. Cohen and Gabriel M. Scheinmann, "Can Europe Fill the Void in U.S. Military Leadership? *Orbis* 58, no. 1 (Winter 2014): 45.

112. "Searching for Deterrence: Ukraine Crisis Exposes Gaps between Berlin and

NATO," *Spiegel Online International,* April 7, 2014, www.spiegel.de/international/germany/ukraine-crisis-exposes-gaps-between-berlin-and-nato-a-962978.html.

113. Timothy Garton Ash, "The Crisis of Europe: How the Union Came Together and Why It's Falling Apart," *Foreign Affairs,* September/October 2012, www.foreignaffairs.com/articles/138010/timothy-garton-ash/the-crisis-of-europe.

114. Josef Joffe, *The Myth of America's Decline: Politics, Economics, and a Half Century of False Prophecies* (New York: Liveright, 2014), 247.

115. Cohen and Scheinmann, "Can Europe Fill the Void?," 49–54.

116. Robert Samuelson, "Russia's Threat of Stopping Natural Gas Exports," *Daily Journal,* March 31, 2014, www.daily-journal.com/opinion/columnists/national/robert-samuelson-russia-s-threat-of-stopping-natural-gas-exports/article_a57d191e-407c-5e21-92e0-de5c532c9bb4.html.

117. Markus Feldenkirchen, Christiane Hoffmann, and René Pfister, "Germany's Choice: Will It Be America or Russia?" July 10, 2014, *Spiegel Online International,* www.spiegel.de/international/germany/as-us-scandals-grow-germans-seek-greater-political-independence-a-979695.html.

118. Michael R. Gordon, "France's Sale of 2 Ships to Russians Is Ill-Advised, U.S. Warns," *New York Times,* May 14, 2014, www.nytimes.com/2014/05/15/world/europe/frances-sale-of-2-warships-to-russia-worries-us.html.

119. "Ukraine Crisis: France Halts Warship Delivery to Russia," *BBC News Europe,* September 3, 2014, www.bbc.com/news/world-europe-29052599.

120. Anthony Faiola, "In Court of Public Opinion, Putin Goes on Trial," *Washington Post,* July 20, 2014, www.washingtonpost.com/world/europe/in-court-of-public-opinion-putin-goes-on-trial/2014/07/20/6849d4ff-cf71-43e9-aefd-154a172a1545_story.html.

121. Jonathan Freedland, "U.S. Elections: Obama Wows Berlin Crowd with Historic Speech," *Guardian,* July 24, 2008, www.theguardian.com/global/2008/jul/24/barackobama.uselections2008.

122. Barack Obama, "Full Transcript of Obama's Speech [in Berlin]," *CNNPolitics.com,* July 24, 2008, http://edition.cnn.com/2008/POLITICS/07/24/obama.words/.

123. Aubrey Bloomfield, "Barack Obama Berlin Speech: No Rock Star Reception This Time," *Policy.Mic,* June 19, 2013, http://mic.com/articles/49725/barack-obama-berlin-speech-no-rock-star-reception-this-time.

124. Kori Schake, "How to Lose Friends and Alienate Allies: Why America's Friends in Europe Are Wishing for the Good Old Days of George W. Bush," *Foreign Policy,* June 30, 2014, www.foreignpolicy.com/articles/2014/06/30/why_the_obama_administration_is_making_europe_miss_george_w_bush.

125. "Polish President Accuses Obama of Betraying Poland," *Telegraph,* August 6, 2012, www.telegraph.co.uk/news/worldnews/europe/poland/9456610/Polish-president-accuses-Obama-of-betraying-Poland.html.

126. Lech Walesa, quoted in John Bachman and Jim Meyers, "Lech Walesa: Obama Doesn't Care If US Remains World Superpower, *Newsmax,* February 16, 2014, www.

newsmax.com/Headline/lech-walesa-obama-leadership-disappointment/2014/02/16/id/553062/.

127. Lech Walesa, quoted in Michael Dorstewitz, "Obama's a Dangerous Disappointment to the World, Ex-president of Poland Tells CNN," *Bizpac Review,* January 2, 2014, www.bizpacreview.com/2014/01/02/obamas-a-dangerous-disappointment-to-world-ex-president-of-poland-tells-cnn-91739.

128. James P. Rubin, "Reassuring Eastern Europe," *New York Times,* June 11, 2014, www.nytimes.com/2014/06/12/opinion/reassuring-eastern-europe.html.

129. Krzysztof Kubiak, quoted in Peter Baker and Rick Lyman, "Obama, in Poland, Renews Commitment to Security," *New York Times,* June 3, 2014, www.nytimes.com/2014/06/04/world/europe/obama-in-europe.html.

130. Rubin, "Reassuring Eastern Europe."

131. Radoslaw Sikorski, quoted in "SikorskiGate, Part I," XX Committee, June 22, 2014, www.20committee.com/2014/06/22/sikorskigate-part-i/; see also Rick Lyman, "Tapes Said to Reveal Polish Minister Disparaging U.S. Ties," *New York Times,* June 22, 2014, www.nytimes.com/2014/06/23/world/europe/tapes-said-to-reveal-polish-minister-disparaging-us-ties.html.

132. Roger Cohen, "An Ally Offended," *New York Times,* February 13, 2014, www.nytimes.com/2014/02/14/opinion/cohen-an-ally-offended.html.

133. David Francis and Dan Murphy, "At Berlin Wall Fall Celebration, Old Allies Ask Where Is Obama," *Christian Science Monitor,* November 9, 2009, www.csmonitor.com/World/Global-News/2009/1109/at-berlin-wall-fall-celebration-old-allies-ask-where-is-obama.

134. Cameron Abadi, "The Betrayal of Angela Merkel," *New Republic,* November 2, 2013, www.newrepublic.com/article/115442/angela-merkel-spying-us-just-lost-very-good-friend.

135. Clemens Binninger, quoted in Philip Oltermann and Spencer Ackerman, "Germany Asks Top US Intelligence Official to Leave Country over Spy Row," *Guardian,* July 10, 2014, www.theguardian.com/world/2014/jul/10/germany-asks-top-us-intelligence-official-spy-row.

136. Roger Cohen, "A Much Less Special Relationship," *New York Times,* August 30, 2013, www.nytimes.com/2013/08/31/opinion/cohen-a-much-less-special-relationship.html.

137. Patrick Goodenough, "Obama Says He's 'Neutral' over Falklands but Seems to Tilt toward Argentina," CNS News, April 17, 2012, cnsnews.com/news/article/obama-says-he-s-neutral-over-falklands-seems-tilt-toward-argentina.

138. Matthew Moore, Gordon Rayner, and Christopher Hope, "WikiLeaks Cables: US Agrees to Tell Russia Britain's Nuclear Secrets," *Telegraph,* February 4, 2011, www.telegraph.co.uk/news/worldnews/wikileaks/8304654/WikiLeaks-cables-US-agrees-to-tell-Russia-Britains-nuclear-secrets.html; and Nile Gardiner, "The Obama Administration Betrays Britain to Appease the Russians over New START," *Telegraph,* February 4, 2011, http://blogs.telegraph.co.uk/news/nilegardiner/100074846/the-obama-administration-betrays-britain-to-appease-the-russians-over-new-start/.

139. Robert G. Kaufman, "A Two-Level Interaction: Structure, Stable Liberal

Democracy, and U.S. Grand Strategy," *Security Studies* 3, no. 4 (Summer 1994): 678–717.

140. Robert Kagan, *Of Paradise and Power: America and Europe in the New World Order* (New York: Alfred A. Knopf, 2003), 3–4.

141. Robert Cooper, *The Breaking of Nations: Order and Chaos in the Twenty-First Century* (New York: Atlantic Monthly Press, 2004), 34–35.

142. Lord Ismay, quoted in Octavian Manea, "Lord Ismay Restated," *Small Wars Journal,* November 18, 2010, www.smallwarsjournal.com/blog/lord-ismay-restated.

143. Robert G. Kaufman, "The First Principles of Ronald Reagan's Foreign Policy," *Heritage Foundation First Principles Series Report #40,* November 1, 2011, www.heritage.org/research/reports/2011/11/the-first-principles-of-ronald-reagans-foreign-policy.

144. David J. Kramer, "The Dangerous Mr. Putin," *American Interest,* August 15, 2014, www.the-american-interest.com/articles/2014/08/15/the-dangerous-mr-putin/.

5. The Obama Doctrine Meets the Middle East and Afghanistan

1. Robert D. Blackwill and Meghan L. O'Sullivan, "America's Energy Edge: The Geopolitical Consequences of the Shale Revolution," *Foreign Affairs,* March/April 2014, www.foreignaffairs.com/articles/140750/robert-d-blackwill-and-meghan-l-osullivan/americas-energy-edge.

2. David H. Petraeus, "How We Won in Iraq," *Foreign Policy,* October 29, 2013, www.foreignpolicy.com/articles/2013/10/29/david_petraeus_how_we_won_the_surge_in_iraq; and Peter R. Mansoor, *Surge: My Journey with General David Petraeus and the Remaking of the Iraq War* (New Haven: Yale University Press, 2014).

3. Martin S. Indyk, Kenneth G. Lieberthal, and Michael E. O'Hanlon, *Bending History: Barack Obama's Foreign Policy* (Washington, D.C.: Brookings Institution Press, 2012), 70–140.

4. Barack Obama, "Remarks by the President at the United States Military Academy Commencement Ceremony," West Point, N.Y., May 28, 2014, www.whitehouse.gov/the-press-office/2014/05/28/remarks-president-united-states-military-academy-commencement-ceremony.

5. Robert G. Kaufman, *In Defense of the Bush Doctrine* (Lexington: University Press of Kentucky, 2007), 43–46.

6. Barack Obama, "Remarks by the President on a New Beginning," Cairo University, Cairo, Egypt, June 4, 2009, www.whitehouse.gov/the-press-office/remarks-president-cairo-university-6-04-09; David Brooks, "The Chicago View," *New York Times,* June 5, 2009, www.nytimes.com/2009/06/05/opinion/05brooks.html?_r=0; and Victor Davis Hanson, "Obama's Hazy Sense of History," *National Review,* August 28, 2014, www.nationalreview.com/article/386498/obamas-hazy-sense-history-victor-davis-hanson.

7. Ryan Lizza, "The Consequentialist: How the Arab Spring Remade Obama's Foreign Policy," *New Yorker,* May 2, 2011, www.newyorker.com/magazine/2011/05/02/the-consequentialist.

8. Mark Mazzetti and Helene Cooper, "U.S. Officials and Experts at Odds on Threat Posed by ISIS," *New York Times,* August 22, 2014, www.nytimes.com/2014/08/23/us/politics/us-isnt-sure-just-how-much-to-fear-isis.html.

9. James S. Robbins, "Obama's Middle East Policy in Tatters," *USA Today,* March 20, 2013, www.usatoday.com/story/opinion/2013/03/20/obamas-middle-east-policy-in-tatters-column/2004343/.

10. Indyk, Lieberthal, and O'Hanlon, *Bending History,* 212.

11. Fareed Zakaria, "Inside Obama's World: The President Talks to TIME about the Changing Nature of American Power," *Time,* January 19, 2012, http://swampland.time.com/2012/01/19/inside-obamas-world-the-president-talks-to-time-about-the-changing-nature-of-american-power/; and Vali Nasr, *The Dispensable Nation: American Foreign Policy in Retreat* (New York: Doubleday, 2013), 197–98.

12. Barack Obama, "Remarks by President Obama to the Turkish Parliament," Ankara, Turkey, April 6, 2009, www.whitehouse.gov/the_press_office/Remarks-By-President-Obama-To-The-Turkish-Parliament.

13. Michael Rubin, "Turkey, from Ally to Enemy," *Commentary,* July 1, 2010, www.commentarymagazine.com/article/turkey-from-ally-to-enemy/.

14. Erik Meyersson and Dani Rodrik, "Erdogan's Coup: The True State of Turkish Democracy," *Foreign Affairs,* May 26, 2014, www.foreignaffairs.com/articles/141464/erik-meyersson-and-dani-rodrik/erdogans-coup; for a defense of Erdogan this writer finds unpersuasive, see Daron Acemoglu, "The Failed Autocrat: Despite Erdogan's Ruthlessness, Turkey's Democracy Is Still on Track," *Foreign Affairs,* May 22, 2014, www.foreignaffairs.com/articles/141444/daron-acemoglu/the-failed-autocrat.

15. Elana Beiser, "Second Worst Year on Record for Jailed Journalists," Committee to Protect Journalists, December 18, 2013, http://cpj.org/reports/2013/12/second-worst-year-on-record-for-jailed-journalists.php.

16. Freedom House, "Freedom in the World 2013: Turkey," www.freedomhouse.org/report/freedom-world/2013/turkey.

17. Graham E. Fuller, *Turkey and the Arab Spring: Leadership in the Middle East* (Squamish, B.C.: Bozorg Press, 2014), 318–85; and Soner Cagaptay, *The Rise of Turkey: The Twenty-First Century's First Muslim Power* (Lincoln: University of Nebraska Press, 2014), 55–69.

18. Recep Tayyip Erdogan, quoted in Hillel Fradkin and Lewis Libby, "Erdogan's Grand Vision: Rise and Decline," *World Affairs Journal,* March/April 2013, www.worldaffairsjournal.org/article/erdogan%E2%80%99s-grand-vision-rise-and-decline.

19. Piotr Zalewski, "How Turkey Went from 'Zero Problems' to Zero Friends," *Foreign Policy,* August 22, 2013, www.foreignpolicy.com/articles/2013/08/21/how_turkey_foreign_policy_went_from_zero_problems_to_zero_friends.

20. Kenneth Roth, "Turkey's Tyrant in the Making," *Foreign Policy,* May 12, 2014, www.foreignpolicy.com/articles/2014/05/12/turkey_tyrant_in_the_making_erdogan_akp_politics_democracy.

21. Jonathan Schanzer, "An Unhelpful Ally," *Wall Street Journal,* June 25,

2014, http://online.wsj.com/articles/how-turkey-is-exacerbating-the-mideast-crisis-1403722487; and Ben Hubbard and Ceylan Yeginsu, "After Opening Way to Rebels, Turkey Is Paying Heavy Price," *New York Times,* June 24, 2014, www .nytimes.com/2014/06/25/world/europe/after-opening-way-to-rebels-turkey-is-paying-heavy-price.html?smid=tw-share&r=1&referr=.

22. Mohammad Abdel Kader, "Turkey's Relationship with the Muslim Brotherhood," *Al Arabiya News,* October 14, 2013, http://english.alarabiya.net/en/perspective/alarabiya-studies/2013/10/14/Turkey-s-relationship-with-the-Muslim-Brotherhood.html.

23. Daniel Pipes, "On Second Thought . . . Maybe That Israeli Apology to Turkey Was a Good Idea," *Lion's Den,* March 29, 2013, www.danielpipes.org/blog/2013/03/on-second-thought-maybe-that-israeli-apology-to.

24. Recep Tayyip Erdogan, quoted in "Israel War on Gaza Reminiscent of Hitler Genocide: Erdogan," e*PressTV,* August 1, 2014, www.presstv.com/detail/2014/08/01/373633/israels-gaza-war-reminiscent-of-hitler/.

25. Schanzer, "An Unhelpful Ally."

26. David Ignatius, "Turkey Blows Israel's Cover for Iranian Spy Ring," *Washington Post,* October 16, 2013, www.washingtonpost.com/opinions/david-ignatius-turkey-blows-israels-cover-for-iranian-spy-ring/2013/10/16/7d9c1eb2-3686-11e3-be86-6aeaa439845b_story.html.

27. Michael Rubin, "Turkey Betrays Spies to Iran," *American Enterprise Institute Ideas,* October 17, 2013, www.aei-ideas.org/2013/10/turkey-betrays-spies-to-iran/.

28. Adam Entous and Joe Parkinson, "Turkey's Spymaster Plots Own Course on Syria," *Wall Street Journal,* October 10, 2013, http://online.wsj.com/news/articles/SB10001424052702303643304579107373585228330.

29. Anthony Faiola and Souad Mekhennet, "In Turkey, a Late Crackdown on Islamist Fighters," *Washington Post,* August 12, 2014, www.washingtonpost.com/world/how-turkey-became-the-shopping-mall-for-the-islamic-state/2014/08/12/5eff70bf-a38a-4334-9aa9-ae3fc1714c4b_story.html.

30. Tim Arango, "Turkey Denies Reports of Deal for Use of Its Bases in the Fight against Islamic State," *New York Times,* October 13, 2014, www.nytimes.com/2014/10/14/world/europe/not-so-fast-turkey-says-on-us-use-of-air-bases.html?_r=0.

31. Desmond Butler, "US Embassy: Turkey, US Sign Deal to Train, Arm Syrian Rebels," Military.com, February 20, 2015, www.military.com/daily-news/2015/02/20/turkey-us-sign-deal-to-train-arm-syrian-rebels.html.

32. Blaise Misztal, Halil Karaveli, and Svante Cornell, "Foreign Policy Reset Unlikely under President Erdogan," *American Interest,* August 7, 2014, www.the-american-interest.com/2014/08/07/foreign-policy-reset-unlikely-under-president-erdogan/.

33. Daniel Pipes, "Talking Turkey with an Islamist Academician," *Washington Times,* August 27, 2014, www.washingtontimes.com/news/2014/aug/27/pipes-talking-turkey-with-an-islamist-academician/print/.

34. Ibid.

35. Eric Schmitt and Kareem Fahim, "ISIS Intensifies Siege of Kurdish Enclave in Syria," *New York Times,* October 10, 2014, www.nytimes.com/2014/10/11/world/middleeast/isis-intensifies-siege-of-kurdish-enclave-in-syria.html.

36. Interview with Behlul Ozkan, "Early Writings Reveal the Real Davutoglu," *Al-Monitor,* August 13, 2014, www.al-monitor.com/pulse/originals/2014/08/zaman-davutoglu-ideologue-behlul-ozkan-academic-akp-islamic.html#.

37. Ibid.

38. Misztal, Cornell, and Karaveli, "Foreign Policy Reset Unlikely under President Erdogan."

39. Fareed Zakaria, "Who Lost Iraq? The Iraqis Did, with an Assist from George W. Bush," *Washington Post,* June, 12, 2014, www.washingtonpost.com/opinions/fareed-zakaria-who-lost-iraq-the-iraqis-did-with-an-assist-from-george-w-bush/2014/06/12/35c5a418-f25c-11e3-914c-1fbd0614e2d4_story.html.

40. Leslie H. Gelb, "Iraq Is Vietnam 2.0 and U.S. Drones Won't Solve the Problem," *Daily Beast,* June 12, 2014, www.thedailybeast.com/articles/2014/06/12/iraq-is-vietnam-2-0-and-u-s-drones-won-t-solve-the-problem.html.

41. Barack Obama, "Statement by the President on Iraq," August 9, 2014, www.whitehouse.gov/the-press-office/2014/08/09/statement-president-iraq.

42. David H. Petraeus, "How We Won in Iraq," *Foreign Policy,* October 29, 2013, www.foreignpolicy.com/articles/2013/10/29/david_petraeus_how_we_won_the_surge_in_iraq.

43. Joe Biden, in an interview on *Larry King Live,* CNN, February 10, 2010, www.cnn.com/TRANSCRIPTS/1002/10/lkl.01.html.

44. Dexter Filkins, "In Extremists' Iraq Rise, America's Legacy," *New Yorker,* June 11, 2014, www.newyorker.com/news/news-desk/in-extremists-iraq-rise-americas-legacy.

45. Leon Panetta and Jim Newton, *Worthy Fights: A Memoir of Leadership in War and Peace* (New York: Penguin Press, 2014), 394–95.

46. John McCain, as quoted by Kevin Baron, "McCain Calls for Obama's National Security Team to Resign over Iraq," *Defense One,* June 12, 2014, www.defenseone.com/politics/2014/06/mccain-calls-obamas-national-security-team-resign-over-iraq/86377/.

47. Indyk, Lieberthal, O'Hanlon, *Bending History,* 83.

48. On the issue of hasty withdrawal, Obama has his share of liberal as well as conservative critics. For the former, see Nasr, *The Dispensable Nation,* 201, 211–12.

49. Andrew C. McCarthy, "Don't Blame Iraq on Obama Alone," *National Review Online,* June 14, 2014, www.nationalreview.com/article/380398/dont-blame-iraq-obama-alone-andrew-c-mccarthy.

50. Jennifer Rubin, "Hillary Clinton's Latest Falsehood on Iraq," *Washington Post,* June 26, 2014, www.washingtonpost.com/blogs/right-turn/wp/2014/06/26/hillary-clintons-latest-falsehood-on-iraq/.

51. Dexter Filkins, "What We Left Behind," *New Yorker,* April 28, 2014, www.newyorker.com/magazine/2014/04/28/what-we-left-behind.

52. Sami al-Askari, as quoted in ibid.

53. Debate transcript, Commission on Presidential Debates, Lynn University,

Boca Raton, Fla., October 22, 2012, http://debates.org/index.php?page=october-22-2012-the-third-obama-romney-presidential-debate.

54. Ben Rhodes, quoted in Filkins, "What We Left Behind."

55. Ibid.

56. Bob Woodward, *Obama's Wars* (New York: Simon and Schuster, 2010), offers the full story, which largely corresponds with the account of Robert Gates.

57. Robert M. Gates, *Duty: Memoirs of a Secretary at War* (New York: Alfred A. Knopf, 2014), 335–86, 468–521.

58. Mark Landler, "U.S. Troops to Leave Afghanistan by the End of 2016," *New York Times,* May 27, 2014, www.nytimes.com/2014/05/28/world/asia/us-to-complete-afghan-pullout-by-end-of-2016-obama-to-say.html.

59. Matthew Rosenberg, "Afghans to Alter the Government," *New York Times,* July 13, 2014, www.nytimes.com/2014/07/14/world/asia/afghans-to-alter-the-government-constitution-following-election.html; and Declan Walsh and Azam Ahmed, "Mending Alliance, U.S. and Afghanistan Sign Long-Term Security Agreement," *New York Times,* September 30, 2014, www.nytimes.com/2014/10/01/world/asia/afghanistan-and-us-sign-bilateral-security-agreement.html.

60. Nasr, *Dispensable Nation,* 61–94.

61. Gates, *Duty,* 477.

62. Nasr, *Dispensable Nation,* 66–94.

63. Barack Obama, quoted in Karen DeYoung, "Obama to Leave 9,800 Troops in Afghanistan," *Washington Post,* May 27, 2014, www.washingtonpost.com/world/national-security/obama-to-leave-9800-us-troops-in-afghanistan-senior-official-says/2014/05/27/57f37e72-e5b2-11e3-a86b-362fd5443d19_story.html.

64. Robert Gates, quoted in Bob Woodward, "Robert Gates, Former Defense Secretary, Offers Harsh Critique of Obama's Leadership in 'Duty,'" *Washington Post,* January 7, 2012, www.washingtonpost.com/world/national-security/robert-gates-former-defense-secretary-offers-harsh-critique-of-obamas-leadership-in-duty/2014/01/07/6a6915b2-77cb-11e3-b1c5-739e63e9c9a7_story.html.

65. Gates, *Duty,* 496.

66. Ibid, 569.

67. Lizza, "The Consequentialist: How the Arab Spring Remade Obama's Foreign Policy."

68. Nasr, *Dispensable Nation,* 165.

69. Walter Russell Mead, "The Failed Grand Strategy in the Middle East," *Wall Street Journal,* August 24, 2013, http://online.wsj.com/news/articles/SB10001424127887324619504579028923699568400.

70. Michael R. Gordon and Mark Landler, "In Crackdown Response, U.S. Temporarily Freezes Some Military Aid to Egypt," *New York Times,* October 9, 2013, www.nytimes.com/2013/10/10/world/middleeast/obama-military-aid-to-egypt.html?pagewanted=all.

71. Abe Greenwald, "He Made It Worse: Obama's Middle East," *Commentary,* May 1, 2014, www.commentarymagazine.com/article/hes-made-it-worse-obamas-middle-east/.

72. Cliff Smith, "Dictatorships and Double Standards, Redux," *Daily Caller,* August 20, 2013, http://dailycaller.com/2013/08/20/dictatorships-and-double-standards-redux/.

73. Jeane J. Kirkpatrick, "Dictatorships and Double Standards," *Commentary,* November 1, 1979, www.commentarymagazine.com/articles/dictatorships-double-standards/.

74. Lizza, "The Consequentialist: How the Arab Spring Remade Obama's Foreign Policy."

75. David D. Kirkpatrick, "A Deadly Mix in Benghazi," *New York Times,* December 28, 2013, www.nytimes.com/projects/2013/benghazi/#/?chap=O.

76. James Mann, *The Obamians: The Struggle inside the White House to Redefine American Power* (New York: Viking, 2012), 299–300.

77. Barack Obama, quoted in Thomas L. Friedman, "Obama on the World," *New York Times,* August 8, 2014, www.nytimes.com/2014/08/09/opinion/president-obama-thomas-l-friedman-iraq-and-world-affairs.html.

78. Kaufman, *In Defense of the Bush Doctrine,* 69–77.

79. Ibid.

80. Ibid.

81. James Traub, "Is Libya beyond Repair?" *Foreign Policy,* November 1, 2013, www.foreignpolicy.com/articles/2013/11/01/is_libya_beyond_repair.

82. Raphael Cohen and Gabriel Scheinmann, "Lessons from Libya: America Can't Lead from Behind," *Time,* February 15, 2014, http://ideas.time.com/2014/02/15/lessons-from-libya-america-cant-lead-from-behind/.

83. Nick Cumming-Bruce, "Death Toll in Syria Estimated at 191,000," *New York Times,* August 22, 2014, www.nytimes.com/2014/08/23/world/middleeast/un-raises-estimate-of-dead-in-syrian-conflict-to-191000.html?_r=0.

84. Patrick Goodenough, "Syrian President Assad Regarded as a 'Reformer,' Clinton Says," CNS News, March 28, 2011, http://www.cnsnews.com/news/article/syrian-president-assad-regarded-reformer-clinton-says; and Michael Slackman, "Kerry Tries to Nudge Syria to Re-engage with the U.S.," *New York Times,* April 1, 2010, www.nytimes.com/2010/04/02/world/middleeast/02syria.html.

85. Fiona Hill, "Putin Scores on Syria: How He Got the Upper Hand—and How He Will Use It," *Foreign Affairs,* September 11, 2013, www.foreignaffairs.com/articles/139905/fiona-hill/putin-scores-on-syria.

86. Fouad Ajami, "Obama's Syria Debacle Laid Bare," *Wall Street Journal,* February 20, 2014, www.hoover.org/research/obamas-syria-debacle-laid-bare.

87. Olivier Knox, "Kerry Vows 'Unbelievably Small' Strike on Syria," *Yahoo News,* September 9, 2013, http://news.yahoo.com/-kerry-vows-%E2%80%98unbelievably-small%E2%80%99-strike-on-syria--150302777.html.

88. Peter Baker, "Brief Respite for the President, but No Plan B on Syria," *New York Times,* September 15, 2013, www.nytimes.com/2013/09/16/world/middleeast/brief-respite-for-president-but-no-plan-b-on-syria.html?pagewanted=all.

89. Max Boot, "Russia's Absurd Proposal on Syria's Weapons," *Commen-*

tary, September 9, 2013, www.commentarymagazine.com/2013/09/09/kerrys-unserious-proposal/.

90. Jeffrey Goldberg, "Hillary Clinton: 'Failure' to Help Syrian Rebels Led to the Rise of ISIS," *Atlantic*, August 10, 2014, www.theatlantic.com/international/archive/2014/08/hillary-clinton-failure-to-help-syrian-rebels-led-to-the-rise-of-isis/375832/.

91. Paul Szoldra, "Obama's 2 Previous Defense Secretaries Are Criticizing His ISIS Policy," *Business Insider*, September 19, 2014, www.businessinsider.com/gates-panetta-iraq-syria-2014-9.

92. Marc Lynch, "Would Arming Syria's Rebels Have Stopped the Islamic State?" *Washington Post*, August 11, 2014, www.washingtonpost.com/blogs/monkey-cage/wp/2014/08/11/would-arming-syrias-rebels-have-stopped-the-islamic-state/.

93. Barack Obama, "Statement by the President on ISIL," September 10, 2014, www.whitehouse.gov/the-press-office/2014/09/10/statement-president-isil-1; and Friedman, "Obama on the World."

94. George W. Bush, "Transcript: President Bush Addresses Nation on the Iraq War," *Washington Post*, January 10, 2007, www.washingtonpost.com/wp-dyn/content/article/2007/01/10/AR2007011002208.html.

95. Patricia Zengerle and Mark Hosenball, "U.S. Spy Chiefs Say Number of Foreign Militants in Syria Rises," Reuters, January 29, 2014, www.reuters.com/article/2014/01/29/us-usa-security-syria-idUSBREA0S1XL20140129.

96. Interview with K. T. McFarland, "Inside ISIS' Network of Wealth," *On the Record with Greta Van Susteren*, August 21, 2014, www.foxnews.com/on-air/on-the-record/2014/08/22/inside-isis-network-wealth.

97. Stuart Varney, "ISIS' Thirst for Oil Could Lead to Global Financial Disaster," *Fox News*, August, 22, 2014, http://video.foxnews.com/v/3743606529001/isis-thirst-for-oil-could-lead-to-global-financial-disaster/#sp=show-clips.

98. Richard Grenell, "ISIS Speech: Obama Has Long History of Downplaying Threat from Islamic Terrorists," *Fox News*, September 9, 2014, www.foxnews.com/opinion/2014/09/09/isis-speech-obama-has-long-history-downplaying-threat-from-islamic-terrorists/.

99. Marc A. Thiessen, "Obama Failed to Stop the Islamic State When He Had the Chance," *Washington Post*, July 28, 2014, www.washingtonpost.com/opinions/obama-failed-to-stop-the-islamic-state-when-he-had-the-chance/2014/07/28/7b883e38-1652-11e4-9349-84d4a85be981_story.html.

100. David Remnick, "Going the Distance: On and Off the Road with Barack Obama," *New Yorker*, January 27, 2014, www.newyorker.com/magazine/2014/01/27/going-the-distance-2?currentPage=all.

101. David Ignatius, "James Clapper: We Underestimated the Islamic State's 'Will to Fight,'" *Washington Post*, September 18, 2014, www.washingtonpost.com/opinions/david-ignatius-we-underestimated-the-islamic-state-james-clapper-says/2014/09/18/f0f17072-3f6f-11e4-9587-5dafd96295f0_story.html.

102. Missy Ryan, "Islamic State Threat 'Beyond Anything We've Seen': Pen-

tagon," *Reuters*, August 21, 2014, www.reuters.com/article/2014/08/21/us-usa-islamicstate-idUSKBN0GL24V20140821.

103. Michael R. Gordon and Helene Cooper, "U.S. General Says Raiding Syria Is Key to Halting ISIS," *New York Times*, August 21, 2014, www.nytimes.com/2014/08/22/world/middleeast/isis-believed-to-have-as-many-as-17000-fighters.html.

104. Wesley Lowery, "Biden to Islamic State: We Will Follow You 'to the Gates of Hell,'" *Washington Post*, September 3, 2014, www.wasingtonpost.com/blogs/post-politics/wp/2014/09/03/biden-to-islamic-state-we-will-follow-you-to-the-gates-of-hell/.

105. Barack Obama, "Transcript: President Obama's Aug. 28 Remarks on Ukraine, Syria and the Economy," *Washington Post*, August, 28, 2014, www.washingtonpost.com/politics/transcriptpresident-obamas-aug-28-remarks-on-ukraine-and-syria/2014/08/28/416f1336-2eec-11e4-bb9b-997ae96fad33_story.html.

106. Obama, "Statement by the President on ISIL," September 10, 2014.

107. For a splendid exposition about what Islamism is, the danger it poses, and its implications for the struggles the Unites States faces in the Middle East, see Mary R. Habeck, *Knowing the Enemy: Jihadist Ideology and the War on Terror* (New Haven: Yale University Press, 2006). See also Efraim Karsh, *Islamic Imperialism: A History* (New Haven: Yale University Press, 2006).

108. Editorial Board, "President Obama's Strategy Can't Only Be to Shoot Terrorists from the Air," *Washington Post*, September 11, 2014, www.washingtonpost.com/opinions/president-obamas-strategy-cant-only-be-to-shoot-terrorists-from-the-air/2014/09/11/063d6750-39cc-11e4-9c9f-ebb47272e40e_story.html; and Katherine Zimmerman, "Yemen Model Won't Work in Iraq, Syria," *Washington Post*, July 17, 2014, www.washingtonpost.com/opinions/the-yemen-model-wont-work-in-iraq-syria/2014/07/17/ba0ae414-0d18-11e4-8341-b8072b1e7348_story.html.

109. Obama, "Statement by the President on ISIL," September 10, 2014.

110. Ibid.

111. Jeff Shesol, "Obama's Coalition of the Willing and Unable," *New Yorker*, September 11, 2014, www.newyorker.com/news/news-desk/obamas-new-war-isis.

112. Michael O'Hanlon, "Beyond Air Strikes: The Obama Administration's Plan for an Iraqi National Guard," *Foreign Affairs*, September 12, 2014, www.foreignaffairs.com/articles/141984/michael-ohanlon/beyond-air-strikes.

113. Robin Simcox, "Go Big or Go Home: Iraq Needs U.S. Ground Troops More Than Ever," *Foreign Affairs*, August 12, 2014, www.foreignaffairs.com/articles/141873/robin-simcox/go-big-or-go-home.

114. Kenneth M. Pollack, "An Army to Defeat Assad: How to Turn Syria's Opposition into a Real Fighting Force," *Foreign Affairs*, September/October 2014, www.foreignaffairs.com/articles/141848/kenneth-m-pollack/an-army-to-defeat-assad.

115. Anne Barnard and David D. Kirkpatrick, "Arabs Give Tepid Support to U.S. Fight against ISIS," *New York Times*, September 11, 2014, www.nytimes.com/2014/09/12/world/middleeast/arabs-give-tepid-support-to-us-fight-against-isis.html.

116. Kristina Wong, "Robert Gates: Obama Will Need Ground Troops," *The Hill* (from an interview on *CBS This Morning*), September 17, 2014, http://thehill.com/policy/defense/218003-robert-gates-troops-needed-to-defeat-isis.

117. Emily Schultheis, "Republicans' Newest 2014 Weapon: Foreign Policy," *National Journal,* September 10, 2014, www.nationaljournal.com/politics/republicans-newest-2014-weapon-foreign-policy-20140910.

118. Henry Kissinger, quoted in an interview with NPR staff, "Henry Kissinger's Thoughts on the Islamic State, Ukraine and 'World Order,'" NPR, September 6, 2014, www.npr.org/2014/09/06/346114326/henry-kissingers-thoughts-on-the-islamic-state-ukraine-and-world-order.

119. Jeffrey Goldberg, "Obama to Iran and Israel: 'As President of the United States, I Don't Bluff,'" *Atlantic,* March 2, 2012, www.theatlantic.com/international/archive/2012/03/obama-to-iran-and-israel-as-president-of-the-united-states-i-dont-bluff/253875/.

120. Barack Obama, quoted in Jeffrey Goldberg, "Obama to Israel—Time Is Running Out," *BloombergView,* March 2, 2014, www.bloombergview.com/articles/2014-03-02/obama-to-israel-time-is-running-out.

121. Kenneth M. Pollack, *Unthinkable: Iran, the Bomb, and American Strategy* (New York: Simon and Schuster, 2013), 118–21.

122. Ibid., 123–24.

123. Ibid., 128.

124. Katie Harris, "Rouhani Dismisses Claims of Iran's Nuclear Weapons," *Time,* September 19, 2013, http://world.time.com/2013/09/19/rouhani-dismisses-claims-of-irans-nuclear-weapons/.

125. Mark Landler, "Rice Offers a More Modest Strategy for Mideast," *New York Times,* October 26, 2013, www.nytimes.com/2013/10/27/world/middleeast/rice-offers-a-more-modest-strategy-for-mideast.html.

126. Barack Obama, "Remarks by President Obama in Address to the United Nations General Assembly," New York, September 24, 2013, www.whitehouse.gov/the-press-office/2013/09/24/remarks-president-obama-address-united-nations-general-assembly.

127. Jeff Mason and Yeganeh Torbati, "Obama Pledges Diplomacy with Iran, but He and Rouhani Don't Meet," Reuters, September 25, 2013, www.reuters.com/article/2013/09/25/us-un-obama-speech-idUSBRE98N0TU20130925.

128. Anne Gearan and Joby Warrick, "World Powers Reach Nuclear Deal with Iran to Freeze Its Nuclear Program," *Washington Post,* November 24, 2013, www.washingtonpost.com/world/national-security/kerry-in-geneva-raising-hopes-for-historic-nuclear-deal-with-iran/2013/11/23/53e7bfe6-5430-11e3-9fe0-fd2ca728e67c_story.html.

129. Michael R. Gordon and Eric Schmitt, "Negotiators Put Final Touches on Iran Accord," *New York Times,* January 12, 2014, www.nytimes.com/2014/01/13/world/middleeast/iran-nuclear-deal.html.

130. Kenneth Pollack, "Confidence Enrichment: The Nuclear Deal with Iran Was about Trust, Not Verification," *Foreign Affairs,* November 25, 2013, www.foreignaffairs.com/articles/140290/kenneth-pollack/confidence-enrichment.

131. John Bolton, "Don't Forget Iran's Nuclear Program," *Newsmax,* September 15, 2014, www.newsmax.com/Newsfront/Iran-nuclear-weapons-IAEA-John-Bolton/2014/09/15/id/594640/.

132. John Bolton, "Abject Surrender by the United States: What Does Israel Do Now?" *Weekly Standard,* November 24, 2013, www.weeklystandard.com/blogs/abject-surrender-united-states_768140.html.

133. Michael Warren, "Foreign Policy Experts to Congressional Leaders: Enforce Iranian Compliance with Nuclear Deal," *Weekly Standard,* January 9, 2014, www.weeklystandard.com/blogs/foreign-policy-experts-congressional-leaders-enforce-iranian-compliance-nuclear-deal_774057.html.

134. Laurence Norman, "Iran Nuclear Talks Extended until Late November," *Wall Street Journal,* July 18, 2014, http://online.wsj.com/articles/iran-nuclear-talks-to-be-extended-until-late-november-1405719102.

135. Michael Rubin, *Dancing with the Devil: The Perils of Engaging Rogue Regimes* (New York: Encounter Books, 2014), 72–84.

136. Robert G. Kaufman, "Delusional Enthusiasm for Iran Negotiations," *Orange County Register,* October 2, 2013, www.ocregister.com/articles/iran-528885-nuclear-regime.html.

137. Robert G. Kaufman, "An Ignominious Deal for the U.S., Mideast," *Orange County Register,* December 1, 2013, www.ocregister.com/articles/iran-539170-nuclear-iranian.html.

138. Rubin, *Dancing with the Devil,* 72–84, 309–26.

139. Ali Alfoneh and Reuel Marc Gerecht, "The Man and the Myth: The Many Faces of Hassan Rouhani," *Weekly Standard,* July 14, 2014, www.weeklystandard.com/articles/man-and-myth_796083.html#; and Reuel Marc Gerecht, "The New Rouhani: Same as the Old Rouhani," *Weekly Standard,* October 7, 2013, www.weeklystandard.com/articles/new-rouhani_757227.html.

140. Quoted in Daniel Halper, "Iran's Rouhani: 'World Powers Surrendered to Iranian Nation's Will,'" *Weekly Standard,* January 14, 2014, www.weeklystandard.com/blogs/irans-rouhani-world-powers-surrendered-iranian-nations-will_774616.html.

141. Kenneth M. Pollack, "The Right Way to Press Iran," *New York Times,* May 6, 2014, www.nytimes.com/2014/05/07/opinion/the-right-way-to-press-iran.html?_r=0.

142. Pollack, *Unthinkable,* 304–5.

143. Ibid., 393–422.

144. Pollack, "The Right Way to Press Iran."

145. Peter Kenyon, "The Stickiest Issues in the Iran Nuclear Talks," NPR, September 16, 2014, www.npr.org/blogs/parallels/2014/09/16/348903293/with-a-deadline-looming-irans-nuclear-talks-reopen-in-new-york.

146. John Kerry, quoted in Justyna Pawlak and Parisa Hafezi, "U.S. Warns on Iran 'Breakout' Capability as Nuclear Talks Start," Reuters, April 8, 2014, www.reuters.com/article/2014/04/08/us-iran-nuclear-idUSBREA370FD20140408.

147. John Harney, "Iran Fails to Address All Nuclear Concerns, U.N. Says," *New York Times,* September 5, 2014, www.nytimes.com/2014/09/06/world/middleeast/iran-fails-to-address-all-nuclear-concerns-un-says.html.

148. Jay Solomon and Carol E. Lee, "Obama Wrote Secret Letter to Iran's Khamenei about Fighting Islamic State," *Wall Street Journal,* November 6, 2014, http://online.wsj.com/articles/obama-wrote-secret-letter-to-irans-khamenei-about-fighting-islamic-state-1415295291.

149. Michael Doran and Max Boot, "Obama's Losing Bet on Iran," *New York Times,* January 15, 2014, www.nytimes.com/2014/01/16/opinion/obamas-losing-bet-on-iran.html.

150. Kenneth N. Waltz, "Why Iran Should Get the Bomb: Nuclear Balancing Would Mean Stability," *Foreign Affairs,* July/August 2012, www.foreignaffairs.com/articles/137731/kenneth-n-waltz/why-iran-should-get-the-bomb; and Stephen M. Walt, "What's Really at Stake in the Iranian Nuclear Deal," *Foreign Policy,* November 25, 2013, www.foreignpolicy.com/posts/2013/11/25/iran_the_us_and_the_middle_east_balance_of_power.

151. Paul Pillar, "We Can Live with a Nuclear Iran," *Washington Monthly,* March/April 2012, www.washingtonmonthly.com/magazine/marchapril_2012/features/we_can_live_with_a_nuclear_ira035772.php?page=all.

152. Doran and Boot, "Obama's Losing Bet on Iran."

153. Indyk, Lieberthal, and O'Hanlon, *Bending History,* 112.

154. Wire staff, "Sarkozy, Obama Bemoan Netanyahu over Open Mic," CNN, November 8, 2011, www.cnn.com/2011/11/08/world/europe/france-sarkozy-netanyahu/.

155. Bret Stephens, "Obama's Curious Rage: Calm When It Comes to Putin, ISIS and Hamas, but Furious with Israel," *Wall Street Journal,* September 1, 2014, http://online.wsj.com/articles/bret-stephens-obamas-curious-rage-1409610734.

156. David Rothkopf, "The U.S.–Israel Relationship Arrives at a Moment of Reckoning," *Foreign Policy,* August 26, 2014, www.foreignpolicy.com/articles/2014/08/26/a_conversation_with_martin_indyk_netanyahu_gaza_israel_palestine_hamas.

157. Indyk, Lieberthal, O'Hanlon, *Bending History,* 116.

158. Ibid., 118–19.

159. Goldberg, "Obama to Israel—Time Is Running Out."

160. Martin Gilbert, *In Ishmael's House: A History of Jews in Muslim Lands* (New Haven: Yale University Press, 2010), 2–5.

161. Goldberg, "Obama to Israel—Time Is Running Out"; and Kaufman, *In Defense of the Bush Doctrine,* 46.

162. For the definitive contemporary account of Kerry's peace talks, see Ben Birnbaum and Amir Tibon, "The Explosive, Inside Story of How John Kerry Built an Israel-Palestine Peace Plan—and Watched It Crumble," *New Republic,* July 20, 2014, www.newrepublic.com/article/118751/how-israel-palestine-peace-deal-died.

163. For an excellent book skeptical of whether the Palestinian Authority is reconciled to Israel's existence, see Efraim Karsh, *Palestine Betrayed* (New Haven: Yale

University Press, 2010). For a more positive assessment of the Palestinian Authority, see Jimmy Carter, *Palestine: Peace Not Apartheid* (New York: Simon and Schuster, 2006).

164. Indyk, quoted in Rothkopf, "The U.S.–Israel Relationship Arrives at a Moment of Reckoning."

165. Josh Rogin, "Exclusive: Kerry Warns Israel Could Become 'An Apartheid State,'" *Daily Beast,* April 27, 2014, www.thedailybeast.com/articles/2014/04/27/exclusive-kerry-warns-israel-could-become-an-apartheid-state.html.

166. Rothkopf, "The U.S.–Israel Relationship Arrives at a Moment of Reckoning."

167. David Ignatius, "John Kerry's Big Blunder in Seeking an Israel-Gaza Cease-Fire," *Washington Post,* July 28, 2014, www.washingtonpost.com/opinions/david-ignatius-john-kerrys-big-blunder-in-seeking-an-israel-gaza-cease-fire/2014/07/28/ab3fbfd2-1686-11e4-9349-84d4a85be981_story.html.

168. Walter Russell Mead, "The Gaza War: When Strategies Collide," *American Interest,* July 25, 2014, www.the-american-interest.com/wrm/2014/07/25/the-gaza-war-when-strategies-collide/.

169. Ibid.

170. Editorial Board, "The U.S. Should Push for the Disarming of Hamas in Gaza-Israel Cease-Fire," *Washington Post,* July 23, 2014, www.washingtonpost.com/opinions/the-us-should-push-for-the-disarming-of-hamas-in-gaza-israel-cease-fire/2014/07/23/7c2d1d9e-1284-11e4-8936-26932bcfd6ed_story.html.

171. Michael Oren, "Israel Must Be Permitted to Crush Hamas," *Washington Post,* July 24, 2014, www.washingtonpost.com/opinions/michael-oren-israel-must-be-permitted-to-crush-hamas/2014/07/24/bd9967fc-1350-11e4-9285-4243a40ddc97_story.html.

172. Jeffrey Goldberg, "The Crisis in U.S.–Israel Relations Is Officially Here," *Atlantic,* October 28, 2014, www.theatlantic.com/international/archive/2014/10/the-crisis-in-us-israel-relations-is-officially-here/382031/.

173. James Zogby, "More to the U.S.–Israel Spat Than Meets the Eye," *Huffington Post,* November 1, 2014, www.huffingtonpost.com/james-zogby/more-to-the-us-israel-spa_b_6086338.html.

174. John Hudson, "The White House Distances Itself from Netanyahu 'Chickenshit' Comment," *Foreign Policy,* October 29, 2014, http://thecable.foreignpolicy.com/posts/2014/10/29/white_house_distances_itself_from_netanyahu_chickenshit_comment.

175. Stephen M. Walt, "Netanyahu's Not Chickenshit, the White House Is," *Foreign Policy,* October 31, 2014, www.foreignpolicy.com/articles/2014/10/31/netanyahu_s_not_chickenshit_israel_united_states_special_relationship_obama.

6. The Obama Doctrine's Asian Pivot

1. Aaron L. Friedberg, *A Contest for Supremacy: China, America, and the Struggle for Mastery in Asia* (New York: W. W. Norton, 2011), 254.

2. United States Census Bureau, "Foreign Trade: Trade in Goods with Asia," July 2014, www.census.gov/foreign-trade/balance/c0016.html.

3. Hillary Clinton, "America's Pacific Century," *Foreign Policy,* October 11, 2011, www.foreignpolicy.com/articles/2011/10/11/americas_pacific_century.

4. "China GDP Annual Growth Rate, 1989–2015," *Trading Economics,* 2015, www.tradingeconomics.com/china/gdp-growth-annual.

5. Fareed Zakaria, *The Post-American World* (New York: W. W. Norton, 2008), 100–144; and Kishore Mahbubani, *The New Asian Hemisphere: The Irresistible Shift of Global Power to the East* (New York: Public Affairs, 2008).

6. Mike Bird, "China Just Overtook the US as the World's Largest Economy," *Business Insider,* October 8, 2014, www.businessinsider.com/china-overtakes-us-as-worlds-largest-economy-2014-10.

7. Tom Murse, "How Much U.S. Debt Does China Really Own?" *About News,* 2014, http://usgovinfo.about.com/od/moneymatters/ss/How-Much-US-Debt-Does-China-Own.htm.

8. Josef Joffe, "China's Coming Economic Slowdown," *Wall Street Journal,* October 25, 2013, http://online.wsj.com/articles/SB10001424052702304402104579151511303083436.

9. Nicholas Eberstadt, "China's Coming One-Child Crisis," *Wall Street Journal,* November 26, 2013, http://online.wsj.com/articles/SB10001424052702304791704579216630468814424.

10. Josef Joffe, *The Myth of America's Decline: Politics, Economics, and a Half Century of False Prophecies* (New York: Liveright, 2014), 129–268.

11. Joffe, "China's Coming Economic Slowdown."

12. Charles Krauthammer, "Decline Is a Choice: The New Liberalism and the End of American Ascendancy," *Weekly Standard,* October 19, 2009, www.weeklystandard.com/Content/Public/Articles/000/000/017/056lfnpr.asp#.

13. Paul Krugman, "In Defense of Obama," *Rolling Stone,* October 8, 2014, www.rollingstone.com/politics/news/in-defense-of-obama-20141008.

14. George P. Shultz, "How to Get America Moving Again," *Wall Street Journal,* August 8, 2014, http://online.wsj.com/articles/george-p-shultz-how-to-get-america-moving-again-1407536979.

15. "China's Military Spending: At the Double," *Economist,* March 15, 2014, www.economist.com/news/china/21599046-chinas-fast-growing-defence-budget-worries-its-neighbours-not-every-trend-its-favour.

16. Adam P. Liff and Andrew S. Erickson, "Demystifying China's Defense Spending: Less Mysterious in the Aggregate," *China Quarterly* 216 (December 2013): 805–30.

17. Hans-Dieter Evers and Solvay Gerke, "The Strategic Importance of the Straits of Malacca for World Trade and Regional Development," Center for Development Research, Department of Political and Cultural Change, www.academia.edu/1585485/The_Strategic_Importance_of_the_Straits_of_Malacca_for_World_Trade_and_Regional_Development.

18. Bryan McGrath and Seth Cropsey, "The Real Reason China Wants Aircraft Carriers," *Real Clear Defense,* April 16, 2014, www.realcleardefense.com/articles/2014/04/16/the_real_reason_china_wants_aircraft_carriers.html.

19. Andrew F. Krepinevich, "China's 'Finlandization' Strategy in the Pacific," *Wall Street Journal,* September 11, 2010, http://online.wsj.com/articles/SB10001424052748704164904575421753851404076.

20. James Holmes, "Does India Still Fear China's Growing Military Might?" *National Interest,* June 24, 2014, http://nationalinterest.org/feature/does-india-still-fear-chinas-growing-military-might-10731.

21. Ibid.

22. National Defense Panel, "Ensuring a Strong Defense for the Future," National Defense Panel Review of the 2014 Quadrennial Defense Review, July 31, 2014, www.usip.org/sites/default/files/Ensuring-a-Strong-U.S.-Defense-for-the-Future-NDP-Review-of-the-QDR.pdf.

23. Jim Talent, "China Rising," *National Review,* August 25, 2014, www.nationalreview.com/article/386230/china-rising-jim-talent.

24. Seth Cropsey, "A Naval Disaster in the Making," *Weekly Standard,* October 6, 2014, 18–20, www.weeklystandard.com/articles/naval-disaster-making_806166.html.

25. Michael Raska, "Submarine Modernization in East Asia," *Diplomat,* July 14, 2014, http://thediplomat.com/2014/07/submarine-modernization-in-east-asia/.

26. Mackenzie Eaglen, "Cutting Navy While Obama Pivots to Asia Does Not Add Up," *Breaking Defense,* March 30, 2012, http://breakingdefense.com/2012/03/navy-shrinking-while-obama-pivots-to-asia-does-not-add-up/.

27. Talent, "China Rising."

28. Ibid.

29. National Defense Panel, "Ensuring a Strong National Defense for the Future," 11–12.

30. Robert S. Ross, "The Problem with the Pivot," *Foreign Affairs,* November/December, 2012, www.foreignaffairs.com/artcles/138211/robert-s-ross/the-problem-with-the-pivot.

31. For a more nuanced, sophisticated, and conditional version of Ross's argument, see Andrew J. Nathan and Andrew Scobell, *China's Search for Security* (New York: Columbia University Press, 2012), 278–317, 345–59.

32. Martin Fackler, "Amid Chinese Rivalry, Japan Seeks More Muscle," *New York Times,* December 17, 2013, www.nytimes.com/2013/12/18/world/asia/japan-moves-to-strengthen-military-amid-rivalry-with-china.html?_r=0; Keith Bradsher, "Philippine Leader Sounds Alarm on China," *New York Times,* February 4, 2014, www.nytimes.com/2014/02/05/world/asia/philippine-leader-urges-international-help-in-resisting-chinas-sea-claims.html; and Robert D. Kaplan, *Asia's Cauldron; The South China Sea and the End of a Stable Pacific* (New York: Random House, 2014).

33. Robert Jervis, *Perception and Misperception in International Politics* (Prince-

ton: Princeton University Press, 1976), 58–113; and Donald Kagan, *On the Origins of War and the Preservation of Peace* (New York: Doubleday, 1995).

34. Joffe, *The Myth of America's Decline*, 144–49.

35. Heritage Foundation, "2014 Index of Economic Freedom, China," www. heritage.org/index/country/china.

36. Freedom House, "Freedom in the World 2014, China," https://freedom-house.org/report/freedom-world/2014/china-0#.VGGLmIdvvRw.

37. Editors, "Document 9: A ChinaFile Translation: How Much Is a Hardline Party Directive Shaping China's Current Political Climate?" *ChinaFile*, November 8, 2013, www.chinafile.com/document-9-chinafile-translation.

38. Chris Buckley, "China Takes Aim at Western Ideas," *New York Times*, August 19, 2013, www.nytimes.com/2013/08/20/world/asia/chinas-new-leader-ship-takes-hard-line-in-secret-memo.html?pagewanted=all&_r=0.

39. Martin Lee, "Who Will Stand with Hong Kong?" *New York Times*, October 3, 2014, www.nytimes.com/2014/10/04/opinion/martin-lee-hong-kongs-great-test. html.

40. Jeff Bader, quoted in William Wan, "Ex-Obama Adviser on Hong Kong: 'We Have to Focus on Reality,'" *Washington Post*, October 2, 2014, www.washingtonpost.com/ blogs/worldviews/wp/2014/10/02/ex-obama-adviser-on-hong-kong-we-have-to-focus-on-reality/.

41. David Shambaugh, quoted in Mark Landler, "An Inconvenient Protest for Both China and the U.S.," *New York Times*, October 3, 2014, www.nytimes. com/2014/10/04/world/asia/an-inconvenient-protest-for-china-and-us-relations-obama-jinping.html.

42. Carl Minzner, "China Is Again Slowly Turning in on Itself," *Los Angeles Times*, October 18, 2014, www.latimes.com/opinion/op-ed/la-oe-1019-minzner-end-of-china-reform-20141019-story.html#page=1.

43. Christopher Layne, "From Preponderance to Offshore Balancing: America's Future Grand Strategy," *International Security* 22, no. 1 (Summer 1997): 86–124; and Barry R. Posen, *Restraint: A New Foundation for U.S. Grand Strategy* (Ithaca: Cornell University Press, 2014).

44. John J. Mearsheimer, "A Return to Offshore Balancing," *Newsweek*, December 30, 2008, www.newsweek.com/return-offshore-balancing-82925; and Stephen M. Walt, "Offshore Balancing: An Idea Whose Time Has Come," *Foreign Policy*, November 2, 2011, www.foreignpolicy.com/posts/2011/11/02/ offshore_balancing_an_idea_whose_time_has_come.

45. Robert G. Kaufman, "To Balance or to Bandwagon? Alignment Decisions in 1930s Europe," *Security Studies* 1, no. 3 (Spring 1992): 417–47.

46. Robert Haddick, *Fire on Water: China, America, and the Future of the Pacific* (Annapolis: Naval Institute Press, 2014), 42.

47. Ibid., 43.

48. See entries by Daniel W. Drezner, Robert S. Ross, Avery Goldstein, Randall L. Schweller and Xiaoyu Pu, Alastair Iain Johnston, and Sean M. Lynn-Jones in *The*

United States and China: A Batch from International Security (MIT Press Batches), Kindle ed. (Cambridge: MIT Press, 2014).

49. Robert G. Sutter, *China's Rise in Asia: Promises and Perils* (Lanham, Md.: Rowman and Littlefield, 2005); and Ross, "The Problem with the Pivot."

50. David Shambaugh, *China Goes Global: The Partial Power* (New York: Oxford University Press, 2013), 308–9.

51. Bill Clinton, *My Life* (New York: Alfred A. Knopf, 2004), 956–57.

52. G. John Ikenberry, "The Illusion of Geopolitics: The Enduring Power of the Liberal Order," *Foreign Affairs*, May/June, 2014, www.foreignaffairs.com/articles/141212/g-john-ikenberry/the-illusion-of-geopolitics.

53. Avery Goldstein, *Rising to the Challenge: China's Grand Strategy and International Security* (Stanford: Stanford University Press, 2005), 204–19.

54. Andrew J. Nathan and Andrew Scobell, *China's Search for Security* (New York: Columbia University Press, 2012), 345–58; and Henry A. Kissinger, *On China* (New York: Penguin Press, 2011), 487–530.

55. Ross Terrill, *The New Chinese Empire: And What It Means for the United States* (New York: Basic Books, 2003), 3–4.

56. Arthur Waldron, "Deterring China," *Commentary*, October 1, 1995, www.commentarymagazine.com/articles/deterring-china/.

57. Friedberg, *A Contest for Supremacy;* and Michael Pillsbury, "The Sixteen Fears: China's Strategic Psychology," *Survival: Global Politics and Strategy"* 54, no. 5 (October 2012): 149–82.

58. Friedberg, *A Contest for Supremacy;* and Pillsbury, "The Sixteen Fears."

59. Gordon G. Chang, "The Coming Collapse of China: 2012 Edition," *Foreign Policy*, December 29, 2011, www.foreignpolicy.com/articles/2011/12/29/the_coming_collapse_of_china_2012_edition.

60. Arthur Waldron, "The Chinese Sickness," *Commentary*, July 1, 2003, www.commentarymagazine.com/articles/the-chinese-sickness/.

61. Aaron L. Friedberg, *Beyond Air-Sea Battle: The Debate over US Military Strategy in Asia* (London: Routledge, 2014).

62. Constantine C. Menges, *China: The Gathering Threat* (Nashville: Nelson Current, 2005), 1–40.

63. Friedberg, *Beyond Air-Sea Battle,* 59.

64. Robert Gilpin, "The Theory of Hegemonic War," *Journal of Interdisciplinary History* 18, no. 4 (Spring 1988): 591–613.

65. John J. Mearsheimer, "Can China Rise Peacefully?" *National Interest,* October 25, 2014, http://nationalinterest.org/commentary/can-china-rise-peacefully-10204.

66. Kaplan, *Asia's Cauldron,* 7.

67. Ibid., 17–18.

68. Jeffrey A. Bader, *Obama and China's Rise: An Insider's Account of America's Asia Strategy* (Washington, D.C.: Brookings Institution Press, 2012), 1–8.

69. Martin S. Indyk, Kenneth G. Lieberthal, and Michael E. O'Hanlon, *Bend-*

ing History: Barack Obama's Foreign Policy (Washington, D.C.: Brookings Institution, 2012), 31.

70. H. Clinton, "America's Pacific Century."

71. Mark Landler, "Clinton Seeks a Shift on China," *New York Times,* February 13, 2009, www.nytimes.com/2009/02/14/world/asia/14diplo.html?_r=0.

72. "Clinton Softens Her Tone on China," *New York Times,* February 20, 2009, www.nytimes.com/2009/02/20/world/asia/20iht-clinton.4.20337969.html.

73. H. Clinton, *Hard Choices,* 491–506.

74. Michael Wines, "China Leader Warns Iran Not to Make Nuclear Arms," *New York Times,* January 20, 2012, www.nytimes.com/2012/01/21/world/asia/chinese-leader-wen-criticizes-iran-on-nuclear-program.html.

75. Indyk, Lieberthal, and O'Hanlon, *Bending History,* 38.

76. Bader, *Obama and China's Rise,* 26–39, 83–93.

77. "In Focus: North Korea's Nuclear Threats," *New York Times,* April 16, 2013, www.nytimes.com/interactive/2013/04/12/world/asia/north-korea-questions.html.

78. Sharon LaFraniere, "On North Korea, China Prefers Fence," *New York Times,* May 23, 2010, www.nytimes.com/2010/05/24/world/asia/24china.html.

79. Barack Obama, quoted in "Obama: U.S. Will Defend South Korea," CBS News, November 23, 2010, www.cbsnews.com/news/obama-we-will-defend-south-korea/.

80. David E. Sanger and Mark McDonald, "South Koreans and U.S. to Stage a Joint Exercise," *New York Times,* November 23, 2010, www.nytimes.com/2010/11/24/world/asia/24nkorea.html?pagewanted=all; and Martin Fackler, "U.S. and South Korea Begin Joint Naval Exercises," *New York Times,* November 27, 2010, www.nytimes.com/2010/11/28/world/asia/28korea.html.

81. Choe Sang-Hun, "South Korea Approves Free Trade Pact with U.S.," *New York Times,* November 22, 2011, www.nytimes.com/2011/11/23/business/global/seoul-votes-a-chaotic-yes-to-free-trade-with-us.html?pagewanted=all.

82. Bader, *Obama and China's Rise,* 40–47.

83. Martin Fackler, "Rebuilding Lives and American Ties to Japan," *New York Times,* March 22, 2011, www.nytimes.com/2011/03/23/world/asia/23reagan.html?pagewanted=all.

84. Dan Twining, "The Obama Administration Gets Indonesia Right and Burma Wrong," *Foreign Policy,* July 31, 2009, http://shadow.foreignpolicy.com/posts/2009/07/31/the_obama_administration_gets_indonesia_right_and_burma_wrong.

85. Murray Hiebert, Ted Osius, and Gregory B. Poling, "A U.S.–Indonesia Partnership for 2020: Recommendations for Forging a 21st Century Relationship," *CSIS Report,* September 2013, http://csis.org/files/publication/130917_Hiebert_USIndonesiaPartnership_WEB.pdf.

86. Kaplan, *Asia's Cauldron,* 8, 9, 41.

87. Jane Perlez, "American and Chinese Navy Ships Nearly Collided in South China Sea," *New York Times,* December 14, 2013, www.nytimes.com/2013/12/15/world/asia/chinese-and-american-ships-nearly-collide-in-south-china-sea.html.

88. Robert Haddick, "America Has No Answer to China's Salami-Slicing," *War on the Rocks,* February 6, 2014, http://warontherocks.com/2014/02/america-has-no-answer-to-chinas-salami-slicing/#_.

89. Michael Pillsbury, *The Hundred-Year Marathon: China's Secret Strategy to Replace America as the Global Superpower* (New York: Henry Holt, 2015), 35–36.

90. Michael Mazza, "Biden and Hagel Appease China at Allies' Expense," *National Interest,* December 11, 2013, http://nationalinterest.org/commentary/biden-hagel-appease-china-allies-expense-9541.

91. Jane Perlez, "Japan's Leader Compares Strain with China to Germany and Great Britain in 1914," *New York Times,* January 23, 2014, www.nytimes.com/2014/01/24/world/asia/japans-leader-compares-strain-with-china-to-germany-and-britain-in-1914.html.

92. Bradsher, "Philippine Leader Sounds Alarm on China."

93. Kaplan, *Asia's Caldron,* 51–70.

94. StMA, "Obama Admin Gets Tougher with China over South China Sea Claims," Consortium of Defense Analysts, February 9, 2014, http://cofda.wordpress.com/2014/02/09/obama-admin-gets-tougher-on-china-over-south-china-sea-claims/.

95. Trefor Moss, "America's Pivot to Asia: A Report Card," *Diplomat,* May 5, 2013, http://thediplomat.com/2013/05/americas-pivot-to-asia-a-report-card/.

96. Barack Obama, "Remarks by President Obama and Benigno Aquino III of the Philippines in Joint Press Conference," Manila, Philippines, April 28, 2014, www.whitehouse.gov/the-press-office/2014/04/28/remarks-president-obama-and-president-benigno-aquino-iii-philippines-joi.

97. Andrew Browne, "Asian Nations' Fears of War Elevated as China Flexes Muscle, Study Finds," *Wall Street Journal,* July 14, 2014, http://online.wsj.com/articles/asian-nations-fears-of-war-elevated-as-china-flexes-muscle-study-finds-1405361047.

98. "How Asians View Each Other," Pew Research Global Attitudes Project, July 14, 2014, www.pewglobal.org/2014/07/14/chapter-4-how-asians-view-each-other/.

99. "Asia Is Undergoing the Fastest Military Buildup on the Planet," *Economist,* March 26, 2012, www.businessinsider.com/military-spending-in-southeast-asia-is-skyrocketing-2012-3; and Stockholm International Peace Research Institute, "Military Spending Continues to Fall in the West but Rises Everywhere Else, Says SIPRI," April 14, 2014, www.sipri.org/media/pressreleases/2014/Milex_April_2014.

100. Rahul Bedi, "New Naval Base Coming Up Near Visakhapatnam," *IHS Jane's Business Standard,* August 26, 2014, www.business-standard.com/article/current-affairs/new-naval-base-coming-up-near-visakhapatnam-114082601458_1.html.

101. Kaplan, *Asia's Cauldron,* 35.

102. Japanese Ministry of Defense, "Defense of Japan 2014: Security Environment Surrounding Japan: Section 3, China," www.mod.go.jp/e/publ/w_paper/pdf/2014/DOJ2014_1-1-3_web_1031.pdf.

103. "Japan's Military Spending: Tooling Up," *Economist,* September 1, 2014, www.economist.com/blogs/banyan/2014/09/japans-military-spending.

104. Paul J. Leaf, "Promise and Potential Peril: Japan's Military Normalization," *Diplomat,* September 4, 2014, http://thediplomat.com/2014/09/promise-and-potential-peril-japans-military-normalization/.

105. Sadanand Dhume, quoted in "AEI Reactions to Obama's Upcoming Asia Trip," *AEIdeas,* October 2, 2013, www.aei.org/publication/aei-reactions-to-obamas-upcoming-asia-trip/.

106. Jane Perlez, "Cancellation of Trip by Obama Plays to Doubts of Asia Allies," *New York Times,* October 4, 2013, www.nytimes.com/2013/10/05/world/asia/with-obama-stuck-in-washington-china-leader-has-clear-path-at-asia-conferences.html?pagewanted=all.

107. Rizal Sukma, quoted in ibid.

108. National Defense Panel, "Ensuring a Strong U.S. Defense for the Future."

109. Katrina McFarland, quoted in Zachary Fryer-Biggs, "DoD Official: Asia Pivot 'Can't Happen' Due to Budget Pressures," *Defense News,* March 4, 2014, www.defensenews.com/article/20140304/DEFREG02/303040022/DoD-Official-Asia-Pivot-Can-t-Happen-Due-Budget-Pressures.

110. Admiral Jonathan W. Greenert, U.S.N., and General Norton A. Schwartz, U.S.A.F., "Air-Sea Battle," *American Interest,* February 20, 2012, www.the-american-interest.com/2012/02/20/air-sea-battle/.

111. Friedberg, *Beyond Air-Sea Battle,* 73–149; and Haddick, *Fire on Water,* 160–218.

112. Chuck Hagel, quoted in Christopher J. Griffin and Robert Zarate, "FPI Bulletin: Risks and Reality in the Defense Budget," *Foreign Policy Initiative,* February 26, 2014, www.foreignpolicyi.org/content/fpi-bulletin-risks-and-reality-defense-budget.

113. Jonathan Greenert, quoted in Ernesto Londoño, "Hagel Seeks to Reassure Allies in Asia amid Questions about U.S. Commitment," *Washington Post,* April 5, 2014, www.washingtonpost.com/world/asia_pacific/hagel-seeks-to-reassure-allies-in-asia-amid-questions-about-us-commitment/2014/04/05/2feda9b8-6d92-4609-89c6-ba3fb85d5e99_story.html.

114. Pillsbury, *The Hundred-Year Marathon,* 141.

115. Kaplan, *Asia's Cauldron,* 30.

116. Gardiner Harris, "Years after Obama Hailed Warming Ties with India, the Temperature Has Fallen," *New York Times,* March 31, 2014, www.nytimes.com/2014/04/01/world/asia/years-after-obama-hailed-warming-ties-with-india-the-temperature-has-fallen.html.

117. Robert D. Blackwill, "The India Imperative," *National Interest,* Summer 2005, 10.

118. Robert Kagan, "India Is Not a Precedent," *Washington Post,* March 12, 2006, B07, www.washingtonpost.com/wp-dyn/content/article/2006/03/10/AR2006031001865.html.

119. Editorial Board, "India-America Relations on Edge," *New York Times,* January 14, 2014, www.nytimes.com/2014/01/15/opinion/india-america-relations-on-edge.html.

120. Walter Russell Mead, "Why Syria Isn't the Big Story This Week," *American Interest,* August 31, 2013, www.the-american-interest.com/2013/08/31/why-syria-isnt-the-big-story-this-week/.

121. For the definitive history of India since independence, see Ramachandra Guha, *India after Gandhi: The History of the World's Largest Democracy* (New York: Ecco, 2007).

122. Council on Foreign Relations, "Indian Prime Minister Narendra Modi on India's Economy and U.S.–India Relations," September 29, 2014, www.cfr.org/india/indian-prime-minister-narendra-modi-indias-economy-us-india-relations/p33535.

123. Maitreesh Ghatak and Sanchari Roy, "Modinomics: Do Narendra Modi's Economic Claims Add Up?" *Guardian,* March 13, 2014, www.theguardian.com/commentisfree/2014/mar/13/modinomics-narendra-modi-india-bjp.

124. Naazneen Karmali, "India Election Result: Narendra Modi Sweeps to Victory, Indian Stocks Soar," *Forbes,* May 16, 2014, www.forbes.com/sites/naazneenkarmali/2014/05/16/india-election-resultnarendra-modi-sweeps-to-victory-sensex-soars/.

125. "Modi Beefs Up Indian Military," *American Interest,* July 14, 2014, www.the-american-interest.com/2014/07/14/modi-beefs-up-indian-military/.

126. Lisa Curtis, "An Opportunity to Reenergize U.S.–India Relations," Heritage Foundation, August 16, 2014, www.heritage.org/research/reports/2014/09/an-opportunity-to-reenergize-usindia-relations-lisa-curtis.

127. Ellen Barry, "Narendra Modi's Ambitious Agenda Will Face Difficult Obstacles," *New York Times,* May 16, 2014, www.nytimes.com/2014/05/17/world/asia/india-elections.html.

128. For a highly negative account of what Modi represents (the antithesis of this writer's view), see Pankaj Mishra, "Modi's Idea of India," *New York Times,* October 24, 2014, www.nytimes.com/2014/10/25/opinion/pankaj-mishra-nirandra-modis-idea-of-india.html.

129. Gardiner Harris, "India's Muslims Wary of Rising Political Star," *New York Times,* March 3, 2014, www.nytimes.com/2014/03/04/world/asia/indias-muslims-wary-of-rising-political-star.html.

130. Niharika Mandhana and William Mauldin, "Indian Leader Modi Moves Closer to U.S. as Differences Persist," *Wall Street Journal,* September 30, 2014, http://online.wsj.com/articles/obama-narendra-modi-meet-at-white-house-in-first-formal-talks-1412089904.

131. Council on Foreign Relations, "Indian Prime Minister Narendra Modi."

132. Curtis, "An Opportunity to Reenergize U.S.–India Relations."

133. Associated Press, "Obama, Modi Declare Era of 'New Trust' in US–India Relations," *Daily Mail,* January 26, 2015, www.dailymail.co.uk/wires/ap/article-2925366/Obama-received-warmly-India-seeks-policy-advances.html.

134. Landler, "An Inconvenient Protest for Both China and the U.S."

135. Ibid.

136. John Kerry, "China, America and Our Warming Planet," *New York Times,* November 11, 2014, www.nytimes.com/2014/11/12/opinion/john-kerry-our-historic-agreement-with-china-on-climate-change.html.

137. Carol E. Lee, Jeremy Page, and William Mauldin, "U.S., China Reach New Climate, Military Deal," *Wall Street Journal,* November 12, 2014, http://online.wsj.com/articles/u-s-china-ready-deals-to-avert-military-confrontations-1415721451.

138. Ibid.

139. Roger Cohen, "Asia's American Angst," *New York Times,* October 16, 2014, www.nytimes.com/2014/10/17/opinion/roger-cohen-asias-american-angst.html?_r=0.

140. Ibid.

Conclusion

1. Samuel P. Huntington, *American Politics: The Promise of Disharmony* (Cambridge: Belknap Press of Harvard University Press, 1981), 246–50.

2. Samuel P. Huntington, *The Third Wave: Democratization in the Late Twentieth Century* (Norman: University of Oklahoma Press, 1993).

3. Josef Joffe, *The Myth of America's Decline: Politics, Economics, and a Half Century of False Prophesies* (New York: Liveright, 2014), 264–67.

4. Huntington, *The Third Wave.*

5. Strobe Talbott, "Rethinking the Red Menace," *Time,* January 1, 1990.

6. See, e.g., John Patrick Diggins, *Ronald Reagan: Fate, Freedom and the Making of History* (New York: W. W. Norton, 2007); James Mann, *The Rebellion of Ronald Reagan: A History of the End of the Cold War* (New York: Viking, 2009); Justin Vaïsse, *Neoconservatism: The Biography of a Movement,* trans. Arthur Goldhammer (Cambridge: Belknap Press of Harvard University Press, 2010); and Jack F. Matlock Jr., *Superpower Illusions: How Myths and False Ideologies Led America Astray—and How to Return to Reality* (New Haven: Yale University Press, 2010).

7. Beth A. Fischer, *The Reagan Reversal: Foreign Policy and the End of the Cold War* (Columbia: University of Missouri Press, 1997).

8. Mann, *The Rebellion of Ronald Reagan,* 280–320; and Vaïsse, *Neoconservatism,* 196–97.

9. John Lewis Gaddis, *We Now Know: Rethinking Cold War History* (New York: Oxford University Press, 1997).

10. For a detailed and compelling account of the genesis and implementation of Reagan's strategy to defeat the Soviet Union, see Peter Schweizer, *Reagan's War: The Epic Story of His Forty-Year Struggle and Final Triumph over Communism* (New York: Doubleday, 2002).

11. Ronald Reagan, "Remarks and a Question-and-Answer Session at the University of Virginia," Charlottesville, December 16, 1988, www.reagan.utexas.edu/archives/speeches/1988/121688b.htm.

12. Ibid.

13. Jonathan Haslam, *Russia's Cold War: From the October Revolution to the Fall of the Wall* (New Haven: Yale University Press, 2011), 399.

14. Jeane J. Kirkpatrick, *Dictatorships and Double Standards: Rationalism and Reason in Politics* (New York: Simon and Schuster, 1982).

15. Winston S. Churchill, "Dictators and the Covenant," in *Winston S. Churchill: His Complete Speeches, 1897–1963,* ed. Robert Rhodes James, 8 vols. (New York: Chelsea House, 1974), 6:5717–21.

16. Jeffrey H. Anderson, "Is Defense Spending Driving Our Debt?," *Weekly Standard,* July 8, 2011, www.weeklystandard.com/blogs/defense-spending-driving-our-debt_576430.html.

17. Ronald Reagan, *An American Life* (New York: Simon and Schuster, 1990), 410.

18. Francis Fukuyama—a critic of neoconservatism—points out compellingly the many and deep affinities between Reagan and neoconservatives. See Francis Fukuyama, *America at the Crossroads: Democracy, Power, and the Neoconservative Legacy* (New Haven: Yale University Press, 2006), 45–46.

19. Charles Krauthammer, *Democratic Realism: An American Foreign Policy for a Unipolar World* (Washington, D.C.: American Enterprise Institute Press, 2004), 1–21.

20. Reagan, "The Brotherhood of Man."

21. NSDD 75, 3.

22. John Lewis Gaddis, *Surprise, Security, and the American Experience* (Cambridge: Harvard University Press, 2004).

23. Daniel Henninger, "Father of the Bush Doctrine: The Saturday Interview with George Shultz," *Wall Street Journal,* April 29, 2006, A8, http://online.wsj.com/news/articles/SB114626915007139434.

24. Robert D. Kaplan, *Asia's Cauldron: The South China Sea and the End of a Stable Pacific* (New York: Random House, 2014), 25.

25. Aristotle, *Nicomachean Ethics,* trans. Robert C. Bartlett and Susan D. Collins (Chicago: University of Chicago Press, 2011), 115–34.

Epilogue

1. Martin Dempsey, quoted in Greg Jaffe, "Obama Budget's Boost for Military Spending Points to Brewing National Security Debate," *Washington Post,* February 1, 2015, www.washingtonpost.com/politics/obama-budgets-boost-for-military-spending-points-to-brewing-national-security-debate/2015/02/01/914c5030-a967-11e4-a2b2-776095f393b2_story.html.

2. Barack Obama, *National Security Strategy,* February 2015, www.whitehouse.gov/sites/default/files/docs/2015_national_security_strategy.pdf.

3. David Adesnik and Christopher J. Griffin, "FPI Fact Sheet: Defense Budgeting in Context," Foreign Policy Initiative, March 17, 2015, www.foreignpolicyi.org/content/fpi-fact-sheet-defense-budgeting-in-context.

4. Helene Cooper, "Obama's Defense Budget Aims Higher, and at Overseas Conflicts," *New York Times,* February 2, 2015, www.nytimes.com/2015/02/03/us/politics/obamas-budget-seeks-534-billion-for-pentagon.html?_r=0.

5. Jaffe, "Obama Budget's Boost for Military."

6. Ian Talley and Lingling Wei, "Momentum Builds to Label Chinese Yuan a Reserve Currency," *Wall Street Journal*, April 1, 2015, www.wsj.com/articles/momentum-builds-to-label-chinese-yuan-a-reserve-currency-1427926918?KEYWORDS=China+IMF.

7. Trefor Moss, "China Expands Islands in Disputed Waters, Photos Show," *Wall Street Journal*, April 14, 2015, www.wsj.com/articles/china-expands-islands-in-disputed-waters-photos-show-1429011466?KEYWORDS=south+china+sea.

8. Obama, *National Security Strategy*, February 2015.

9. Steven Mufson and David Nakamura, "Obama: China Has Benefited by U.S. Presence in Asia," *Washington Post*, April 28, 2015, www.washingtonpost.com/blogs/post-politics/wp/2015/04/28/obama-and-japanese-leader-vow-closer-ties-70-years-after-the-end-of-world-war-ii/.

10. Aaron L. Friedberg, "The Sleeper Issue of 2016 Is China," *Politico*, May 11, 2015, www.politico.com/magazine/story/2015/05/2016-elections-beijing-117831.html#.VVVJKGbyofo.

11. Paul Stronski, "Broken Ukraine: The Mess Isn't All Russia's Fault," *Foreign Affairs*, March 17, 2015, www.foreignaffairs.com/articles/143268/paul-stronski/broken-ukraine.

12. Paul Sonne and Jay Solomon, "Russia Lifts Its Ban on Delivery of S-300 Surface-to-Air Missile System to Iran," *Wall Street Journal*, April 13, 2015, www.wsj.com/articles/russia-lifts-its-ban-on-sales-of-s-300-missiles-to-iran-1428935224.

13. Michael R. Gordon, "Kerry Arrives in Russia for Talks with Vladimir Putin on Cooperation," *New York Times*, May 12, 2015, www.nytimes.com/2015/05/13/world/europe/vladimir-putin-john-kerry-russia-sochi-ukraine-syria.html?_r=0; and Felicia Schwartz and Alan Cullison, "Softer Tone but No Breakthroughs in U.S.–Russia Talks," *Wall Street Journal*, May 12, 2015, www.wsj.com/articles/kerry-arrives-in-russia-for-first-direct-talks-with-putin-in-two-years-1431416574.

14. Anne Applebaum, "How to Make the World's Madmen Think Twice," *Washington Post*, April 2, 2015, www.washingtonpost.com/opinions/make-the-madmen-think-twice/2015/04/02/e2340ad2-d960-11e4-ba28-f2a685dc7f89_story.html.

15. John McCain, quoted in Kyle Balluck, "McCain: 'I'm Ashamed of My Country,'" *The Hill*, February 22, 2015, http://thehill.com/policy/defense/233442-mccain-im-ashamed-of-my-country.

16. Paul McLeary, "More Pentagon Generals Line Up to Proclaim Russia's 'Existential' Threat to U.S.," *Foreign Policy*, July 14, 2015, foreignpolicy.com/2015/07/14/more-pentagon-generals-line-up-to-proclaim-russia-existential-threat-to-u-s/.

17. Lally Weymouth, "Egyptian President Abdel Fatal al-Sissi, Who Talks to Netanyahu 'a Lot,' Says His Country Is in Danger of Collapse," *Washington Post*, March 12, 2015, www.washingtonpost.com/opinions/egypts-president-says-he-talks-to-netanyahu-a-lot/2015/03/12/770ef928-c827-11e4-aa1a-86135599fb0f_story.html.

18. Orient Advisory Group, "Middle East Briefing: Why Jordan Put Its Army on Alert March 16—and Why Its Foreign Minister Went to Iran a Week Earlier," *Middle East Briefing,* March 23, 2015, http://mebriefing.com/?p=1578.

19. Ali al-Mujahed and Hugh Naylor, "Bombers Strike Rebel-Linked Mosques during Friday Prayers in Yemen," March 20, 2015, www.washingtonpost.com/world/middle_east/reports-suicide-bombers-strike-rebel-linked-mosque-in-yemen/2015/03/20/bd36caba-cef4-11e4-a2a7-9517a3a70506_story.html.

20. Karam Shoumali and Ceylan Yeginsu, "Turkey Says Suicide Bombing Kills at Least 30 in Suruc, Near Syria," *New York Times,* July 20, 2015, www.nytimes.com/2015/07/21/world/europe/suruc-turkey-syria-explosion.html?_r=0.

21. Stephen F. Hayes and Thomas Joscelyn, "How America Was Misled on al Qaeda's Demise," *Wall Street Journal,* March 5, 2015, www.wsj.com/articles/stephen-hayes-and-tomas-joscelyn-how-america-was-misled-on-al-qaedas-demise-1425600796.

22. Jennifer Griffin and Lucas Tomlinson, "Army Chief Odierno, in Exit Interview, Says US Could Have 'Prevented' ISIS Rise," *FoxNews.com,* July 22, 2015, www.foxnews.com/politics/2015/07/22/exclusive-army-chief-odierno-in-exit-interview-says-us-could-have-prevented/.

23. Eric Schmitt, "Iran Sent Arms to Iraq to Fight ISIS, U.S. Says," *New York Times,* March 16, 2015, www.nytimes.com/2015/03/17/world/middleeast/iran-sent-arms-to-iraq-to-fight-isis-us-says.html.

24. Michael Doran, "Obama's Secret Iran Strategy," *Mosaic Magazine,* February 2, 2015, http://mosaicmagazine.com/essay/2015/02/obamas-secret-iran-strategy/.

25. Liz Sly, "Petraeus: The Islamic State Isn't Our Biggest Problem in Iraq," *Washington Post,* March 20, 2015, www.washingtonpost.com/blogs/worldviews/wp/2015/03/20/petraeus-the-islamic-state-isnt-our-biggest-problem-in-iraq/.

26. Walter Russell Mead, "Captain Obama and the Great White Whale," *American Interest,* March 20, 2015, www.the-american-interest.com/2015/03/20/captain-obama-and-the-great-white-whale/.

27. Helene Cooper, "Saudi Arabia Says King Won't Attend Meetings in U.S.," *New York Times,* May 10, 2015, www.nytimes.com/2015/05/11/world/middleeast/saudi-arabia-king-wont-attend-camp-david-meeting.html?_r=0.

28. Charles Krauthammer, "The Fatal Flaw in the Iran Deal," *Washington Post,* February 26, 2015, www.washingtonpost.com/opinions/the-fatal-flaw-in-the-iran-deal/2015/02/26/9186c70e-bde1-11e4-8668-4e7ba8439ca6_story.html.

29. Joint Comprehensive Plan of Action (full text of Iran nuclear deal), Vienna, July 14, 2015, http://apps.washingtonpost.com/g/documents/world/full-text-of-the-iran-nuclear-deal/1651/.

30. Ibid.

31. Thomas L. Friedman, "A Good Bad Deal?" *New York Times,* July 1, 2015, www.nytimes.com/2015/07/01/opinion/thomas-friedman-a-good-bad-deal.html?smid=tw-TomFriedman&seid=auto&_r=0.

32. Henry Kissinger and George P. Shultz, "The Iran Deal and Its Conse-

quences," *Wall Street Journal,* April 7, 2015, www.wsj.com/articles/the-iran-deal-and-its-consequences-1428447582.

33. Henry Kissinger, *World Order* (New York: Penguin Press, 2014), 165–66.

34. Thomas L. Friedman, "Iran and the Obama Doctrine," *New York Times,* April 5, 2015, www.nytimes.com/2015/04/06/opinion/thomas-friedman-the-obama-doctrine-and-iran-interview.html.

35. Rick Gladstone, "Strait of Hormuz Once Again at Center of U.S.–Iran Strife," *New York Times,* May 1, 2015, www.nytimes.com/2015/05/02/world/middleeast/strait-of-hormuz-once-again-at-center-of-us-iran-strife.html.

36. "Remarks by President Obama's to the United Nations General Assembly," www.whitehouse.gov/the-press-office/2015/09/28/remarks-president-obama-united-nations-general-assembly.

37. For a chilling and definitive account of this lamentable trend, see Michael B. Oren, *Ally: My Journey across the American-Israeli Divide* (New York: Random House, 2015).

38. Michael Warren, "Hillary Silent on Obama Threats to Israel," *Weekly Standard,* March 19, 2015, www.weeklystandard.com/blogs/hillary-silent-obama-threats-israel_892358.html.

39. Marco Rubio, "Obama Administration's Treatment of Israel Is a 'Historic and Tragic Mistake,'" Senate floor speech, March 19, 2015, www.rubio.senate.gov/public/index.cfm/press-releases?ID=4123bbf1-c114-4b4c-9998-421ba6dac2d2.

40. "A Conversation with Marco Rubio," remarks made at the Council on Foreign Relations, May 13, 2015, www.cfr.org/united-states/conversation-marco-rubio/p36511.

41. Bret Stephens, "An Unteachable President," *Wall Street Journal,* September 28, 2015, www.wsj.com/articles/an-unteachable-president-1443485444.

42. Jeffrey Goldberg, "'Look . . . It's My Name on This': Obama Defends the Iran Nuclear Deal," *Atlantic,* May 21, 2015, www.theatlantic.com/international/archive/2015/05/obama-interview-iran-isis-israel/393782/.

43. Ibid.

44. Ibid.

45. Rubio, "Obama Administration's Treatment of Israel."

46. "A Conversation with Marco Rubio."

47. Lindsey Graham, "Lindsey Graham on Iran's Nuclear Program," remarks made at the Council on Foreign Relations, March 23, 2015, www.cfr.org/iran/conversation-lindsey-graham/p36291.

Select Bibliography

Ajami, Fouad. *The Syrian Rebellion*. Stanford, Calif.: Hoover Institution Press, 2012.

Applebaum, Anne. *Gulag: A History*. New York: Doubleday, 2003.

———. "How to Make the World's Madmen Think Twice." *Washington Post,* April 2, 2015, www.washingtonpost.com/opinions/make-the-madmen-think-twice/2015/04/02/e2340ad2-d960-11e4-ba28-f2a685dc7f89_story.html.

———. *Iron Curtain: The Crushing of Eastern Europe, 1944–1956*. New York: Doubleday, 2012.

Aron, Leon. *Yeltsin: A Revolutionary Life*. New York: St Martin's Press, 2000.

Auslin, Michael. "Obama's Asia Policy Flounders." *Commentary*, March 17, 2015, www.commentarymagazine.com/2015/03/17/obamas-asia-policy-flounders/.

Bacevich, Andrew J. *The Limits of Power: The End of American Exceptionalism*. New York: Metropolitan Books, 2008.

———. *Washington Rules: America's Path to Permanent War*. New York: Metropolitan Books, 2010.

Boot, Max. "More 'Daylight' between Netanyahu's Israel and the U.S.—Is That What Obama Wants?" *Los Angeles Times,* March 19, 2015, www.latimes.com/opinion/op-ed/la-oe-0320-boot-israel-election-20150320-story.html.

Bourne, Peter C. *Jimmy Carter: A Comprehensive Biography from Plains to Post-Presidency*. New York: Scribner's, 1997.

Brinkley, Douglas. *The Unfinished Presidency: Jimmy Carter's Quest for Global Peace*. New York: Viking, 1998.

Brooks, Stephen G., G. John Ikenberry, and William C. Wohlforth. "Lean Forward: In Defense of American Engagement." *Foreign Affairs,* January/February 2013, www.foreignaffairs.com/articles/138468/stephen-g-brooks-g-john-ikenberry-and-william-c-wohlforth/lean-forward.

Brooks, Stephen G., and William C. Wohlforth. *World Out of Balance: International Relations and the Challenge of American Primacy*. Princeton: Princeton University Press, 2008.

Brzezinski, Zbigniew. *The Grand Chessboard: American Primacy and Its Geostrategic Imperatives*. New York: Basic Books, 1997.

Bush, George W. *Decision Points*. New York: Crown Books, 2010.

Cagaptay, Soner. *The Rise of Turkey: The Twenty-First Century's First Muslim Power*. Lincoln: University of Nebraska Press, 2014.

Carter, Jimmy. *Palestine: Peace Not Apartheid*. New York: Simon and Schuster, 2006.

Chollet, Derek, and James Goldgeier. *America between the Wars: From 11/9 to 9/11; The Misunderstood Years between the Fall of the Berlin Wall and the Start of the War on Terror.* New York: Public Affairs, 2008.

Churchill, Winston S. "Dictators and the Covenant." December 21, 1937. In *Winston S. Churchill: His Complete Speeches, 1897–1963.* Edited by Robert Rhodes James. Vol. 6. London: Chelsea House, 1974.

Clinton, Hillary Rodham. "America's Pacific Century." *Foreign Policy,* October 11, 2011, www.foreignpolicy.com/articles/2011/10/11/americas_pacific_century.

———. *Hard Choices.* New York: Simon and Schuster, 2014.

———. "Transcript: Senate Confirmation Hearing: Hillary Clinton." *New York Times,* January 13, 2009, www.nytimes.com/2009/01/13/us/politics/13text-clinton.html?pagewanted=all&_r=0.

Commission on Presidential Debates. Debate Transcript. "President Barack Obama and Former Gov. Mitt Romney, R-Mass., Participate in a Candidates Debate." Lynn University, Boca Raton, Fla., October 22, 2012, http://debates.org/index.php?page=october-22–2012-the-third-obama-romney-presidential-debate.

Cooper, Robert. *The Breaking of Nations: Order and Chaos in the Twenty-First Century.* New York: Atlantic Monthly Press, 2004.

Council on Foreign Relations. "Transcript: Indian Prime Minister Narendra Modi on India's Economy and U.S.–India Relations." September 29, 2014, www.cfr.org/india/indian-prime-minister-narendra-modi-indias-economy-us-india-relations/p33535.

Doran, Michael. "Obama's Secret Iran Strategy." *Mosaic Magazine,* February 2, 2015, http://mosaicmagazine.com/essay/2015/02/obamas-secret-iran-strategy/.

Dueck, Colin. *Hard Line: The Republican Party and U.S. Foreign Policy since World War II.* Princeton: Princeton University Press, 2010.

———. *The Obama Doctrine: American Grand Strategy Today.* New York: Oxford University Press, 2015.

Fischer, Beth. *The Reagan Reversal: Foreign Policy and the End of the Cold War.* Columbia: University of Missouri Press, 1997.

Flynn, Michael T. "Why the Iraq Offensive Will Fail." *Politico,* February 20, 2015, www.politico.com/magazine/story/2015/02/why-the-iraq-offensive-will-fail-115356.html#.VRWPUGYqofo.

Fox, Richard Wightman. *Reinhold Niebuhr: A Biography.* New York: Pantheon, 1985.

Fradkin, Hillel, and Lewis Libby. "Erdogan's Grand Vision: Rise and Decline." *World Affairs Journal,* March/April 2013, www.worldaffairsjournal.org/article/erdogan%E2%80%99s-grand-vision-rise-and-decline.

Friedberg, Aaron L. *Beyond Air-Sea Battle: The Debate over US Military Strategy in Asia.* London: Routledge, 2014.

———. *A Contest for Supremacy: China, America, and the Struggle for Mastery in Asia.* New York: W. W. Norton, 2011.

———. "The Sleeper Issue of 2016 Is China." *Politico,* May 11, 2015, www

.politico.com/magazine/story/2015/05/2016-elections-beijing-117831.html#
.VVVJKGbyofo.

Friedman, Thomas L. "Clinton's Foreign Policy Agenda Reaches across Broad Spectrum." *New York Times,* October 4, 1992, www.nytimes.com/1992/10/04/
us/1992-campaign-issues-foreign-policy-looking-abroad-clinton-foreign-policy
.html.

————. "Iran and the Obama Doctrine." *New York Times,* April 5, 2015, www
.nytimes.com/2015/04/06/opinion/thomas-friedman-the-obama-doctrine-and-
iran-interview.html.

————. "Obama on the World." *New York Times,* August 8, 2014, www.nytimes
.com/2014/08/09/opinion/president-obama-thomas-l-friedman-iraq-and-
world-affairs.html.

————. "Obama's Foreign Policy Book." *New York Times,* May 31, 2014, www
.nytimes.com/2014/06/01/opinion/sunday/friedman-obamas-foreign-policy-
book.html.

Fukuyama, Francis. *America at the Crossroads: Democracy, Power, and the Neoconservative Legacy.* New Haven: Yale University Press, 2006.

Fulbright, J. William. *The Arrogance of Power.* New York: Random House, 1966.

Fuller, Graham E. *Turkey and the Arab Spring: Leadership in the Middle East.* Squamish, B.C.: Bozorg Press, 2014.

Gaddis, John Lewis. *The Cold War: A New History.* New York: Penguin Press, 2005.

————. *Strategies of Containment: A Critical Appraisal of American National Security
Policy during the Cold War.* New York: Oxford University Press, 2005.

Gates, Robert M. *Duty: Memoirs of a Secretary at War.* New York: Alfred A. Knopf,
2014.

Gerecht, Reuel Marc. "The New Rouhani: Same as the Old Rouhani." *Weekly Standard,* October 7, 2013, www.weeklystandard.com/articles/new-rouhani_757227
.html.

Gilbert, Martin. *In Ishmael's House: A History of Jews in Muslim Lands.* New Haven:
Yale University Press, 2010.

Gilpin, Robert. "The Theory of Hegemonic War." *Journal of Interdisciplinary History*
18, no. 4 (Spring 1988): 591–613.

Glick, Caroline. *The Israeli Solution: A One-State Plan for Peace in the Middle East.*
New York: Crown Forum, 2014.

Glynn, Patrick. *Closing Pandora's Box: Arms Races, Arms Control, and the History of
the Cold War.* New York: Basic Books, 1992.

Goldberg, Jeffrey. "The Crisis in U.S.–Israel Relations Is Officially Here." *Atlantic,* October 28, 2014, www.theatlantic.com/international/archive/2014/10/
the-crisis-in-us-israel-relations-is-officially-here/382031/.

————. "Hillary Clinton: 'Failure' to Help Syrian Rebels Led to the Rise of ISIS."
Atlantic, August 10, 2014, www.theatlantic.com/international/archive/2014/08/
hillary-clinton-failure-to-help-syrian-rebels-led-to-the-rise-of-isis/375832/.

————. "Obama to Iran and Israel: 'As President of the United States, I Don't Bluff.' "

Atlantic, March 2, 2012, www.theatlantic.com/international/archive/2012/03/obama-to-iran-and-israel-as-president-of-the-united-states-i-dont-bluff/253875/.

Gordon, Michael R. "Kerry Suggests There Is a Place for Assad in Syria Talks." *New York Times,* March 15, 2015, www.nytimes.com/2015/03/16/world/middleeast/kerry-suggests-there-is-a-place-for-assad-in-syria-talks.html?_r=0.

Gordon, Michael R., and David E. Sanger. "Iran Agrees to Detailed Nuclear Outline, First Step toward a Wider Deal." *New York Times,* April 2, 2015, www.nytimes.com/2015/04/03/world/middleeast/iran-nuclear-talks.html?_r=0.

Graham, Lindsey. "Lindsey Graham on Iran's Nuclear Program." Remarks made at the Council on Foreign Relations, March 23, 2015, www.cfr.org/iran/conversation-lindsey-graham/p36291.

———. Transcript of interview by Chuck Todd. *Meet the Press,* March 8, 2015, www.nbcnews.com/meet-the-press/meet-press-transcript-march-8-2015-n323726.

Greenwald, Abe. "He Made It Worse: Obama's Middle East." *Commentary,* May 1, 2014, www.commentarymagazine.com/article/hes-made-it-worse-obamas-middle-east/.

Guha, Ramachandra. *India after Gandhi: The History of the World's Largest Democracy.* New York: Ecco, 2007.

Gulick, Edward V. *Europe's Classical Balance of Power.* 1955. Reprint. New York: W. W. Norton, 1967.

Haass, Richard N. *Foreign Policy Begins at Home: The Case for Putting America's House in Order.* New York: Basic Books, 2013.

Habeck, Mary R. *Knowing the Enemy: Jihadist Ideology and the War on Terror.* New Haven: Yale University Press, 2006.

Hanson, Victor Davis. *The Savior Generals: How Five Great Commanders Saved Wars That Were Lost: From Ancient Greece to Iraq.* New York: Bloomsbury Press, 2013.

Haslam, Jonathan. *Russia's Cold War: From the October Revolution to the Fall of the Wall.* New Haven: Yale University Press, 2011.

Hayes, Stephen F., and Thomas Joscelyn. "How America Was Misled on al Qaeda's Demise." *Wall Street Journal,* March 5, 2015, www.wsj.com/articles/stephen-hayes-and-tomas-joscelyn-how-america-was-misled-on-al-qaedas-demise-1425600796.

Henninger, Daniel. "Father of the Bush Doctrine: The Saturday Interview with George Shultz." *Wall Street Journal,* April 29, 2006, http://online.wsj.com/news/articles/SB114626915007139434.

Hodgson, Godfrey. *The Myth of American Exceptionalism.* New Haven: Yale University Press, 2009.

House, Karen Elliot. *On Saudi Arabia: Its People, Past, Religion, Fault Lines—and Future.* New York: Alfred A. Knopf, 2012.

Hudson, John. "The White House Distances Itself from Netanyahu 'Chickenshit' Comment." *Foreign Policy,* October 29, 2014, http://thecable.foreignpolicy.com/posts/2014/10/29/white_house_distances_itself_from_netanyahu_chickenshit_comment.

Huntington, Samuel P. *American Politics: The Promise of Disharmony.* Cambridge: Belknap Press of Harvard University Press, 1981.

———. *The Third Wave: Democratization in the Late Twentieth Century.* Norman: University of Oklahoma Press, 1993.

Ikenberry, G. John. *Liberal Leviathan: The Origins, Crisis, and Transformation of the American World Order.* Princeton: Princeton University Press, 2011.

Inboden, Will. "Looking for an Obama Doctrine That Doesn't Exist." *Foreign Policy,* September 16, 2013, http://shadow.foreignpolicy.com/posts/2013/09/16/looking_for_an_obama_doctrine_that_doesnt_exist.

Indyk, Martin S., Kenneth G. Lieberthal, and Michael E. O'Hanlon. *Bending History: Barack Obama's Foreign Policy.* Washington, D.C.: Brookings Institution Press, 2012.

Joffe, Josef. *The Myth of America's Decline: Politics, Economics, and a Half Century of False Prophecies.* New York: Liveright, 2014.

Kagan, Donald. *On the Origins of War and the Preservation of Peace.* New York: Doubleday, 1995.

Kagan, Robert. *Dangerous Nation: America's Place in the World, from Its Earliest Days to the Dawn of the Twentieth Century.* New York: Alfred A. Knopf, 2006.

———. *The World America Made.* New York: Alfred A. Knopf, 2012.

Kaplan, Robert D. *Asia's Cauldron: The South China Sea and the End of a Stable Pacific.* New York: Random House, 2014.

Karsh, Efraim. *Islamic Imperialism: A History.* New Haven: Yale University Press, 2006.

———. *Palestine Betrayed.* New Haven: Yale University Press, 2010.

Kaufman, Robert G. "E. H. Carr, Winston Churchill, Reinhold Niebuhr, and Us: The Case for Principled, Prudential Democratic Realism." *Security Studies* 5, no. 2 (December 1995): 314–53.

———. *Henry M. Jackson: A Life in Politics.* Seattle: University of Washington Press, 2000.

———. *In Defense of the Bush Doctrine.* Lexington: University Press of Kentucky, 2007.

———. "A Two-Level Interaction: Structure, Stable Liberal Democracy, and U.S. Grand Strategy." *Security Studies* 3, no. 4 (Summer 1994): 678–717.

Kennan, George F. *American Diplomacy, 1900–1950.* Chicago: University of Chicago Press, 1951.

———. *Realities of American Foreign Policy.* Princeton: Princeton University Press, 1954.

Kerry, John. "China, America and Our Warming Planet." *New York Times,* November 11, 2014, www.nytimes.com/2014/11/12/opinion/john-kerry-our-historic-agreement-with-china-on-climate-change.html.

———. "Interview with David Gregory." *Meet the Press,* March 2, 2014, www.state.gov/secretary/remarks/2014/03/222721.htm.

Kirkpatrick, Jeane J. *Dictatorships and Double Standards: Rationalism and Reason in Politics.* New York: Simon and Schuster, 1982.

Kissinger, Henry A. *Diplomacy*. New York: Simon and Schuster, 1994.

———. *On China*. New York: Penguin Press, 2011.

———. *World Order*. New York: Penguin Press, 2014.

———. *A World Restored: Metternich, Castlereagh, and the Problem of Peace, 1812–22*. Boston: Houghton Mifflin, 1957.

Kissinger, Henry, and George P. Schultz. "The Iran Deal and Its Consequences." *Wall Street Journal*, April 7, 2015, www.wsj.com/articles/the-iran-deal-and-its-consequences-1428447582.

Kloppenberg, James T. *Reading Obama: Dreams, Hope, and the American Political Tradition*. Princeton: Princeton University Press, 2010.

Krauthammer, Charles. "Decline Is a Choice: The New Liberalism and the End of American Ascendancy." *Weekly Standard*, October 19, 2009, www.weeklystandard.com/Content/Public/Articles/000/000/017/056lfnpr.asp#.

———. *Democratic Realism: An American Foreign Policy for a Unipolar World*. Washington, D.C.: American Enterprise Institute Press, 2004.

———. "The Fatal Flaw in the Iran Deal." *Washington Post*, February 26, 2015, www.washingtonpost.com/opinions/thefatal-flaw-in-the-iran-deal/2015/02/26/9186c70e-bde1-11e4-8668-4e7ba8439ca6_story.html.

———. "The Iran Deal: Anatomy of a Disaster." *Washington Post*, April 9, 2015, www.washingtonpost.com/opinions/the-iran-deal-anaomy-of-adisaster/2015/04/09/11bdf9ee-dee7-11e4-a1b8-2ed88bc190d2_story.html.

———. "No Peace in Our Time." *Washington Post*, March 19, 2015, www.washingtonpost.com/opinions/no-peace-in-our-time/2015/03/19/8df19520-ce61-11e4-a2a7-9517a3a70506_story.html.

Krugman, Paul. "In Defense of Obama." *Rolling Stone*, October 8, 2014, www.rollingstone.com/politics/news/in-defense-of-obama-20141008.

Layne, Christopher. "From Preponderance to Offshore Balancing: America's Future Grand Strategy." *International Security* 22, no. 1 (Summer 1997): 86–124.

———. "This Time It's Real: The End of Unipolarity and the Pax Americana." *International Studies Quarterly* 56, no. 1 (2012): 203–13.

Lewis, Bernard. *What Went Wrong? The Clash between Islam and Modernity in the Middle East*. 2002. Reprint. New York: Harper Perennial, 2003.

Lewis, Bernard, and Buntzie Ellis Churchill. *Notes on a Century: Reflections of a Middle East Historian*. New York: Viking, 2012.

Lucas, Edward. *The New Cold War: Putin's Russia and the Threat to the West*. Revised edition. New York: Palgrave Macmillan, 2014.

Mackinder, Halford J. *Democratic Ideals and Reality: A Study in the Politics of Reconstruction*. New York: Henry Holt, 1919.

Mankoff, Jeffrey. *Russian Foreign Policy: The Return of Great Power Politics*. 2nd edition. Lanham, Md.: Rowman & Littlefield, 2011.

Mann, James. *The Obamians: The Struggle inside the White House to Redefine American Power*. New York: Viking, 2012.

Maraniss, David. *Barack Obama: The Story*. New York: Simon and Schuster, 2012.

Martel, William C. "America's Grand Strategy Disaster." *National Interest,* June 9, 2014, http://nationalinterest.org/feature/americas-grand-strategy-disaster-10627.

May, Ernest R., Ed. *American Cold War Strategy: Interpreting NSC 68.* New York: St. Martin's, 1993.

McCarthy, Andrew C. *Spring Fever: The Illusion of Islamic Democracy.* New York: Encounter Books, 2013.

Mead, Walter Russell. "Captain Obama and the Great White Whale." *American Interest,* March 20, 2015, www.the-american-interest.com/2015/03/20/captain-obama-and-the-great-white-whale/.

———. "The Failed Grand Strategy in the Middle East." *Wall Street Journal,* August 24, 2013, http://online.wsj.com/news/articles/SB1000142412788732461950457902892369956840

———. "The Return of Geopolitics: The Revenge of the Revisionist Powers." *Foreign Affairs,* May/June 2014, www.foreignaffairs.com/articles/141211/walter-russell-mead/the-return-of-geopolitics.

———. *Special Providence: American Foreign Policy and How It Changed the World.* New York: Alfred A. Knopf, 2001.

Mearsheimer, John. "Rebalancing the Middle East." *Newsweek,* November 28, 2008, www.newsweek.com/john-mearsheimer-rebalancing-middle-east-85225.

———. "A Return to Offshore Balancing." *Newsweek,* December 30, 2008, www.newsweek.com/return-offshore-balancing-82925.

———. *The Tragedy of Great Power Politics.* New York: W. W. Norton, 2001.

Mearsheimer, John, and Stephen M. Walt. *The Israel Lobby and U.S. Foreign Policy.* New York: Farrar, Straus and Giroux, 2007.

Meyersson, Erik, and Dani Rodrik. "Erdogan's Coup: The True State of Turkish Democracy." *Foreign Affairs,* May 26, 2014, www.foreignaffairs.com/articles/141464/erik-meyersson-and-dani-rodrik/erdogans-coup.

Micklethwait, John, and Adrian Wooldridge. *The Fourth Revolution: The Global Race to Reinvent the State.* New York: Penguin Press, 2014.

Misztal, Blaise, Halil Karaveli, and Svante Cornell. "Foreign Policy Reset Unlikely under President Erdogan." *American Interest,* August 7, 2014, www.the-american-interest.com/2014/08/07foreign-policy-reset-unlikely-under-president-erdogan/.

Morgenthau, Hans J. *Politics among Nations: The Struggle for Power and Peace.* 6th edition. Revised by Kenneth Thompson. New York: Alfred A. Knopf, 1985.

———. *Scientific Man vs. Power Politics.* Chicago: University of Chicago Press, 1946.

Moseley, Carys. "Reinhold Niebuhr's Approach to the State of Israel: The Ethical Promise and Theological Limits of Christian Realism." *Studies in Christian-Jewish Relations* 4, no. 1 (2009), http://ejournals.bc.edu/ojs/index.php/scjr/article/view/1517/1370.

Motyl, Alexander J. "Trusting or Containing Putin?" *World Affairs,* February 13, 2015, www.worldaffairsjournal.org/blog/alexander-j-motyl/trusting-or-containing-putin.

Muravchik, Joshua. *Making David into Goliath: How the World Turned against Israel.* New York: Encounter Books, 2014.

Murdock, Clark A., Ryan Crotty, and Angela Weaver. *Building the 2021 Affordable Military.* Lanham, Md.: Rowman and Littlefield, June 2014.

Nasr, Vali. *The Dispensable Nation: American Foreign Policy in Retreat.* New York: Doubleday, 2013.

Nathan, Andrew J., and Andrew Scobell. *China's Search for Security.* New York: Columbia University Press, 2012.

National Defense Panel. "Ensuring a Strong U.S. Defense for the Future." National Defense Panel Review of the 2014 Quadrennial Defense Review, July 31, 2014, www.usip.org/sites/default/files/Ensuring-a-Strong-U.S.-Defense-for-the-Future-NDP-Review-of-the-QDR.pdf.

National Security Decision Directive (NSDD) 75. "U.S. Relations with the U.S.S.R." January 17, 1983, Records Declassified and Released by the National Security Council. Ronald Reagan Presidential Library.

National Security Study Directive (NSSD) 11-82. August 21, 1982. Ronald Reagan Presidential Library.

Nau, Henry. *Conservative Internationalism: Armed Diplomacy under Jefferson, Polk, Truman, and Reagan.* Princeton: Princeton University Press, 2013.

Netanyahu, Benjamin. "The Complete Transcript of Netanyahu's Address to Congress." *Washington Post,* March 3, 2015, www.washingtonpost.com/blogs/post-politics/wp/2015/03/03/full-text-netanyahus-address-to-congress/.

Niebuhr, Reinhold. *The Children of Light and the Children of Darkness: A Vindication of Democracy and a Critique of Its Traditional Defense.* New York: Scribner's, 1940.

———. *Christianity and Power Politics.* New York: Scribner's, 1940.

———. *Moral Man and Immoral Society: A Study in Ethics and Politics.* New York: Charles Scribner's Sons, 1932.

———. "Our Stake in Israel." *New Republic,* February 3, 1957, www.newrepublic.com/book/review/our-stake-in-the-state-israel.

———. "Winston Churchill and Great Britain." In *A Reinhold Niebuhr Reader.* Edited by Charles E. Brown. Philadelphia: Trinity Press, 1992.

Nye, Joseph S., Jr. *The Future of Power.* New York: Public Affairs, 2011.

———. *Soft Power: The Means to Success in World Politics.* New York: Public Affairs, 2004.

Obama, Barack. "Against Going to War in Iraq." Speech made at the Federal Plaza in Chicago, October 2, 2002, http://obamaspeeches.com/001-2002-Speech-Against-the-Iraq-War-Obama-Speech.htm.

———. *The Audacity of Hope: Thoughts on Reclaiming the American Dream.* New York: Crown, 2006.

———. "Breaking the Cold War Mentality." *Sundial,* March 10, 1983, 1–3.

———. *Dreams from My Father: A Story of Race and Inheritance.* New York: Times Books, 1995.

———. "Full Transcript of Obama's Speech [in Berlin]." *CNNPolitics.com*, July 24, 2008, http://edition.cnn.com/2008/POLITICS/07/24/obama.words/.

———. *National Security Strategy*. February 2015, www.whitehouse.gov/sites/default/files/docs/2015_national_security_strategy.pdf.

———. "News Conference by President Obama." Strasbourg, France, April 4, 2009, www.whitehouse.gov/the-press-officenews-conference-president-obama-4042009.

———. "Obama Flashback: The Day I'm Inaugurated Muslim Hostility Will Ease." New Hampshire Public Radio, November 21, 2007, www.breitbart.com/Breitbart-TV/2012/09/14/FLASHBACK-Obama-The-Day-Im-Inaugurated-Muslim-Hostility-Will-Ease.

———. "President Obama's Message on Nowruz." March 19, 2015, http://iipdigital.usembassy.gov/st/english/texttrans/2015/03/20150320314370.html#axzz3VbPfWacL.

———. "Remarks by President Barack Obama in Prague as Delivered." Prague, Czech Republic, April 5, 2009, www.whitehouse.gov/the_press_office/Remarks-By-President-Barack-Obama-In-Prague-As-Delivered.

———. "Remarks by President Obama and Benigno Aquino III of the Philippines in Joint Press Conference." Manila, Philippines, April 28, 2014, www.whitehouse.gov/the-press-office/2014/04/28/remarks-president-obama-and-president-benigno-aquino-iii-philippines-joi.

———. "Remarks by President Obama and President Medvedev of Russia at New START Treaty Signing Ceremony and Press Conference." Prague, Czech Republic, April 8, 2010, www.whitehouse.gov/the-press-office/remarks-president-obama-and-president-medvedev-russia-new-start-treaty-signing-cere.

———. "Remarks by President Obama at the League of Conservation Voters Capital Dinner." Washington, D.C., June 25, 2014, www.whitehouse.gov/the-press-office/2014/06/25/remarks-president-league-conservation-voters-capital-dinner.

———. "Remarks by President Obama in Address to the United Nations General Assembly." New York, September 24, 2013, www.whitehouse.gov/the-press-office/2013/09/24/remarks-president-obama-address-united-nations-general-assembly.

———. "Remarks by President Obama to the Turkish Parliament." Ankara, Turkey, April 6, 2009, www.whitehouse.gov/the_press_office/Remarks-By-President-Obama-To-The-Turkish-Parliament.

———. "Remarks by the President at the Acceptance of the Nobel Peace Prize." Oslo, Norway, December 10, 2009, www.whitehouse.gov/the-press-office/remarks-president-acceptance-nobel-peace-prize.

———. "Remarks by the President at the Morning Plenary Session of the United Nations Climate Change Conference." Copenhagen, Denmark, December 18, 2009, www.whitehouse.gov/the-pressoffice/remarks-president-morning-plenary-session-united-nations-climate-change-conference.

———. "Remarks by the President at the New Economic School Graduation." Moscow, Russia, July 7, 2009, www.whitehouse.gov/the-press-office/remarks-president-new-economic-school-graduation.

————. "Remarks by the President at the United States Military Academy Commencement Ceremony." West Point, N.Y., May 28, 2014, www.whitehouse.gov/the-press-office/2014/05/28/remarks-president-united-states-military-academy-commencement-ceremony.

————. "Remarks by the President in Address to the Nation on Syria." September 10, 2013, www.whitehouse.gov/the-press-office/2013/09/10/remarks-president-address-nation-syria.

————. "Remarks by the President in State of the Union Address." U.S. Capitol, January 20, 2015, www.whitehouse.gov/the-press-office/2015/01/20/remarks-president-state-union-address-january-20-2015.

————. "Remarks by the President on a New Beginning." Cairo University, Cairo, Egypt, June 4, 2009, www.whitehouse.gov/the_press_office/Remarks-by-the-President-at-Cairo-University-6-04-09.

————. "Remarks by the President to the United Nations General Assembly," New York, September 23, 2009, www.whitehouse.gov/the-press-office/remarks-president-united-nations-general-assembly.

————. "Renewing American Leadership." *Foreign Affairs*, July/August 2007, www.foreignaffairs.com/articles/62636/barack-obama/renewing-american-leadership.

————. "Statement by the President on Iraq." August 9, 2014, www.whitehouse.gov/the-press-office/2014/08/09/statement-president-iraq.

————. "Statement by the President on ISIL." September 10, 2014, www.whitehouse.gov/the-press-office/2014/09/10/statement-president-isil-1.

————. "Statement by the President on Syria." August 31, 2013, www.whitehouse.gov/the-press-office/2013/08/31/statement-president-syria.

————. "Statement by the President on Ukraine." July 29, 2014, www.whitehouse.gov/the-press-office/2014/07/29/statement-president-ukraine.

————. "Transcript: President Obama's Aug. 28 Remarks on Ukraine, Syria and the Economy." *Washington Post*, August 28, 2014, www.washingtonpost.com/politics/transcriptpresident-obamas-aug-28-remarks-on-ukraine-and-syria/2014/08/28/416f1336–2eec-11e4-bb9b-997ae96fad33_story.html.

Panetta, Leon, with Jim Newton. *Worthy Fights: A Memoir of Leadership in War and Peace*. New York: Penguin Press, 2014.

Parker, Ashley. "Impasse with Congress Imperils Authorization to Combat ISIS." *New York Times*, March 11, 2015, www.nytimes.com/2015/03/12/us/politics/a-rift-imperils-authorization-to-combat-isis.html.

Paul, Rand. "How U.S. Interventionists Abetted the Rise of ISIS." *Wall Street Journal*, August 27, 2014, www.wsj.com/articles/rand-paul-how-u-s-interventionists-abetted-the-rise-of-isis-1409178958.

————. "Transcript of Rand Paul's Heritage Foundation Speech." News.Mic, February 6, 2013, http://mic.com/articles/25024/rand-paul-speech-full-text-transcript.

Petraeus, David H. "How We Won in Iraq." *Foreign Policy*, October 29, 2013, www.foreignpolicy.com/articles/2013/10/29/david_petraeus_how_we_won_the_surge_in_Iraq.

Pillar, Paul. "We Can Live with a Nuclear Iran." *Washington Monthly*, March/April

2012, www.washingtonmonthly.com/magazine/marchapril_2012/features/we_can_live_with_a_nuclear_ira035772.php?page=all.

Pillsbury, Michael. *The Hundred-Year Marathon: China's Secret Strategy to Replace America as the Global Superpower.* New York: Henry Holt, 2015.

———. "The Sixteen Fears: China's Strategic Psychology." *Survival: Global Politics and Strategy* 54, no. 5 (October 2012): 149–82.

Pipes, Daniel. *In the Path of God: Islam and Political Power.* New York: Basic Books, 1983.

———. "On Second Thought . . . Maybe That Israeli Apology to Turkey Was a Good Idea." *Lion's Den,* March 29, 2013, www.danielpipes.org/blog/2013/03/on-second-thought-maybe-that-israeli-apology-to.

———. "There Are No Moderates: Dealing with Fundamentalist Islam." *National Interest,* Fall 1995, www.danielpipes.org/274/there-are-no-moderates-dealing-with-fundamentalist-islam.

Pollack, Kenneth M. "Confidence Enrichment: The Nuclear Deal with Iran Was about Trust, Not Verification." *Foreign Affairs,* November 25, 2013, www.foreignaffairs.com/articles/140290/kenneth-pollack/confidence-enrichment.

———. *Unthinkable: Iran, the Bomb, and American Strategy.* New York: Simon and Schuster, 2013.

Poroshenko, Petro. "Crimea Is Still Ukraine." *Wall Street Journal,* March 19, 2015, www.wsj.com/articles/petro-poroshenko-crimea-is-still-ukraine-1426797603.

Posen, Barry R. *Restraint: A New Foundation for U.S. Grand Strategy.* Ithaca: Cornell University Press, 2014.

———. "We Can Live with a Nuclear Iran." *New York Times,* February 27, 2006, www.nytimes.com/2006/02/27/opinion/27posen.html?pagewanted=all&_r=0.

Power, Samantha. "Force Full." *New Republic,* March 3, 2003, www.newrepublic.com/article/srebenica-liberalism-balkan-united%20nations.

———. *A Problem from Hell: America and the Age of Genocide.* New York: Basic Books, 2002.

President of the United States. *National Security Strategy.* May 2010, www.whitehouse.gov/sites/default/files/rss_viewer/national_security_strategy.pdf.

Putin, Vladimir V. "Address by President of the Russian Federation." Kremlin, Moscow, March 18, 2014, http://eng.kremlin.ru/news/6889.

———. "Address to the Federal Assembly of the Russian Federation." Kremlin, Moscow, April 25, 2005, http://archive.kremlin.ru/eng/speeches/2005/04/25/2031_type70029type82912_87086.shtml.

———. "A Plea for Caution from Russia." *New York Times,* September 11, 2013, www.nytimes.com/2013/09/12/opinion/putin-plea-for-caution-from-russia-on-syria.html?pagewanted=all.

———. "Speech and the Following Discussion at the Munich Conference on Security Policy." Munich, Germany, February 10, 2007, http://archive.kremlin.ru/eng/speeches/2007/02/10/0138_type82912type82914type82917type84779_118123.shtml.

Reagan, Ronald. "Address before a Joint Session of Congress on the State of the Union." January 25, 1988, www.reagan.utexas.edu/archives/speeches/1988/012588d. htm.

——. "Address from the Brandenburg Gate." West Berlin, June 12, 1987, http://millercenter.org/president/speeches/speech-3415.

——. *An American Life.* New York: Simon and Schuster, 1990.

——. "The Brotherhood of Man." Remarks at the Westminster College Cold War Memorial, Fulton, Mo., November 19, 1990, www.pbs.org/wgbh/americanexperience/features/primary-resources/reagan-brotherhood/.

——. *Reagan, in His Own Hand: The Writings of Ronald Reagan That Reveal His Revolutionary Vision for America.* Edited by Kiron K. Skinner, Annelise Anderson, and Martin Anderson. New York: Free Press, 2001.

——. "Remarks and a Question-and-Answer Session at the University of Virginia." Charlottesville, December 16, 1988, www.reagan.utexas.edu/archives/speeches/1988/121688b.htm.

——. "Remarks at the Annual Convention of the National Association of Evangelicals." Orlando, Fla., March 8, 1983, www.reagan.utexas.edu/archives/speeches/1983/30883b.htm.

Remnick, David. *The Bridge: The Life and Rise of Barack Obama.* New York: Alfred A. Knopf, 2010.

Renshon, Stanley A. *Barack Obama and the Politics of Redemption.* New York: Routledge, 2011.

Romney, Mitt. "Obama's Worst Foreign-Policy Mistake." *Washington Post,* July 6, 2010, www.washingtonpost.com/wp-dyn/content/article/2010/07/05/AR2010070502657.html.

Rose, Gideon. *Crisis in Ukraine.* New York: Council on Foreign Relations, 2014.

Ross, Dennis. *The Missing Peace: The Inside Story of the Fight for Middle East Peace.* New York: Farrar, Straus and Giroux, 2004.

Rothkopf, David. "The U.S.–Israel Relationship Arrives at a Moment of Reckoning." *Foreign Policy,* August 26, 2014, www.foreignpolicy.com/articles/2014/08/26/a_conversation_with_martin_indyk_netanyahu_gaza_israel_palestine_hamas.

Rubin, Michael. *Dancing with the Devil: The Perils of Engaging Rogue Regimes.* New York: Encounter Books, 2014.

Rubio, Marco. "A Conversation with Marco Rubio." Remarks made at the Council on Foreign Relations, May 13, 2015, www.cfr.org/united-states/conversation-marco-rubio/p36511.

——. "Obama Administration's Treatment of Israel Is a 'Historic and Tragic Mistake.'" Senate floor speech, March 19, 2015, www.rubio.senate.gov/public/index.cfm/press-releases?ID=4123bbf1-c114–4b4c-9998–421ba6dac2d2.

Satter, David. *It Was a Long Time Ago, and It Never Happened Anyway: Russia and the Communist Past.* New Haven: Yale University Press, 2012.

Schake, Kori. "How to Lose Friends and Alienate Allies: Why America's Friends in Europe Are Wishing for the Good Old Days of George W. Bush." *For-*

eign Policy, June 30, 2014, www.foreignpolicy.com/articles/2014/06/30/ why_the_obama_administration_is_making_europe_miss_george_w_bush.

Schweller, Randall L. *Maxwell's Demon and the Golden Apple: Global Discord in the New Millennium.* Baltimore: Johns Hopkins University Press, 2014.

Sestanovich, Stephen. *Maximalist: America in the World from Truman to Obama.* New York: Alfred A. Knopf, 2014.

Shambaugh, David. *China Goes Global: The Partial Power.* New York: Oxford University Press, 2013.

Shanker, Thom, and Helene Cooper. "Pentagon Plans to Shrink Army to Pre–World War II Level." *New York Times,* February 23, 2014, www.nytimes.com/2014/02/24/us/politics/pentagon-plans-to-shrink-army-to-pre-world-war-ii-level.html.

Shesol, Jeff. "Obama's Coalition of the Willing and Unable." *New Yorker,* September 11, 2014, www.newyorker.com/news/news-desk/obamas-new-war-isis.

Shultz, George P. "How to Get America Moving Again." *Wall Street Journal,* August 8, 2014, http://online.wsj.com/articles/george-p-shultz-how-to-get-america-moving-again-1407536979.

———. *Turmoil and Triumph: My Years as Secretary of State.* New York: Scribner's, 1993.

Solomon, Jay, and Carol E. Lee. "Iran's Ayatollah Sends New Letter to Obama amid Nuclear Talks." *Wall Street Journal,* February 13, 2015, www.wsj.com/articles/irans-ayatollah-sends-new-letter-to-obama-amid-nuclear-talks-1423872638.

———. "Obama Wrote Secret Letter to Iran's Khamenei about Fighting Islamic State." *Wall Street Journal,* November 6, 2014, http://online.wsj.com/articles/obama-wrote-secret-letter-to-irans-khamenei-about-fighting-islamic-state-1415295291.

Spykman, Nicholas J. *America's Strategy in World Politics: The United States and the Balance of Power.* 1942. Reprint. New Brunswick, N.J.: Transaction Publishers, 2012.

Stephens, Bret. *America in Retreat: The New Isolationism and the Coming Global Disorder.* New York: Sentinel, 2014.

Sutter, Robert G. *China's Rise in Asia: Promises and Perils.* Lanham, Md.: Rowman and Littlefield, 2005.

Terrill, Ross. *The New Chinese Empire: And What It Means for the United States.* New York: Basic Books, 2003.

Thornton, Bruce S. *The Wages of Appeasement: Ancient Athens, Munich, and Obama's America.* New York: Encounter Books, 2011.

"Top Military Chief Voices Concerns about Fight against ISIS." Associated Press, March 11, 2015, www.newsmax.com/Newsfront/dempsey-raises-concerns-isis/2015/03/11/id/629536/.

United States Department of Defense. "Remarks by Secretary Hagel and Gen. Dempsey on the Fiscal Year 2015 Budget Preview in the Pentagon Briefing Room." February 24, 2014, http://archive.defense.gov/Transcripts/Transcript.aspx?TranscriptID=5377.

———. "Sustaining U.S. Global Leadership: Priorities for 21st Century Defense." January 2012, www.defense.gov/news/defense_strategic_guidance.pdf.

United States Department of State. "Text of the New START Treaty." Prague, April 8, 2010, www.state.gov/documents/organization/140035.pdf.

Walt, Stephen M. "Is Barack Obama More of a Realist Than I Am?" *Foreign Policy*, August 19, 2014, www.foreignpolicy.com/articles/2014/08/19/is_barack_obama_more_of_a_realist_than_i_am_stephen_m_walt_iraq_russia_gaza.

———. "The Myth of American Exceptionalism." *Foreign Policy*, October 11, 2011, www.foreignpolicy.com/articles/2011/10/11/the_myth_of_american_exceptionalism.

———. "Netanyahu's Not Chickenshit, the White House Is." *Foreign Policy*, October 31, 2014, www.foreignpolicy.com/articles/2014/10/31/netanyahu_s_not_chickenshit_israel_united_states_special_relationship_obama.

———. *Taming American Power: The Global Response to U.S. Primacy*. New York: W. W. Norton, 2005.

———. "What's Really at Stake in the Iranian Nuclear Deal." *Foreign Policy*, November 25, 2013, www.foreignpolicy.com/posts/2013/11/25/iran_the_us_and_the_middle_east_balance_of_power.

Waltz, Kenneth N. *Theory of International Politics*. Reading, Mass.: Addison-Wesley, 1979.

———. "Why Iran Should Get the Bomb: Nuclear Balancing Would Mean Stability." *Foreign Affairs*, July/August 2012, www.foreignaffairs.com/articles/137731/kenneth-n-waltz/why-iran-should-get-the-bomb.

Weigel, George. *American Interests, American Purpose: Moral Reasoning and U.S. Foreign Policy*. New York: Praeger, 1989.

———. *The Cube and the Cathedral*. New York: Basic Books, 2006.

Wolfers, Arnold. *Discord and Collaboration: Essays on International Politics*. Baltimore: Johns Hopkins University Press, 1962.

Woodward, Bob. *Obama's Wars*. New York: Simon and Schuster, 2010.

Yglesias, Matthew. "Obama: The Vox Conversation, Part Two: Foreign Policy." *Vox*, January 23, 2015, www.vox.com/a/barack-obama-interview-vox-conversation/obama-foreign-policy-transcript.

Zakaria, Fareed. "Inside Obama's World: The President Talks to TIME about the Changing Nature of American Power." *Time*, January 19, 2012, http://swampland.time.com/2012/01/19/inside-obamas-world-the-president-talks-to-time-about-the-changing-nature-of-american-power/.

———. "Netanyahu Enters Never-Never Land." *Washington Post*, March 5, 2015, www.washingtonpost.com/opinions/netanyahu-enters-never-never-land/2015/03/05/2f279c3c-c372-11e4-ad5c-3b8ce89f1b89_story.html.

———. "Obama's Disciplined Leadership Is Right for Today." *Washington Post*, May 29, 2014, www.washingtonpost.com/opinions/fareed-zakaria-obamas-disciplined-leadership-is-right-for-today/2014/05/29/7b4eb460-e76d-11e3-afc6-a1dd9407abcf_story.html.

————. "Obama the Realist." *Newsweek,* December 4, 2009, www.newsweek.com/zakaria-obama-realist-75621.

————. "On Ukraine, Obama Must Lead from the Front." *Washington Post,* March 13, 2014, www.washingtonpost.com/opinions/fareed-zakaria-on-ukraine-obama-must-lead-from-the-front/2014/03/13/10b9359a-aaea-11e3-af5f-4c56b834c4bf_story.html.

————. "Stop Searching for an Obama Doctrine." *Washington Post,* July 6, 2011, www.washingtonpost.com/opinions/stop-searching-for-an-obama-doctrine/2011/07/06/gIQAQMmI1H_story.html.

————. "Who Lost Iraq? The Iraqis Did, with an Assist from George W. Bush." *Washington Post,* June, 12, 2014, www.washingtonpost.com/opinions/fareed-zakaria-who-lost-iraq-the-iraqis-did-with-an-assist-from-george-w-bush/2014/06/12/35c5a418-f25c-11e3–914c-1fbd0614e2d4_story.html.

Index

CPSIA information can be obtained at www.ICGtesting.com
Printed in the USA
BVOW08*2223250316

441659BV00001B/1/P

5042